D1124583

Severe Behavior Disorders in the Mentally Retarded

Nondrug Approaches to Treatment

Edited by

Rowland P. Barrett

Brown University Program in Medicine
Emma Pendleton Bradley Hospital
East Providence, Rhode Island

PLENUM PRESS • NEW YORK AND LONDON

Library of Congress Cataloging in Publication Data

Main entry under title:

Severe behavior disorders in the mentally retarded.

(Applied clinical psychology)
Includes bibliographies and index.
1. Mental retardation—Complications and sequelae. 2. Mental illness—Treatment. 3. Behavior modification. I. Barrett, Rowland P. II. Series. [DNLM: 1. Behavior Therapy. 2. Mental Disorders—complications. 3. Mental Retardation—complications. WM 307.M5 S498]
RC451.4.M47S48   1986   616.85'88   85-30087
ISBN 0-306-42162-3

© 1986 Plenum Press, New York
A Division of Plenum Publishing Corporation
233 Spring Street, New York, N.Y. 10013

Printed in the United States of America

To Chris,
Sarah, Ethan, and Jessica
and to Michael L.,
a past source of inspiration

Contributors

PATRICK K. ACKLES, Illinois Institute for the Study of Developmental Disabilities, University of Illinois at Chicago, Chicago, Illinois

ROWLAND P. BARRETT, Department of Psychiatry and Human Behavior, Brown University Program in Medicine, Emma Pendleton Bradley Hospital, East Providence, Rhode Island

KAREN S. BUDD, Meyer Children's Rehabilitation Institute, University of Nebraska Medical Center, Omaha, Nebraska

JANIS CHADSEY-RUSCH, Department of Special Education, University of Illinois, Champaign, Illinois

THOMAS M. DILORENZO, Department of Psychology, University of Missouri, Columbia, Missouri

PAMELA L. FABRY, Meyer Children's Rehabilitation Institute, University of Nebraska Medical Center, Omaha, Nebraska

LINDA FITZPATRICK GOURASH, Department of Psychiatry, Western Psychiatric Institute and Clinic, University of Pittsburgh School of Medicine, Pittsburgh, Pennsylvania

ROBERT G. GRIFFITH, Elwyn Institutes' National Rehabilitation Center, Philadelphia, Pennsylvania

BARBARA HAWK, Biological Sciences Research Center, University of North Carolina, Chapel Hill, North Carolina

MICHEL HERSEN, Department of Psychiatry, Western Psychiatric Institute and Clinic, University of Pittsburgh School of Medicine, Pittsburgh, Pennsylvania

MICHAEL L. JONES, Bureau of Child Research, University of Kansas, Lawrence, Kansas

MARY MARGARET KERR, Department of Psychiatry, Western Psychiatric Institute and Clinic, University of Pittsburgh School of Medicine, Pittsburgh, Pennsylvania

JENNIFER LATTIMORE, Department of Human Development, University of Kansas, Lawrence, Kansas

EDWARD J. NUFFIELD, Department of Psychiatry, Western Psychiatric Institute and Clinic, University of Pittsburgh School of Medicine, Pittsburgh, Pennsylvania

THOMAS H. OLLENDICK, Department of Psychology, Virginia Polytechnic Institute and State University, Blacksburg, Virginia

DENNIS H. REID, Western Carolina Center, Morganton, North Carolina

TODD R. RISLEY, Department of Psychology, University of Alaska, Anchorage, Alaska

FRANK R. RUSCH, Department of Special Education, University of Illinois, Chapaign, Illinois

MAUREEN M. SCHEPIS, Western Carolina Center, Morganton, North Carolina

CAROLYN S. SCHROEDER, Biological Sciences Research Center, University of North Carolina, Chapel Hill, North Carolina

STEPHEN R. SCHROEDER, Biological Sciences Research Center, University of North Carolina, Chapel Hill, North Carolina

EDWARD S. SHAPIRO, School Psychology Program, Lehigh University, Bethlehem, Pennsylvania

GARY R. ULICNY, Department of Human Development, University of Kansas, Lawrence, Kansas

Foreword

It is well known that behavior problems are a salient characteristic of children and adults with mental retardation. That is not to say that all persons with mental retardation experience behavior disorders; however, most studies indicate that the incidence of emotional disturbance in this population is four to six times greater than that observed in similar intellectually nonhandicapped children and adults. It is equally well known that the principal form of treatment accorded clients with mental retardation and behavior disorders is pharmacotherapy or the prescription of behavior modifying drugs. Recent studies show that 6 out of every 10 individuals with mental retardation have been prescribed drugs as treatment for disorders of emotion or behavior. Unfortunately, further studies indicate that only one or 2 out of every 10 clients receiving medication are determined to be "responders," such that some therapeutic benefit is derived from their drug treatment.

As noted by the title, the single major thrust of this volume is to review approaches to the treatment of behavior disorders in persons with mental retardation from a *nondrug* perspective. This requires the presentation of a wide range of material on treatment: basic behavior modification programming, cognitive-behavioral strategies, habilitative approaches, counseling and psychotherapy, designing therapeutic living environments, managing medical factors bearing relevance to emotional illness, intervening with families, training special education teachers and direct care staff, and supplying information on the client's rights to obtain treatment in the least restrictive and least intrusive manner. The present text accomplishes this review in a thorough and superb fashion, while presenting convincing evidence of the effectiveness and applicability of each technique to the behavior disorders commonly experienced by persons with mental retardation. Moreover, the implicit notion that several among the therapeutic techniques reviewed will, in all likelihood, need to be simultaneously applied if a comprehensive approach to treatment is to be attained, may be among the more important contributions of the book. As the overwhelming majority of mental health professionals will freely admit, managing the so-called dually diagnosed client, who has both an emotional or behavioral disturbance and mental retardation, is no easy task and requires a well coordinated and integrated multimodel approach to therapy. The present text supplies state-of-the-art information on each of the treatment modalities proven as effective therapies for use with this population, which makes this book required reading for all psychiatrists, psychologists, pediatricians, special educators, social workers, and other mental health professionals serving persons with mental retardation.

JEAN K. ELDER

Commissioner
Administration on Developmental
*   Disabilities*
Washington, DC

Preface

During the past 5 years, the issue of mental health within the mentally retarded population has emerged as a major area of both scientific and clinical interest. From the scientific perspective, books by Matson and Barrett (1982), Menolascino and McCann (1983), Sigman (1985), and Szymanski and Tanguay (1980) have reviewed the empirical data and provided unequivocal testimony that mentally retarded children, adolescents, and adults may present with behavior characteristic of psychiatric disturbance covering the full range of DSM-III (American Psychiatric Association, 1980) diagnostic categories at a rate four to six times greater than that observed in the intellectually nonimpaired population. This is not to say that psychiatric disturbance is a fixed result of mental retardation. It does, however, firmly establish the presence of emotional and behavior disorders as a salient feature of the various mental retardation subtype diagnoses.

Clinical interest in the assessment and treatment of behavior disorders within the mentally retarded population has in the past, as it continues presently, to focus largely on the effectiveness of pharmacotherapy and behavior modification approaches. Drug therapies, which in the 1960s involved the nearly exclusive use of neuroleptic medications, have evolved to further include stimulant and antidepressant medications in the 1970s, as well as experimental drugs like carbamazepine, propranolol, fenfluramine, and naloxone hydrochloride in the 1980s. Operant conditioning approaches to the treatment of behavior disorders in the mentally retarded have similarly evolved, beginning with the reinforcement therapy techniques of the early 1960s, the use of punishment in the late 1960s, the growing doctrine of least aversive procedures characteristic of the 1970s, and the recently acknowledged utility of combining approaches to treatment that marks the 1980s.

This volume has been prepared with recent history particularly in mind. As more and better controlled drug studies appear in the mental retardation literature, testifying to low rates of efficacy and an alarmingly high probability of side effects, nondrug approaches to therapy have gathered momentum and appear to be emerging strongly as the treatments of choice. Of concern, however, is the failure of these approaches to be comprehensive in nature. The majority of treatment programs presently serving the mentally retarded are critically unidimensional. That is, they are either strictly "behavioral" or strictly "psychodynamic," and fail to recognize the potential benefit of addressing problem behavior from a multimodal perspective that simultaneously utilizes a variety of proven therapies.

Such is the principal goal of this book: To advise the reader that, in the very least, a half-dozen separate approaches to the treatment of behavior disorders in the mentally retarded exist, that each of the approaches is highly compatible for use with one or more of the others, and that such an integration is necessary to achieving a comprehensive treatment plan. In addition, it is hoped that the reader will recognize that there is more to the development of a comprehensive treatment protocol than the simultaneous use of two or more therapies. It should be apparent that the assessment and management of an enormous variety of medical factors that may bear relevance to the behavior disorder are of paramount importance. Similarly, the need to educate, train, and otherwise involve parents, family members, teachers, and direct care staff is considered essential to both the attainment of a comprehensive treatment plan and a successful outcome resulting from such planning.

As a final note, it should be emphasized that the intent of this volume is not to be considered as *antidrug*, particularly on the mere fact that it chooses to review nondrug approaches to the treatment of behavior disorders in the mentally retarded. Most professionals have witnessed, on more than one occasion, the suppression of significantly disordered behavior in certain mentally retarded clients that could be solely attributed to the carefully planned and conscientious use of various medications, including psychotropic drugs. This book, like any other professional book, seeks to purvey among its readership certain information and, perhaps, a message. A number of federally funded, multicenter drug studies addressing behavior disorders in the mentally retarded have been and continue to be successfully operated on a national basis. The results of these studies, unfortunately, have been equivocal. Perhaps the time has arrived to integrate additional nondrug approaches to treatment, either singularly or in combination with medications, within the existing drug protocols. It is hoped that the contents of this volume will prepare clinicians and applied researchers for just such a large and challenging task.

ROWLAND P. BARRETT

References

American Psychiatric Association. (1980). *Diagnostic and statistical manual of mental disorders* (3rd ed.). Washington, DC: American Psychiatric Association.

Matson, J. L., & Barrett, R. P. (Eds.). (1982). *Psychopathology in the mentally retarded.* New York: Grune & Stratton.

Menolascino, F. J., & McCann, B. M. (Eds.). (1983). *Mental health and mental retardation: Bridging the gap.* Baltimore: University Park Press.

Sigman, M. (Ed.). (1985). *Children with dual diagnosis: Mental retardation and mental illness.* Orlando: Grune & Stratton.

Szymanski, L. S., & Tanguay, P. (Eds.). (1980). *Emotional disorders of mentally retarded persons.* Baltimore: University Park Press.

Contents

Chapter 3

BEHAVIOR MODIFICATION: SELF-CONTROL AND COGNITIVE PROCEDURES   61

Edward S. Shapiro

Chapter 6

ASSESSING AND MANAGING MEDICAL FACTORS   157

Linda Fitzpatrick Gourash

Chapter 7

COUNSELING AND PSYCHOTHERAPY   207

Edward J. Nuffield

Chapter 8

PARENT AND FAMILY TRAINING   235

Karen S. Budd and Pamela L. Fabry

Chapter 9

TEACHER AND SCHOOL PERSONNEL TRAINING   273

Mary Margaret Kerr

Chapter 10

DIRECT CARE STAFF TRAINING   297

Dennis H. Reid and Maureen M. Schepis

Chapter 11

STRATEGIES FOR EVALUATING TREATMENT
EFFECTIVENESS   323

Rowland P. Barrett, Patrick K. Ackles, and Michel Hersen

Chapter 12

ADMINISTRATIVE CONSIDERATIONS AND
RESPONSIBILITIES: LEGAL AND ETHICAL ISSUES   359

Robert G. Griffith

1

Behavior Modification
Reinforcement

BARBARA HAWK, STEPHEN R. SCHROEDER, AND
CAROLYN S. SCHROEDER

Introduction

Intervention procedures based upon reinforcement have been successfully used to modify behavior of mentally retarded persons across many
populations, settings, and target behaviors (Schroeder, Mulick, &
Schroeder, 1979; Whitman & Scibak, 1979). Reinforcement approaches
are particularly salient with severely and profoundly retarded people
because of the critical importance of changing dangerous and/or maladaptive behavior patterns. This is paired with a growing desire on the
part of many agencies, institutions, and parent advocate groups to use
nonpunitive methods of behavior modification whenever possible.

When one leaves the laboratory and enters the applied setting, for
research or clinical purposes, the issues involved with behavior change
and reinforcement greatly increase in complexity. How does one decide
what to reinforce? Who defines behavior as good, bad, or in need of
change, and how does one do so? Do we really know how to judge
behaviors as to whether they are appropriate or inappropriate? If the
goal is to eliminate undesirable behaviors, how can training sessions be
maintained and generalized across days and settings? Can desirable
behaviors be substituted for inappropriate behaviors, and how? How
does one establish that a certain condition, such as food or an activity,

BARBARA HAWK, STEPHEN R. SCHROEDER AND CAROLYN S. SCHROEDER • Biological Sciences
Research Center, University of North Carolina, Chapel Hill, North Carolina 27514.   We
wish to acknowledge Grant Nos. HD-03110, HD-16834, MCH Project 916, and EPA
No. CR 809992 for support of the authors during the writing of this project.

is indeed reinforcing? Does this vary across clients? Can the reinforcement value of certain events or activities be modified or increased?

Applying principles of reinforcement to the severely and profoundly mentally retarded raises additional questions. What implications does their seriously limited behavior repertoire hold for the process of reinforcement (e.g., what behaviors are available to reinforce; and, what reinforcing conditions—food, praise, preferred activity—are actually viable options for a particular client?). Does he or she "learn" the contingency between behavior and reinforcers? If so, what implications does this have for people whose "learning" abilities are quite compromised? Will a profoundly mentally retarded person "learn" relationships between events in the same manner as mildly retarded or learning—disabled persons? Moreover, do we understand reinforcement well enough to actually answer these questions?

This chapter will provide an overview of several contemporary concepts of reinforcement from the basic research literature and their implications for current methods of applying reinforcement and for existing theories of reinforcement usage with mentally retarded people. This body of knowledge will then be specifically related to the behavior disorders commonly observed in the mentally retarded. Implications with regard to both research and treatment will be discussed. Reinforcement can be used to increase desired behavior, decrease undesired behavior, or both. The classes of "reinforcement" to be discussed include positive reinforcement, negative reinforcement, and extinction (or lack of reinforcement).

Fundamental Properties of Operants

A fundamental principle of operant analysis is the *law of effect* that holds that the strength of conditioning is developed and maintained by its reinforcing consequences. The question is how. Thorndike's view was that new behavior was "stamped in" through the mechanism of reinforcement, the implication being that the reinforced behavior somehow gained strength over other possible behaviors in a given situation. Rate of response was proposed by Skinner (1938) as the index of the strength of that acquisition, and this is the index that has been used most frequently in behavior modification research. However, one can raise many objections to response rate as an index of strength. A most obvious one is that rate of response is not a homogeneous dimension of behavior but a summary of the relative contribution of responding plus not responding. Dramatically different spatial or temporal topo-graphies can yield the same overall rate of responding. If rate is com-posed of these different response classes, does it index response strength, or does it reflect changes in the contribution of one class of behavior to the overall form of a larger response class? For instance, are biting, kicking, and verbal threats part of a response class we call *aggression*? What are the parameters of these behaviors that led us to call them aggression?

In recent years, the preceding problems have been the stimulus for some of the most heuristic analyses of behavior, including Herrn-stein's matching law (1970), Baum's (1973) correlation-based law of effect, Staddon and Simmelhag's (1971) study of the adaptive characteristics of operants, and Rachlin and Burkhard's (1978) multidimensional analysis of operants. However, Nevin's (1974) analysis seems to incorporate a description of response strength most clearly releated to behavior inter-vention research. His model takes as the definition of a response class the sum of all its constituents (e.g., force, duration, and latency), all of which may be essential dimensions of the response. The strength of the behavior is equal to the consistency of all of these dimensions when the response is emitted over a variety of circumstances. Consistency implies a strong response, and variability implies a weaker response. This is not a new theme for research among the mentally retarded. The thesis that response consistency (or variability) among the mentally retarded is more characteristic of their adaptive responding than response rate has been the subject of a substantial amount of research (see Baumeister & Kellas, 1968).

What does such research tell us about treating severe behavior disorders? First, the idea that rate of responding is the only or even the best measure of response strength for any operant behavior, let alone response topographies, is far from settled. Second, consistency across settings and resistance to change are important antecedents and possible parameters of behaviors. Third, other dimensions of behavior besides rate ought to be investigated as indexes of response strength (besides the currently prevalent use of complaints by caregivers, accident reports, nurses' notes, etc.). For instance, if one looks at the temporal course of interresponse times of severe behavior problems exhibited by mentally retarded persons, it is apparent that there often are identifiable patterns of responding. The most obvious one is "break-run" responding, where some clients distribute their interresponse times (IRT) rather randomly. For others (e.g., self-restrainers or clients who appear to fit the escape/ avoidance explanation of self-injurious behavior, SIB), their IRT distri-bution is negatively skewed because of very high-rate SIB contingent on release. Often, SIB continues until the client is restrained again. It is very important to analyze the relevance of the behavioral measure of response to be used, lest an inappropriate behavioral intervention be designed. For instance, rate of response is often not appropriate for reflecting infrequent behaviors like aggression or pica, whereas latency to first response may be more appropriate (Schroeder, Mulick, & Rojahn, 1980).

Types of Positive Reinforcement

A *positive reinforcer* is a stimulus that increases the probability of recurrence of some response. Whether a particular stimulus is actually reinforcing for a particular person usually is defined empirically by whether, in fact, the frequency of that response *increases* when followed by a particular stimulus. In other words, no object or operation can be presumed to be reinforcing until demonstrated as such by operational definition. Positive reinforcers may take on many forms. Perhaps the best-known category is that of *primary reinforcers*, such as food. Cereal pieces, crackers, M & Ms, raisins, ice cream, and juice tend to be most frequently employed and best received by children. Concern about sugar intake has prompted a search for "healthier" edibles. This issue will continue to pose a challenge of finding edibles that not only contain nutrients rather than sugar but that taste good enough to be worth working for (i.e., to be reinforcing). A common problem with edible reinforcers is satiation. Once a person is no longer hungry, food will decline in value and will not longer be reinforcing or worth working for. Thus, although edibles may be a potent reinforcer, other reinforcers must eventually be employed. Further, because most natural settings do not routinely distribute food in recognition of some behavior, other types of reinforcements need to be used that have a higher probability of occurring naturally. Very often the search for natural reinforcers for severely mentally handicapped people can require much ingenuity. Furthermore, the relative dimensions of a reinforcer may be its sensory quality and may include such variables as warmth, texture, vibration, or the control of selection or use of a particular possession such as a toy or string. The evaluation of reinforcers is an area of behavioral research that needs to be greatly developed (Cataldo & Risley, 1974; Favell & Cannon, 1976).

The most powerful *secondary* or conditioned type of reinforcement is social reinforcement. This includes attention, verbal praise, hugs, pets or other affectionate contact enjoyed by a particular person, and smiles. Social reinforcement may be effective on its own from the start of a behavior change program, or it may have to be paired initially with a primary reinforcer such as food, with the food systematically faded as social attention increases in value or, at least, becomes a salient cue that food is forthcoming! Social reinforcement does not tend to produce satiation, which is another advantage. It is also less disruptive; whereas food administration stops ongoing activity temporarily, social attention can be given in the midst of such activity. However, an important variable to keep in mind when using social reinforcement is whether such reinforcement is actually occurring. For example, a teacher may be asked to praise a child's sitting quietly at story time, and the teacher may report that she or he is praising the child; however, careful observation may show that the teacher's perspective is overestimating the true occurrence of praise. It may also be that the teacher is actually praising the child, but that the child seems to need "more" than what is being given at that point in time. Again, *reinforcement* is defined by whether a particular stimulus actually increases the magnitude of some response. The mere intention to do so does not warrant the approach being termed reinforcement.

Some people respond well to *information feedback*, or simply being given feedback about their performance. This has proven effective in some workshop situations, where information about how many units a client finished and how much the client earned that day or that hour provide sufficient incentive for continued performance. Feedback may take many forms and, once again, is empirically determined by what produces the desired behavior change. Verbal feedback may be sufficient for some clients (Schroeder & Schroeder, 1982). For others, graphs or pictures may be a more easily understood feedback system (Jens & Shores, 1969). Grades may be an effective feedback in classroom settings (Kazdin, 1982a). At times, feedback alone is sufficient reinforcement. Frequently, however, it must be paired with social reinforcement (as is often the case in the naturally occurring environment) to be effective. The condition under which feedback is effective must be determined by careful observation and analysis.

Tokens are conditioned reinforcers such as stars, check marks, poker chips, or points that are accumulated and exchanged for "back-up reinforcers" of the client's choice (Kazdin, 1982a; Schroeder & Schroeder, 1982). When a whole ward, classroom, or unit uses such a system it is called a *token economy*, with the tokens serving as "currency" to buy desired edibles, activities, and privileges. Thus, satiation can be avoided because when one food or activity loses its appeal, the client can simply choose another. Both token economies and individual token systems have been shown to be effective with mentally retarded people (Kazdin, 1977, 1982c; Kazdin & Bootzin, 1972).

How Are Reinforcers Identified?

Although the previously mentioned forms of reinforcement depend on stimuli that are "different" from the response class to be reinforced, high-probability behaviors can also serve as reinforcers for lower probability behaviors. This is an example of the *Premack principle*, which states that, given any two responses in an operant procedure, the more probable response will reinforce the less probable response. For example, most children engage in outdoor play at a very high frequency but clean their rooms at a very low frequency. Outdoor play can be made contingent upon a clean room, and hence it serves as a reinforcer for a nonpreferred activity. Similarly, a mentally retarded client who likes to engage in stereotyped rocking might respond to rocking as reinforcement for gradually extended periods of sitting still and working, with the eventual goal of little, or no, rocking in a more adaptive context (e.g., use of a rocking chair).

Timberlake and Allison (1974) have added to the Premack principle their belief that response deprivation, not probability differential, is the key factor in producing the reinforcement effect. Specifically, deprivation is created by providing less than the baseline level of contingent (reinforcing) activity. Thus, in order to maintain the baseline level of the desired, or high-probability behavior (rocking), the person must perform the less preferred behavior (sitting) at a level higher than its baseline. Support for this hypothesis has been provided in two studies of academic performance in a first grade and an Educable Mentally Retarded (EMR) classroom (Konarski, Johnson, Crowell, & Whitman, 1980; Konarski, Crowell, Johnson, & Whitman, 1982). In the latter, math and reading times were manipulated such that the more probable activity served as reinforcement for the less likely activity, as established by individual baseline observations on each child. The instrumental (less probable but desired) response increased when response deprivation of the reinforcing response (more probable behavior) was present but not when it was absent.

This model becomes increasingly complex when one considers a behavior reperotire of more than two behaviors. Under such circumstances, "substitution" is likely to occur, such that the instrumental and reinforcing (or contingent) behaviors are not the only ones to change, either in frequency or total time engaged in each. Bernstein and Ebbesen (1978) conducted a study of three adults engaging in their normal leisure activities in a laboratory apartment. After baseline measurements, they manipulated the requirements for instrumental and contingent responding, varying which activities were designated "instrumental" and "contingent," based on baseline observations and subsequent activity levels, through various phases of the experiment. They found "selective sub-stitution," or an increase in an unrestricted activity to a level greater than would be expected by simple proportional redistribution, to be a "reliable phenomenon." The authors suggested that this substitution may be a function of how response classes are defined. For example, when sewing was restricted for one subject contingent upon some other activity, time spent doing embroidery increased from 6% to 22%, when its expected change value was only to 8%. Obviously, sewing and embroidery can be viewed as similar behaviors and belonging to the same response class. However, because they were not defined as such, unexpected results were obtained. Bernstein and Ebbesen (1978) con-cluded that reducing access to contingent response will not exclusively determine an increase in instrumental response; however, if the instru-mental and contingent responses are substitutable activities (i.e., sewing and embroidery), reducing the contingent response will strongly influ-ence an increase in the instrumental response. It is clear that very thor-ough baseline observations must be made if we are to intelligently and successfully influence behavior change in a complex human repertoire. This will be discussed in greater detail later in the chapter.

Staddon (1979) has proposed a mathematical model to predict func-tional relationships between instrumental and contingent responses under different reinforcement schedules. He proposes that a homeostatic bal-ance is involved, encompassing three basic ideas: (a) the sum of behavior during a fixed time period is a constant; (b) people seek a certain dis-tribution of activities; and (c) if constraints on this distribution are imposed, they will change their activity distribution in a way that min-imizes deviation from their perferred distribution. This model seems basically in agreement with Bernstein and Ebbesen's (1978) concept of *response classes and selective substitution.* However, it could also be inter-preted to suggest other behavioral distributions that may be based on individual idiosyncracies rather than on response classes understood or defined by the experimenter or therapist. Again, only careful baseline observations will provide clues in individual cases.

Building Response Repertoires with Positive Reinforcement

Shaping and Priming Responses

Often additional assistance beyond reinforcement is required to increase a behavior or to initially establish it. This is particularly salient to intervention procedures because severely mentally retarded persons frequently lack desirable, reinforcible behaviors in their limited repertoire.

One cannot reinforce a behavior that is not there! In such a case, if some undesirable behavior is suppressed, another undesirable behavior may take its place. Thus, either the presence or creation of some specific, desired behavior must be planned. *Shaping* refers to systematically reinforcing successively closer approximations to the desired response. For example, a client may not have sufficient work skills to complete any tasks. He or she could first be reinforced for approaching the table; then for sitting for a predetermined, short length of time; then for looking at a puzzle; then for allowing a teacher to guide his or her hand through placing a puzzle piece; then for placing it himself or herself. Another procedure is known as *response priming*. This refers to any action that initiates the early steps in a sequence of behaviors culminating in the desired response. When a behavior involves many steps, the reinforcement is a strong reinforcer for the final step but a very delayed and thus weak reinforcer for the initial steps of the sequence. Thus, a behavioral sequence involving many steps is less likely to get started. Prompting the initial steps is often necessary, and once started, a sequence is much more likely to continue to completion and reinforcement. Such prompts can eventually be faded as the behavioral sequence becomes more strongly established in the peson's repertoire. Because satiation can occur and because preferred reinforcers may capriciously change, reinforcer sampling can be helpful in ensuring that the contingencies employed are indeed reinforcing. Further, this sampling can "prime" or motivate the person because it provides a concrete example of what payoff lies at the end of some task or behavior and thus helps initiate the behavioral sequence.

Schedules of Reinforcement

One must establish not only which behavior to reinforce and with which reinforcer, but one must devise also a *schedule* that dictates when responses will be reinforced. In general, *continuous reinforcement*, or reinforcing every appropriate response, will establish a behavior most quickly; however, that behavior will also be most easily and quickly extinguished once reinforcement is not continuously forthcoming. *Intermittent reinforcement* refers to providing reinforcement after several appropriate responses instead of after every one. Although behaviors require a longer period to be established under intermittent reinforcement, they are also more resistant to extinction. Kazdin (1982b) used the slot machine as a prime example of such resilience in the face of infrequent reinforcement.

Intermittent reinforcement schedules can be broken down into two general categories: *ratio and interval schedules*. A ratio schedule is one in which every behavior is reinforced (i.e., reinforcement is dependent upon occurrence of a specified number of behaviors). In an interval schedule, reinforcement is contingent upon a certain length of time during which the response is performed at least once. Each of these schedules can be either *fixed or variable*. A fixed schedule holds ratio or interval specifications constant, whereas a variable schedule changes the requirements periodically. An example of a fixed ratio schedule is requiring a client to place three blocks in a can or to smile appropriately at two different staff members before being reinforced. On a variable ratio schedule, reinforcement might be given after placement of three blocks, then after two more, then after four more, and so on. In a fixed interval schedule, the first response occurring after the specified (constant) time interval has elapsed is reinforced. With a variable interval schedule, the time interval would vary. With intermittent reinforcement under fixed schedules, behaviors tend to be established more easily, but they also extinguish more easily, whereas a variable schedule will require more time and effort to establish a behavior that will then extinguish more slowly. Similarly, a behavior that has been strengthened or established under a continuous reinforcement schedule may only be emitted when that reinforcer is present. On the other hand, under a variable schedule, especially if that schedule also includes different therapists or caretakers and/or takes place in different settings, the behavior may be emitted in a more consistent manner. Thus, interresponse times may also decrease (e.g., the behavior will occur more frequently).

Latency and Magnitude of Reinforcement

Along with the schedule of reinforcement, other factors need to be considered in maximizing the effectiveness of a reinforcement program. Delay of reinforcement can be an important variable. The closer the temporal proximity of the instrumental behavior and reinforcer, the stronger the reinforcer's value will be. Immediate reward is often necessary to establish a behavior, but one must consider that in a naturally occurring environment, reinforcement will likely not always be immediate. Delay can be gradually increased until it (hopefully) reaches a level that is not too disruptive to the normal flow of events in a particular setting but still maintains the desired behavior.

Magnitude, amount, or frequency of reinforcement is another variable. A greater amount of intensity of reinforcement will more strongly increase the desired behavior; however, this must be balanced with satiation considerations. A common paradigm for studying self-control is to see if people will tolerate a longer delay for a greater reward. Anderson (1978) found that younger, more immature children preferred a smaller but immediate reward, whereas older children were able to wait for the larger reward. This has implications for the mentally retarded in that reward may need to be fairly immediate until the behaviors are quite firmly established. It also suggests that "mediating reinforcers" may be used. For example, using praise to encourage a client through a long task or behavioral sequence and then giving an edible reinforcer at completion may effectively modify behavior. Quality of reinforcers can be another important variable. Obviously, good-tasting edibles provide more incentive than stale ones, and having a variety of reinforcers available can allow one to sidestep the problem of satiation.

Maintaining and Generalizing Reinforcement

Another component of maximizing reinforcement is *generalization*. One would hope not to have to follow a client from setting to setting, reinforcing every desired behavior ad infinitum. Rather, the goal is to find a way for that behavior to maintain itself. Unfortunately, the natural social reinforcement one would assume should follow desirable behavior change is not always forthcoming. Baer and Wolf (1967) state that "behavioral changes should endure over time only a little longer than the contingencies responsible for them endure. . . . Thus, current technological research is increasingly aimed at arranging behavior modification procedures so as to make the eventual [reinforcement] as late as possible" (pp. 2–3). They go on to propose making use of "natural communities of reinforcement" by "trapping" the person. In this approach, a simple response is required to gain entry into the reinforcement community, whereupon that community will provide continuing reinforcement for continuing behavior change. This has been effectively demonstrated in preschools (Allen, Hart, Buell, Harris, & Wolf, 1964; Baer & Wolf, 1967; Harris, Johnston, Kelley, & Wolf, 1964; Johnston, Kelley, Harris, & Wolf, 1966). For example, in cases where either a client lacked an "entry response" or the community was not responding adequately, "priming" (Baer & Wolf, 1967) could be employed. This would involve shaping the client's behavior to gain entry into the community of reinforcement, and then training the client to solicit reinforcement from the community. Once this interaction was begun, it should then perpetuate itself through a mutual reinforcement value to both parties.

Negative Reinforcement

Negative reinforcement refers to the strengthening or increasing of some behavior because it allows escape from, or avoidance of, some aversive event. Thus, the aversive event is the contingent stimulus, and the strengthened behavior is the instrumental response. Negative reinforcement differs from positive reinforcement only in that a stimulus is *removed* with negative reinforcement and *presented* with positive reinforcement. Negative reinforcement is not considered to be very effective in eliminating undesirable behaviors. Whaley and Tough (1968) used electric shock and a buzzer as an ongoing aversive event from which a mentally retarded child could escape by holding a toy (which was incompatible with head banging). Multiple toys were used during the conditioning sequence, and headbanging was successfully eliminated. Timeout from reinforcement and/or from the opportunity to earn tokens has also been used as a negative reinforcement procedure. Combining positive reinforcement for desirable behaviors with negative reinforcement for undesired behaviors has been effective and seems only sensible. In general, however, negative reinforcement appears to serve best as a last option. Kazdin (1982a) cites the following potential problems with negative reinforcement: (a) Aversive conditions must be employed frequently and/or for long periods of time before an appropriate behavior may occur. Thus, this procedure is even more susceptible to undesirable side effects than are punishment procedures, which rely on severe but infrequent aversive events. Such side effects include disruptive or distressing emotional reactions, inappropriate escape behavior, aggression, and the perpetuation of a negative reinforcement cycle instead of moving into a more positive system. (b) Unless the termination of the aversive condition is carefully controlled so that the desired behavior does occur and is indeed reinforced, inappropriate behaviors will be strengthened instead. In cases where positive reinforcement is sorely lacking or difficult to administer, negative reinforcement may be a viable option. However, one would question the ethicality of accepting such an environment as is. It would seem wise to consider modifying the environment first so that positive reinforcement is a more viable option (see Chapter 7).

Differential Reinforcement of Other Behavior (DRO)

One usually thinks of positive reinforcement in terms of increasing desired behavior. However, it can also be used to decrease undesirable behavior through differential reinforcement of other behavior, or DRO. The client is reinforced for a response defined as the absence of the undesired response. Because no particular alternative behavior is specified, this procedure has also been called differential reinforcement of not responding (Zeiler, 1977) and, indeed, "no response" may be the most preferable response in a client's repertoire. However, this points out a problem with DRO, because no response is rarely near the top of someone's behavioral hierarchy, and almost any other behavior in a repertoire will be more likely to occur. One hopes that a client's repertoire contains behaviors that are positive, so as to avoid reinforcing other undesirable behaviors in lieu of the target behavior. But this may not be the case, and care must be taken not to inadvertently reinforce other unacceptable behaviors simply because the target behavior has been absent for its specified period of time.

Poling and Ryan (1982), in a review of the DRO literature, concluded that DRO procedures work more quickly than extinction procedures. However, a DRO procedure requires a reinforcer that is stronger than the reinforcer maintaining the undesired behavior. Often it may be difficult to meet this requirement. Our knowledge of deprivation effects suggests that mild food deprivation would increase the reinforcement value of food. However, deprivation is considered to be unethical and is usually precluded by institutional policies. Further, studies have shown effectiveness of DRO over short periods of time but not over long periods of time (Poling & Ryan, 1982). It is impractical to expect the availability of staff to provide a client with reinforcement every 30 seconds throughout the day. Paired with this is the possibility that, as DRO intervals increase, the quality or magnitude of the reinforcer may have to increase in order to maintain its superior strength over the target behavior's reinforcer. These factors suggest that the long-term efficacy of DRO is still unknown.

Differential Reinforcement of Incompatibile Behavior (DRI)

A related procedure is known as DRI, or differential reinforcement of incompatible behavior. There continues to be some controversy over the importance of reinforcing some behavior that is specifically incompatible with the target behavior. Some researchers maintain that the critical factor is the efficiency of the alternative behavior at gaining reinforcement (Lovaas, Freitag, Gold, & Kassorla, 1965; Peterson & Peterson, 1968). Others (Young & Wincze, 1974) have clearly shown that the incompatibility of the alternative response to the target response is indeed a key factor. Tarpley and Schroeder (1979) compared DRO and DRI procedures in an attempt to decrease self-injurious behavior (SIB) in three profoundly mentally retarded persons. They found DRI to be more effective than DRO in controlling SIB and discussed possible reasons for this. It may not simply be reinforcement that is at issue. Tarpley and Schroeder (1979) suggested that the conjoint contingency of no-SIB and emitting an incompatible behavior, in this case ball play with the therapist, established a social interaction that also competed with SIB. Thus, social interaction may be an activity that holds reinforcement value in addition to the reinforcement given for the specified incompatible behavior.

Extinction

Extinction means noncontingently withholding reinforcement from some response that had previously been reinforced. It assumes that the behavior to be extinguished has been established as being reinforcing to the client. To withhold reinforcement of a behavior, in practice, generally means to ignore it. Extinguishing a previously positively reinforced behavior will be affected by how entrenched the behavior is (i.e., what type of reinforcement schedule it was subjected to). An intermittently reinforced behavior will require much more time and effort to extinguish than will a continuously reinforced behavior (Kazdin, 1982b). Similarly, the quality and magnitude of the previous reinforcer will contribute to the tenacity of the behavior (Kazdin, 1982b). These variables should be carefully considered in developing expectations or predictions for an extinction program. Identifying the reinforcer(s) of some behavior may not be as easy as it sounds. Different settings may provide different types of reinforcement, or multiple reinforcers may be at work in one setting. Careful observation and thought are required in order to establish a behavior as reinforcing. Continuing observations throughout an extinction program will help tease out what events are reinforcing a behavior, and such a program may have to follow a stepwise progression as new reinforcers come to light. Controlling the withholding of the reinforcers may not be easy, but it is critical to do so. Allowing even one bit of reinforcement to occur may cause a dramatic prolongation of the extinction process (Schroeder & Schroeder, 1982).

There are some additional problems with extinction, as well. First, extinction procedures rarely produce immediate results. In fact, the most frequent initial response is an *extinction burst*, or sudden increase in undesired behavior. A common example of this is the child who successfully whines at the grocery store until she or he gets a toy, candy bar, or the like. The first time mother ignores such whining, increased whining leading to a full-fledged tantrum is quite likely to ensue. The mentally retarded person will react in a similar manner to being ignored, in that his or her SIB and aggression will likely increase, both to test the limits of this new contingency (being ignored) and as an expression of frustration over it. Sometimes, self-injurious behavior may be far too dangerous to allow potential further damage. In such cases, extinction is not an appropriate procedure to use. In cases of nondangerous but extremely disruptive behavior, such as screaming, one should consider whether the people around the client can realistically tolerate such an extinction burst. If not, some other procedure should be employed. Second, *spontaneous recovery* of the behavior, without reinforcement may occur. It is usually weaker than its initial strength and should reextinguish more quickly. However, it is critical that the therapist not be surprised by spontaneous recovery and inadvertently reinforce this unexpected reappearance or presume that extinction was ineffective because of the recurrence of the problem behavior. Third, extinction procedures may produce side effects such as a negative emotional response (e.g., frustration, anger, aggression). Kazdin (1982b) points out that there should be "no net loss in reinforcement" (i.e., as the undesirable behavior is being extinguished some other, more desirable behavior(s) must be positively reinforced).

Extinction Plus Reinforcement of Alternative Responding (EXT ALT-R)

A procedure that uses extinction as a component is EXT ALT-R, or extinction plus reinforcement of alternative behaviors (Leitenberg, Rawson, & Bath, 1970). This procedure has been shown to be more effective than DRO or extinction alone in both animal studies (Mulick, Leitenberg, & Rawson, 1976) and with a chronic ruminative vomiter (Mulick, Schroeder, & Rojahn, 1980). Its advantage over DRO procedures is that it places a smaller time demand on staff persons; undesirable behavior is ignored, and only specific alternatives are reinforced. Thus, the therapist or staff member is not tied to a tightly timed, continuous DRO schedule.

Selective Reinforcement of Response Classes

Behavior does not occur in a vaccum but in the context of a stream of other behavior clusters. How does one decide what to reinforce and what not to reinforce? A behavioral event may be defined operationally in terms of its covariants. Covariation can exist in two forms: (a) transitional changes in the instrumental behavior stream (e.g., extinction burst), and (b) changes in other behaviors as a function of target behavior change. Covariation can be a function of the reinforcing or punishing effects of a particular contingent stimulus, the relationship of a target behavior to a broader response class, or changes in setting conditions such that other behaviors are subsequently affected by existing reinforcement contingencies (Schroeder & MacLean, 1982).

The Stochastic Model

Changes in other behaviors have been examined in terms of various theoretical models. The *stochastic model* (Baumeister & Rollings, 1976; Lovaas, Freitag, Gold, & Kassorla, 1965) views stereotyped behavior as a probabilistic event. That is, within a person's behavioral hierarchy, if a given behavior is suppressed, or not reinforced, the next behavior in the hierarchy will appear, and so on. This model also encompasses behavioral chains. For example, Jackson, Johnson, Ackron, and Crowley (1975) successfully intervened in a chronic behavioral chain of ruminative vomiting by providing a thick milkshake 90 minutes after mealtime as an "alternative reinforcement" for hunger (as opposed to the previous reinforcer: reverse peristalsis, which was then reinforced by rumination). Thus, by "sidestepping" a behavioral chain, the probability of undesired behaviors would be decreased, with a concurrent increase in more desirable behaviors through additional positive reinforcement. Staddon's (1979) operant probability model is also relevant to covariant behaviors. As one behavior is suppressed, other behaviors will change in frequency in such a way as to minimize the difference between the original hierarchy and the modifications imposed by the therapist. Thus, consideration of response classes is important. Thorough behavioral observations can provide information about possible response classes of each individual. For example, SIB may appear to be a single response class. Upon further examination, however, a particular subject may show both socially related SIB, such as self-biting or head banging, and more sensorially reinforcing SIB, such as pica or rumination. Intervention with head banging would be more likely to affect other socially related SIBs, and perhaps even other behaviors, than it would the sensorily motivated SIB.

Correlational Models

Correlational models of covariation focus on behavioral clusters, defined by their stable appearance across settings and time during baseline observations (Schroeder & MacLean, 1982). These clusters might reasonably be viewed as response classes and can certainly provide descriptive information that eventually may lead to a conceptual framework for defining what is reinforcing for mentally retarded persons. At the least, it provides information to the therapist about where covariation will be most likely to occur (i.e., in other behaviors within the same cluster as the target behavior). If covariation occurs outside that cluster, one might posit (a) that clusters are not the only organization of response classes, and/or (b) other factors are at work creating differential reinforcement. Some examples follow in the following paragraphs.

One such factor that can affect covariation is noncontingent suppression of behavior. For example, Rojahn, Schroeder, and Mulick (1980) examined the use of self-protective devices such as helmets and straitjackets with three profoundly mentally retarded adults. Such devices were used specifically to control self-injurious behaviors such as pica and rectal digging. However, observational data showed that although such devices were successful in preventing these target behaviors, they also decreased all desirable behaviors including work, play, and social interaction. Further, stereotypy increased, and appropriate attention from teachers decreased. Thus, a very narrow-band intervention had extremely broad, far-reaching consequences. Other studies (Rollings, Baumeister, & Baumeister, 1977; Schroeder & MacLean, 1983) have also found interaction with, or proximity to, people to influence covariation with self-injurious or stereotypic behavior.

Careful baseline observations may also suggest that modifying some behavior other than the initially defined target behavior may be more efficacious. As Voeltz and Evans (1982) have observed:

> The concept of treatment validity requires not only that a selected target behavior can be modified, but that this change is non-trivial in the context of the client's needs. Knowledge of behavioral interrelationships would provide empirical grounds for the selection of one target behavior in preference to another. For example, a hierarchical organization of responses—such that one is a prerequisite to others—could affect the advice a clinician provides a caregiver that a behavior identified by the latter for intervention might not influence the client's repertoire as broadly as some more fundamental alternative. (p. 132)

Kazdin (1982b) has observed that it may still be premature to demand that a conceptual framework elaborate the bases of response covariations without more systematic descriptive information about how behaviors are, in fact, organized.

Programming Considerations

An important consideration in developing a treatment program is the history of such programs in the past. The use of positive reinforcement, especially DRI and DRO programs, has proven fairly successful across a variety of behavior problems, including some as recalcitrant as severe SIB (Rojahn, Schroeder, & Mulick, 1980; Schroeder, Mulick, & Schroeder, 1979; Tarpley & Schroeder, 1979). However, the "price" of such success has typically been the involvement of a psychologist and more than one extra staff member (to serve as "therapist(s)," in addition to the health care technician staff) for intense periods of time. These time periods have been either of short duration, in a sense "removed" from the typical daily routine, or they have been integrated into the client's daily schedule at the expense of much additional time and energy from additional staff. These "successes" usually deteriorate as staffing patterns return to normal. In one large SIB study, only 2 clients out of 52 had maintained any behavioral control over their SIB at a 2-year follow-up (Schroeder, Kanoy, Thios, Mulick, Rojahn, Stephens, & Hawk, 1982). This poses a difficult question: what is missing from our programs that would help maintain improvement—or even maximize the probability of improvement in the first place?

One place to look is to the learning literature. Do we really understand the process by which the severely and profoundly mentally retarded learn, or change behavioral hierarchies? The answer, from several camps, is a resounding "not exactly." Certainly, given a particular stimulus, we can predict certain responses for given persons based on their unique repertoire and on the extant body of literature. But the underlying learning process still holds some mysteries.

Catania (1973), in summarizing the animal learning literature, which has perhaps the soundest theoretical research base, concludes that "even the definition of learning is potentially controversial, for the phenomena of learning are varied even though they share the same name" (p. 32). But when we try to apply various theories to the ecological social structure and learning processes observed in institutions, we find little help from the animal literature. The learned helplessness model (Abramson, Seligman, & Teasdale, 1978) would predict that institutional residents are likely to learn that their behavior will not be responded to contingently or consistently and hence will become apathetic. Although a certain amount of inertia appears to exist on many wards, there is also more than enough undesired behavior to call the usefulness of this model into question.

If we look to the human cognitive-learning literature, we find the "developmental versus difference" controversy, which focuses on mentally retarded persons who are not "organically impaired" and who have IQs greater than 50 (Weisz & Yates, 1981). Zigler, Weisz, and other developmental theorists believe that such persons learn in exactly the same manner as persons with normal intelligence but at a slower rate and with a lower ceiling for learning capacity (Weisz & Zigler, 1979; Zigler, 1967, 1969). The difference theorists, on the other hand, believe that mentally retarded persons actually learn in a manner that is qualitatively different from normal-IQ persons. Following an extensive and careful analysis of the extant literature, Weisz and Yates (1981) concluded that the developmentalists' "similar structure" hypothesis is indeed supported for nonorganically impaired retarded persons. Further, these mentally retarded persons seem to use the same cognitive processes (as measured with Piagetian techniques) as do normal persons. However, neither side addresses the learning process that occurs in people with IQs less than 50 and who are theorized to be "organically impaired." Further, "organically impaired" has yet to be clinically or operationally defined accurately (Baumeister & MacLean, 1979). Still, the "difference" theory probably more accurately reflects learning processes in the severely and profoundly retarded. Unfortunately, the state of the art seems to be no more specific than simply "different." It is clear that a profoundly mentally retarded person may evidence severe neurological impairment and may even evidence observable gross brain damage (Baumeister & MacLean, 1979). However, our understanding of neuroanatomy and neurophysiology is not sufficient to tie specific brain damage (when damage can even be specified) to specific types of impaired functioning in any predictive manner. Further, the "splinter skills" present in many severely and profoundly retarded persons make it difficult to predict learning potential, even with the aid of a good assessment of developmental level. For example, a client with poor fine motor skills and no self-help skills may learn some very basic language. This would suggest that there is additional learning potential present, and yet that client may have extreme difficulty learning further skills.

These *how* and *how much* learning questions are just as elusive and controversial in the mental retardation literature itself. A past issue of *Analysis and Intervention in Development Disabilities* (1981) addressed itself exclusively to the topic Are All Children Educable? Not only is there uncertainty about how the mentally retarded learn, but there is also a great deal of sociopolitical controversy and uncertainty over what is a reasonable "price" for such learning. This brings us full circle to our original challenge: How do we maximize our probability of successfully changing the aberrant behaviors of our clients, and how do we ensure that such behaviors can be maintained over a long period of time, in the client's natural setting, with the most economical allocation of staff resources possible.

Is there something missing in our present treatment programs? Can we change some as yet unaccounted-for variables to increase our chance for success? A combination of motivation theory, ecobehavioral assessment, and the infant–child development literature may lend some answers. Motivation has been conceived of as the clustering of setting factors that reliably occasion behavior (Carr, 1977). It is an umbrella encompassing reinforcement and other variables. It appears that both incentive motivation, or drive induction, and drive reduction contribute to motivation in any given circumstance. The external aspects of motivation are easy to observe: a person's interest in some reinforcer (evidenced by his or her attending to it, trying to get it, etc.). Internal (sensory, emotional) aspects are not always so easy to observe. We can infer that food will reinforce best under relative states of deprivation (i.e., just before mealtimes, rather than just after). But there may be other contributions to internal motivation that are inferred from the child development literature. In a commentary on Patterson's (1980) monograph on aggressive children and their mothers, Maccoby (1980) states:

> The behavior modification view point leads to a search for specific contingencies for specific kinds of behavior, and it is here that I suspect the point of view does us a disservice by narrowing the search too much. What leads children to want to do what their parents want done? . . . To accept the legitimacy of the parent's authority . . . ? We know from the work on intrinsic motivation that simply having received a rich diet of "positive reinforcement" in the past probably does not provide the whole answer. The prior history of the relationship is surely something that matters a great deal in determining whether a child complies willingly with a given demand, and the relationship is not adequately described in terms of what the parents have reinforced or punished the children for. The quality of the attachment that was built up at an earlier time probably has something to do with it; so does the parent's skill in mood-setting before a request is made; so does a history of mutually rewarding joint activities including play; so does the parent's willingness to reciprocate with compliance to reasonable demands from the child. (pp. 58–59)

Perhaps, as Maccoby charges, limiting our conceptualization to behavior theory does narrow our search. That is always a possibility with any theory; in fact, all of research is based on failing to confirm the null hypothesis, not on definitively confirming some alternative hypothesis. On the other hand, Maccoby has also raised a challenge to us as behaviorists to broaden our own viewpoint. The behavioral literature does, in fact, contain some helpful hints.

Wahler's (1980) research on insular (isolated) mothers has shown that his behavioral program worked as long as relationship with the therapist continued but that without such a relationship, the negative aspects of the mother's environment reassumed control, and the mother was subsequently unable to maintain the program. Patterson (1980) has noted that many aggressive children are not positively reinforced for their aggressive behavior, as had been previously assumed. Rather, aggression is negatively reinforced by its success in stopping parental demands and intrusions.

Wahler's (1980) results suggest that there is something about the relationship to the therapist that must be accounted for. In a presidential address to APA Division 33, Marie Skodak Crissey (1975) presented a historical overview of the mentally retarded in the United States. Many of the current, "new" behavior change techniques were used 150 years ago by Itard and Seguin. Seguin, in fact, catalyzed the development of educational institutions ("training schools") for the mentally retarded in the northwestern United States and developed many successful educational programs. Crissey raised the pointed question, why has it been necessary to rediscover these ideas, again and again? She goes on to conclude:

> I realize that there has been one consistent omission from my discussion. I have discussed "the retarded" movements, trends, and developments. This is the objective approach we think is appropriate. Sadly, we mislead ourselves. It is people, individual people, who make the difference in other people. It was Sequin's enthusiasm that inspired his teachers to work, to invest, and to influence from 5:30 in the morning when the children wake to 8:30 at night when they went to bed. It was he and his disciples who changed the "hopeless idiots" into functioning citizens. Howe, Richards, Bernstein, Mogridge, and many others who headed up institutions in this country did the same. While they were there, colony programs, family live-in cottages, and all kinds of innovations were tried and were successful. An institution is but the lengthened shadow of the person at the head of it. When Dye left the institution of Glenwood, the project that had seen a dozen children transformed from unquestioned retardation to normal was discontinued. Everything that had made this dramatic demonstration possible was still there, except for the superintendent who approved and encouraged it and for Harold Skeels, who with his quiet but persistent visits gave ideas to the ward attendants and showed a warmth and love of the children and affectionate support to the inmates who were in the background but indispensable. When these two men were not there, there was nothing. (pp. 807–808)

Thus, the larger context in which behavior management occurs is crucial to the success and maintenance of individual behavior programs.

Negative reinforcement, as an ongoing behavior management process (e.g., in institutions), is also a force to be reckoned with. Behavioral research had dealt with these factors but not in a consistent manner. Most behavior programs for the mentally retarded, especially in institutions, do not deal directly with these variables and the effect they have on the clients' behavioral repertoires.

Ecobehavioral research has addressed this second issue. Many studies have shown that, in order to reverse such a negative reinforcement cycle, one must increase the general level of positive reinforcement so that the environment offers something more intrinsically rewarding than "bad behavior" (i.e., disruptive behavior, aggression, SIB) (Horner, 1980; Williams, Schroeder, Eckerman, & Rojahn, 1983). In other words, there must be a minimum level of positive reinforcement within an environment in order for there to be a reasonable probability of positive behavior change. A big part of this "minimum level of reinforcement" is likely to be social interaction between staff and client (Tarpley & Schroeder, 1979). Thus, one factor in the success of a difficult behavior program (as programs for difficult behaviors typically are) is "deinstitutionalizing" and "rehumanizing" the institutional (or home) environment. Although Maccoby's (1980) conceptualization cannot be precisely and operationally defined and measured as yet, she and Crissey (1975) offer us a critical conceptual challenge to incorporate into our efforts to ensure, through careful assessment and planning, an optimally reinforcing environment as a backdrop to behavioral intervention with severe behavior disorders.

This is especially important because of the increasing trend toward employing reinforcement procedures instead of punishment or aversive procedures whenever possible. Intrusive procedures will likely become increasingly difficult to gain approval for and, as such, reinforcement procedures will be increasingly challenged by more difficult cases. Success may depend on our ability to take a broader look at treatment objectives (e.g., Voeltz & Evans's treatment validity, more thorough ecobehavioral assessment, consideration of social variables described by Maccoby and Crissey) and approach a higher level of conceptualization with an equally advanced assessment and intervention technology.

Summary

The use of reinforcement in behavior management programs for mentally retarded people is having widespread appeal and support, given the deemphasis on restrictive punishment procedures. This chapter has outlined the types of reinforcements and some of the factors affecting the power of reinforcement in changing behavior. The effective use of reinforcement requires careful observation and analysis of the client's behavior as well as the environment and caregiver behaviors. The goal of any behavior management program should be to develop behaviors that are desirable and helpful to the person for whom the program is being written. The behaviors should also be able to be maintained in the environment in which the person lives. The specifics of doing this at a predictable and effective level in terms of empirical and practical evidence are poorly articulated at this time. Important considerations for the professional developing the behavior management programs based on reinforcement include (a) examination of the parameters of behavior by which operant response classes are identified; (b) clearly establishing the conditions under which a stimulus is expected to be a reinforcer; (c) developing a programmatic strategy for building response repertoires; (d) matching the appropriate reinforcement techniques to antecedant conditions that affect objectives for intervention, generalization, and maintenance; (e) assessment of change not only in terms of rate of target behaviors but also reorganization of a client's covariant behaviors and how they affect the broader community of reinforced or punished behaviors; and (f) relating all of the foregoing to the ecological context in which the client lives.

References

Abramson, L. Y., Seligman, M. E. P., & Teasdale, J. D. (1978). Learned helplessness in humans: Critique and reformulation. *Journal of Abnormal Psychology, 87,* 49–74.
Allen, K. E., Hart, B. M., Buell, J. S., Harris, F. R., & Wolf, M. M. (1964). Effects of social reinforcement on isolate behavior of a nursery school child. *Child Development, 35,* 511–519.
Anderson, W. (1978). A comparison of self-destruction with self-verbalization under moralistic vs. instrumental rationales in a delay of gratification paradigm. *Cognitive Therapy and Research, 2,* 299–303.
Are all children educable? (1981). Special Issue. *Analysis and Intervention in Developmental Disabilities, 1,* 1–108.
Baer, D. M., & Wolf, M. M. (1967). *The entry into natural communities of reinforcement.* Paper presented at the meeting of the American Psychological Association, Washington, DC.
Baum, W. M. (1973). The correlation-based law of effect. *Journal of the Experimental Analysis of Behavior, 20,* 137–153.
Baumeister, A. A., & Kellas, G. (1968). Response variability among the retarded. In N. R. Ellis (Ed.), *International review of research in mental retardation* (Vol. 3). New York: Academic Press.
Baumeister, A. A., & MacLean, W. E. (1979). Brain damage and mental retardation. In N. R. Ellis (Ed.), *Handbook of mental deficiency, psychological theory and research* (2nd ed.). Hillsdale, NJ: Erlbaum.
Baumeister, A. A., & Rollings, P. (1976). Self-injurious behavior. In N. R. Ellis (Ed.), *International review of research in mental retardation* (Vol. 9). New York: Academic Press.

Bernstein, D. J., & Ebbesen, E. B. (1978). Reinforcement and substitution in humans: A multiple-response analysis. *Journal of Experimental Analysis of Behavior, 30,* 243–253.

Carr, E. G. (1977). The motivation of self-injurious behavior. *Psychological Bulletin, 84,* 800–816.

Cataldo, M., & Risley, T. (1974). Evaluation of living environments: The MANIFEST description of ward activities. In W. Davidson, H. Clark, & L. Hamerlynck (Eds.), *Evaluation of social programs in community residential and school settings.* Champaign, IL: Research Press.

Catania, A. C. (1973). The nature of learning. In J. A. Nevin & G. B. Reynolds (Eds.), *The study of behavior.* Glenview, IL: Scott, Foresman, & Co.

Crissey, M. S. (1975, August). Mental retardation: Past, present and future. *American Psychologist,* pp. 800–808.

Favell, J. E., & Cannon, P. R. (1976). Evaluation of entertainment materials for severely retarded persons. *American Journal of Mental Deficiency, 81,* 357–361.

Harris, F. R., Johnston, M. K., Kelley, C. S., & Wolf, M. M. (1964). Effects of positive social reinforcement on regressed crawling of nursery school child. *Journal of Educational Psychology, 55,* 35–41.

Herrnstein, R. J. (1970). On the law of effect. *Journal of Experimental Analysis of Behavior, 13,* 243–266.

Horner, R. D. (1980). The effects of an environmental "enrichment" program on the behavior of institutionalized profoundly retarded children. *Journal of Applied Behavior Analysis, 13,* 473–491.

Jackson, G. M., Johnson, C. R., Ackron, G. S., & Crowley, R. (1975). Food satiation as a procedure to decelerate vomiting. *American Journal of Mental Deficiency, 80,* 223–227.

Jens, K. E., & Shores, R. E. (1969). Behavioral graphs as reinforcers for work behavior of mentally retarded adolescents. *Education and Training of the Mentally Retarded, 4,* 21–28.

Johnston, M. K., Kelley, C. S., Harris, F. R., & Wolf, M. M. (1966). An application of reinforcement principles to development of motor skills of a young child. *Child Development, 37,* 377–387.

Kazdin, A. E. (1977). *The token economy.* New York: Plenum Press.

Kazdin, A. E. (1982a). *Behavior modification in applied settings* (2nd ed.). Homewood, IL: The Dorsey Press.

Kazdin, A. E. (1982b). Symptom substitution, generalization and response covariation: Implication for psychotherapy outcome. *Psychological Bulletin, 91*(2), 349–365.

Kazdin, A. E. (1982c). The token economy: A decade later. *Journal of Applied Behavioral Analysis, 15,* 431–445.

Kazdin, A. E., & Bootzin, R. L. (1972). The token economy: An examination of issues. *Journal of Applied Behavior Analysis, 5,* 343–372.

Konarski, E. A., Johnson, M. R., Crowell, C. R., & Whitman, T. L. (1980). Response deprivation and reinforcement in applied settings: A preliminary analysis. *Journal of Applied Behavior Analysis, 13,* 599–609.

Konarski, E. A., Crowell, C. R., Johnson, M. R., & Whitman, T. L. (1982). Response deprivation, reinforcement, and instrumental academic performance in an EMR classroom. *Behavior Therapy, 13,* 94–102.

Leitenberg, H., Rawson, R. A., & Bath, K. (1970). Reinforcement of competing behavior during extinction. *Science, 169,* 301–303.

Lovaas, O. I., Freitag, G., Gold, V. J., & Kassorla, I. (1965). Experimental studies in childhood schizophrenia: Analysis of self-destructive behavior. *Journal of Experimental Child Psychology, 2,* 67–84.

Maccoby, E. E. (1980). Commentary and reply to Patterson, G. R. Mothers: The Unacknowledged Victims. *Monographs of the Society of Research in Child Development, 45*(5), 56–63.

Mulick, J. A., Leitenberg, H., & Rawson, R. (1976). Alternative response training, differential reinforcement of other behavior and extinction in squirrel monkeys (*Saimiri-sciureus*). *Journal of the Experimental Analysis of Behavior, 25,* 311–320.

Mulick, J. A., Schroeder, S. R., & Rojahn, J. (1977). *A comparison of four procedures for the treatment of chronic ruminative vomiting.* Paper presented at the Gathinburg Conference on Mental Retardation, Gathinburg, Tennessee.

Mulick, J., Schroeder, S. R., & Rojahn, J. (1980). Chronic ruminative vomiting: A comparison of four procedures for treatment. *Journal of Autism and Developmental Disorders, 10,* 203–213.

Nevin, J. A. (1974). Response strength in multiple schedules. *Journal of Experimental Analysis of Behavior, 21,* 389–408.

O'Leary, K. D., & Drabman, R. (1971). Token reinforcement programs in the classroom: A review. *Psychological Bulletin, 75,* 379–398.

Patterson, G. R. (1980). Mothers: The unacknowledged victims. *Monographs of the Society for Research in Child Development, 45*(5), 1–55.

Peterson, R., & Peterson, L. (1968). The use of positive reinforcement in the control of self-destructive behavior in a retarded boy. *Journal of Experimental Child Psychology, 6,* 351–360.

Poling, A., & Ryan, C. (1982). Differential reinforcement of other behavior schedules. *Behavior Modification, 6*(1), 3–21.

Rachlin, H., & Burkhard, B. (1978). Temporal triangle: Response substitution in instrumental conditioning. *Psychological Review, 85,* 22–47.

Rojahn, J., Schroeder, S. R., & Mulick, J. (1980). Ecological assessment of self-protective restraints for the chronically self-injurious. *Journal of Autism and Developmental Disorders, 10,* 99–65.

Rollings, J. P., Baumeister, A., & Baumeister, A. (1977). The use of overcorrection procedures to eliminate stereotyped behaviors in retarded individuals. *Behavior Modification, 1,* 29–46.

Schroeder, C. S., & Schroeder, S. R. (1982). Behavior theory and practice. In J. Paul & J. Epanchin (Eds.), *Educating emotionally disturbed children.* Columbus, OH: Charles E. Merrill.

Schroeder, S. R., & MacLean, W. (1982). *If it isn't one thing, it's another: Experimental analysis of covariation in behavior management data of severely disturbed retarded persons.* Paper presented at Lake Wilderness Conference on the Impact of Residential Environments on Retarded Persons and Their Care Providers; also at Association for Behavior Analysis annual meeting, Milwaukee, Wisconsin.

Schroeder, S. R., Mulick, J. A., & Schroeder, C. S.(1979). Management of severe behavior problems of the retarded. In N. R. Ellis (Ed.), *Handbook of mental deficiency, psychological theory and research* (2nd ed.). Hillsdale, NJ: Erlbaum.

Schroeder, S. R., Mulick, J. A., & Rojahn, J. (1980). The definition, taxonomy, epidemiology, and ecology of self-injurious behavior. *Journal of Autism and Developmental Disorders, 10,* 417–432.

Schroeder, S. R., Kanoy, R., Thios, S., Mulick, J., Rojahn, J., Stephens, M., & Hawk, B. (1982). Antecedent conditions affecting management and maintenance of programs for the chronically self-injurious. In J. Hollis & C. E. Myers (Eds.), *Life threatening behavior: Analysis and intervention.* Washington, DC: AAMD Monograph Series, No. 5.

Skinner, B. F. (1938). *The behavior of organisms.* New York: Appleton-Century-Crofts.

Staddon, J. E. R. (1979). Operant behavior as adaptation to constraint. *Journal of Experimental Psychology, 103(1),* 48–67.

Staddon, J. E. R., & Simmelhag, V. L. (1971). The "superstitution" experiment: A reexamination of its implications for the principles of adaptive behavior. *Psychological Review, 76,* 3–43.

Tarpley, H. D., & Schroeder, S. R. (1979). Comparison of DRO and DRI on rate of suppression of self-injurious behavior. *American Journal of Mental Deficiency, 84(2),* 188–194.

Timberlake, W., & Allison, J. (1974). Response deprivation: An empirical approach to instrumental performance. *Psychological Review, 81,* 146–164.

Voeltz, L. M., & Evans, I. M. (1982). The assessment of behavior interrelationships in child behavior therapy. *Behavioral Assessment, 4,* 131–165.

Wahler, R. G. (1980). The insular mother: Her problems in parent–child treatment. *Journal of Applied Behavior Analysis, 13(2),* 207–219.

Weisz, J. R., & Yates, K. O. (1981). Cognitive development in retarded and nonretarded persons: Piagetian tests of the similar structure hypothesis. *Psychological Bulletin, 90(1),* 153–178.

Weisz, J. R., & Zigler, E. (1979). Cognitive development in retarded and nonretarded persons: Piagetian tests of the similar sequence hypothesis. *Psychological Bulletin, 86,* 831–851.

Whaley, D. L., & Tough, J. (1968). Treatment of a self-injurious mongoloid with shock-induced suppression and avoidance. *Michigan Department of Mental Health, 4.*

Whitman, T. L., & Scibak, J. W. (1979). Behavior modification research with the severely and profoundly retarded. In N. Ellis (Ed.), *Handbook of mental deficiency, psychological theory and research* (2nd ed.). Hillsdale, NJ: Erlbaum.

Williams, J. L., Schroeder, S. R., Eckerman, P. A., & Rojahn, J. (1983). Time-out from positive reinforcement procedures with mentally retarded persons: An ecobehavioral review and analysis. In S. E. Breuning, J. L. Matson, & R. P. Barrett (Eds.), *Advances in mental retardation and developmental disabilities* (Vol. 1). Greenwich, CT: JAI Press.

Young, J. A., & Wincze, J. P. (1974). The effects of the reinforcement of compatible and incompatible behaviors on the self-injurious and related behaviors of a profoundly retarded female adult. *Behavior Therapy, 2,* 614–623.

Zeiler, M. D. (1977). Schedules of reinforcement: The controlling variables. In W. K. Honig & J. E. R. Staddon (Eds.), *Handbook of operant behavior,* Englewood Cliffs, NJ: Prentice-Hall.

Zigler, E. (1967). Familial mental retardation: A continuing dilemma. *Science, 155,* 292–298.

Zigler, E. (1969). Developmental vs. difference theories of mental retardation and the problem of motivation. *American Journal of Mental Deficiency, 73,* 536–556.

2

Behavior Modification
Punishment

Thomas M. DiLorenzo and Thomas H. Ollendick

Introduction

Definition

Punishment is a greatly misunderstood procedure, perhaps due in part to definitional inconsistencies. There appear to be at least two distinct definitions of punishment: one definition is espoused by the professional community (i.e., behavioral clinicians and researchers), and one definition is promulgated by the lay community. The lay definition refers to any stimulus considered unpleasant to most people in our society. Thus, shouting, spanking, and cursing generally would be considered punishers. This definition differs markedly from the definition used in the behavior modification literature. Azrin and Holz (1966) define punishment as *"a reduction of the future probability of a specific response as a result of the immediate delivery of a stimulus for that response. The stimulus is designated as a punishing stimulus; the entire process is designated as punishment"* (p. 381). Note that the behavioral definition describes a process in which three essential components are outlined: (a) a behavior is defined; (b) a punishing stimulus is administered; and (c) a decrease is observed in the behavior. The lay definition more aptly defines aversive stimuli with no functional process necessarily delineated. Because the two definitions are so different, much confusion is generated when communication between these communities is initiated. This confusion

Thomas M. DiLorenzo • Department of Psychology, University of Missouri, Columbia, Missouri 65211. Thomas H. Ollendick • Department of Psychology, Virginia Polytechnic Institute and State University, Blacksburg, Virginia 24061.

often leads to a negative emotional reaction by the lay community concerning the use of punishment in a therapeutic sense. Consider the following quote that attempts to define the use of punishment in behavior therapy but that instead exemplifies the type of erroneous information disseminated to the public.

> Many parents scold or spank their children to train them. Such punishment, or "negative reinforcement," also brings about the desired behavior. But negative reinforcement breeds hostility: therefore, professional behavior therapists don't use it. (Ubell, 1983, p. 17)

This quote was taken from the popular newspaper magazine, *Parade*. Punishment, in the therapeutic sense, has been defined incorrectly, and it has been equated with negative reinforcement that also is incorrect (Michael, 1975).

In this chapter, we have attempted to dispel some of this confusion and misunderstanding by presenting data from empirical studies in the behavior modification literature that define and elaborate on various therapeutic punishment procedures. Furthermore, we will document the effective and durable effects of punishment and the efficient reduction of human suffering and dysfunction with less pain than if no punishment procedure were initiated at all (Azrin & Holz, 1966; Gardner, 1969; Johnston, 1972; Matson & DiLorenzo, 1984).

Historical Perspective and Basic Principles

Punishment and aversive events are not new nor infrequently encountered in everyday life. Kazdin (1980) has noted

> aversive techniques are deeply enmeshed in many social institutions including government and law (e.g., fines and imprisonment), education (e.g., failing grades on exams, expulsion, and probation), religion (e.g., damnation), international relations (e.g., military coercion), and normal social intercourse (e.g., discrimination, disapproval, humiliation, and social stigma). Routine interactions of most individuals with both physical and social environments result in aversive events ranging from a burn on a hot stove to verbal abuse from an acquaintance. (p. 161)

The difference between these aversive events and punishment is that punishment is

> presented in a planned and systematic fashion in order to decelerate certain types of behavior (i.e., surplus behavior). Although punishment techniques are employed, the obvious goal *is not* punishment per se. Quite to the contrary, the terminal goal is rehabilitation or improvement in the patient's psychological condition. (Bellack & Hersen, 1977, p. 216)

Many of the clinical applications in behavioral psychology (i.e., behavior therapy and behavior modification) have been based on basic animal research. Punishment is no different. The definition of punishment just presented was based on animal research and published in a seminal chapter by Azrin and Holz in 1966. Most of the punishment research conducted up to the time these researchers presented their findings was designed to define characteristics, determinants, and outcomes of punishment procedures. After reviewing the relevant data, Azrin and Holz (1966) delineated 14 considerations or guidelines that would make punishment maximally effective. These considerations are vital to the use of therapeutic punishment (as will become evident as each punishment procedure is defined) and are here summarized as they relate to clinical practice.

1. The client should not be able to escape or terminate the punishing stimulus.
2. The punishing stimulus should be fairly intense such that a reduction in the maladaptive behavior is observed.
3. The punishing stimulus should be delivered after every occurrence of the targeted behavior.
4. The punishing stimulus should be administered immediately after the maladaptive response.
5. The punishing stimulus should not be gradually increased but administered at maximum intensity.
6. The punishing stimulus should be administered in brief periods of time.
7. The punishing stimulus should not be differentially associated with the delivery of reinforcement.
8. The punishing stimulus should be a discriminative stimulus for extinction. That is, no reinforcement will be provided for the response.
9. Reinforcement for the maladaptive response should be assessed and removed.
10. The maladaptive behavior should not be positively reinforced at the same time that it is being punished.
11. Alternative responses to the punished response should be available and reinforced.
12. If an alternative response is not available in the situation where the maladaptive response is being punished, a different situation should be available to receive reinforcement.
13. If the punishing stimulus cannot be delivered in certain situations, a conditioned punishing stimulus should be given.

14. If a particular punishing stimulus cannot be used, then a reduction in positive reinforcement may be used as punishment (e.g., time-out and response cost).

Although most of the guidelines define conditions under which the punishing stimulus should be administered, several guidelines (i.e., 11 and 12) detail the need for reinforcement procedures in conjunction with the punishment procedures. The following section elaborates on this premise.

On The Need for Reinforcement While Using Punishment

Look for Behavioral Deficits

The intervention of choice varies as a function of how the target behavior is defined (Bellack & Hersen, 1977). If the problem behavior is conceptualized as a behavioral deficit, reinforcement programs are implicated as the treatment of choice. Conversely, if the problem behavior is conceptualized as a behavioral excess, punishment programs are implicated as the treatment of choice. The clinician should attempt to define most problem behaviors as deficits so that reinforcement programs may be designed. This does not appear to be a problem in many cases. Even some behavioral excesses can be reconceptualized as behavioral deficits. For example, disruptive out-of-seat behavior (i.e., a behavioral excess) could be redefined as infrequent in-seat behavior (i.e., a behavioral deficit).

Bellack and Hersen (1977) define at least three factors of which deficits may be categorized.

> First, the environment might not provide adequate prompts (S^Ds) for the [person] to emit a response already in his repertoire. Second, a response in the repertoire might be prompted, but fails to appear because its occurrence is not maintained by reinforcement. Third, the response simply might not be in the [person's] repertoire (i.e., a skill deficit). (p. 174)

These factors should be assessed with each client when program development is initiated. However, if the problem behavior is ultimately defined as a behavioral excess and some punishment procedure has been selected, reinforcement programs still must be initiated.

Why Reinforcement is Necessary when Using Punishment

As noted earlier, two guidelines for increasing the effectiveness of punishment detail the need for reinforcement procedures in conjunction with punishment. One of the justifiable criticisms of punishment is that it teaches the client what behaviors *not to exhibit* but does not teach what behavior *to exhibit*. Therefore, alternative adaptive responses should be prompted and reinforced. This point cannot be overstated. *No punishment program should ever be initiated without a reinforcement program overtly expressed and initiated either before or in addition to the punishment program.* There is no reason to expect an adaptive behavior, which is not being emitted at the present time, will increase unless reinforcement for the desired response occurs. This statement is a simple principle of learning, and yet it is often ignored.

Types of Reinforcement Schedules Used with Punishment

Several specific types of reinforcement schedules have been used in punishment programs. These schedules have been referred to as differentiation schedules or differential reinforcement of positive and/or neutral behaviors.

"In differentiation schedules reinforcers are presented when a response or a group of responses displays a specified property" (Zeiler, 1977, p. 203). At least four differentiation schedules have been defined in the behavioral literature (Deitz, Repp, & Deitz, 1976; Ferster & Skinner, 1957; Luiselli, Colozzi, Helfen, & Pollow, 1980; Repp & Brulle, 1981; Reynolds, 1968). *Differential reinforcement of other behavior* (DRO) is defined as the delivery of reinforcement when the targeted behavior has not been emitted for a specified interval. *Differential reinforcement of low rates of responding* (DRL) is defined as the delivery of reinforcement when the rate of responding of the targeted behavior is less than or equal to some specified criterion. *Differential reinforcement of incompatible responding* (DRI) is defined as the delivery of reinforcement for responses that are topographically incompatible with the targeted behavior. *Differential reinforcement of alternative behavior* (DRA) is defined as the delivery of reinforcement for adaptive behaviors that are not necessarily topographically incompatible with the targeted behavior (Repp & Brulle, 1981).

In the rest of this chapter, we will define specific punishment procedures (i.e., overcorrection, time-out from reinforcement, use of punishing stimuli, physical restraint, and response cost) and provide specific treatment considerations that should be assessed when applying these techniques. In addition, some issues related to practical application of the procedures will be presented. Finally, extinction will be considered as a reductive procedure, specific issues that are important to consider when using punishment will be presented, and ethical and legal issues will be discussed.

Overcorrection (A Work Procedure)

Definition

Azrin and Foxx introduced overcorrection in the early 1970s as a viable method to reduce maladaptive behavior (Azrin & Foxx, 1971; Foxx & Azrin, 1972, 1973). As originally conceptualized:

> The general rationale of the proposed restitution procedure is to educate the offender to assume individual responsibility for the disruption caused by his misbehavior by requiring him to restore the disturbed situation to a greatly improved state. (1972, p. 16)

Although overcorrection has been defined as an educative procedure or as a type of reinforcement, Axelrod, Brantner, and Meddock (1978) note that because the purpose of overcorrection is to decrease the frequency, duration, and/or intensity of the inappropriate behavior that precedes the application of the overcorrection technique, it is, by definition, punishment.

Overcorrection has been defined as a two-stage process whereby the client must provide some work and expend some effort for some disruption. The first stage, referred to as *restitution overcorrection*, requires the client to restore the area that was disturbed to its original condition. For example, if a client kicked over a bucket of water, he or she would be required to mop the disturbed area (restitution) as well as clean and/ or mop other adjoining areas (overcorrection). Therefore, the required work would result in considerably more effort than merely reversing the original disruptive behavior. The purpose for the extended effort is to make the task particularly aversive by doing additional repetitive tasks that result in increased expenditure of effort (Matson & DiLorenzo, 1984).

The second stage, defined as *positive practice overcorrection*, requires the client to practice appropriate modes of responding in situations where that individual normally misbehaves (Azrin & Powers, 1975; Foxx & Martin, 1975). For example, after the individual completes restitution overcorrection, the bucket would be set up again in the disrupted area, and the client would be required to walk past and around the bucket appropriately (positive practice). This task would be repeated 10 to 20 times (overcorrection) (Matson & DiLorenzo, 1984).

Treatment Considerations

Three treatment considerations are addressed: (a) topographical similarity; (b) latency of implementation; and (c) duration of the procedure. As originally conceptualized, the overcorrection response should be similar to the misbehavior. However, the results of research addressing this point are equivocal. Many early studies utilized responses that were topographically similar to the maladaptive behavior. For example, Foxx and Azrin's oral hygiene procedure had been used for mouthing of objects (Foxx & Azrin, 1973), biting (Foxx & Azrin, 1972), and coprophagy (Foxx & Martin, 1975). In addition, Harris and Romanczyk (1976) required arm and head exercises contingent on head-banging.

However, several studies have demonstrated suppressive effects with topographically dissimilar behaviors. Doke and Epstein (1975) and Epstein, Doke, Sajwaj, Sorrell, and Rimmer (1974) treated inappropriate vocal and nonvocal behaviors with topographically dissimilar overcorrection responses. In addition, Ollendick, Matson, and Martin (1978) and Wells, Forehand, Hickey, and Green (1977) demonstrated that dissimilar overcorrection responses could reduce the incidence of the targeted response. However, it is suggested that overcorrection may be more effective when topographically similar responses are used and that learning of appropriate incompatible behaviors may occur only when these same responses are chosen (Ollendick & Matson, 1978).

Latency of implementation of the overcorrection contingency is the second consideration. Little research has been conducted on the effectiveness of immediate versus delayed consequation of the overcorrection procedure. Although Azrin and Powers (1975) demonstrated equal effectiveness of immediate and delayed application of the overcorrection contingency, a number of methodological shortcomings make the results inconclusive. In actual practice, we would suspect that it is better to consequate the misbehavior as soon after it occurs as possible.

The third treatment consideration involves the duration of the work procedure. A wide variety of durations of the overcorrection procedure have been successfully utilized to control maladaptive behavior including 30 seconds (Smeets, Elson, & Clement, 1975), 1 minute (Freeman, Graham, & Ritvo, 1975), 3 minutes (Nunn & Azrin, 1976), 5 minutes (Ollendick & Matson, 1976), 10 minutes (Harris & Romanczyk, 1976), 30 minutes (Foxx & Azrin, 1972), 1 hour (Azrin & Wesolowski, 1975b), and 2 hours (Foxx, 1976a). In addition, several studies (Foxx, 1977; Foxx & Azrin, 1973; Ollendick & Matson, 1976; Sumner, Meuser, Hsu, & Morales, 1974) demonstrated that increasing the duration of the overcorrection procedure increased its effectiveness.

Types of Problems Treated

Overcorrection has been proven to be very effective in reducing a broad range of maladaptive behaviors. Table 1 has a representative listing of studies noting the problem behaviors treated and population. It

Table 1. Overcorrection Studies

Study	Population	Behaviors treated
Azrin, Gottlieb, Hughart, Wesolowski, & Rahn (1975)	Retarded children	Self-stimulatory rocking and hand movements
Azrin, Kaplan, & Foxx (1973)	Retarded adults	Various self-injurious behaviors
Azrin, Sneed, & Foxx (1973)	Retarded adults	Enuresis
Azrin & Wesolowski (1974)	Retarded adults	Stealing
Azrin & Wesolowski (1975a)	Retarded adults	Self-injurious vomiting
Azrin & Wesolowski (1975b)	Retarded adults	Floor sprawling
Barrett & Shapiro (1980)	Retarded child	Self-injurious hair pulling
Drabman, Cruz, Ross, & Lynd (1979)	Retarded children	Drooling
Foxx (1976b)	Retarded adult	Public disrobing
Foxx & Azrin (1972)	Retarded adults	Aggressive behavior
Foxx & Azrin (1973)	Retarded children	Self-stimulatory mouthing and head weaving
Foxx & Martin (1975)	Retarded adults	Self-injurious pica and coprophagy
Harris & Romanczyk (1976)	Retarded child	Self-injurious head banging
Luiselli, Helfen, Pemberton, & Reisman (1977)	Retarded child	Self-stimulatory repetitive masturbation
Martin & Matson (1978)	Retarded adult	Disruptive vocalizations
Matson & Stephens (1981)	Retarded adults	Various stereotypies
Measel & Alfieri (1976)	Retarded children	Self-injurious head banging
O'Brien & Azrin (1972)	Retarded adults	Inappropriate eating behavior
Ollendick, Matson, & Martin (1978)	Retarded adults	Self-stimulatory head shaking and nose touching
Rollings, Baumeister, & Baumeister (1977)	Retarded adult	Self-stimulatory rocking
Townsend & Marholin (1978)	Retarded child	Self-stimulatory rocking
Webster & Azrin (1973)	Retarded adults	Disruptive behaviors

can be seen that overcorrection has been used to treat self-stimulatory behaviors, self-injurious behaviors, aggressive behaviors, and other disruptive or maladaptive behaviors.

Advantages of Overcorrection

There are several distinct advantages to using overcorrection. First, it is quite effective. Controlling a maladaptive behavior in a few sessions is more the rule than the exception (Matson & DiLorenzo, 1984). Second, overcorrection has been shown to be more effective than a number of other procedures including verbal warnings, restraint, simple correction, contingent social isolation, extinction, and reinforcement alone. Third, overcorrection appears to be readily accepted by staff and the lay community. Fourth, as noted earlier, overcorrection is very effective with a broad range of problems and with both mentally retarded adults and children.

Time-Out from Reinforcement

Definition

Time-out from reinforcement, or simply time-out, has been defined in a number of ways. Some researchers have defined *time-out* as the removal of all positive reinforcers from a certain period of time (Kazdin, 1980; Wells & Forehand, 1981). Others define time-out as removing an individual from positively reinforcing events (Bellack & Hersen, 1977). Still others define it as a combination of the preceding (Harris & Ersner-Hershfield, 1978; Plummer, Baer, & LeBlanc, 1977; Rimm & Masters, 1979).

Harris and Ersner-Hershfield's (1978) definition appears to be rather comprehensive and will be used here. Time-out is defined as

> removing attention or another reinforcing event upon emission of the target behavior. This removal is marked clearly by such events as removing the subject from the room, physical withdrawal of the therapist, or other discrete acts that signal the withdrawal of reinforcement. Return of access to reinforcement may be contingent upon cessation of the target behavior. This procedure is often called time-out but is more actively punishing than most definitions of time-out permit. (p. 1356)

Parameters of Time-Out

Ten specific parameters by which time-out is suggested to be maximally effective have been delineated (Hobbs & Forehand, 1977; MacDonough & Forehand, 1973; Matson & DiLorenzo, 1984; Solnick, Rincover, & Peterson, 1977; White, Nielsen, & Johnson, 1972). The first parameter is *duration*. Effective time-out durations have ranged from 10 seconds to 3 hours, although most studies have used time-out durations of from 5 to 20 minutes. Rimm and Masters (1979) suggest "5 minutes is a reasonable rule-of-thumb for initial implementation" (p. 187). There are several important points to consider when deciding on the duration of time-out periods. Time-out periods that are too short may be ineffective (Rimm & Masters, 1979; Sailor, Guess, Rutherford,

& Baer, 1968), and time-out periods that are too long may decrease the opportunity for the clients to learn more adaptive behaviors, subject a person to an unnecessary aversive experience, and increase the rate of deviant behavior (Sailor *et al.*, 1968; White *et al.*, 1972).

The second parameter, *presence of a stimulus to indicate the onset of time-out*, refers to a nonverbal signal that time-out is beginning or has ended. No definitive data are available concerning the efficacy of this procedure.

The third parameter *contrasts instructing a client to go to a time-out room with physically placing him or her in the room.* Although no comparative data exist, it is generally agreed that a minimal amount of force should be used to minimize injury and/or modeling of agressive behavior.

The next parameter involves *schedules* of time-out. Clark, Rowbury, Baer, and Baer (1973) compared four intermittent schedules of time-out, and their results suggest an inverse nonlinear relationship between the percentage of responses punished and the frequency of the response. At this time, the data suggest that a continuous schedule should be used for initial suppression of the targeted behavior; however, an intermittent schedule may be effective for maintenance (Matson & DiLorenzo, 1984).

The fifth parameter, *location* of time-out, refers to the actual physical location where the client is placed. The client may be placed either in a separate area or room or isolated in the same area where the act took place. Although MacDonough and Forehand (1973) suggest that the major advantage to the separate-area technique is the probability that positive reinforcement will be effectively removed, recent court decisions have severely restricted the use of exclusionary time-outs in many institutional settings. Therefore, other forms of time-out should be explored including a requirement to stand in the corner (Barrett, 1969; Hobbs, Forehand, & Murray, 1978), use of a time-out chair (Carlson, Arnold, Becker, & Madsen, 1968), use of a modified time-out room (Harris, Ersner-Hershfield, Kaffashan, & Romanczyk, 1974; Kendall, Nay, & Jeffers, 1975), and nonexclusionary techniques (Foxx & Shapiro, 1978).

Response-contingent versus a fixed duration time-out is the next parameter. Patterson and White (1970) have suggested the use of response-contingent time-out, and a number of studies have utilized this technique. Hobbs and Forehand (1975) compared contingent and noncontingent release from time-out, and their conclusions indicated that contingent release was more effective and less disruptive than noncontingent release. The critical variable appears to be the reinforcement of adaptive behavior at the time of the release.

Although Parameters 7 and 8 (i.e., a verbal warning before the administration of contingent time-out and the use of an explanation for time-out) have some heuristic value, their use appears to be less important with a mentally retarded population as opposed to a normal child population because higher level cognitive functioning is implicated as the important dimension (Wilson & Lyman, 1982). The ninth parameter involves *the reinforcing value of the natural environment* and is critically important to time-out. Theoretically, time-out from reinforcement presumes the prior establishment of reinforcement in the natural environment (Matson & DiLorenzo, 1984). If this were not the case, the observed reductions in behavior when using time-out may be due to the aversive nature of the time-out room and not the removal of reinforcement. If reinforcement does not exist in the natural environment, time-out may fit a negative reinforcement paradigm or serve as an escape (Plummer *et al.*, 1977; Solnick *et al.*, 1977) from the dreary institutional environment or demanding learning situations to which clients are exposed (Carr, Newsom, & Binkoff, 1976).

Baum (1973) suggests that just referring to the punishing situation is not enough. Instead, the relationship between situations before and after a punishing stimulus is delivered may better define the reinforcing and punishing effects of the stimulus. Solnick *et al.* (1977) examined this situation by establishing a time-out contingency with a 16-year-old mentally retarded boy in both an enriched and impoverished environment. Time-out was effective only in the enriched environment condition, suggesting the reinforcing value of the natural environment is an important issue.

The final parameter has been defined by Hobbs and Forehand (1977) as *presence versus absence of an adult* during time-out and by Matson and DiLorenzo (1984) as *subject removal versus specific reinforcer removal*. Specific reinforcers that have been removed during time-out include parental attention (Forehand, Roberts, Doleys, Hobbs, & Resick, 1976; Scarboro & Forehand, 1975), television and music (Greene & Hoats, 1969; Greene, Hoats, & Hornick, 1970; Hauck & Martin, 1970; Ritschl, Mongrella, & Presbie, 1972), food (Barton, Guess, Garcia, & Baer, 1970; Martin, MacDonald, & Omichinski, 1971; O'Brien & Azrin, 1972), and visual field (Barrett, Staub, & Sisson, 1983; Lutzker, 1978; McGonigle, Duncan, Cordisco, & Barrett, 1982; Rincover & Devany, 1982; Singh, Beale, & Dawson, 1981; Zegiob, Alford, & House, 1978). In addition, several researchers (Foxx & Shapiro, 1978; Husted, Hall, & Agin, 1971; Spitalnik & Drabman, 1976) have suggested innovative forms of nonexclusionary time-out procedures. For example, Spitalnik and Drabman (1976) designed a reinforcement and time-out procedure for two mentally retarded children. Time-out was defined as "the interruption of an ongoing reinforcement system, for a fixed time period, contingent upon the emission of inappropriate behavior" (p. 17). When a time-out was warranted, an orange card was placed on the child's desk at which time reinforcement was not dispensed.

Types of Problems Treated

Time-out has been empirically validated as an efficacious approach in perhaps more studies, for more populations, and more problem behaviors than any other punishment procedure. Table 2 has a representative listing of studies noting the problem behavior treated and the population. A wide variety of problematic behaviors have been treated including aggressive and disruptive behaviors, self-injurious behaviors, abusive verbal behaviors, inappropriate eating behaviors, and noncompliant behaviors.

Advantages of Time-Out

There are a number of advantages to using time-out. First, a number of very short durations have been quite effective in controlling maladaptive behaviors. This major advantage eliminates prolonged confinement periods that increase the probability that appropriate behaviors will occur and be reinforced. Another advantage is that time-out can be rather portable and adaptable. Third, time-out removes the individual from the situation that may be reinforcing the maladaptive behavior.

Also, positive side effects have been observed including increases in participation in ward activities and interactions (Barrett, 1969; Bostow & Bailey, 1969; Brawley, Harris, Allen, Fleming, & Peterson, 1969; Hamilton, Stephens, & Allen, 1967; Sachs, 1973) and increases in appropriate eating behavior (Edwards & Lilly, 1966; Martin et al., 1971).

A fifth advantage addresses the issue of the increased potential for physical harm with extremely disruptive behaviors. When time-out is conducted appropriately, there is a decrease in the likelihood of physical harm done to the individual and/or others around that person as well as fewer disruptions to the physical environment (Bellack & Hersen, 1977; Matson, Ollendick, & DiLorenzo, 1980).

Also, time-out is relatively easy to teach to staff members or family who will be administering the procedure (Barrett, 1969; Laws, Brown, Epstein, & Hocking, 1971; Nordquist & Wahler, 1973). A method such as time-out also decreases the need for psychotrophic medications used as chemical restraints (Matson & DiLorenzo, 1984).

Table 2. Time-Out Studies

Study	Population	Behaviors treated
Adams, Klinge, & Keiser (1973)	Retarded child	Self-injurious behaviors
Anderson, Herrmann, Alpert, & Dancis (1975)	Retarded child	Self-injurious behaviors
Azrin & Foxx (1971)	Retarded adults	Incontinence
Barton, Guess, Garcia, & Baer (1970)	Retarded children	Inappropriate mealtime behaviors
Bostow & Bailey (1969)	Retarded adult	Abusive verbal behaviors
Brawley, Harris, Allen, Fleming, & Peterson (1969)	Retarded child	Self-injurious behaviors
Calhoun & Lima (1977)	Retarded child	Disruptive behaviors
Calhoun & Matherne (1975)	Retarded child	Aggressive behaviors
Cayner & Kiland (1974)	Retarded adults	Disruptive behaviors
Clark, Rowbury, Baer, & Baer (1973)	Retarded child	Aggressive behaviors
Doyleys, Wells, Hobbs, Roberts, & Cartelli (1976)	Retarded children	Noncompliant behaviors
Hamilton & Stephens (1967)	Retarded adult	Self-stimulatory behaviors
Hamilton, Stephens, & Allen (1967)	Retarded adults	Aggressive behaviors
Husted, Hall, & Agin (1971)	Retarded children	Self-injurious behavior
Iwata & Lorentzson (1976)	Retarded adult	Seizurelike behavior
Mansdorf (1977)	Retarded adult	Noncompliant behavior
Martin, MacDonald, & Omichinski (1971)	Retarded children	Inappropriate eating behavior
O'Brien, Bugle, & Azrin (1972)	Retarded child	Inappropriate eating behavior
Pendergrass (1972)	Retarded children	Noncompliant behaviors
Reichle, Brubakken, & Tetreault (1976)	Retarded child	Perseverative speech
Solnick, Rincover, & Peterson (1977)	Retarded child	Self-injurious behavior
Spitalnik & Drabman (1976)	Retarded children	Inappropriate speech
Tate & Baroff (1966)	Retarded child	Self-injurious behavior
Vukelich & Hake (1971)	Retarded adult	Aggressive behavior
Wiesen & Watson (1967)	Retarded child	Noncompliant behavior
Winkler (1977)	Retarded adult	Disruptive behavior

In addition, when release of time-out is contingent on appropriate behaviors, not only are these behaviors reinforced, but also the release may serve as a negative reinforcer for the development of behaviors that are incompatible with the targeted behavior (Matson *et al.*, 1980). Finally, time-out interrupts a situation that has explosive potential. The staff person (or family member) as well as the client can use this interval to consider his or her own behavior, to calm down, and to review alternative appropriate behaviors (Kanfer & Phillips, 1970).

Punishing Stimuli

At the present time, overcorrection and time-out are the most widely used punishment procedures. However, this was not always the case. During the late 1960s and early 1970s when much punishment research was being conducted with animals, the application of punishment procedures was just being started with humans. During this time, very specific punishing stimuli were presented upon the emanation of maladaptive behavior. Although punishing stimuli are used relatively less often than overcorrection and time-out, procedures utilizing these stimuli remain as viable options to treat extreme forms of maladaptive behavior.

Definition and Types

Researchers originally considered punishing stimuli to be quite specific as opposed to elaborate procedures (i.e., overcorrection and time-out). Therefore, any specific stimulus that reduces the future probability that a response will occur would be considered a punishing stimulus. Contingent electric shock was the first punishing stimulus that was thoroughly researched with humans.

A procedure utilizing contingent electric shock as the punishing stimulus would be conducted as follows. Immediately following an operationally defined behavior that the clinician is attempting to suppress, an electrical charge is presented through two electrodes placed either on the fingers, forearms, legs, or feet of the client (Rimm & Masters, 1979). The electrodes are fastened with elastic or cloth strips and electrode paste is used to increase conductance (Bellack & Hersen, 1977). An inductorium device is used to supply the electric current through the electrodes (Galbraith, Byrick, & Rutledge, 1970; Pfeiffer & Johnson, 1968; Royer, Rynearson, Rice, & Upper, 1971).

Contingent electric shock *is not* the same procedure as electroconvulsive shock therapy (ECT). ECT is a procedure designed to change the mood of an individual who has been diagnosed with some form of psychopathology such as psychotic depression. The electrical current is directed through the brain, and the voltage is quite high.

Quite differently, contingent electric shock is aimed at the suppression of a particular maladaptive behavior such as head banging and, therefore, its purpose is more specific than ECT. In addition, contingent electric shock is administered to one of the limbs (never to the brain or trunk) and involves no convulsions, no loss of consciousness, and no tissue damage as might be expected from ECT (Craven, 1970). Finally, the voltage used with contingent electric shock is fairly low in comparison with ECT. Lovaas and Simmons (1969) report that the shock felt like "a dentist drilling on an unanesthetized tooth" (p. 149). Typically, the shock is presented for less than 1 second. The voltage, duration of the charge, and the focus of the charge on the body are of considerable importance both in the purpose of treatment and type of effects achieved.

Other stimuli that have been administered contingent on the emission of maladaptive behaviors and that have resulted in the reduction of the behavior include noxious substances. Noxious substances are defined as any substances that are not physically harmful but that are unpleasant for the client to either hear, ingest, or smell (Matson & DiLorenzo, 1984). In addition, for a noxious substance to be considered a punishing stimulus, it must fulfill all the other properties of punishing stimuli (i.e., consistent application, reduction in behavior observed, etc.). Some examples would include lemon juice (Apolito & Sulzer-Azaroff, 1981; Cook, Altman, Shaw, & Blaylock, 1978; Marholin, Luiselli, Robinson, & Lott, 1980), aromatic ammonia (Altman, Haavik, & Cook, 1978; Tanner & Zeiler, 1975), ice (Drabman, Ross, Lynd, & Cordua, 1978), noise (Barrett, 1962), water squirts (Robinson, Hughes, Wilson, Lahey, & Haynes, 1974), and mouthwash (Matson & Ollendick, 1976; Pollow, McPhee, Luiselli, & Marholin, 1980).

Finally, there are a number of other stimuli that have been used to decrease the frequency of problematic behaviors. Some of these punishing stimuli include reprimands or verbal commands (Baumeister & Forehand, 1972; Kazdin, 1971), slaps (Koegel & Covert, 1972; Koegel, Firestone, Kramme, & Dunlap, 1974; Marshall, 1966; Romanczyk, 1977), and shaking (Risley, 1968).

Treatment Considerations

There are several treatment conditions specific for the use of contingent electric shock. First, high quality brand-name equipment should be purchased, and only specially trained personnel should be permitted to use it. These persons should be aware of the potential hazards when using this type of equipment.

Because humans differ in their sensitivity to shock, *a priori* decisions regarding shock intensities should be avoided. Instead, the clinician should choose the minimal level of shock that will produce the desired effects.

Placement of the electrodes is critical. As noted, the electrodes should not be placed on the head or torso. The electrodes should be placed approximately 2 inches apart on the same limb. Therefore, the current will travel a very short distance. Additional safety precautions include avoiding water on the floor and metal objects. Finally, the shock unit should be battery operated. This would decrease the potential hazard of an undue amount of shock, and the battery operated units are much smaller and therefore more portable (Matson & DiLorenzo, 1984).

There are several treatment considerations that should be addressed in the use of noxious substances and other punishing stimuli. As with contingent electric shock, the least amount or degree of the punishing stimulus that achieves the desired effects should be administered. This will help to prevent the potential for physical harm and abuse. In addition, great care should be taken to administer the stimuli each time the maladaptive behavior occurs in a precise manner. Given the nature of these stimuli, variability of administration could be a problem. Finally, although not empirically validated, it would appear that the stimulus should be topographically specific to the problem behavior. For example, water squirts or mouthwash applied to the self-injurious behavior of lip biting may prove to be more effective than noise.

Types of Problems Treated

Because of the wide array of punishing stimuli, a number of problem behaviors have been treated successfully. Table 3 presents several studies noting the populations, behaviors treated, and types of punishing stimuli used with each. As can be seen in the table, self-injurious behaviors, self-stimulatory behaviors, and aggressive behaviors have been treated with a variety of punishing stimuli.

Advantages of Punishing Stimuli

There are at least three advantages to using contingent electric shock. First, when used appropriately, effects are observed very quickly with no physical harm done to the client. Second, administration of the stimulus is quite precise. It can be specified in terms of milliamperes and volts in minute amounts that are consistent across the time that the electrical discharge occurs and across administrations (Matson & DiLorenzo, 1984). Third, the shock can be applied directly to the body part where the maladaptive behavior occurs, assuming arms or legs are implicated.

Table 3. Punishing Stimuli Studies

Study	Population	Behaviors treated	Punishing stimulus
Altman, Haavik, & Cook (1978)	Retarded children	Self-injurious behaviors	Aromatic ammonia
Apolito & Sulzer-Azaroff (1981)	Retarded child	Chronic vomiting	Lemon juice
Baumeister & Forehand (1972)	Retarded children	Body rocking	Verbal commands and contingent electric shock
Browning (1971)	Retarded/Autistic children	Aggressive behavior	Contingent electric shock
Koegel & Covert	Austistic children	Self-stimulating behavior	Slaps
Lovaas & Simmons (1969)	Retarded children	Self-injurious behaviors	Contingent electric shock
Matson & Ollendick (1976)	Retarded adult	Biting	Mouthwash
Pollow, McPhee, Luiselli, & Marholin (1980)	Retarded child	Vocal disruptions	Mouthwash
Robinson, Hughes, Wilson, Lahey, & Haynes (1974)	Autistic children	Self-stimulating behavior	Water squirts
Sajwaj, Libet, & Agras (1974)	An infant	Chronic rumination	Lemon juice
Tate & Baroff (1966)	Retarded/Autistic child	Self-injurious head banging	Contingent electric shock

With other punishing stimuli, effects also are observed quickly even with severe and highly resistant behaviors. Also, as with contingent electric shock, noxious substances and other punishing stimuli can be topographically similar to the maladaptive behavior. Finally, noxious stimuli have been considered less objectionable than contingent electric shock (Luiselli, 1981). Because some similar behaviors have been successfully treated with both noxious substances and contingent electric shock, it would be important to consider these noxious stimuli first when designing a program.

Physical Restraint

Definition

Traditionally, *physical restraint* has referred to the use of leather or cloth bracelets to restrict the movement of a client's limbs (Rosen & DiGiacomo, 1978). Physical restraint had been used primarily with psychotic clients to control violent behavior (Abroms, 1968; Bursten, 1975;

Wells, 1972). However, physical restraint in the behavior modification literature refers to a very different procedure. Matson and DiLorenzo (1984) have referred to physical restraint as a special case of time-out where a client is removed from an environment that is highly reinforcing. These authors define physical restraint as the physical restriction of the movement of a person's limbs (e.g., holding the limb behind the person's back) for a specified brief period of time. The procedure is initiated, contingent on the emission of a specific behavior that is functionally related to the limbs involved in the procedure. Finally, the expressed purpose of the procedure is to decrease the future probability of the occurrence of the targeted behavior. This procedure is a relatively new advancement in the behavioral literature, and therefore, little research has been conducted using physical restraint.

Treatment Considerations

Matson and DiLorenzo (1984) suggest that because physical restraint is a type of time-out procedure, it should be used only after consideration has been made of the procedures, rules, and guidelines ascribed to time-out. As mentioned earlier, some potential considerations would be duration, location, schedules, response-contingent versus fixed duration, warnings, explanations, and reinforcing value of the natural environment. In addition, the weight, height, and strength of the client should be taken into consideration because the clinician would want to avoid a confrontation that could produce injury to both the client and clinician.

Types of Problems Treated

Although physical restraint has been a widely used technique in dealing with self-injurious behavior of mentally retarded clients (Baumeister & Rollings, 1976), it has not been researched extensively. An example of the procedure recently was documented by Rapoff, Altman, and Christophersen (1980). They used brief physical restraint successfully to reduce the self-hitting of a mentally retarded child. During the treatment phase, upon each occurrence of the child's hitting, the teacher held both hands behind his back for 30 seconds. Using a reversal design, the behavior was observed to be functionally controlled by the treatment phases.

Other behaviors that have been reduced successfully using physical restraint include inappropriate eating behavior (Henricksen & Doughty, 1967), crawling behavior (O'Brien, Azrin, & Bugle, 1972), self-destructive behavior (Saposnek & Watson, 1974), and soiling accidents (Giles & Wolf, 1966).

Advantages of Physical Restraint

Most of the advantages delineated with time-out also apply to physical restraint. This type of procedure may also prove to be an effective method to reduce self-injury where placement in a time-out room may prove to be inappropriate.

Response Cost (A Penalty Procedure)

Definition

Response cost is a punishment procedure based primarily on assessing fines or withdrawing positive reinforcers. Typically, response cost is one part of token economy systems. In the reinforcement component of a token economy, individuals earn tokens or some other form of tangible product for exhibiting appropriate behavior. At some later time, they are given the opportunity to trade the tokens for reinforcers. If the individual exhibits inappropriate or maladaptive behavior, tokens will be removed or fines assessed.

Overview

Response cost has been documented as a very effective procedure for reducing certain behaviors, although it has not been researched extensively. Few published reports have discussed the potential application of response cost with mentally retarded clients. In one example, Kazdin (1973) treated 40 mentally retarded adults for speech dysfluencies. He compared response cost (i.e., withdrawal of tokens), aversive sound stimulation (i.e., a loud noise), information feedback, and a no-treatment control. Response cost proved to be more effective than aversive sound stimulation, and both were superior to the other two groups. Also, the author noted that response cost led to greater response generalization (i.e., suppression of related but nonpunished speech dysfluencies).

Extinction

Definition

Although in a technical sense, *extinction* is not considered a punishment procedure because a specific stimulus is not applied (Azrin & Holz, 1966; Matson & DiLorenzo, 1984), it will be discussed briefly because a reduction in the future probability of a response is observed when the procedure is used correctly. Harris and Ersner-Hershfield (1978) define extinction as the

> withholding of previously given positive reinforcement following the emission of the target behavior. No discriminative cues, such as environmental changes or verbal warnings, are given. For example, in using an extinction procedure to treat tantrums, the therapist simply ignores the tantrum behavior and proceeds as though nothing has happened. (pp. 1355–1356)

Extinction is probably one of the most widely *attempted* procedures and likewise the most widely misunderstood. Clear and serious associated effects accompany and probably outweigh its use in most circumstances. These effects are detailed in the next section.

Treatment Considerations

Matson and DiLorenzo (1984) outlined 12 treatment considerations when using extinction. Although space does not permit us to list all of these, we will highlight the most important. First, the ease with which a response is extinguished is directly related to the frequency of the response-reinforcement relationship. That is, those responses that are continuously reinforced are much easier to extinguish than intermittently reinforced responses (Kazdin, 1980). Most responses in everyday life are intermittently reinforced.

Second, *every* response must be consequated. If not, an intermittent reinforcement schedule is produced, and the response is maintained indefinitely. Third, responses are harder to extinguish if (a) the behavior has been greatly reinforced; (b) the behavior has been in existence a long time; and (c) the behavior has been exposed to extinction repeatedly. All three of the preceding are typically true of resistant high-rate maladaptive behaviors exhibited by the general population and specifically, mentally retarded clients. Fourth, extinction is a gradual process. It usually takes a long time for extinction to work. Therefore, high-rate self-injurious behaviors should not be exposed to extinction. Fifth, extinction "bursts" should be expected. Extinction bursts are defined as increases in the maladaptive behavior to above baseline levels after an initial decrease has been observed. This phenomenon occurs because of an attempt by the client to regain the reinforcement that is no longer dispensed.

Because of the serious nature of many of the maladaptive behaviors emitted by mentally retarded clients, extinction is simply not suggested as a treatment of choice in most instances. It is simply too difficult to ignore extremely harmful behaviors for long periods of time. We are not saying that extinction is not an effective procedure if the preceding treatment considerations are observed. However, in most applied settings, it is virtually impossible to gain the amount of control necessary to make the procedure effective.

Issues in Implementing Punishment Procedures

Kazdin (1980) suggests some general considerations that should be heeded before selecting a procedure to implement, including

> severity of behavior, the danger of the behavior to the client or the others, the ease of implementing the technique in a particular setting, and the training required of the person(s) who will administer the program. (p. 179)

In addition, several specific steps should be followed. A good functional analysis of the behavior and the situation is necessary. A functional analysis involves the operational definition of the problem behavior and a thorough assessment of the antecedent and consequent conditions that control the behavior. For example, if *head banging* (i.e., head hit against the floor or wall) was defined as the maladaptive behavior, the clinician should observe what behaviors or environmental events occur just before the client headbangs (e.g., client is asked to begin working on a project) and what behaviors or environmental events occur just after the head-banging incident (e.g., the work assignment is terminated). In this example, it may be speculated that the head banging serves as a stimulus to avoid work and is being negatively reinforced by the termination of the work assignment.

The antecedent and consequent conditions are termed the *controlling variables* and general patterns of antecedent–behavior–consequence should be delineated. Consequent to this functional analysis, a procedure should be selected that would manipulate the controlling variables in the most efficacious way to change the behavior in a desirable and predictable direction (Schreibman & Koegel, 1981). An attempt should be made to define the behavior as a deficit so that reinforcement programs may be initiated. However, if the behavior is defined as an excess, the clinician may refer to the preceding sections to decide what punishment programs have been designed to treat the maladaptive behavior in the past and/or what programs are most suited for treating the present problem.

Next, Azrin and Holz's (1966) 14 considerations-guidelines should be consulted. An attempt should be made to meet as many considerations as possible. Finally, the clinician should refer to the treatment considerations listed under the punishment procedure selected, and each guideline should be observed. Johnston (1972) has noted:

> It must be stressed that the successful use of the punishment paradigm cannot be reduced simply to such a concise summary of principles; these basic principles must be expanded in application to a variety of procedural details, the importance of any one of which will vary with each situation. Ignoring any one of these variables certainly does not doom necessarily any particular manipulation of therapeutic endeavor: rather, the probability of maximally effective results from any punishment paradigm is increased to the extent that such factors are carefully considered in the design and execution of the study or therapeutic attempt. (p. 1034)

In addition to the actual construction of the program, clinical and staffing demands must be assessed (Matson & Kazdin, 1981). These demands refer to practical considerations such as proficiency of staff in applying punishment programs and a sufficient number of staff to employ the procedures. Considerable variability may exist in staff ability to execute the contingencies depending upon the type and frequency of the targeted behavior, the environment in which assessment and training occur, and characteristics of the client (Matson & DiLorenzo, 1984).

Another important practical concern is the training of staff. In addition to a simple explanation of the procedure, supervised hands-on instruction, role plays, and feedback are absolutely necessary. This is not an easy task, and often it is quite time consuming, difficult to implement, and requires continued supervision (Kazdin & Moyer, 1976; Matson & Ollendick, 1977). This training is necessary, though, because most caregivers will not have the requisite skills prior to the development of the program.

Finally, consistency is critically important. Kazdin (1980) suggests that the major contribution of behavior modification programs is to "ensure that consequences are delivered systematically and consistently so that they produce the desired results" (p. 57). Consistency, in this respect, takes the form of consequences delivered. Schreibman and Koegel (1981) suggest the following guidelines:

> 1. *The consequence must be contingent upon the behavior.* This means that to be effective a consequence must follow *only* the specific target behavior and be

present *immediately* upon the behavior's occurrence. . . . 2. *The consequence delivery must be consistent.* If a consequence is to be effective, it must be presented in the same manner and contingent upon the same behavior across trials. . . . 3. *The consequence must be delivered in an unambiguous manner.* The nature of the consequence must always be clear to the [client]. . . . 4. *The consequence should be easily discriminable.* The therapist must make the consequence obvious to the [client]. The best way to do this is to present the stimulus strongly and to minimize extraneous cues at the time. (pp. 520–521)

After the program has been designed, implemented, and encouraging results are observed, the clinician must focus on maintenance and generalization of treatment gains. In a seminal paper on generalization, Stokes and Baer (1977) observed:

> Traditionally, many theorists have considered generalization to be a *passive* phenomenon. Generalization was not seen as an operant response that could be programmed, but as a description of a "natural" outcome of any behavior-change process. . . . Even though the literature shows many instances of generalization, it is still frequently observed that when a change in behavior has been accomplished through experimental contingencies, then that change is manifest where and when those contingencies operate, and is often seen in only transitory forms in other places and at other times. The frequent need for generalization of therapeutic behavior change is widely accepted, but it is not always realized that generalization does not automatically occur simply because a behavior change is accomplished. Thus, the need actively to *program* generalization, rather than passively to expect it as an outcome of certain training procedures, is a point requiring both emphasis and effective techniques. (pp. 349–350)

Several pragmatic techniques have been suggested to help maintain and generalize treatment effects (Kazdin, 1980). First, the changed behavior should be brought under the control of natural contingencies. Some behaviors are consistently reinforced or punished in the client's natural environment. The clinician should focus on these behaviors and consequate them as they would be in the natural environment (e.g., praise or reprimands). Second, naturally occuring reinforcers should be programmed into the treatment plan. For example, fade the use of tangible reinforcers and replace them with social reinforcers.

Third, the actual contingencies used to change the behavior should be removed or faded gradually. Fourth, a number of stimuli should be used to cue the contingencies. Therefore, the desired behavior will be cued more often and in more situations.

Fifth, after the behavior is well established, continuously reinforced or punished responses should be put on intermittent schedules. Sixth, immediate reinforcement should be delayed slowly. Most reinforcers in the natural environment are delayed. Seventh, and finally, a number of caregivers and peers should be used as behavior change agents because the client will have contact with these people in a variety of situations.

As can be seen from this section, not only is the design of the punishment program specific, time-consuming, and laborious at times, but also critical aspects of clinical and staffing demands must be observed and dealt with for these programs to be successful. Also, maintenance and generalization should not be expected to just happen but should be programmed.

Ethical and Legal Issues

Although Chapter 11 in this text has been devoted solely to legal and ethical issues involved in working with mentally retarded clients, several important issues related specifically to punishment must be covered. A committee appointed by the Association for Advancement of Behavior Therapy (1977) developed a set of questions that addressed ethical issues in the practice of behavior therapy. They are presented as a means of assessing ethical issues related to punishment programs.

1. Have the goals of treatment been adequately considered?
2. Has the choice of treatment methods been adequately considered?
3. Is the client's participation voluntary?
4. When another person or an agency is empowered to arrange for therapy, have the interests of the subordinated client been sufficiently considered?
5. Has the adequacy of treatment been evaluated?
6. Has the confidentiality of the treatment relationship been protected?
7. Does the therapist refer the clients to other therapists when necessary?
8. Is the therapist qualified to provide treatment?

Although all are important, several appear to be especially cogent questions to be asked when using punishment. Concerning the question of adequacy of treatment choice, several individuals have suggested the need for a formal review process before implementing any punishment program. Morris and Brown (1983) have expressed the need for both internal and external review boards. The internal review board would assess the actual punishment program as to its goals, its clarity, staffing needs and training, and data collection devices. The external review board would have a more global function to serve as an advocate for clients' rights.

A second question involves informed consent. Most mentally retarded clients who would benefit from punishment programs would not be able to meet the three requirements for informed consent: competence, knowledge, and volition. *Competence* refers to the individual's ability to make a well-reasoned decision. *Knowledge* requires that the individual understand the treatment and alternatives and be aware of potential risks and benefits. *Volition* is defined as agreement to participate without coercion. Special care must be taken to ensure that mentally retarded clients' rights are not being violated if the preceding criteria cannot be met. Either family involvement in the client's treatment planning or review boards would be essential in this respect.

A third question involves the delineation of exactly who the client is. The clinician may have to decide if the intervention is designed to help the individual or to establish rules or regulations for the institution or parents to increase conformity and convenience (Bellack & Hersen, 1977; Brown, Wienckowski, & Stolz, 1975).

A final issue related to ethical behavior involves the qualifications of the therapist and referral and/or consultation when skills of the therapist are inadequate. Rimm and Masters (1979) note: "In no case should [punishment procedures] be employed without the direct supervision of doctorally trained therapists who are experts in the use of such techniques" (p. 320). Considering the fact that there are not many individuals who would meet this requirement, consultation may prove to be the next best answer. If an institution, school, or individual is considering the use of punishment and a trained therapist is not on staff, the institution would be bound ethically to seek such an individual through consultation (Matson & DiLorenzo, 1984).

Conclusions

This chapter was designed to provide the reader with an overview of punishment procedures that have been defined and researched in the behavior modification literature. In addition, specific treatment considerations, types of problem behaviors treated, and advantages of each technique were presented. Finally, some practical issues in the implementation of punishment programs and ethical and legal issues were discussed.

Because the reader has had the opportunity to see how punishment is defined and used in behavior modification, we would like to return to an issue that was mentioned in the introduction, namely the difference between the lay definition and the behavioral definition of punishment.

We feel that it was unfortunate for early researchers to choose the label *punishment* to identify the set of procedures that we have discussed in this chapter. There is no obscuring the fact that the word *punishment* immediately brings to mind awful connotations of aversive events in daily life. However, there is little correlation between these daily life events and the procedures that we have discussed, neither in terms of purpose nor intent.

Punishment, as used by the general public, involves an emotional angry reaction due to frustration and feelings of personal intrusion and usually serves no other function than to rebel, act on vengeance, or simply "make life tough" for someone with whom we are interacting. These forms of aversive events usually are not meant to change behavior but simply to castigate. A person needs to look no farther than *Webster's Seventh New Collegiate Dictionary*'s definition of punish:

> 1a: to impose a penalty on for a fault, offense, or violation b: to inflict a penalty for the commission of (an offence) in retribution or retaliation 2a: to deal with roughly or harshly b: to inflict injury upon; HURT. (p. 693)

This is clearly not the aim of the procedures that we have discussed. Nevertheless, we feel certain that our aim will be misunderstood by those who react to the connotations of the terminology we have inherited.

Our actual aim is one that we share with most people. We are all constantly attempting to change our own and others' behavior, often in an eliminative fashion. Simple examples include losing weight, quitting smoking, and reducing alcohol consumption. The general public is often not successful because of a lack of knowledge of basic principles of behavior. Those researchers who are working in the area of "therapeutic punishment" are simply trying to delineate basic principles by which the systematic and successful reduction or elimination of behavior may be realized. Perhaps the answer to the confusion between the lay community and professionals comes not from qualifying what we do but in changing the name. The connotations ascribed to the word *punishment*, in all likelihood, will not change. Furthermore, we are not sure that they should. Instead, it might be more parsimonious to say that we do not punish but that we simply attempt to reduce maladaptive behaviors.

References

Abroms, G. M. (1968). Setting limits. *Archives of General Psychiatry, 19,* 113–119.
Adams, K. M., Klinge, V. K., & Keiser, T. W. (1973). The extinction of a self-injurious behavior in an epileptic child. *Behaviour Research and Therapy, 11,* 351–356.

Altman, K., Haavik, S., & Cook, J. W. (1978). Punishment of self-injurious behavior in natural settings using contingent aromatic ammonia. *Behaviour Research and Therapy, 16,* 85–96.

Anderson, L. T., Herrmann, L., Alpert, M., & Dancis, J. (1975). Elimination of self-mutilation in Lesch-Nyhan disease. *Pediatric Research, 9,* 257.

Apolito, P. M., & Sulzer-Azaroff, B. (1981). Lemon-juice therapy: The control of chronic vomiting in a twelve-year-old profoundly retarded female. *Education and Treatment of Children, 4,* 339–347.

Association for Advancement of Behavior Therapy. (1977). Ethical issues for human service. *Behavior Therapy, 8,* 763–764.

Axelrod, S., Brantner, J. P., & Meddock, T. D. (1978). Overcorrection: A review and critical analysis. *The Journal of Special Education, 12,* 367–391.

Azrin, N. H., & Foxx, R. M. (1971). A rapid method of toilet training the institutionalized retarded. *Journal of Applied Behavior Analysis, 4,* 89–99.

Azrin, N. H., & Holz, W. C. (1966). Punishment. In W. K. Honig (Ed.), *Operant behavior: Areas of research and application.* New York: Appleton-Century-Crofts.

Azrin, N. H., & Powers, M. A. (1975). Eliminating classroom disturbances of emotionally disturbed children by positive practice procedures. *Behavior Therapy, 6,* 525–534.

Azrin, N. H., & Wesolowski, M. D. (1974). Theft reversal: An overcorrection procedure for eliminating stealing by retarded persons. *Journal of Applied Behavior Analysis, 7,* 577–582.

Azrin, N. H., & Wesoloski, M. D. (1975a). Eliminating habitual vomiting in a retarded adult by positive practice and self-correction. *Journal of Behavior Therapy and Experimental Psychiatry, 6,* 145–148.

Azrin, N. H., & Wesolowski, M. D. (1975b). The use of positive practice to eliminate persistent floor sprawling by profoundly retarded persons. *Behavior Therapy, 6,* 627–631.

Azrin, N. H., Kaplan, S. J., & Foxx, R. M. (1973). Autism reversal: Eliminating stereotyped self-stimulation of retarded individuals. *American Journal of Mental Deficiency, 78,* 241–248.

Azrin, N. H., Sneed, T. J., & Foxx, R. M. (1973). Dry bed: A rapid method of eliminating enuresis of the retarded. *Behavior Therapy, 11,* 427–434.

Azrin, N. H., Gottlieb, L., Hughart, L., Wesolowski, M. D., & Rahn, T. (1975). Eliminating self-injurious behavior by educative procedures. *Behaviour Research and Therapy, 13,* 101–111.

Barrett, B. (1962). Reduction in rate of multiple tics by free operant conditioning methods. *Journal of Nervous and Mental Disease, 135,* 187–195.

Barrett, B. (1969). Behavior modification in the home: Parents adapt laboratory-developed tactics to bowel-train a 5½ year old. *Psychotherapy: Theory, Research and Practice, 6,* 172–176.

Barrett, R. P., & Shapiro, E. S. (1980). Treatment of stereotyped hairpulling with overcorrection: A case study with long term follow-up. *Journal of Behavior Therapy and Experimental Psychiatry, 11,* 317–320.

Barrett, R. P., Staub, R. W., & Sisson, L. A. (1983). Treatment of compulsive rituals with visual screening: A case study with long-term follow-up. *Journal of Behavior Therapy and Experimental Psychiatry, 14,* 55–59.

Barton, E. S., Guess, D., Garcia, E., & Baer, D. M. (1970). Improvement of retardates mealtime behaviors by timeout procedures using multiple baseline techniques. *Journal of Applied Behavior Analysis, 3,* 77–84.

Baum, W. M. (1973). The correlation-based law of effect. *Journal of the Experimental Analysis of Behavior, 20,* 137–153.

Baumeister, A. A., & Forehand, R. (1972). Effects of contingent shock and verbal command on body rocking of retardates. *Journal of Clinical Psychology, 28,* 586–590.

Baumeister, A. A., & Rollings, J. P. (1976). Self-injurious behavior. In N. R. Ellis (Ed.), *International review of research in mental retardation.* New York: Academic Press.

Bellack, A. S., & Hersen, M. (1977). *Behavior modification: An introductory textbook.* New York: Oxford University Press.

Bostow, D., & Bailey, J. B. (1969). Modification of severe disruptive and aggressive behavior using brief timeout and reinforcement procedures. *Journal of Applied Behavior Analysis, 2,* 31–37.

Brawley, E. R., Harris, F. R., Allen, K. E., Fleming, R. S., & Peterson, R. F. (1969). Behavior modification of an autistic child. *Behavioral Science, 14,* 87–97.

Brown, B. S., Wienckowski, L. A., & Stolz, S. B. (1975). *Behavior modification: Perspective on a current issue.* U.S. Department of Health, Education, and Welfare Publication (No. ADM 75-202). Washington, DC: U.S. Government Printing Office.

Browning, R. M. (1971). Treatment effects of a total behavior modification program with five autistic children. *Behaviour Research and Therapy, 9,* 319–327.

Bursten, B. (1975). Using mechanical restraints on acutely disturbed psychiatric patients. *Hospital and Community Psychiatry, 26,* 757–759.

Calhoun, K. S., & Lima, P. P. (1977). Effects of varying schedules of timeout on high and low rate behaviors in a retarded girl. *Journal of Behavior Therapy and Experimental Psychiatry, 8,* 189–194.

Calhoun, K. S., & Matherne, P. (1975). The effects of varying schedules of time-out on aggressive behavior of a retarded girl. *Journal of Behavior Therapy and Experimental Psychiatry, 6,* 139–143.

Carlson, C. S., Arnold, C. R., Becker, W. C., & Madsen, C. H. (1968). The elimination of tantrum behavior of child in an elementary classroom *Behaviour Research and Therapy, 6,* 117–119.

Carr, E. G., Newsom, C. D., & Binkoff, J. A. (1976). Stimulus control of self-destructive behavior in a psychotic child. *Journal of Abnormal Child Psychology, 4,* 139–153.

Cayner, J. J., & Kiland, J. R. (1974). Use of brief time out with three schizophrenic patients. *Journal of Behavior Therapy and Experimental Psychiatry, 5,* 141–145.

Clark, H. B., Rowbury, T., Baer, C. M., & Baer, D. M. (1973). Timeout as a punishing stimulus in continuous and intermittent schedules. *Journal of Applied Behavior Analysis, 6,* 443–455.

Cook, J. W., Altman, K., Shaw, J., & Blaylock, M. (1978). Use of contingent lemon juice to eliminate public masturbation by a severely retarded boy. *Behaviour Research and Therapy, 16,* 131–134.

Craven, W. F. (1970). Protecting hospitalized patients from electrical hazards. *Hewlett-Packard Journal, 21,* 11–17.

Deitz, S. M., Repp, A. C., & Deitz, D. E. D. (1976). Reducing inappropriate classroom behavior of retarded students through three procedures of differential reinforcement. *Journal of Mental Deficiency Research, 20,* 155–170.

Doke, L. A., & Epstein, L. H. (1975). Oral overcorrection: Side effects and extended applications. *Journal of Experimental Child Psychology, 20,* 469–511.

Doyles, D. M., Wells, K. C., Hobbs, S. A., Roberts, M. W., & Cartelli, L. M. (1976). The effects of social punishment on noncompliance: A comparison with time out and positive practice. *Journal of Applied Behavior Analysis, 9,* 471–482.

Drabman, R. S., Ross, J. M., Lynd, R. S., & Cordua, E. D. (1978). Retarded children as observers, mediators, and generalization programmers using an icing procedure. *Behavior Modification, 2,* 371–385.

Drabman, R. S., Cruz, G. C., Ross, J., & Lynd, S. (1979). Suppression of chronic drooling in mentally retarded children and adolescents: Effectiveness of a behavioral treatment package. *Behavior Therapy, 10,* 46–56.

Edwards, M., & Lilly, R. T. (1966). Operant conditioning: An application to behavioral problems in groups. *Mental Retardation, 4,* 18–20.

Epstein, L. H., Doke, L. A., Sajwaj, T. E., Sorrell, S., & Rimmer, B. (1974). Generality and side effects of overcorrection. *Journal of Applied Behavior Analysis, 7,* 385–390.

Ferster, C. B., & Skinner, B. F.(1957). *Schedules of reinforcement.* Englewood Cliffs, NJ: Prentice-Hall.

Forehand, R., Roberts, M., Doleys, D., Hobbs, S., & Resick, P. (1976). An examination of disciplinary procedures with children. *Journal of Experimental Child Psychology, 21,* 109–120.

Foxx, R. M. (1976a). Increasing a mildly retarded woman's attendance at self-help classes by overcorrection and instruction. *Behavior Therapy, 7,* 390–396.

Foxx, R. M. (1976b). The use of overcorrection to eliminate the public disrobing (stripping) of retarded women. *Behaviour Research and Therapy, 14,* 53–61.

Foxx, R. M. (1977). Attention training: The use of overcorrection avoidance to increase the eye contact of autistic and retarded children. *Journal of Applied Behavior Analysis, 10,* 489–499.

Foxx, R. M., Azrin, N. H. (1972). Restitution: A method of eliminating aggressive-disruptive behavior of retarded and brain damaged patients. *Behaviour Research and Therapy, 10,* 15–27.

Foxx, R. M., & Azrin, N. H. (1973). The elimination of autistic self-stimulatory behavior by overcorrection. *Journal of Applied Behavior Analysis, 6,* 1–14.

Foxx, R. M., & Martin, E. D. (1975). Treatment of scavenging behavior (coprophagy and pica) by overcorrection.*Behaviour Research and Therapy, 13,* 153–163.

Foxx, R. M., & Shapiro, S. T. (1978). The timeout ribbon: A nonexclusionary timeout procedure. *Journal of Applied Behavior Analysis, 11,* 125–136.

Freeman, B. J., Graham, V., & Ritvo, E. R. (1975). Reduction of self-destructive behavior by overcorrection. *Psychological Reports, 37,* 446.

Galbraith, D. A., Byrick, R. J., & Rutledge, J. T. (1970). An aversive conditioning approach to the inhibition of chronic vomiting. *Canadian Psychiatric Association Journal, 15,* 311–313.

Gardner, W. I. (1969). Use of punishment procedures with the severely retarded: A review. *American Journal of Mental Deficiency, 74,* 86–103.

Giles, D. K., & Wolf, M. M. (1966). Toilet training institutionalized, severe retardates: An application of operant behavior modification procedures. *American Journal of Mental Deficiency, 70,* 766–780.

Greene, R. J., & Hoats, D. L. (1969). Reinforcing capabilities of television distortion. *Journal of Applied Behavior Analysis, 2,* 139–141.

Greene, R. J., Hoats, D. L., & Hornick, A. J. (1970). Music distortion: A new technique for behavior modification. *Psychological Record, 20,* 107–109.

Hamilton, J. W., & Stephens, L. Y. (1967). Reinstating speech in an emotionally disturbed, mentally retarded young woman. *Journal of Speech and Hearing Disorders, 32,* 383–389.

Hamilton, J. W., Stephens, L. Y., & Allen, P. (1967). Controlling aggressive and destructive behavior in severely retarded institutionalized residents. *American Journal of Mental Deficiency, 71,* 852–856.

Harris, S. L., & Ersner-Hershfield, R. (1978). Behavioral suppression of seriously disruptive behavior in psychotic and retarded patients: A review of punishment and its alternatives. *Psychological Bulletin, 85,* 1352–1375.

Harris, S. L., & Romanczyk, R. (1976). Treating self-injurious behavior of a retarded child by overcorrection. *Behavior Therapy, 7,* 235–239.

Harris, S. L., Ersner-Hershfield, R., Kaffashan, L. C., & Romanczyk, R. G. (1974). The portable time-out room. *Behavior Therapy, 5,* 687–688.

Hauck, L. P., & Martin, P. L. (1970). Music as a reinforcer in patient-controlled duration of time-out. *Journal of Music Therapy, 7,* 43–53.

Henricksen, K., & Doughty, R. (1967). Decelerating undesired mealtime behavior in a group of profoundly retarded boys. *American Journal of Mental Deficiency, 72,* 40–44.

Hobbs, S. A., & Forehand, R. (1975). Effects of differential release from timeout on children's deviant behavior. *Journal of Behavior Therapy and Experimental Psychiatry, 6,* 256–257.

Hobbs, S. A., & Forehand, R. (1977). Important parameters in the use of timeout with children: A re-examination. *Journal of Behavior Therapy and Experimental Psychiatry, 8,* 365–370.

Hobbs, S. A., Forehand, R., & Murray, R. (1978). Effects of various durations of timeout on the noncompliant behavior of children. *Behavior Therapy, 9,* 652–656.

Husted, J. R., Hall, P., & Agin, B. (1971). The effectiveness of time-out in reducing maladaptive behavior of autistic and retarded children. *Journal of Psychology, 79,* 189–196.

Iwata, B. A., & Lorentzson, A. M. (1976). Operant control of seizure-like behavior in an institutionalized retarded adult. *Behavior Therapy, 1,* 247–251.

Johnston, J. M. (1972). Punishment of human behavior. *American Psychologist, 27,* 1033–1054.

Kanfer, F., & Phillips, J. (1970). *Learning foundations of behavior therapy.* New York: Wiley.

Kazdin, A. E. (1971). The effect of response cost in suppressing behavior in a prepsychotic retardate. *Journal of Behavior Therapy and Experimental Psychiatry, 2,* 137–140.

Kazdin, A. E. (1973). The effect of response cost and aversive stimulation in suppressing punished and nonpunished speech dysfluencies. *Behavior Therapy, 4,* 73–82.

Kazdin, A. E. (1980). *Behavior modification in applied settings* (2nd ed.). Homewood, IL: The Dorsey Press.

Kazdin, A. E., & Moyer, W. (1976). Teaching teachers to use behavior modification. In S. Yen & R. McIntire (Eds.), *Teaching behavior modification.* Kalamazoo, MI: Behaviordelia.

Kendall, P. C., Nay, W. R., & Jeffers, J. (1975). Timeout duration and contrast effects: A systematic evaluation of a successive treatments design. *Behavior Therapy, 6,* 609–615.

Koegel, R. L., & Covert, A. (1972). The relationship of self-stimulation to learning in autistic children. *Journal of Applied Behavior Analysis, 5,* 381–387.

Koegel, R. L., Firestone, P. B., Kramme, K. W., & Dunlap, G. (1974). Increasing spontaneous play by suppressing self-stimulation in autistic children. *Journal of Applied Behavior Analysis, 7,* 521–528.

Laws, D. R., Brown, R. A., Epstein, J., & Hocking, N. (1971). Reduction of inappropriate social behavior in distrubed children by an untrained paraprofessional therapist. *Behavior Therapy, 2,* 519–533.

Lovaas, O. I., & Simmons, J. Q. (1969). Manipulation of self-destruction in three retarded children. *Journal of Applied Behavior Analysis, 2,* 143–157.

Luiselli, J. K. (1981). Behavioral treatment of self-stimulation: Review and recommendations. *Education and Treatment of Children, 4*, 375–392.

Luiselli, J. K., Helfen, C. S., Pemberton, B. W., & Reisman, J. (1977). The elimination of a child's in-class masturbation by overcorrection and reinforcement. *Journal of Behavior Therapy and Experimental Psychiatry, 8*, 201–204.

Luiselli, J. K., Colozzi, G. A., Helfen, C. S., & Pollow, R. S. (1980). Differential reinforcement of incompatible behavior (DRI) in treating classroom management problems of developmentally disabled children. *The Psychological Record, 30*, 261–270.

Lutzker, J. R. (1978). Reducing self-injurious behavior by facial screening. *American Journal of Mental Deficiency, 82*, 510–513.

MacDonough, T. S., & Forehand, R. (1973). Response-contingent timeout: Important parameters in behavior modification with children. *Journal of Behavior Therapy and Experimental Psychiatry, 4*, 231–236.

Mansdorf, I. J. (1977). Reinforcer isolation: An alternative to subject isolation in time-out from positive reinforcement. *Journal of Behavior Therapy and Experimental Psychiatry, 8*, 391–393.

Marholin, D., Luiselli, J. K., Robinson, M., & Lott, I. (1980). Response-contingent taste aversion in treating chronic ruminative vomiting of institutionalized profoundly retarded children. *Journal of Mental Deficiency Research, 24*, 47–56.

Marshall, G. R. (1966). Toilet training of an autistic eight-year-old through conditioning therapy: A case report. *Behaviour Research and Therapy, 4*, 242–245.

Martin, G. L., MacDonald, S., & Omichinski, M. (1971). An operant analysis of response interactions during meals with severely retarded girls. *American Journal of Mental Deficiency, 76*, 68–75.

Martin, J., & Matson, J. L. (1978). Eliminating the inappropriate vocalizations of a retarded adult by overcorrection. *Scandinavian Journal of Behavior Therapy, 7*, 203–209.

Matson, J. L., & DiLorenzo, T. M. (1984). *Punishment and its alternatives: A new perspective for behavior modification.* New York: Springer.

Matson, J. L., & Kazdin, A. E. (1981). Punishment in behavior modification: Pragmatic, ethical and legal issues. *Clinical Psychology Review, 1*, 197–210.

Matson, J. L., & Ollendick, T. H. (1976). Elimination of low frequency biting. *Behavior Therapy, 7*, 410–412.

Matson, J. L., & Ollendick, T. H. (1977). Issues in toilet training. *Behavior Therapy, 8*, 549–553.

Matson, J. L., & Stephens, R. M. (1981). Overcorrection treatment of stereotyped behaviors. *Behavior Modification, 5*, 491–502.

Matson, J. L., Ollendick, T. H., & DiLorenzo, T. M. (1980). Time-out and the characteristics of mentally retarded institutionalized adults who do or do not receive it. *Mental Retardation, 18*, 181–184.

McGonigle, J. J., Duncan, D. V., Cordisco, L., & Barrett, R. P. (1982). Visual screening: An alternative method for reducing stereotypic behavior. *Journal of Applied Behavior Analysis, 15*, 461–468.

Measel, L. J., & Alfieri, P. A. (1976). Treatment of self-injurious behavior by a combination of reinforcement for incompatible behavior and overcorrection. *American Journal of Mental Deficiency, 2*, 147–153.

Michael, J. (1975). Positive and negative reinforcement, a distinction that is no longer necessary; or a better way to talk about bad things. *Behaviorism, 3*, 33–44.

Morris, R. J., & Brown, D. K. (1983). Legal and ethical issues in behavior modification with mentally retarded persons. In J. L. Matson & F. Andrasik (Eds.), *Treatment issues and innovations in mental retardation.* New York: Plenum Press.

Nordquist, V. M., & Wahler, R. G. (1973). Naturalistic treatment of an autistic child. *Journal of Applied Behavior Analysis, 6,* 79–87.

Nunn, R. G., & Azrin, N. H. (1976). Eliminating nail-biting by the habit reversal procedure. *Behaviour Research and Therapy, 14,* 65–67.

O'Brien, F., & Azrin, N. H. (1972). Developing proper mealtime behaviors of the institutionalized retarded. *Journal of Applied Behavior Analysis, 5,* 389–399.

O'Brien, F., Azrin, N. H., & Bugle, C. (1972). Training profoundly retarded children to stop crawling. *Journal of Applied Behavior Analysis, 5,* 131–137.

O'Brien, F., Bugle, C., & Azrin, N. H. (1972). Training and maintaining a retarded child's proper eating. *Journal of Applied Behavior Analysis, 5,* 67–72.

Ollendick, T. H., & Matson, J. L. (1976). An initial investigation into the parameters of overcorrection. *Psychological Reports, 39,* 1139–1142.

Ollendick, T. H., Matson, J. L. (1978). Overcorrection: An overview. *Behavior Therapy, 9,* 830–842.

Ollendick, T. H., Matson, J. L., & Martin, J. E. (1978). Effectiveness of hand overcorrection for topographically similar and dissimilar self-stimulatory behaviors. *Journal of Experimental Child Psychology, 25,* 396–403.

Patterson, G. R., & White, G. D. (1970). It's a small world: The application of "timeout from reinforcement." In F. H. Kanfer & J. S. Phillips (Eds.), *Learning foundations of behavior therapy.* New York: Wiley.

Pendergrass, V. E. (1972). Time-out from positive reinforcement following persistent, high-rate behavior in retardates. *Journal of Applied Behavior Analysis, 5,* 85–91.

Pfeiffer, E. A., & Johnson, J. B. (1968). A new electrode for the application of electrical shock in aversive conditioning therapy. *Behaviour Research and Therapy, 6,* 393–394.

Plummer, S., Baer, D. M., & LeBlanc, J. M. (1977). Functional considerations in the use of procedural time-out and an effective alternative. *Journal of Applied Behavior Analysis, 10,* 689–705.

Pollow,R. S., McPhee, D. F., Luiselli, J. K., & Marholin, D. (1980). *Assessment and treatment of high rate vocal disruption in a developmentally disabled child: Contingent application of mouthwash as a response-inhibitory technique.* Unpublished manuscript.

Rapoff, M. A., Altman, K., & Christophersen, E. R. (1980). Elimination of a retarded blind child's self-hitting by response-contingent brief restraint. *Education and Treatment of Children, 3,* 231–236.

Reichle, J., Brubakken, D., & Tetreault, G. (1976). Eliminating perseverative speech by positive reinforcement and time-out in a psychotic child. *Journal of Behavior Therapy and Experimental Psychiatry, 1,* 179–183.

Repp, A. C., & Brulle, A. R. (1981). Reducing aggressive behavior of mentally retarded persons. In J. L. Matson & J. R. McCartney (Eds.), *Handbook of behavior modification with the mentally retarded.* New York: Plenum Press.

Reynolds, G. S. (1968). *A primer on operant conditioning.* Glenview, IL: Scott, Foresman.

Rimm, D. C., & Masters, J. C. (1979). *Behavior therapy: Techniques and empirical findings* (2nd ed.). New York: Academic Press.

Rincover, A., & Devany, J. (1982). The application of sensory extinction procedures to self-injury. *Analysis and Intervention in Developmental Disabilities, 2,* 67–81.

Risley, T. R. (1968). The effects and side effects of punishing the autistic behaviors of a deviant child. *Journal of Applied Behavior Analysis, 1,* 21–34.

Ritschl, C., Mongrella, J., & Presbie, R. J. (1972). Group time-out from rock and roll music and out-of-seat behavior of handicapped children while riding a school bus. *Psychological Reports, 31,* 967–973.

Robinson, E., Hughes, H., Wilson, D., Lahey, B. B., Haynes, S. N. (1974). *Modification of self-stimulatory behaviors of autistic children through contingent water squirts.* Paper presented at the meeting of the Association for the Advancement of Behavior Therapy, Chicago.

Rollings, J. P., Baumeister, A. A., & Baumeister, A. A. (1977). The use of overcorrection procedures to eliminate the stereotyped behaviors of retarded individuals: An analysis of collateral behaviors and generalization of suppressive effects. *Behavior Modification, 1,* 29–46.

Romanczyk, R. G. (1977). Intermittent punishment of self-stimulation: Effectiveness during application and extinction. *Journal of Consulting and Clinical Psychology, 45,* 53–60.

Rosen, H., & DiGiacomo, J. N. (1978). The role of physical restraint in the treatment of psychiatric illness. *The Journal of Clinical Psychiatry, 135,* 325–328.

Royer, F. L., Rynearson, R., Rice, W., Upper, D. (1971). An inexpensive quickly built shockgrid for use with humans. *Behavior Therapy, 2,* 251–252.

Sachs, D. A. (1973). The efficacy of time-out procedures in a variety of behavior problems. *Journal of Behavior Therapy and Experimental Psychiatry, 4,* 237–242.

Sailor, W., Guess, D., Rutherford, G., & Baer, D. M. (1968). Control of tantrum behavior by operant techniques during experimental verbal training. *Journal of Applied Behavior Analysis, 1,* 237–243.

Sajwaj, T., Libet, J., & Agras, S. (1974). Lemon juice therapy: The control of life-threatening rumination in a six-month-old infant. *Journal of Applied Behavior Analysis, 7,* 557–563.

Saposnek, D. T., & Watson, L. S. (1974). The elimination of the self-destructive behavior of a psychotic child: A case study. *Behavior Therapy, 5,* 79–89.

Scarboro, M. E., & Forehand, R. (1975). Effects of two types of response-contingent timeout on compliance and oppositional behavior of children. *Journal of Experimental Child Psychology, 19,* 151–164.

Schreibman, L., & Koegel, R. L. (1981). A guideline for planning behavior modification programs for autistic children. In S. M. Turner, K. S. Calhoun, & H. E. Adams (Eds.), *Handbook of clinical behavior therapy.* New York: Wiley.

Singh, N. N., Beale, I. L., & Dawson, M. J. (1981). Duration of facial screening and suppression of self-injurious behavior: Analysis using an alternating treatments design. *Behavioral Assessment, 3,* 411–420.

Smeets, P. M., Elson, L. E., & Clement, A. (1975). Eliminating nasal discharge in a multihandicapped deaf child. *Journal of Behavior Therapy and Experimental Psychiatry, 6,* 264–266.

Solnick, J. V., Rincover, A., & Peterson, C. R. (1977). Some determinants of the reinforcing and punishing effects of timeout. *Journal of Applied Behavior Analysis, 10,* 415–424.

Spitalnik, R., & Drabman, R. (1976). A classroom timeout procedure for retarded children. *Journal of Behavior Therapy and Experimental Psychiatry, 7,* 17–21.

Stokes, T. F., & Baer, D. M. (1977). An implicit technology of generalization. *Journal of Applied Behavior Analysis, 10,* 349–367.

Sumner, J. G., Meuser, S. T., Hsu, L., & Morales, R. G. (1974). Overcorrection treatment for radical reduction of aggressive-disruptive behavior in institutionalized mental patients. *Psychological Reports, 35,* 655–662.

Tanner, B. A., & Zeiler, M. (1975). Punishment of self-injurious behavior using aromatic ammonia as the aversive stimulus. *Journal of Applied Behavior Analysis, 8,* 53–57.

Tate, B. G., & Baroff, G. S. (1966). Aversive control of self-injurious behavior in a psychotic boy. *Behavior Research and Therapy, 4,* 281–287.

Townsend, N. M., & Marholin, D. (1978). Practice makes perfect: The elimination of stereotyped body-rocking through positive practice. *Scandinavian Journal of Behaviour Therapy, 7,* 195–201.

Ubell, E. (1983, March). Health on parade. *Parade,* p. 17.

Vukelich, R., & Hake, D. F. (1971). Reduction of dangerously aggressive behavior in a severely retarded resident through a combination of positive reinforcement procedures. *Journal of Applied Behavior Analysis, 4,* 215–225.

Webster, D. R., & Azrin, N. H. (1973). Required relaxation: A method of inhibiting agitative-disruptive behavior of retardates. *Behaviour Research and Therapy, 11,* 67–78.

Wells, D. A. (1972). The use of seclusion on a university hospital psychiatric floor. *Archives of General Psychiatry, 26,* 410–413.

Wells, K. C., & Forehand, R. (1981). Childhood behavior problems in the home. In S. M. Turner, K. S. Calhoun, & H. E. Adams (Eds.), *Handbook of clinical behavior therapy.* New York: Wiley.

Wells, K. C., Forehand, R., Hickey, K., & Green, R. (1977). Effects of a procedure derived from the overcorrection principle on manipulated and nonmanipulated behaviors. *Journal of Applied Behavior Analysis, 10,* 679–687.

White, G. D., Nielsen, G., & Johnson, S. M. (1972). Timeout duration and suppression of deviant behavior in children. *Journal of Applied Behavior Analysis, 5,* 111–120.

Wiesen, A. E., & Watson, E. (1967). Elimination of attention seeking behavior in a retarded child. *American Journal of Mental Deficiency, 72,* 50–52.

Wilson, D. R., & Lyman, R. D. (1982). Time-out in the treatment of childhood behavior problems: Implementation and research issues. *Child and Family Behavior Therapy, 4,* 5–20.

Winkler, R. C. (1971). Reinforcement schedules for individual patients in a token economy. *Behavior Therapy, 2,* 534–537.

Zegiob, L., Alford, G. S., & House, A. (1978). Response suppressive and generalization effects of facial screening on multiple self-injurious behaviors in a retarded boy. *Behavior Therapy, 9,* 688.

Zeiler, M. (1977). Schedules of reinforcement: The controlling variables. In W. K. Honig & J. E. R. Staddon (Eds.), *Handbook of operant behavior.* Englewood Cliffs, NJ: Prentice-Hall.

3

Behavior Modification
Self-Control and Cognitive Procedures

EDWARD S. SHAPIRO

Introduction

Research evidence has clearly demonstrated that the behavior of mentally retarded persons can be modified using the techniques of behavior management. Specifically, the principles of reinforcement and punishment are quite powerful in effecting change among the variety of academic, behavioral, and vocational problems facing those working with mentally retarded individuals (see Chapters 1 and 2 of this volume). Strategies used to effect changes, however, are for the most part controlled by an external agent such as a teacher, parent, or therapist. Typically, these external agents decide when the targeted subject has met the required contingencies and administered the appropriate consequences. The person learns to behave in the desired way in order to either receive the specific positive reinforcement offered by the external agent or to avoid the aversive consequences that will occur should the undesirable behavior be emitted. Although these procedures are highly effective, they are often found to result in behavior change that is discriminated to the conditions present when the external agent implemented the procedure. In other words, when the external agent or other discriminable stimuli are absent, the behavior change ceases to be present.

An excellent example of this problem can be seen in comparing child behavior in two very different settings, school and home. Often, when a behavior modification program is implemented in the classroom to control for disruptive behavior, for example, the child's behavior changes dramatically within the classroom but remains the same at home.

EDWARD S. SHAPIRO • School Psychology Program, Lehigh University, Bethlehem, Pennsylvania 18015.

A common explanation of this phenomenon is simply that the child responds to the contingencies that are arranged by the environment. Because the school setting has provided consequences for appropriate behavior that are reinforcing, the child's behavior changes. At home, those consequences are not being applied, so the child's behavior remains as it had been.

An alternative approach to the externally initiated modification of behavior has been the use of self-control. Loosely defined, *self-control* places the contingencies controlling behavior within the individual's control rather than in the hands of an external agent. Instead of the antecedents and consequences being arranged by the teacher or parent, the same response-contingent behaviors are consequated by the individual themselves. In more technical terms, Kanfer (1971) and Thoresen and Mahoney (1974) have defined self-control as a response that occurs in a situation where there is a low probability of occurrence. Essentially, a self-controlled response is one that has not often occurred in the past but continues to be performed over time. The distinct advantage of self-control over externally controlled behavior is the fact that the conditions under which the client's behavior is changed are not discriminated to certain individuals, times, or settings.

The development of strategies to achieve self-control can probably best be categorized based on one of two sets of principles. Roberts and Dick (1982), in their review of self-control strategies in the classroom, separated the methodologies as either self-control through contingency management or self-control through cognitive change. Although other categorizations have also been suggested, such as self-control via behavioral antecedents versus behavioral consequences (O'Leary & Dubey, 1979), the division of procedures as proposed by Roberts and Dick (1982) provides a consistent conceptual scheme for classifying behavior.

Procedures that are identified as using contingency management involve those techniques in which an individual is taught to apply some specific consequence for engaging in a behavior. The application of self-recording, self-reinforcement, or self-punishment contingent on the occurrence of the response are all examples of such procedures. In each of these cases, because the individual is instructed to consequate (i.e., apply consequences following) occurrences of their behaviors, the method is categorized as based upon contingency management.

Techniques that utilize cognitive change procedures are quite different in scope. Whereas self-controlling methods based on contingency management aim at consequating specific responses, the focus of intervention using cognitive change procedures emphasizes the modification of thought and other processes that mediate the overt behavior response.

In essence, cognitive change strategies attempt to modify one's thought processes and basic problem-solving skills rather than concentrate on the specific behavior at hand. Examples of self-control procedures based on cognitive change would be self-instruction training and the imagery-based techniques used to reduce anxiety such as desensitization.

Although self-control strategies have been developed and researched primarily with nonmentally retarded populations, there has been a significant number of attempts to demonstrate the usefulness of self-control with mentally retarded children, adolescents, and adults (see Shapiro, 1981, and Litrownik, 1982, for excellent reviews of this literature). Further, those strategies identified as based on contingency management as well as those based on cognitive change have been successful in modifying the behavior of mentally retarded persons.

Methods of Self-Control Through Contingency Management

As indicated previously, self-control established through the principles of contingency management involves techniques whereby an individual consequates the occurrences of his or her own behavior. The exact nature of the consequences imposed will vary from recording the presence of the behaviors through providing reinforcement or punishment to oneself. The critical feature of such approaches to self-control are their response-contingent relationships to the occurrence of behavior.

The one procedure that is probably the most frequently used self-control technique is self-monitoring. Basically, self-monitoring is a technique that incorporates several components. Each component may also be useful in isolation or in combination with others. Kanfer (1971) identified the three components of self-monitoring as *self-observation, self-evaluation,* and *self-recording*. Self-observation requires the individual to simply be aware that the specified behavior has occurred. For example, in weight control programs, one may be instructed to take note of how long it takes to finish a meal. As long as no other component of the self-monitoring process, such as recording the length of time it takes to eat each meal or whether one meets some preestablished duration for finishing is employed, the behavior would be characterized as *self-observation* (also called self-assessment) alone. Self-evaluation requires the person to not only observe the presence of the target behavior but also to decide if the behavior meets some preestablished criterion. Using the same weight control example, a person who was instructed to take at least 30 minutes eating time per meal would be performing self-evaluation by noting whether the criterion had been met.

Self-recording, the final component of self-monitoring, requires a permanent record (usually written or mechanical) to be made of the targeted response. Again, following the weight control example used before, the entering of the exact time it takes to finish a meal would constitute the data of self-recording.

Although self-monitoring is considered to incorporate all three component skills, self-observation, self-evaluation, and self-recording, it is possible for some of these procedures to occur in isolation. For example, it is not uncommon for individuals interested in behavior change to simply make a "mental note" when certain behaviors are occurring. One could observe how many sweets were eaten each day, how many cigarettes were smoked, how often one called out in class, how many worksheets were completed, and so forth. Such procedures could be conceptualized as self-observation alone because no comparisons to expected performance levels (self-evaluation) nor permanent records (self-recording) were made. Additionally, one could self-record without self-observation or self-evaluation. This would be done by having another individual indicate whether the behavior should be recorded. If the individual recorded the data him or herself, self-recording alone would have occurred. Similarly, self-evaluation could be performed independently of the other components by having an observer inform the targeted person that the specified behavior had occurred but have the individual him or herself determine if their behavior met or did not meet the established criterion. As long as the observation and recording were completed by someone other than the subject, self-evaluation alone would be occurring.

It is clear that it is typically not the case that self-observation or self-evaluation would be performed in isolation. More commonly, they are incorporated into the procedures of self-monitoring. The actual technique of self-monitoring is quite straightforward. Ciminero, Nelson, and Lipinski (1977) provide an excellent review of specific techniques of self-monitoring that will be summarized here. Interested readers should consult Ciminero et al. (1977) for more detail on the variety of self-monitoring procedures.

The most common procedure of self-monitoring involves having the individual keep a frequency count of the target behavior. This data may be obtained by having the person count every episode of the behavior within a specified time period (event sampling) or only monitor oneself at certain times each day (time sampling). Numerous mechanical devices are available to assist in the collection of self-monitoring data. Paper-and-pencil techniques, grocery store counters, and timing devices have all been suggested.

Although the methodology of self-monitoring is straightforward, the effects resulting from engaging in self-monitoring are not nearly as simple. It has been extensively demonstrated that the presence of observers may result in behavior change in target subjects under observation (Kent & Forster, 1977; Kent, O'Leary, Diament, & Dietz, 1974). Similarly, behavior change may be reactive when one monitors oneself. That is, the process of observing, evaluating, and recording one's own behavior may result in changes in the targeted response. Such effects, although valuable for therapeutic purposes, can cause difficulty when self-monitoring is intended to be used as an assessment device because behavior may be altered during initial baseline data collection periods. Likewise, because reactivity of self-monitoring is difficult to predict, one may be disheartened by the lack of behavior change evident when the procedure is being used as an intervention strategy. Despite the attempts of numerous authors to delineate those conditions that may enhance reactivity (e.g., Nelson, 1977; Shapiro, 1983), the occurrence of reactive self-monitoring still appears to be quite idiosyncratic.

The process of self-monitoring clearly involves techniques that require the ability of persons to engage in self-controlling behavior. In fact, self-monitoring has been identified as the first step toward self-reinforcement and ultimate self-management (Thoresen & Mahoney, 1974). Because self-monitoring requires a high degree of independence, it is unlikely to expect mentally retarded individuals, who, by definition, are highly dependent on others for their needs (Mahoney & Mahoney, 1976; Robinson & Robinson, 1976), to have the ability to develop self-monitoring skills without instruction. As a result, a number of studies have attempted to demonstrate the ability of mentally retarded individuals to learn self-monitoring.

One of the first systematic attempts to teach self-monitoring and other self-control skills to mentally retarded persons was the result of a research program sponsored by the U.S. Office of Education, Bureau of Education for the Handicapped, and reported in a series of studies by Litrownik and his colleagues. In the first of those studies, Litrownik, Freitas, and Franzini (1978) attempted to teach self-monitoring to moderately mentally retarded children. Thirty children between the ages of 7 and 11 years were selected based on their ability to exhibit prerequisite discrimination skills necessary to perform the experimental tasks. The children were assigned to either a training, attention-control, or no-treatment control group. One of the training tasks required children to perform a paper-and-pencil match-to-sample. Stimuli included on the task were either shape or body parts. They were instructed to monitor themselves each time they matched body parts. The other task involved a bowling game similar to the one employed by Bandura (1976). Each time a child rolled a ball down the alley, a score was shown directly above the game. The children were instructed to monitor themselves each time a score of 10 was obtained.

The generalization tasks involved two tasks analogous to the training tasks. One was a pursuit rotor task where a score of 10 required a self-monitored response. The other task was a paper-and-pencil match-to-sample of vehicles and letters. Self-monitoring on this task was required each time a vehicle was matched.

Following a pretest on the training tasks, the children assigned to the training group received two sessions of up to 40 minutes during which the self-monitoring was taught using a combination of modeling, prompting, and reinforcement. In addition, a videotape was shown to the children to aid in the training of self-monitoring for the bowling task. Children in the yoked-attention control group were given the opportunity to perform an equal number of trials to their yoked training group partner but did not receive the benefits of the self-monitoring training package. Posttesting and assessment of generalization were performed immediately following the training sessions and again approximately 1 week later.

Results of the Litrownik *et al.* (1978) study were quite straightforward. At pretesting, all children performed at chance levels of self-monitoring on all tasks. Following training, those children in the training group displayed a significantly higher number of accurate self-monitored responses compared to either control group that did not differ from each other. The findings were present on both training and generalization tasks. In addition, they were still evident during the follow-up period 1 week after training ended.

Quite clear in the results of Litrownik *et al.* (1978) is the demonstration that moderately mentally retarded children are capable of learning to engage in self-monitoring. However, their study specifically makes note that despite instructions to do so, self-monitoring would not develop without training in the specific component skills that comprise self-monitoring.

An additional skill related to self-monitoring is the ability to set realistic standards for one's own performance. This skill was evaluated in a study conducted by Litrownik, Cleary, Lecklitner, and Franzini (1978).

Twenty-four moderately mentally retarded children, aged 9 and 10, were assigned to one of three conditions. In two conditions, children were trained in setting performance standards using live and filmed modeling. The third group served as a control. Using the identical bowling laboratory task as in the previous study, subjects observed a model engaged in performance-setting behavior. Results showed that children who had observed a model setting performance standards tended to set their own standards identical to the model.

In the second phase of the study, these same students were trained to set standards based on their own past performance. Again, using live and filmed modeling, it was found that students were able to learn to set their standards for performance on the basis of past performance. Additionally, they demonstrated retention and generalization of these skills when assessed at other times and using a different task.

The previous two studies provide strong evidence that moderately mentally retarded children are quite capable of learning to engage in two critical skills necessary for self-control—self-monitoring and setting performance standards. Although these skills are important for achieving behavioral self-control, the ability of individuals to engage in self-evaluation and self-reinforcement are also relevant. Litrownik, Lecklitner, Cleary, and Franzini (1978) examined this in their continuing series of studies.

Again, a training and a generalization task were identified. On the training task, subjects were required to continue working until a bell was sounded. The bell was controlled by the experimenter so that all children actually completed equal numbers of items. After each trial, children were informed if they had finished or not finished the page. If they had "finished," children were instructed to make either a positive self-evaluation or negative self-evaluation by placing either a "happy face" or green square on a visible felt board. Further, instructions were given for the children to reinforce themselves with an available edible placed in a cup on their desk for each positive self-evaluation.

Two groups of eight students were evaluated on the training and generalization tasks. Each student received an equal number of success and failure trials. Following the pretest, those assigned to the training group received demonstrations and prompting for self-evaluation during a 30-minute period. The first posttest was administered to all children on the following day. Training in self-reward was then given for 30 minutes to the training group. The final posttest was administered on the following day.

Results of the study found that whereas all children initially evaluated themselves and rewarded themselves at chance levels, students exposed to training in the specific skills improved their number of correct self-evaluations and self-rewards. The effects were present on both the training and generalization tasks. An additional finding evident from the data found that improved skills in self-evaluation and self-reinforcement also resulted in increased task performance.

Overall, these studies taken together offer strong evidence that young, moderately mentally retarded children are capable of learning the requisite skills for achieving effective self-management. Although initially performing at chance levels, the providing of training in self-monitoring, self-evaluation, and self-reward resulted in mentally retarded children performing each of these behaviors. Having established the capacity of these children to learn the skills to manage and maintain their own behaviors, Litrownik and his colleagues continued their investigation to determine if similar procedures would also be effective at achieving behavior change. From the perspective of self-control through contingency management, the question was asked whether self-monitoring would be found to be reactive.

Numerous studies of self-monitoring with both mentally retarded and nonmentally retarded individuals have found that behavior may be likely to change simply as a result of performing the self-monitoring process (e.g., Nelson, Lipinski, & Black, 1976; Nelson, Lipinski, & Boykin, 1978). These effects have been labeled as reactive (Kanfer, 1977; Kazdin, 1974; McFall, 1977; Nelson, 1977). Some of the variables which have been identified as potentially related to the occurrence of reactivity in self-monitoring are the valence of the behavior monitored when self-monitoring is performed, the schedule of self-monitoring, and the exact nature of the response monitored. Detailed discussion of studies which have investigated the relationships between these and other variables and reactivity in self-monitoring can be found in Hayes and Cavior (1977), McFall, (1977), Nelson (1977), Hayes (1978) and Shapiro (1983). With mentally retarded individuals, few studies have attempted to explore variables which may be related to reactivity.

Litrownik and Freitas (1980) investigated whether valence of behavior had differential effects on accuracy of self-monitoring in moderately mentally retarded adolescents. Using a laboratory task (bead stringing), subjects were assigned to one of four conditions. In the positive valence group, individuals recorded whether they had finished stringing all beads within the alloted time. The negative valence group recorded if they had not finished. A third group was instructed to record a neutral aspect (red beads) while a fourth group strung beads without self-monitoring.

Following an initial pretest, all students were trained to self-monitor. Instructions to begin differential self-monitoring according to valence were given. An assessment of the subjects accuracy in self-monitoring and their persistence to complete the task were made. A final posttest was then administered. Results found no differences in the subject's ability to acquire self-monitoring skills. All students learned to self-monitor within the allotted number of trials.

Comparison between groups regarding their accuracy of self-monitoring found no differences on the proportion of beads strung or on the number of subjects who persisted at the task. All groups displayed highly accurate self-monitoring on all measures.

Regarding reactivity of self-monitoring, it was found that those subjects recording a positively valenced behavior strung more beads than those recording the negative aspects of behavior. These findings suggest that recording positively valenced behavior may result in significantly greater reactivity in moderately mentally retarded adolescents. However, it was not found that recording negatively valenced behavior resulted in a decrease in performance. This group actually increased from pre- to posttesting. The failure of self-monitoring negatively valenced behavior to result in behavioral decrements casts some doubt on the overall conclusions drawn by Litrownik and Freitas (1980) and suggests a need for further research to clarify their findings.

Nelson, Lipinski, and Boykin (1978) examined the effects of training in self-recording and the use of different types of recording devices on the accuracy and reactivity of adolescent mentally retarded individuals. Following baseline, 10 subjects were given training in self-monitoring skills. Using appropriate verbalizations during a group discussion held in the classroom, individuals were told to count each appropriate verbal statement. Modeling and prompting were provided until subjects made five consecutive correct responses during a role-play session. Five of the subjects were given additional training involving videotaped segments from the regular classroom. Practice was also given for those subjects in the regular classroom setting.

After training was completed, the subjects were instructed to monitor themselves for 15 minutes. Subjects used either a belt-worn or hand-held counting device. Presentation of conditions was counterbalanced to account for sequence effects. Results of the study found that the additional training enhanced the accuracy of self-monitoring. Greater reactivity, however, was not produced. Subjects increased their appropriate verbalizations regardless of whether they received the additional training. Similarly, accuracy and reactivity were not effected by the type of recording device used.

In another study investigating specific variables related to reactivity of self-monitoring with mentally retarded individuals, Zeigob, Klukas, and Junginger (1978) trained a subject to self-monitor nose picking, a problem that had resulted in a number of medical complications. Following baseline, the subjects were trained to self-monitor each episode of nose picking by marking an index card. Training occurred during a single 7-hour period. Beginning on the following day, the subject was instructed to engage in self-monitoring. Following a return to baseline, self-monitoring was reinstated. The use of noncontingent social praise was then added to the self-monitoring procedure.

Results of the study showed self-monitoring alone to be reactive, significantly decreasing the level of nose picking. The inclusion of non-contingent social praise did not significantly reduce the target behavior.

The second case study reported by Zeigob et al. (1978) involved a subject who exhibited stereotyped head rocking. Using the identical methodology as the first case, it was found that self-monitoring was reactive, substantially reducing the head-rocking behavior. The addition of a freedback procedure where the subject's data were displayed on a large, visual graph appeared to have an added therapeutic affect.

An interesting finding in both case studies was the low levels of accuracy of the subject's self-monitoring. Despite their inaccuracy, reactive changes were present. This finding was consistent with other studies that have found reactivity and accuracy to be independent (Hayes & Cavior, 1977; Herbert & Baer, 1972; Lipinski & Nelson, 1974). In general, Zeigob et al.'s results show that self-monitoring may be an effective procedure to reduce undesirable behavior in mentally retarded adolescents.

All the studies previously cited have attempted to teach self-monitoring skills via a single, extended training period. Usually the training is completed using modeling, prompting, and rehearsal until subjects perform at some preset criterion. An alternative methodology involving gradual introduction of self-management has been suggested for training mentally retarded individuals in self-monitoring and other self-management skills.

Robertson, Simon, Packman, and Drabman (1979) examined the use of a self-monitoring procedure to maintain high levels of appropriate behavior achieved through a teacher-controlled token economy in a classroom of mentally retarded children. Following baseline, children were given systematic feedback for 17 days. A timer set by the teacher sounded every 10 minutes at which point children were informed whether they had been "good," "OK," or "not good" during the preceding 10-minute period. Each category of behavior was based on the number of disruptive behaviors during the 10 minutes, although the determination was made based on the teacher's subjective impressions.

In the next phase, students were awarded points (2, 1, or 0) corresponding to their teacher ratings. Accumulated points were exchangeable daily for edibles or access to special activities. Self-management was instituted in the following phase. Subjects were asked to rate themselves and were awarded bonuses for matching the teacher's ratings. During the next series of phases totaling 20 days, matching requirements were gradually faded to eliminate the teacher's evaluation. This was accomplished by having fewer children be given the opportunity to match the teacher's ratings and thus earn the bonus rewards. Points were always given, however, based on the child's self-ratings. At the end of the fading period, students monitored themselves for 13 days without any teacher control. The use of points was then faded across 9 days until baseline conditions again prevailed.

Results of their study showed that mean levels of disruptive behavior across all students were substantially reduced compared to initial baseline levels after systematic feedback was begun. The introduction of the point system and matching reduced the levels even further. Low levels of disruptiveness remained throughout the phases in which children gradually achieved complete self-management. In addition, data reported on the children's accuracy of self-ratings offered strong evidence that the gradual shifting from teacher to child control was successful in training mentally retarded students to learn self-management skills.

Shapiro and his colleagues, in a number of studies, have also used a fading strategy to teach self-management skills. In the first of these investigations, Shapiro and Klein (1980) used a series of verbal prompting and fading procedures to teach four mentally retarded children with severe behavior disorders to self-manage a token economy. Using on-task behavior as the targeted response during a 30-minute independent seatwork period in a classroom, children were gradually taught self-assessment and self-reinforcement sequentially. Following baseline, a token reinforcement program was begun. At predetermined intervals, a bell signaled the teacher to award tokens contingent upon the presence of on-task behavior when the bell sounded. After a brief return to baseline and reimplementation of the program, training in self-assessment was begun. Training proceeded by using a series of gradually faded prompts that required the children to engage in increased self-assessment. When the final fading phase was reached, children were expected to indicate whether they were *on* or *off* task as each interval was signaled by the bell. Following this phase, children were trained in self-reinforcement using a similar prompting and fading procedure. Once both self-assessment and self-reinforcement were trained, students were given no further instruction or prompts. The final self-management phase lasted for 11 days. Follow-up data were collected 8 weeks after the program ended.

Results of the study found that the significant increases in the subjects' on-task behavior evident during the teacher-controlled token economy was maintained throughout training in self-assessment and self-reinforcement (see Figure 1). Similar levels were also evident at follow-up.

Although the study by Shapiro and Klein (1980) provides additional evidence for the effectiveness of self-management procedures with the mentally retarded, it was not designed to answer a number of pertinent research questions. For example, two components of self-management, self-assessment, and self-reinforcement were trained separately. It is possible that providing training in self-assessment may simultaneously teach self-reinforcement. No assessment was performed in the Shapiro and Klein (1980) study to examine the possibility. In addition, no data were reported on the accuracy of self-management. Without such information, it may be difficult to be assured that children actually were engaged in the specified skills. Although a criterion level of appropriate self-management had to be attained before moving to the next prompt level throughout training, the collection of accuracy data may have been useful in explaining some of the individual subject variation evident in the study. Finally, unlike Robertson *et al.* (1979), the token program was not faded completely out of the classroom. It is unknown if the methodology used to teach self-management skills in the Shapiro and Klein (1980) study would result in long-term maintenance of behavior.

Addressing some of these issues, Shapiro, McGonigle, and Ollendick (1981) reported a replication and extension of the previous study. In addition, an attempt was made to determine if instruction alone would result in self-management. Using a population similar to that of Shapiro and Klein (1980), Shapiro *et al.* (1981) evaluated whether training in the individual components of self-management, self-assessment, and self-reinforcement were both necessary to achieve self-management. A classroom-independent seatwork period was chosen as the setting with on-task behavior again serving as the target behavior.

Following baseline, a standard token economy was implemented. Procedures described previously from Shapiro and Klein (1980) were used. After a brief return to baseline and reimplementation of the token economy, self-management procedures were begun.

In previous studies reported by Litrownik and his colleagues, it was clear that simply providing instruction regarding self-management procedures did not produce significant changes in the targeted behavior.

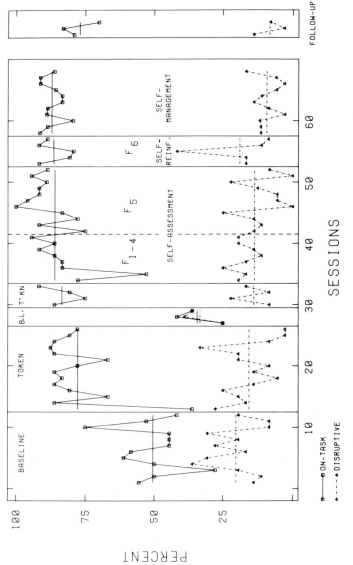

Figure 1. Group mean scores for on-task and disruptive behavior across phases.

The present study attempted to confirm these findings by implementing a brief phase in which the teacher verbally instructed and modeled appropriate self-management prior to the beginning of each day's session. The session was begun without any further training or prompting.

Students were then trained in self-assessment using a procedure similar to that used in Shapiro and Klein (1980). After training was completed, a return to self-management instruction was briefly implemented to probe the effects of self-assessment upon self-reinforcement. In the following phase, self-reinforcement was trained again using procedures described in Shapiro and Klein (1980). Finally, self-management instructions were implemented to assess the effects of training both components of self-management.

Results found that the self-management program was able to maintain levels established during the teacher-controlled token economy. Instruction alone was unable to sustain high levels of on-task behavior (see Figure 2). Examination of the accuracy of self-management reflects more clearly the actual learning of the skills. None of the children initially demonstrated accurate self-assessment or self-reinforcement. After training in self-assessment was completed, one subject also demonstrated accurate self-reinforcement. Two subjects appeared to learn accurate self-assessment and self-reinforcement only after being trained in each component independently. One subject who demonstrated accurate self-assessment after training never became accurate at self-reinforcement. Finally, one subject was unable to learn accurate self-assessment or self-reinforcement (see Table 1).

Overall, the studies by Shapiro and Klein (1980) and Shapiro et al. (1981) provide additional support for the general effectiveness of using self-management procedures with mentally retarded children. However, the lack of uniform results across subjects may cast some doubt as to the conclusions that can be drawn. It is unclear whether variables related to the specific methodology employed in the studies or other individual variables account for the idiosyncratic effects. Regardless, the studies are encouraging in expanding the applicability of self-management to classroom management. One particular research question raised by these studies is whether it is necessary to first bring behavior under external control before shifting to self-control. In both of Shapiro's studies as well as the Robertson et al. (1979) study, behavior was initially brought under the control of teacher-manipulated contingencies. Only after desired levels of behavior were achieved were procedures for achieving self-management introduced. Thus, these studies examined the process of behavioral maintenance rather than behavior change. Because behavior is known to be potentially reactive to self-monitoring, a logical question

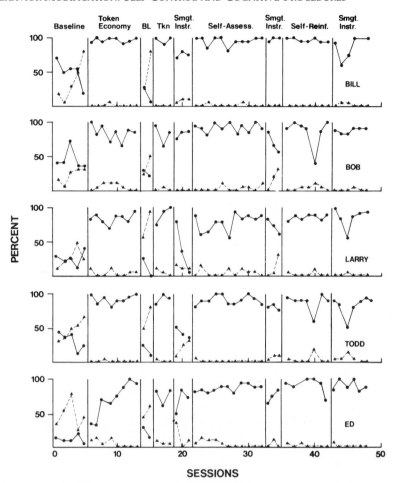

Figure 2. Percentage on-task (●—●) and disruptive (▲—▲) behavior across phases for each individual child. (From "An Analysis of Self-Assessment and Self-Reinforcement in a Self-Managed Token Economy with Mentally Retarded Children" by E. S. Shapiro, J. J. McGonigle, and T. H. Ollendick, 1980, *Applied Research in Mental Retardation, 1,* 234. Copyright 1981 by Pergamon Press. Reprinted by permission.)

would be to ask if the introduction of self-management processes prior to any external token program could result in behavior change.

In a series of three studies reported by Shapiro and Ackerman (1983), the use of self-monitoring as a procedure to increase work productivity among moderately mentally retarded adults in a sheltered workshop setting was examined. In the initial study, the effects of a standard behavior modification program designed to provide contingent

Table 1. Mean Percentage Accuracy of Self-Assessment and Self-Reinforcement across Phases for Each Individual Subject

PHASE	Bill		Bob		Larry		Todd		Ed	
	Assess-ment	Reinforce-ment	Assess-ment	Reinforce-ment	Assess-ment	Reinforce-ment	Assess-ment	Reinforce-ment	Assess-ment	Reinforce-ment
General instructions	68	50	14	20	47	15	35	17	27	20
Self-assessment training	98	—	87	—	88	—	94	—	53	—
General instructions	98	85	60	40	72	37	83	55	42	28
Self-reinforcement training	100	98	96	53	95	94	98	96	48	39
General instructions	94	98	96	36	96	100	89	99	59	29

Note. From "An Analysis of Self-Assessment and Self-Reinforcement in a Self-Managed Token Economy with Mentally Retarded Children" by E. S. Shapiro, J. J. McGonigle, and T. H. Ollendick, 1980, Applied Research in Mental Retardation, 1, 234. Copyright 1981 by Pergamon Press. Reprinted by permission.

social reinforcement and feedback for productive work was implemented in a small classroom isolated from the general workshop environment. Significant increases were observed among all clients compared to matched control subjects who remained in the workshop area. However, when the clients were returned to the workshop, all gains evident as a result of the behavior management program were lost.

Because the improved performance evident through the behavior management program was not maintained when clients returned to the workshop environment, a follow-up study was performed in an attempt to evaluate the use of self-monitoring as a procedure for achieving behavior change, maintenance, and generalization. Prior to beginning that study, however, it was necessary to evaluate what potential contribution to the behavior improvement evident during the behavioral program was due to simply moving clients from the large, distracting workshop environment to the small, self-contained classroom. This was investigated by having clients perform the identical task during two 60-minute periods each day. One period was performed in the workshop, whereas the other was in the small classroom. Comparisons of productivity rates across settings did not differ. Thus, subjects' behavior appeared to be unrelated to simply the change in environments.

The third study in the series examined the use of self-monitoring. Using 12 subjects drawn from the same population, 6 were randomly assigned to receive training in self-monitoring, whereas the other 6 served as the control group. Work productivity remained as the dependent measure. Following baseline, the self-monitoring group was moved to a small classroom for the first 30 minutes of the 60-minute session. In the initial phase, no treatment was begun, thus allowing for an assessment of the effects of simply moving from the workshop to the small, distraction-free classroom. Immediately following the 30-minute session in the classroom (designated as the training period), subjects returned to the large workshop where they were expected to engage in the same pin-sorting task for 30 additional minutes. This later period served as a measure of generalization across time.

During the next phase, experimental subjects were trained in self-monitoring. Using modeling and prompting, subjects were individually instructed to self-monitor by pressing a standard grocery-store counter following each completed packaging of six pins. Subjects were taught to place each package on a counting board until it was filed (five packages) at which time they moved a pointer on a large wheel that kept an additional count (by 5s) of their progress. Thus, there were three self-monitoring responses required of each subject: pressing a grocery-store counter, placing the package on a number line, and moving a pointer on a wheel when five units were completed. Subjects were given prompts and praised for accurate self-monitoring. Over the course of 10 days, the amount of time in which prompting and reinforcement for self-monitoring was given was systematically reduced. Again, as in all phases, subjects returned to the workshop for 30 minutes following training and continued to work under baseline conditions.

After accurate self-monitoring was achieved among all subjects, the next phase begun. During this phase, experimental subjects continued to self-monitor but remained in the workshop setting rather than perform in the small classroom. After the initial 30 minutes, self-monitoring was ended, but subjects continued to work for 30 additional minutes.

In the final phase, the control subjects who had remained under baseline conditions throughout all previous phases were now trained in self-monitoring. As in previous phases, the second 30 minutes of each session was devoted to an assessment of generalization.

Results of the study found self-monitoring to have little effect on the client's productivity. Increases evident in performance (see Figure 3) appeared due to nonspecific effects and were not related to implementation of self-monitoring. In addition, self-monitoring seemed to have little effect on generalization across time. These findings were evident despite the high degree of accuracy of self-monitoring displayed by all clients.

In lieu of the failure of self-monitoring to be reactive, Ackerman and Shapiro (1984) investigated the use of self-monitoring in achieving response generalization across time once behavior was increased using external reinforcement methods. Five moderately mentally retarded clients were selected from the population of a large, sheltered workshop for inclusion in the study. All clients were determined to have counting skills and no physical or behavioral impairments that would interfere with their work productivity.

Subjects were assigned a packaging task that had been contracted from a manufacturer in the local community. The number of assembled packages served as the dependent measure during the study. A 60-minute period each day was divided into two 30-minute segments with the initial 30 minutes designated as the training period and the later 30 minutes as the generalization session. Following baseline, using a multiple baseline across subjects, social praise and pats on the back were given that were contingent upon continued work performance during the training period. Throughout the generalization period, baseline conditions prevailed. In the following phase, subjects were trained in self-monitoring over a 3-day period. After each package was completed,

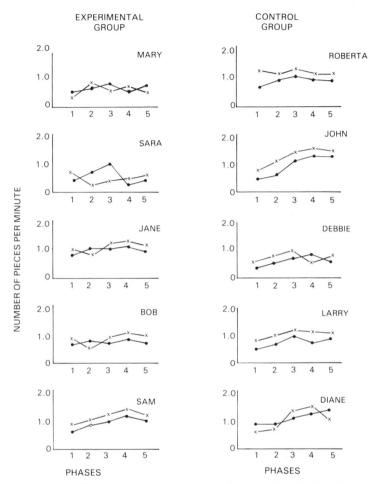

Figure 3. Mean production rates within each phase for individual subjects in experimental and control groups across treatment and generalization periods. (From "Increasing Productivity Rates in Adult Mentally Retarded Clients: The Failure of Self-Monitoring" by E. S. Shapiro and A. Ackerman, 1983, *Applied Research in Mental Retardation, 4*, 177. Copyright 1983 by Pergamon Press. Reprinted by permission.)

clients were taught to push a standard grocery-store counter. Modeling and prompting of the appropriate self-monitoring response was done prior to beginning the first day of training. Once the training session began, verbal and physical prompts for accurate self-monitoring continued for the first 25 minutes of the period on the first day, the first 10 minutes on the second day, and 0 minutes on each successive day. For the time remaining in each 30-minute training period, clients were given the opportunity to self-monitor but were not prompted. This served as a means of assessing client accuracy of self-monitoring and also to fade the prompting procedure. As in the previous phases, baseline conditions continued during the generalization phase.

In the final phase, self-monitoring continued during the training period. During generalization, however, clients were given the opportunity to self-monitor using the same grocery-store counter.

Results of the study are displayed in Figure 4. All subjects were found to have low rates of productivity during baseline. The implementation of the reinforcement procedure resulted in substantial increases in client production. These levels of productivity were maintained when self-monitoring was introduced.

During the generalization periods, clients' productive behavior remained at baseline levels until the phase in which self-monitoring was implemented. Once self-monitoring was begun in the generalization period, productivity improved to levels evident during the initial 30-minute training period. These effects were replicated across all five subjects used in the study.

Of importance in the findings of this study was that self-monitoring again was found to be successful in achieving maintenance of behavior that had been previously increased through reinforcement provided by an external agent. Such external reinforcement, however, resulted in little generalization across a time period when no contingencies were in effect. Although self-monitoring produced some generalization to non-treatment periods, the effect was minimal compared to the change in behavior observed when self-monitoring was implemented during the generalization period. It should be emphasized that baseline conditions had been present for the previous 29 to 36 days and that self-monitoring alone was successful in substantially increasing the subject's behavior.

The results of the Ackerman and Shapiro (1984) study suggest that self-monitoring may be an effective mechanism for obtaining generalization once behavioral levels have been improved using external reinforcement. One question that may be asked is if self-monitoring alone prior to any external reinforcement phase could have resulted in behavior change. Although not addressed in the present study, results from Shapiro and Ackerman (1983) cited previously would support the idea that self-monitoring alone may not be consistently capable of increasing productive behavior of mentally retarded clients. A particular limitation of the present investigation, however, was that generalization was only assessed across one stimulus dimension—time. To investigate whether the effects evident in the present study could be found across tasks as

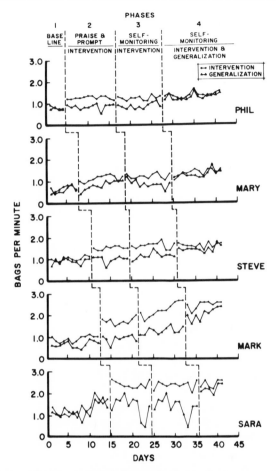

Figure 4. Number of pieces completed per minute by clients across days of program. Phase 1—baseline. Phase 2—reinforcement by external agent. Phase 3—self-monitoring in training period only. Phase 4—self-monitoring in training and generalization periods. (From "Self-Monitoring and Work Productivity with Mentally Retarded Adults" by A. Ackerman and E. S.Shapiro, 1984, *Journal of Applied Behavior Analysis, 17,* 406. Copyright 1984 by *Journal of Applied Behavior Analysis.* Reprinted by permission.)

well as time, Shapiro and Hoyt (1983) attempted to replicate the Ackerman and Shapiro (1984) study.

Four mentally retarded clients employed at a community work station located at the local utility company participated in the study. Daily sessions were again divided into two 60-minute periods with the initial 30 minutes being designated as the training period and the later as the generalization period. During the training period, subjects were assigned to dismantle gas meter regulators, the job for which they were employed by the gas company. Productivity on the task was assessed based on the total number of pieces disassembled. The task used to assess productivity during the generalization session required the attaching of a piece of string to paper tickets. The number of tickets strung served as the dependent measure.

The methodology described previously by Ackerman and Shapiro (1984) was utilized in the present study. In a multiple-baseline across subjects, following baseline, subjects were given a standard amount of praise and encouragement for continued work during the training period. Self-monitoring was trained in the next phase by using modeling and prompting. Prompts were faded across the initial 3 days of the phase as clients achieved high levels of accuracy. In the final phase, self-monitoring was then introduced during the generalization period.

Results of the study were found to be mixed. Implementation of social praise seemed to have a minimal impact upon the clients' productivity. Self-monitoring also had little effect upon the work behavior of the clients. Interestingly, whereas the subjects did not change their productivity on the generalization task as a result of exposure to either reinforcement or self-monitoring in training, the implementation of self-monitoring during the generalization period resulted in substantial improvements in the client productivity among three of four subjects. These findings are surprising in light of the lack of change noted in the subjects' behavior during the training period.

An extension of this line of investigation with other handicapped populations was reported by Shapiro, Browder, and D'Huyvetters (1984). Four children enrolled in a class for the severely multihandicapped served as subjects. The number of problems completed on assigned math and reading worksheets each day was used as a measure of productivity. Each daily 25-minute work period was divided into three sessions of 15 minutes (Session A), 5 minutes (Session B), and 5 minutes (Session C). Session A was designated as the training period during which token reinforcement and/or self-monitoring were first taught. Sessions B and C served as assessments of generalization. In Session A, children were given a packet of math worksheets with instructions to work independently. During Session B, reading worksheets were assigned, whereas another packet of math worksheets were given for Session C. Thus, Session B served as an assessment of generalization across tasks, whereas Session C assessed generalization across time. Presentation order of Sessions B and C were counterbalanced throughout the study to control for order effects.

Following baseline and a brief phase in which decorative stickers were given for academic performance, using a multiple baseline design across subjects, reinforcement was given contingent upon completing each worksheet. After meeting the criterion for reinforcement, subjects were permitted to play with a chosen toy for the remainder of the session. Baseline conditions prevailed during the generalization sessions throughout the phase.

In the next phase, children were trained in self-monitoring using instruction, modeling, and prompting. Once the session began, subjects continued to receive prompting and verbal praise for self-monitoring. Baseline conditions were again maintained throughout the generalization sessions. Once children had demonstrated accurate self-monitoring, prompting was discontinued. Throughout the following two phases, self-monitoring was sequentially introduced during Sessions B and C as well as during the training session.

Results of the study were quite mixed. Of the four subjects, only two ever achieved accurate levels of self-monitoring. In addition, one subject displayed generalization across both task and time when external reinforcement was implemented during the training session. Overall, the study found that self-monitoring could be learned by some of the children but that no firm conclusions could be drawn regarding the value of self-monitoring in achieving generalization across tasks or time with this population.

What appears clear in examining the results of the series of studies by Shapiro and his colleagues is that self-monitoring does appear to be a viable technique for behavioral maintenance among mentally retarded children and adults. It is not possible to state, however, that self-monitoring can be learned by all mentally retarded individuals. Equally important, even when self-monitoring accuracy can be attained, it appears difficult to predict when self-monitoring will be reactive. In studies reported by Shapiro and Klein (1980), Shapiro and Ackerman (1983), Shapiro and Hoyt (1983), and Shapiro, Browder, and D'Huyvetters (1984), some subjects either could not learn accurately to self-monitor, and/or self-monitoring had little effect on behavior.

It is of interest to review the idiosyncratic nature of self-monitoring effects with the mentally retarded. For example, Shapiro and Klein (1980) reported that one subject who failed to demonstrate either self-assessment or self-reinforcement during the appropriate phase was able to perform accurate self-management later in the study. Although the subject appeared to not be influenced by the training program, she may have learned to engage in the appropriate self-management behaviors through modeling and observing the other children. The potential implications for using peers as models in teaching self-management skills is as of yet unexplored.

Shapiro *et al.* (1980) reported a number of idiosyncratic effects. Among their five subjects, one could learn to self-assess but not to self-reinforce; another could not learn either skill; and a third learned to self-reinforce as a result of training in self-assessment alone. Although some differences in individual characteristics were reported, it was not possible to draw any firm conclusions why such differential effects were evident.

Shapiro *et al.* (1984) found even more idiosyncratic differences in trying to extend self-monitoring to severely multihandicapped children. In an extensive discussion of the potential factors that may have been related to self-management failure, Shapiro *et al.* (1984) noted such variables as prior exposure to self-management, peer imitation, behavioral contrast effects, the presence of interfering behavior, behavioral variability, and the lack of salient discriminative stimuli for self-reinforcement as possibilities. Systematic data were not collected to evaluate which, if any, of these factors may have resulted in the reported mixed results.

Shapiro and Hoyt (1983) again reported such mixed results. In their study, subjects were found to show minimal effects when external reinforcement or self-monitoring was implemented during training periods. In assessing generalization across tasks, however, self-monitoring did result in substantial improvements in three of four subjects.

In addition to Shapiro *et al.*'s consistent reporting of idiosyncratic effects in using self-monitoring with the mentally retarded, Zohn and Bornstein (1980) reported such mixed results in an attempt to improve the work productivity of four moderately mentally retarded adults in a sheltered workshop. Using a training procedure based on modeling, prompting, and practice, two of four subjects showed no reactivity as a result of implementing the self-monitoring procedure.

In contrast to these studies, Ackerman and Shapiro (1984), Gardner, Cole, Berry, and Nowinski (1983), and Gardner, Clees, and Cole (1983), among others, reported studies conducted in applied settings in which idiosyncratic effects among subjects were absent. Given this range of outcomes, what conclusions can be drawn regarding the use of self-monitoring and other self-management procedures with the mentally retarded.

First, it does appear that self-management skills, particularly self-monitoring, can be a viable method for behavioral intervention with the mentally retarded. Quite clearly, self-monitoring, self-assessment, self-evaluation, and self-reinforcement were able to be taught to most mentally retarded individuals of all ages. This is an important finding because one may have hesitated to train individuals in self-control due to their limited cognitive capacities. Such limitations that are inherent to these persons should not play a part in deciding their potential for achieving self-control.

Second, although many mentally retarded individuals could learn to self-manage, some could not. The consistency with which this has been demonstrated should provide a significant impetus for future investigations. It is very important to begin to understand the variables that may be accounting for the mixed effects observed in these studies. Two particular categories of variables in need of exploration are those related to environmental stimuli and personality-behavioral characteristics.

When one examines the studies reported on using self-monitoring with the mentally retarded, one is struck by the different methodologies that have been used to train self-monitoring skills in mentally retarded persons. Litrownik and his colleagues, in their laboratory and analog studies, made use of demonstration, modeling, videotape, and practice trials within a few sessions. Although their methods appeared quite successful in teaching self-monitoring and other self-management skills, the group nature of their analysis obscures any individual differences that may have been present in their data. Thus, it is impossible to determine if any idiosyncratic effects were evident.

In the studies reported by Shapiro and Klein (1980) and Shapiro *et al.* (1980), a verbal prompting and fading procedure was used. Both of those studies required subjects to attain self-assessment and self-reinforcement skills gradually. The studies by Shapiro and his colleagues with adult mentally retarded individuals used a very short period of modeling and prompting to train self-monitoring. Similar methodologies were also used by Zohn and Bornstein (1980) and Gardner, Clees & Cole (1983), although the latter included role playing as well as modeling and prompting.

Given the wide-ranging methods reported for training self-management skills with the mentally retarded, it is possible that the idiosyncratic effects reported in studies may be related to subject receptivity to certain types of training regimens. In other words, it is possible that those clients who did not learn self-management may have successfully acquired the skills if an alternative teaching strategy had been employed. Research that examines and compares the effectiveness of the varying teaching strategies is clearly needed.

Related to the need to explore the values of varying methods for teaching self-management skills is the necessity to examine subject–method interactions. It is entirely possible that certain client characteristics and behaviors interact with specific teaching strategies to result in optimal performance and learning of self-management. Investigations that can aid in better predicting which method is most valuable with specific clients may begin to explain the apparent idiosyncratic differences evident in teaching self-control to mentally retarded persons.

Other environmental variables related to teaching strategies also need to be considered. For example, it is possible that some subjects need additional discriminative stimuli to aid in cuing appropriate self-monitoring. Although the studies by Shapiro and Klein (1980) and Shapiro et al. (1981) included provisions for verbal cuing and fading prompts; subjects who failed to learn the appropriate skills may have needed more concrete, nonverbal cues to perform the specific skill.

In addition to environmental variables, one must also consider certain individual differences that may place limitations on the ability of some subjects to learn self-management. Clearly, there may be a minimal level of cognitive capacity necessary to achieve effective self-management. Individuals functioning in the profound ranges of mental retardation may not be capable of learning the behaviors that are necessary for accurate self-management. Although at least one study has reported success in teaching someone of this functioning level self-management (Bates, Renzaglia, & Clees, 1980), few reports of attempting self-managment with this population are evident in the literature.

More important, perhaps, than levels of cognitive ability may be the specific entering behaviors necessary for accurate self-management. Conceptually, it would seem that individuals would need some type of rudimentary counting or number skills to accurately self-monitor. In addition, a certain degree of attentiveness to one's own behavior may also be needed. At present, investigations that have systematically explored these variables are lacking.

Conclusions

The fact that mentally retarded individuals are capable of learning to self-manage via contingency management procedures should not be surprising. Skills required for self-management appear to be learned in the same way as other behaviors. The particular components are identified, prompted, and reinforced. Over the course of several trials, the individual begins to respond in the manner in which he or she had been taught. An important difference between these strategies and other behavioral techniques, however, remains in who is controlling the consequences. Instead of an external agent such as parent or teacher providing the consequences for behavior, it is controlled by the mentally retarded person.

Despite the differences in methodologies for training self-management, the basic principles are identical. Following the occurrence of behavior, the individual performs some specific act, either self-monitoring, self-evaluation, self-reinforcement, or some combination of these responses. Thus, these activities serve as the response-contingent behaviors that maintain or change the targeted response. Of importance is the minimal effort necessary to train many mentally retarded persons in self-management. Studies have found that self-monitoring, for instance, can be learned by mentally retarded individuals in from just a few minutes to a single, lengthy session. It is clear that most mentally retarded persons are able to learn these skills.

Although self-management through contingency management is a distinct possibility with the mentally retarded, a number of limitations of the procedures currently exist. At present, it is not possible to offer a prediction as to which individuals will be able to learn self-management skills. Studies have been consistent at demonstrating that although many mentally retarded persons will display responsiveness to self-management, others do not. In addition, the wide variety of methodologies that have met with success have not been systematically compared with regard to their effectiveness. Finally, specific subject–method interactions have not been explored. It is possible that in those studies where some subjects failed to learn to self-monitor that accurate self-monitoring may have been possible if a different training methodology had been used.

Self-Control Through Cognitive Change

As noted previously, another general method for achieving self-control involves the modification of thought processes. Unlike the strategies based upon contingency management that attempts to teach self-control by having the individual perform some specific behavior (such as self-monitor or self-assess) following the occurrence of the targeted response, procedures based on cognitive strategies attempt to teach the individual an alternative approach to problem solving that will be applicable to any behavior. An important distinction of cognitive methods of achieving self-control is the intention of cognitive strategies to modify the thought process that mediates the occurrence of observable behavior.

The methods that comprise cognitive change strategies for self-control can be categorized into one of two classes. One type of procedure attempts to modify the individual's self-statements. These techniques have been derived from the work conducted by Luria (1961, 1969), Vygotsky (1962), and others investigating the effects of language upon motor behavior. In the behavioral literature, these procedures have become known as *self-instruction techniques*.

A second set of procedures that attempt to teach self-control through cognitive change are those that can loosely be called *imagery-based*. These techniques rely on the individual's ability to imagine specific stimuli or situations and to react to such imagery in an appropriate manner. Systematic desensitization and its many variants would best represent this set of techniques.

Quite clearly, the methods to be discussed here appear to require a certain level of cognitive ability for success. Given the limited cognitive capacity of mentally retarded persons, one may question whether self-control using these strategies can truly be learned by such individuals. Interestingly, although the research is presently limited, one can respond affirmatively to the question of the efficacy of the procedure.

Most studies that have evaluated cognitively based methods for achieving self-control with mentally retarded persons have concentrated on the technique of self-instruction. First described by Meichenbaum and Goodman (1971), self-instruction involves teaching an individual to make specific self-statements that reflect appropriate competence and problem-solving strategies for the targeted response. For example, in the Meichenbaum and Goodman (1971) study, children identified as impulsive were taught to verbalize the solution to perceptual-motor tasks in an attempt to have them modify their impulsive response style. Verbalizations were initially made aloud and gradually shifted toward covert self-verbalization.

Guralnick (1976) provided one of the first studies employing self-instruction with mentally retarded persons. Using the self-instruction program described by Meichenbaum and Goodman (1971), mildly mentally retarded children were asked to solve perceptual-discrimination problems. Comparisons were made between feedback, modeling, and self-instruction procedures. Results found that only self-instruction led to an increase in correct responding. Although Guralnick's primary purpose was not to examine the viability of using self-instruction with mentally retarded children, the study clearly demonstrated that such a technique may be applicable with this population.

Litrownik and his colleagues also provided some examples of attempts to use self-statements in modifying the behavior of mentally retarded persons. Basing their studies on the work of Masters and Santrock (1976) who found that evaluative and affective self-statements result in differences on task performance, Lecklitner (1977) examined the effects of varying self-statements on the performance of moderately mentally retarded children. Children were asked to perform a handle-turning task while making either positive ("I'm really good at this"), negative ("I'm no good at this"), or neutral ("one, two, one, two") statements after each 10 turns. After 30 minutes of this activity, the children were asked to self-evaluate by selecting one of three cards (happy face, sad face, neutral face) that would show the way they would look if they were telling a friend about what they had just done.

Results of the study found self-verbalization to not differentially effect task performance. In an attempt to explain these results, Lecklitner (1977) noted that only 30 to 40% of the positive and negative self-evaluations appeared to contain the desired effect. In other words, although the subjects were making the desired self-statements, they may not have truly believed or felt such things about their skills. Although this is an interesting suggestion, it is purely speculative and must wait for empirical validation.

Another attempt to use self-verbalization to modify task performance with mentally retarded children was reported by Bender (1977). In her study, moderately mentally retarded children were trained to learn five common motor actions; grasp, lean, leap, crouch, and drag. Training consisted of prompting the children to repeat out loud the specific instruction given by the trainer. Comparison was made to a control group who received the identical motor training but were not instructed to make any self-statements. Thus, the key difference between the two groups was in the statements made in conjunction with the training. Results of the study found that although both groups learned to perform the desired skills equally, the children exposed to verbal mediation spontaneously labeled their action more often than those given motor training alone.

Neither the Lecklitner (1977) nor Bender (1977) study offers strong evidence for the facilitative effect of teaching mentally retarded children self-control through verbal self-statements. Both studies, however, contain methodological flaws that make interpretation quite difficult. In addition, both studies utilized a laboratory setting and laboratory task to assess their effects. The analog nature of such studies does not offer strong evidence for generalizing results to more applied settings.

Burgio, Whitman, and Johnson (1980), Johnston, Whitman, and Johnson (1980), and Whitman and Johnston (1983) reported a series of studies using a standard self-instruction program as described by Meichenbaum and Goodman (1971) with mentally retarded children. In the initial study, Burgio *et al.* (1980) developed a comprehensive self-instruction training program designed to increase attending behavior. Five children were selected for evaluation. Two were targeted for treatment on the basis of their pretreatment levels of distractibility. One child served as a control for comparison purposes and the other two, found to be the least distractible, served as subjects for purposes of social validation (Kazdin, 1977).

Tasks used in their study were arithmetic and printing during training and a phonics task in generalization. Data were obtained on the children's on-task, off-task, academic performance, frequency of self-instruction statements made, and ratings of distractibility. Training was implemented in a multiple baseline across the subjects.

The self-instruction program consisted of six predefined types of verbalizations. Occurrence of any of these was noted: (a) asked a question; (b) answered a question; (c) provided direction how to do the task; (d) reinforced themselves for completing the task; (e) provided a cue to ignore distraction; (f) specified how to cope with task failure. Once self-instruction training produced criteria levels of performance, distractibility inoculation was introduced by providing visual, auditory, and *in vivo* distractions during the training session. The purpose of such training was to simulate potential classroom conditions and teach subjects coping strategies to respond to such stimuli.

Results of the study showed that children receiving self-instruction displayed less off-task behavior in the classroom when compared to baseline levels. It was also found that these children engaged in a high rate of self-instruction statements in the classroom, thus providing validation that the training program was making a significant impact. The children used for comparison did not show changes in either self-instructional behavior or off-task behavior.

Johnston *et al.* (1980) attempted to teach specific addition and subtraction skills to three mildly mentally retarded children. Using procedures based upon Meichenbaum and Goodman's (1971) model, a set of specific self-instructions to teach addition and subtraction regrouping were developed. Subjects were trained first in addition regrouping and then subtraction regrouping using a multiple baseline across subjects and tasks.

Results of the study found training to be highly effective in teaching these skills to the children. Accuracy in each skill was found to substantially improve upon implementation of the training procedure. It was noted, however, that although accuracy increased, the rate of responding actually decreased. Thus, although children became more accurate in their computation, they completed fewer problems. Johnston *et al.* indicated that increases in rate may be evident after more long-term use of self-instruction.

Finally, Whitman and Johnston (1983) published the third in this series of studies demonstrating the effectiveness of self-instruction strategies for teaching skills to mentally retarded individuals. Based on the Johnston *et al.* (1980) study, addition and subtraction regrouping were again the skills to be taught. Nine children were instructed in groups of three using a multiple baseline design. Training was done as described in the previous study and was based upon the Meichenbaum and Goodman (1971) procedure. Data were obtained on task accuracy, number and type of self-verbalizations, and the number of problems completed.

Results of their study replicated earlier findings. Following training, all subjects improved their accuracy on both addition and subtraction regrouping. Similar to the previous study, all children also showed a decrease in the number of problems solved. Whitman and Johnston (1983) noted that one of two reasons may account for their findings. Either performing math problems accurately may take more time or that engaging in overt or covert rehearsal of instructions may inhibit performance levels.

The studies reported here provide an indication that self-instruction can be used as a method for achieving behavior change among mentally retarded children. Although the number of studies using this method is still quite limited, the results do point toward the viability of self-instruction with this population. Additional research must be done, however, to determine the specific limitations and problems with using self-instruction with the mentally retarded.

Although there has been some research demonstrating the applicability of self-instruction training to the mentally retarded, the literature concerning the use of imagery-based cognitive change procedures with the mentally retarded are virtually nonexistent. Only a few published accounts of the use of such procedures in the treatment of the mentally retarded could be found. These studies incorporated variations of desensitization procedures in addition to other cognitive change strategies.

Peck (1977) reported an attempt to compare contact desensitization, vicarious symbol desensitization, and systematic desensitization among 20 mildly mentally retarded adults. All subjects met criteria on a fear of rats or heights in prebaseline assessment. Although the overall results found that contact desensitization was most effective on the variety of measures used to assess the fear, the important finding for the present chapter is that systematic desensitization could be taught to mentally retarded clients. Similar success in using desensitization with a mentally retarded individual was reported by Guralnick (1973) and Riverg (1974).

Harvey, Karan, Bhargava, and Morehouse (1978) used a combination of relaxation training and reinforcing positive, verbal self-statements to reduce aggressive outbursts of a moderately mentally retarded woman. Their results found the application of the treatment package was successful in reducing tantrums across the two different settings.

Matson (1981) reported one of the most extensive studies investigating the fear of social interaction among moderately mentally retarded children. Using a participant modeling procedure, these girls, ages 8 to 10, were taught to greet strangers. During successive sessions, the children first practiced greeting their parents. As the treatment progressed, the children were prompted to greet a stranger in her mother's presence and gradually speak to the stranger as the mother moved further away. Results of the study found all three children to increase the number of spoken words, increase their physical proximity to the stranger, and to report substantial decreases in their self-rating of fearfulness.

Particularly remarkable in the study by Matson (1981) was the clear demonstration of a procedure typically used for treatment of nonmentally retarded persons to young, moderately mentally retarded children. Additionally, few modifications of the procedures appeared necessary for treating these children. Continual applications of techniques such as Matson (1981) used for other problems of mentally retarded individuals are clearly needed.

Although the research is again limited and based purely on reports of single-case studies, it is encouraging to find that such positive results in using imagery-based procedures such as cued relaxation and systematic desensitization can be successful in teaching self-control to the mentally retarded. Combined with the findings reported from the self-instruction literature, it seems clear that such cognitive change procedures may offer an additional method for achieving self-control among the mentally retarded.

General Conclusions

The one broad conclusion that can be drawn from this review of the literature is that self-control is clearly in the realm of possibility of mentally retarded individuals. No longer can one assume that the high degree of dependency on others so prevalent among the mentally retarded population cannot be overcome in these individuals. Although it is evident that mentally retarded individuals are unlikely to acquire skills in self-control without instruction and training, these persons are highly capable of learning the skills that are required for self-control with a minimum of effort. Studies have consistently demonstrated that very little training is needed to achieve self-monitoring or to learn self-instruction. Obviously, these skills that we call self-control or self-management are learned as any other skills are learned. The key difference with the mentally retarded population, however, is that these individuals will not acquire these skills independently but must be taught and reinforced for engaging in such behavior. In essence, it is possible that the high degree of dependency evident among mentally retarded persons is present because we assume that they can not learn to self-manage so we do not try to teach them. Obviously, this is a false and erroneous assumption.

Despite the high degree of optimism inherent in realizing that mentally retarded persons can learn to self-manage and thus decrease the degree of dependence on others, a number of important questions must be answered when using self-control strategies with the mentally retarded. First, it has been painfully clear that all mentally retarded individuals do not learn self-management equally. Some persons seem to not be able to acquire accurate self-monitoring, and others cannot learn to effectively self-assess or self-reinforce. Others can be highly successful. It is important that future research begin to aim at the individual differences that have been consistently appearing among the studies using self-management with the mentally retarded. One must understand the limitations and considerations necessary in choosing clients for whom a self-management program will be implemented. Likewise, it is important to identify the variables that may best predict future success of self-management strategies. The exact nature of the variables that must be explored include a wide range of individual subject characteristics as well as environmental contingencies.

A second important issue that needs to be addressed is to decipher if studies that purport to be teaching mentally retarded clients to self-manage are actually teaching self-management skills. This is an interesting issue that can be approached from both empirical and pragmatic directions. Clients trained to self-monitor are simply being taught to perform some act of assessing and recording their behavior each time it occurs. This is a relatively simple procedure to learn and is similar to training a mentally retarded person to perform an additional step in an assembly task. For example, anyone can be taught to push a response counter button after each package is completed. Such behavior when performed independently may be viewed as self-monitoring. One may question, however, whether self-monitoring is actually occurring unless the individual has some way of recognizing that the counter represents the number of completed items.

Many studies of self-management skills with mentally retarded persons do not examine whether a prerequisite skill such as an understanding of number concepts is related to successful self-monitoring. In other words, it is important for studies to begin to validate whether the responses made by individuals in self-management are meaningful. It is possible that the idiosyncratic effects reported in a number of studies are related to just such variables. Indeed, in at least one study where such entering behaviors were considered (e.g., Ackerman & Shapiro, 1984), all subjects appeared responsive to self-monitoring.

Although it is an important concern to document that subjects do understand what their behavior represents, it must also be recognized that the final measure of success is behavioral change or maintenance, not understanding. On the practical side, if the client's behavior is changed or maintained via self-monitoring, then whether the client understands what that behavior means may be irrelevant. The procedure was effective in achieving the goal. Although this is true, the question still remains whether the outcome was due to self-controlling contingencies or some other extraneous variables and requires validation that self-control is indeed present.

Another important issue to address is the state of the research in self-control with the mentally retarded. Given the number of studies cited in the present chapter, the number of investigations not covered in the review, the wider range of levels of mentally retarded populations with which those strategies have found effective, and the overall success of most studies, it is clear that self-management can be achieved among mentally retarded persons. The techniques specified, especially those based on contingency management, provide a viable procedure for inclusion in the treatment of the mentally retarded. As a result of the strength of studies that have demonstrated that self-management with the mentally retarded works, it is time to move on. We need to begin to refine both our methods and understanding of the parameters that define the use of these procedures with the mentally retarded. We need to determine which individuals are likely to learn self-management and which will not. We need to define more clearly the generalizability of the procedures across stimulus dimensions. We need to determine whether cognitive capacity has any relationship at all to successful self-management. We need to understand the set of entering behaviors that a person must possess to most benefit from our training. In essence, it is time to leave the "it works" research behind us.

In general, the use of self-control with the mentally retarded is no longer a new venture. We have proven that it can be a useful and valuable tool for improving the lives of mentally retarded persons. It is hoped that future research will continue to define and refine the methodology and focus upon the effective parameters of these techniques.

References

Ackerman, A., & Shapiro, E. S. (1984). Self-monitoring and work productivity with mentally retarded adults. *Journal of Applied Behavior Analysis, 17,* 403–407.

Bandura, A. (1976). Self-reinforcement. Theoretical and methodological considerations. *Behaviorism, 4,* 135–155.

Bates, P. Renzaglia, A., & Clees, T. (1980). Improving the work performance of severely/profoundly retarded young adults: The use of a changing criterion procedural design. *Education and Training of the Mentally Retarded, 4,* 95–104.

Bender, N. (1977). Verbal mediation as an instructional technique with young trainable mentally retarded children. *Journal of Special Education, 11,* 449–455.

Burgio, L. D., Whitman, T. L., & Johnson, M. R. (1980). A self-instructional package for increasing attending behavior in educable mentally retarded children. *Journal of Applied Behavior Analysis, 13,* 443–460.

Ciminero, A. C., Nelson, R. O., & Lipinski, D. P. (1977). Self-monitoring procedures. In A. R. Ciminero, K. S. Calhoun, & H. E. Adams (Eds.), *Handbook of behavioral assessment* (pp. 195–232). New York: Wiley.

Gardner, W. I., Clees, T. J., & Cole, C. L. (1983). Self-management of disruptive verbal ruminations by a mentally retarded adult. *Applied Research in Mental Retardation, 4,* 41–58.

Gardner, W. I., Cole, C. L., Berry, D. L., & Nowinski, J. M. (1983). Reduction of disruptive behavior in mentally retarded adults. *Behavior Modification, 7,* 76–96.

Guralnick, M. J. (1973). Behavior therapy with an acrophobic mentally retarded young adult. *Journal of Behavior Therapy and Experimental Psychiatry, 4,* 263–265.

Guralnick, M. J. (1976). Solving complex discrimination problems. Techniques for the development of problem-solving strategies. *American Journal of Mental Deficiency, 21,* 18–25.

Harvey, J. R., Karan, O. C., Bhargava, D., & Morehouse, N. (1978). Relaxation training and cognitive behavior procedures to reduce violent temper outbursts in a moderately mentally retarded woman. *Journal of Behavior Therapy and Experimental Psychiatry, 9,* 347–351.

Hayes, S. C., & Cavior, N. (1977). Multiple tracking and the reactivity of self-monitoring. *Behavior Therapy, 8,* 819–831.

Haynes, S. N. (1978). *Principles of behavioral assessment.* New York: Gardner Press.

Herbert, E. W., & Baer, D. M. (1972). Training parents as behavior modifiers. *Journal of Applied Behavior Analysis, 5,* 139–149.

Johnston, M. B., Whitman, T. L., & Johnson, M. (1980). Teaching addition and subtraction to mentally retarded children: A self-motivational program. *Applied Research in Mental Retardation, 1,* 141–160.

Kanfer, F. H. (1971). The maintenance of behavior by self-generated stimuli and reinforcement. In A. Jacobs & L. B. Sachs (Eds.), *The psychology of private events* (pp. 39–59). New York: Academic Press.

Kanfer, F.H. (1977). The many faces of self-control, a behavior modification changes its focus. In R. B. Stuart (Ed.), *Behavioral self-management: Strategies, techniques, and outcomes* (pp. 1–48). New York: Brunner/Mazel.

Kazdin, A. E. (1974). Self-monitoring and behavior change. In M. J. Mahoney & C E. Thoresen (Eds.), *Self-control: Power to the person* (pp. 218–246). Monterey, CA: Brooks/ Cole.

Kazdin, A. E. (1977). Assessing the clinical or applied importance of behavior change through social validation. *Behavior Modification, 1,* 427–452.

Kent, R. N., & Foster, S. L. (1977). Direct observation procedure: Methodological issues in naturalistic settings. In A. R. Ciminero, K. S. Calhoun, & H. E. Adams (Eds.), *Handbook of behavioral assessment* (pp. 279–328). New York: Wiley.

Kent, R. N., O'Leary, K. D., Diament, C., & Dietz, A. (1974). Expectation biases in observational evaluation of therapeutic change. *Journal of Consulting and Clinical Psychology, 42,* 774–780.

Lecklitner, G. L. (1977). *Self-regulation in the mentally retarded. Effects of self-evaluative statements.* Unpublished master's thesis, San Diego State University.

Lipinski, D., & Nelson, R. O. (1974). The reactivity and unreliability of self-recording. *Journal of Consulting and Clinical Psychology, 42,* 118–123.

Litrownik, A. J. (1982). Special considerations in the self-management training of the developmentally disabled. In P. Karoly & F. H. Kanfer (Eds.), *Self-management and behavior change: From theory to practice* (pp. 315–352). New York: Pergamon Press.

Litrownik, A. J., & Freitas, J. L. (1980). Self-monitoring in moderately retarded adolescents: Reactivity and accuracy as function of valence. *Behavior Therapy, 11,* 245–255.

Litrownik, A. J., Cleary, C. P., Lecklitner, G. L. & Franzini, L. R. (1978). Self-regulation in retarded persons: Acquisition of standards for performance. *American Journal of Mental Deficiency, 83,* 86–89.

Litrownik, A. J., Freitas, J. L., & Franzini, L. R. (1978). Self-regulation in retarded persons: Assessment and training of self-monitoring skills. *American Journal of Mental Deficiency, 82,* 499–506.

Litrownik, A. J., Lecklitner, G. L., Cleary, C. P., & Franzini, L. R. (1978). *Acquisition of self-evaluation and self-reward skills and their effects on performance.* Unpublished manuscript, San Diego State University.

Luria, A. R. (1961). *The role of speech in the regulation of normal and abnormal behavior.* New York: Liveright.

Luria, A. R. (1969). Speech development and the formation of mental processes. In M. Cole & I. Maltzman (Eds.), *A handbook of contemporary Soviet psychology* (pp. 121–162). New York: Basic Books.

Mahoney, M. J., & Mahoney, R. (1976). Self-control techniques with the mentally retarded. *Exceptional Children, 42,* 338–339.

Masters, J. C., & Santrock, J. W. (1976). Studies in the self-regulation of behavior: Effects of contingent cognitive and affective events. *Developmental Psychology, 12,* 334–348.

Matson, J. L. (1981). Assessment and treatment of clinical fears in mentally retarded children. *Journal of Applied Behavior Analysis, 14,* 287–294.

McFall, R. M. (1977). Parameters of self-monitoring. In R. B. Stuart (Ed.), *Behavioral self-management: Strategies, techniques, and outcomes* (pp. 196–214). New York: Brunner/ Mazel.

Meichenbaum, D. H., & Goodman, J. (1971). Training impulsive children to talk to themselves: A means of developing self-control. *Journal of Abnormal Psychology, 77,* 115–126.

Nelson, R. O. (1977). Assessment and therapeutic functions of self-monitoring. In M. Hersen, R. M. Eisler, & P. M. Miller (Eds.), *Progress in behavior modification* (Vol. 5, pp. 273–297). New York: Academic Press.

Nelson, R. O., Lipinski, D. P., & Black, J. L. (1976). The reactivity of adult retardates' self-monitoring: A comparison among behavior of different valences, and a comparison with token reinforcement. *Psychological Record, 26,* 189–201.

Nelson, A. O., Lipinksi, D. R., & Boykin, R. A. (1978). The effects of self-recorders' training and the obtrusiveness of the self-recording device on the accuracy and reactivity of self-monitoring. *Behavior Therapy, 9,* 200–208.

O'Leary, S. D., & Dubey, D. R. (1979). Applications of self-control procedures by children: A review. *Journal of Applied Behavior Analysis, 12,* 449–466.

Peck, D. L. (1977). Desensitization for the treatment of fear in the high level adult retardate. *Behaviour Research and Therapy, 15,* 137–148.

Riverg, B. (1974). Behavior therapy of phobias: A case with gynecomastia and mental retardation. *Mental Retardation, 2,* 44–45.

Roberts, R. N., & Dick, M. L. (1982). Self-control in the classroom: Theoretical issues and practical applications. In T. R. Kratochwill (Ed.), *Advances in school psychology* (Vol. 2, pp. 275–314). Hillsdale, NJ: Erlbaum.

Robertson, S. J., Simon, S. J., Packman, J. J., & Drabman, R. J. (1979). Self-control and generalization procedures in a classroom of disruptive retarded children. *Child Behavior Therapy, 1,* 347–362.

Robinson, H. B., & Robinson, N. M. (1976). *The mentally retarded child: A psychological approach.* New York: McGraw-Hill.

Shapiro, E. S. (1981). Self-control procedures with the mentally retarded student. In M. Husen, R. M. Eisler, & P. M. Miller (Eds.), *Progress in behavior modification* (Vol. 12, pp. 265–297). New York: Academic Press.

Shapiro, E. S. (1983). Self-monitoring. In T. H. Ollendick & M. Hersen (Eds.), *Child behavioral assessment: Principles and procedures* (pp. 148–165). New York: Pergamon Press.

Shapiro, E. S., & Ackerman, A. (1983). Increasing productivity rates in adult mentally retarded clients: The failure of self-monitoring. *Applied Research in Mental Retardation, 4,* 163–181.

Shapiro, E. S., & Hoyt, K. (1983). *Self-monitoring and response generalization: Task specific effects.* Unpublished manuscript, Lehigh University.

Shapiro, E. S., & Klein, R. D. (1980). Self-management of classroom behavior with retarded/disturbed children. *Behavior Modification, 4,* 83–97.

Shapiro, E. S., McGonigle, J. J., & Ollendick, T. H. (1981). An analysis of self-assessment and self-reinforcement in a self-managed token economy with mentally retarded children. *Applied Research in Mental Retardation, 1,* 227–240.

Shapiro, E. J., Browder, D. M., D'Huyvetters, K. K. (1984). Increasing academic productivity of severely, multi-handicapped children with self-management: Idiosyncratic effects. *Analysis and Intervention in Developmental Disabilities, 4,* 171–188.

Thoresen, C. E., & Mahoney, N. J. (1974). *Behavioral self-control.* New York: Holt, Rinehart & Winston.

Vygotsky, L. J. (1962). *Thought and language.* Cambridge, MA: M.I.T. Press.

Whitman, T., & Johnston, M. B. (1983). Teaching addition and subtraction with regrouping to educable mentally retarded children: A group self-instructional training program. *Behavior Therapy, 14,* 127–143.

Zeigob, L., Klukas, N., & Junginger, J. (1978). Reactivity of self-monitoring procedures with retarded adolescents. *American Journal of Mental Deficiency, 83,* 156–163.

Zohn, C. J., & Bornstein, P. H. (1980). Self-monitoring of work performance with mentally retarded adults: Effects upon work productivity, work quality, and on-task behavior. *Mental Retardation, 18,* 19–25.

4

Habilitation Programs

JANIS CHADSEY-RUSCH AND FRANK R. RUSCH

Introduction

There is little doubt that the last decade witnessed major legal, philosophical, and methodological advances that have improved the quality
of life for mentally retarded individuals. Legislation (e.g., P.L. 94–142)
enacted in the mid-1970s has resulted in the majority of mentally retarded
children and youth receiving their education in public schools (Certo,
1983). The philosophical tenets of normalization, although often misunderstood, have led to the wholesale proliferation of ideology that
supports the use of culturally normative procedures to achieve culturally
normative outcomes (Wolfensberger, 1972). Finally, during the last decade a host of behavioral procedures have been developed and critically
evaluated. These methods have shown great promise in treating a wide
variety of clinically relevant problems (cf. *The Journal of the Association
for Persons with Severe Handicaps*, 1975 to the present). Despite these three
influences upon improving quality of life, many mentally retarded persons receive minimal community acceptance.

   Throughout the course of humankind, societies such as ours in the
United States have established customs, laws, and moral codes that
determine "normative" behavior. These norms have set the standards
by which individuals have been judged. Frequently, mentally retarded
adults, like other community members, display behaviors that do not
"fit" community expectations, and consequently are either ostracized,
or what is perhaps worse, ignored. Traditionally, the mental health
profession, with primary responsibility for serving mentally retarded
adults, has adopted to exclude these individuals from mainstream community activities, particulary those individuals who display severe

JANIS CHADSEY-RUSCH AND FRANK R. RUSCH • Department of Special Education, University
of Illinois, Champaign, Illinois 61820.

behavior disorders (e.g., aggression, self-injury). In the United States, prevalent public opinion has forced the extraction of the "problem person" from the community, often to segregated settings (e.g., institutions). In fact, numerous studies have indicated that the presence of maladaptive behaviors and lack of social skills are the major impediments to successful community adjustment (Eyman, O'Connor, Tarjan, & Justice, 1972; Hill & Bruininks, 1981; Windle, Stewart, & Brown, 1961).

The chapters in this text encompass a host of topics, including treatment strategies (e.g., behavior modification, pharmacotherapy), personnel preparation, environmental design, social policy, and regulations and legislation. All of these chapters, but particularly Jones and Risley's discussion (Chapter 7) of ecobehavioral issues, have important implications for habilitation programs. That is, the chapters covered herein, considered from an ecobehavioral framework, directly influence the design of habilitation programs for mentally retarded individuals.

The present chapter is based upon three premises. First, all mentally retarded persons should be involved in habilitation programs, if needed. Indeed, habilitation has been interpreted as a right of mentally retarded persons living in institutions (*Youngberg v. Romeo*, 1982) and is generally believed to be among those rights of mentally retarded persons residing in communities. Second, the goal of habilitation should be the integration of mentally retarded persons into natural communities. Recently, Rusch, Chadsey-Rusch, White, and Gifford (1985) defined *community integration* as "the process of uniting handicapped and nonhandicapped individuals as equal members jointly participating in recreational, residential, and employment settings" (p. 120). Rusch *et al.* defined an *integrated community* as a cohesive network of people and resources, which are linked together by common expectations and shared interests. Cohesive networks are formed when individual differences are accepted and individual growth and development is enhanced by recreational, residential, and employment coordination.

The third premise is that "habilitation programs" need to be defined. Definitions of habilitation programs typically depend upon diagnosis. If the diagnosis is mental illness, treatment is psychiatrically oriented; if the diagnosis is mental retardation, the treatment is usually educationally oriented. The focus of this chapter is upon educationally relevant treatment. Habilitation programs for mentally retarded adults will be stressed, but implications for school-aged children are implied. In the present chapter, the term *habilitation* refers to the process of teaching new skills and behaviors that enable mentally retarded individuals to coexist in natural settings with nonhandicapped individuals.

With these premises in mind, the primary purpose of this chapter is to describe the characteristics of habilitation programs oriented toward community integration and considered within an ecobehavioral framework. First, behavior interrelationships that occur from participation in habilitation programs and the subsequent impact participation has upon severe behavior problems will be discussed. Next, the impact of physical, social, and cultural contexts on habilitation programs will be presented. Third, social validation will be discussed as methodology to establish habilitation goals and to evaluate the results of habilitation efforts in attaining these goals. Finally, future areas of research will be delineated.

Considering Habilitation Programs within an Ecobehavioral Framework

An ecobehavioral perspective has recently been suggested as the overarching framework from which to consider intervention programs for deviant or delayed groups of individuals requiring behavior change (Rogers-Warren & Warren, 1977; Willems, 1977) and specifically, mentally retarded persons (Chadsey-Rusch, 1985; Rusch et al., 1985). Essentially, an ecobehavioral perspective integrates principles and methods from behavioral and ecological psychology. Behavioral psychology, and in particular the behavior analytic approach (Baer, Wolf, & Risley, 1968), consists of the following components: (a) objective analysis of socially important behaviors and reasons for behavior change; (b) direct, repeated measurement of behaviors over time; (c) utilization of replicable training procedures; (d) analysis of data to determine variables responsible for change; (e) evaluation of change so it is of practical importance; and (f) changing behavior so that it is durable and generalizable. Although the behavior analytic approach has proven effective for changing behavior, the approach has not gone without criticism. Within the context of community integration, Rusch and Mithaug (1985) criticized the behavior analytic approach for not specifying the "valued" behaviors to teach. That is, the approach has not offered a methodology for pinpointing the behaviors that are the most critical for insuring "fit" within community settings.

Similarly, Willems (1974) criticized the behavior analytic approach for viewing behavior from too narrow a perspective. Willems stated that the focus of behavior analysis on changing one behavior at a time did not address questions of possible intervention side effects in the environment or across behaviors. An intervention designed to change one behavior may unknowingly effect other undesirable, desirable, or neutral behaviors within an individual's repertoire. Recognizing the need to study behavior interrelationships, and not single behaviors, has also been advocated by Wahler (1975) and Voeltz and Evans (1982).

For these reasons, ecological psychology (Barker, 1968; Brunswik, 1955; Schoggen, 1978), with its focus upon the study of individuals within physical and social milieus, presents a means to study the interdependencies that occur between people, behavior, and physical settings. Ecological theory, particularly applied to habilitation programs, has become the zietgeist in the field of mental retardation (cf. Berkson & Landesman-Dwyer, 1977; Berkson & Romer, 1980; Brooks & Baumeister, 1977; Haywood, Meyers, & Switzky, 1982; Rusch & Mithaug, 1985; Schalock, 1985; Schalock, Karan, & Harper, 1980; Schroeder, Rojahn, & Mulick, 1978; Scott, 1980). It has become increasingly clear that any change in the "environmental system," whether it be between people, behaviors, or physical settings, will result in interdependent changes throughout the system. These changes can occur at varying levels. For example, when a competitively employed, mentally retarded male demonstrates a change in his ability to wash dishes faster, that change may subsequently affect his earning power, which may in turn influence his eligibility for income maintenance benefits (e.g., supplementary security income). Clearly, the behavior of mentally retarded persons must be considered within a variety of systems or contexts because of the potential influence of reciprocal behaviors as well as systems.

Although ecological theory and methods will undoubtedly add much to our efforts to integrate mentally retarded persons into community settings, it is imperative also not to lose sight of the advances made through the use of behavioral techniques. This is particularly important because behavior analysis offers a methodology to change behavior, whereas ecological psychology offers only a methodology to describe behavior. Behavioral methods have been used successfully to teach a variety of community behaviors, including mobility skills (Matson, 1979; Sowers, Rusch, & Hudson, 1979; Spears, Rusch, York, & Lilly, 1981; Vogelsberg & Rusch, 1979), self-care (Horner & Keilitz, 1975; Martin, Rusch, James, Decker, & Trtol, 1982; Nutter & Reid, 1978), social skills (Bates, 1980; Garcia, 1974; Matson & Martin, 1979; Mithaug, 1978; Snell, 1979), money management (Bellamy & Buttars, 1975), telephone use (Smith & Meyers, 1979), leisure activity (Wehman, Renzaglia, Berry, Schutz, & Karan, 1978), and vocational skills (Bellamy, Peterson, & Close, 1975; Close, Irvin, Prehm, & Taylor, 1978; Connis & Rusch, 1980; Irvin, 1976; Wehman, Schutz, Renzaglia, & Karan, 1977).

Habilitation programs that integrate principles and methods from both behavioral and ecological psychology, however, may best serve mentally retarded individuals. When habilitation programs are implemented, any changes that occur need to be monitored with respect to two sets of ecobehavioral variables, including (a) those associated with behavior interrelationships or intrapersonal behaviors that are functionally interdependent, and (b) those that are related to physical, social, or cultural contexts. Implications of these two sets of variables are discussed in the following sections.

Implications for Habilitation Programs: Behavior Interrelationship Variables

Although ecologists believe that, for the most part, behaviors are setting-dependent, certain behaviors or chains of behaviors may be more influenced by changes in intrapersonal behaviors that are functionally interdependent than by specific setting events or external stimuli. Even though environmental events (i.e., antecedents and consequences) play a major role in maintaining a particular behavior, Voeltz and Evans (1982) have argued that behavior interrelationships are just as important to consider. Behavior interrelationships imply that the operant may not be maintained solely by external environmental stimuli but rather may be maintained by other chains or clusters of behaviors displayed by the individual (Voeltz & Evans, 1982). Those who have addressed behavior interrelationships, particularly Wahler (1975) and Voeltz and Evans (1982), assume the ecological perspective. That is, the study of multiple behaviors, rather than single behaviors, is emphasized, and the recognition that changes in one behavior may affect other behaviors is acknowledged.

The study of the ecology of behavior interrelationships has important implications for habilitation programs for mentally retarded persons, particularly those with severe behavior problems. Schroeder, Rojahn, and Mulick (1978) emphasized the importance of studying self-injurious behavior (SIB) from this perspective. Schroeder et al. (1978) devoted part of their analysis of self-injurious behavior to covarying, response topographies. Utilizing ecological interval recording and a series of statistical procedures (e.g., correlational and cluster analysis), temper tantrums (accompanied by aggression and head banging) of a 16-year-old severely mentally retarded youth were treated. In this study, the effects of medication change were monitored across a variety of intrapersonal behaviors (e.g., interactions with other clients, interactions with staff, compliance, work, object play). Further, a number of treatment conditions were assessed: (a) thioridazine was decreased from 150 mg to 100 mg and accompanied by a time-out program; (b) thioridazine was decreased to 0 mg with 5 mg of thiothixene added; and (c) thioridazine remained at 0 mg, but thiothixene was increased to 10 mg. Results suggested that although temper tantrums were best suppressed at 0 mg of thioridazine and 5 mg of thiothixene, the reduction in medication was also related to increased levels of positive client (and staff) behaviors. It appeared that the medication change also affected positive social responses and that changes in these behaviors (both client and staff) were related more to one another than to the suppression of tantrum behavior. Schroeder *et al.* (1978) suggested that if only data on temper tantrums had been collected, and data on other client (and staff) behaviors had been ignored, then one might have easily been misled to believe that the reduction of thioridazine was solely responsible for bringing temper tantrums under control.

Behavior interrelationships need to be assessed not only to discover the most judicious behavior to change but also to determine which behaviors to monitor for intended or unintended side effects after intervention begins (Voeltz & Evans, 1982; Willems, 1974). This is important because the behavior chosen for intervention may not necessarily be the behavior initially targeted for change, particularly if an untargeted behavior is found to be more responsive to intervention, and at the same time, influences the targeted behavior in a positive way. For example, some maladaptive behaviors occur as part of a response chain. If the response chain can be modified or broken by altering behaviors that serve as discriminative stimuli before the problem behavior occurs, or modified by changing the behaviors that develop after the problem behavior occurs, then it may be possible to modify the undesirable behavior without actual direct intervention to it. For example, Jackson, Johnson, Ackron, and Crowley (1975) decelerated vomiting with food satiation by intervening early in the chain of behaviors leading to vomiting. Thus, in some cases, an indirect intervention may be the more effective strategy.

Similarly, some maladaptive behaviors may be more easily modified by teaching alternative or incompatible behaviors that compete with the undesirable behavior. For example, if a mentally retarded person who displays high rates of hand flapping is taught to play video games, there is a high probability that the frequency of hand flapping will decrease because of the incompatible behavior (i.e., playing video games). The differential reinforcement of alternative behaviors or incompatible behaviors as an intervention strategy for decreasing severe behavior problems has direct implications for habilitation programs. Because the goal of habilitation programs should be to teach adaptive behaviors that enable mentally retarded persons to fit into community settings, then the selection of which types of adaptive behaviors that should be taught is critical.

Voeltz and Evans (1983) suggested that some habilitation behaviors may be more important to teach than others, especially if the acquisition of target behaviors leads to multiple behavior improvements (e.g., if teaching an adaptive behavior results in a concomitant decrease in maladaptive behaviors). Because mentally retarded persons do not learn new behaviors rapidly, it behooves habilitation specialists to become adept at selecting these target or *keystone behaviors* (Wahler, 1975) that result in multiple positive effects on other behaviors when acquired (Voeltz & Evans, 1983). Most research has focused upon eliminating maladaptive behaviors and has then noted the collateral effects of these procedures on other behaviors (see Voeltz & Evans, 1982, for a review). Relatively little research has been conducted regarding the effects of teaching habilitative or adaptive behaviors and then noting effects on maladaptive behaviors. The research that has been conducted, however, has shown positive effects, as follows.

Effects of Habilitation Programs on Maladaptive Behaviors

Several studies have clearly demonstrated that behavior interdependencies exist between certain adaptive and maladaptive behaviors. For example, Flavell (1973) reduced the frequency of stereotypic responding in three severely mentally retarded, institutionalized boys by prompting and reinforcing toy play. In another investigation, Azrin, Kaplan, and Foxx (1973) utilized a reinforcement program as one of their independent variables to also change self-stimulatory behaviors. In this study, nine severely and profoundly mentally retarded residents of a state hospital were prompted and reinforced for using recreational and educational materials. Although the reinforcement program significantly reduced self-stimulation to one-third of its baseline level, the program was most successful when combined with an overcorrection procedure.

Horner (1980) compared the effects of an "enriched" physical and social environment to an "austere" environment on the adaptive and maladaptive behaviors of five profoundly mentally retarded clients. In this study, mentally retarded women exhibited a variety of maladaptive behaviors including aggression to others, self-injury, property destruction, and self-stimulation. An extensive list of adaptive behaviors were observed (38), and like the maladaptive behaviors, were coded as being either adult-directed, child-directed, self-directed, or object-directed. In this study (Horner, 1980), the "austere" setting consisted of a typical dayroom in an institution that had been constructed at the turn of the 20th century. The same dayroom was used for the "enriched" setting, except that a large number of toys and objects were added.

The experimental design consisted of 5 conditions with 10 phases. Of particular interest were the comparisons between the effects of the "austere" and "enriched" environmental conditions and the comparison between the "enriched" environment and the "enriched" environment combined with differential reinforcement for adaptive behavior (including prompts to exhibit adaptive responses). The results showed that the presence of toys and objects in the "enriched" environment increased the frequency of adaptive object-directed behavior over baseline levels. These data also showed that maladaptive self-directed behavior decreased, although there was a concomitant increase in maladaptive object-directed behavior. In the comparison between the "enriched" environment and the "enriched" environment combined with differential reinforcement for adaptive behavior, the results showed substantial increases in adaptive behaviors and substantial decreases in maladaptive behaviors when the environment included differential reinforcement.

Horner (1980) concluded that maladaptive self-directed behavior in profoundly mentally retarded females, 9 to 14 years of age, can be decreased as adaptive, object-directed behavior is increased. As evidenced by this study, adaptive responses were successfully increased by prompting and reinforcing interactions with toys and objects. Horner concluded further that merely enriching an environment with toys and objects is not nearly as effective in maintaining adaptive behaviors as is engineering the environment so that mentally retarded individuals can initiate a variety of behaviors that produce reinforcers.

In another study showing the interdependencies between adaptive and maladaptive behaviors, Carr, Newsom, and Binkoff (1980) studied variables controlling aggressive behavior in two mentally retarded children. The results of this study showed that aggression occurred most frequently in demand situations and that when a particular stimulus, which was associated with the termination of demands occurred, aggressive behavior was virtually eliminated. Of particular interest in this study was that escape-motivated aggression for one client was controlled by strengthening an alternative behavior (finger tapping) that functioned as a nonaggressive escape response.

The results from these studies suggest that behavioral interdependencies exist between adaptive and maladaptive behaviors and that reinforcing adaptive behaviors is likely to cause a concomitant decrease in maladaptive responses. None of these studies, however, specifically addressed the issue of whether reinforced adaptive behaviors need to be incompatible with maladaptive behaviors or whether maladaptive behaviors will decrease as a result of any alternative adaptive behavior(s) being taught. If maladaptive behavior decreases only when adaptive behavior is incompatible with it, this implies that the adaptive behavior must be topographically or physically incompatible. For example, in Flavell's (1973) study, toy play would be considered topographically incompatible with those clients who evidence repetitive movements of the limbs (assuming this included the hands). Toy play would not, however, be considered topographically incompatible with those clients who evidenced repetitive movements of the jaw. In this case, toy play would be considered an alternative behavior (i.e., toy play movements and jaw movements are topographically dissimilar and not incompatible). Unfortunately, the dependent variable in Flavell's study was defined broadly to include all stereotypies rather than single behaviors. Thus, even though Flavell showed that stereotypies decreased as a result of toy play, we cannot tell if toy play functioned as an incompatible or alternative behavior. This same problem is also present in studies reported by Azrin *et al.* (1973) and Horner (1980). In the Carr *et al.* (1980) investigation, finger tapping was desecribed as an alternative behavior to aggression. Studies that have specifically discussed the relationship between incompatible and alternative adaptive behaviors and their effects on maladaptive behaviors are discussed in the following section.

Incompatible versus Alternative Behaviors. Young and Wincze (1974) compared the effects of reinforcing incompatible and alternative behaviors on head-to-rail and fist-to-head banging in a profoundly mentally retarded woman. In the first condition, where eye contact was reinforced and self-injurious behaviors (SIB) were extinguished, eye contact increased but SIB remained unchanged. In the next condition, gripping the chair was reinforced. With this procedure, first-to-head banging, which was incompatible with gripping, decreased, but head-to-rail hits, which was not incompatible with gripping, increased. In the third condition, head-to-rail hits decreased when hits were shocked; however, fist-to-head hits increased. Self-injurious behavior was best suppressed when gripping the chair was reinforced and head-to-rail hits were shocked. One conclusion that may be drawn from this study is that maladaptive behaviors were best suppressed when topographically incompatible adaptive behaviors were reinforced. However, this conclusion must be considered in light of certain methodological limitations, for example, multiple-treatment effects.

A similar conclusion was reached in a study reported by Mulick, Hoyt, Rojahn, and Schroeder (1978). Mulick *et al.* found that nail and finger biting decreased when toy play was reinforced, but head bobbing and rocking were unaffected by the intervention. In a slightly different study, Tarpley and Schroeder (1979) compared the effects of differential reinforcement of an incompatible behavior (holding or trading a ball) with the differential reinforcement of other behavior (no hitting for a specific time period) on rates of self-hitting. Tarpley and Schroeder found that reinforcement of an incompatible behavior was more effective in suppressing self-injurious behavior than was reinforcement for other or alternative behaviors.

O'Brien and Azrin (1972a) studied the effects of reinforcing alternative adaptive behaviors on screaming. In this study, an institutionalized client was placed on a token economy program that required increased functional behaviors (e.g., housekeeping, social skills, grooming). As the token economy program increased positive behaviors, it was accompanied by reduced rates of screaming. This study led O'Brien and Azrin to conclude that the acquisition of adaptive or positive behaviors can decrease negative behaviors, even when the two behaviors are physically compatible.

For the most part, these studies suggest that reinforcement of incompatible behaviors is more likely to suppress maladaptive behaviors than reinforcement of alternative behaviors. In the O'Brien and Azrin (1972a) study, it may be that the success of reinforcing alternative behaviors was due to the type of behaviors reinforced. That is, the behaviors (i.e., grooming, social, housekeeping) were dynamic and functional in nature. In the Young and Wincze (1974) study, for example, gripping a chair would more likely be considered nonfunctional. Differences might also be accounted for by the nature of the maladaptive behaviors themselves (i.e., screaming versus self-injurious behavior) or client characteristics (i.e., it is not clear whether the client in the O'Brien and Azrin, 1972a study was mentally retarded).

Social Skills Training. Mulick and Schroeder (1980) suggested that one determinant of maladaptive behavior may be lack of social skills. For example, Talkington, Hall, and Altman (1971) found that more destructive behaviors, such as clothes tearing, window breaking, and furniture upsetting, was exhibited by noncommunicating, severely mentally retarded institutionalized adults than by communicating, severely retarded adults. Both groups, however, did not differ with regard to attacks on themselves or to others.

A number of studies suggest that social skills and communication training, which may include a broad class of behaviors that can generally be considered incompatible with maladaptive behaviors, have been effective in reducing inappropriate behaviors. For example, Casey (1978) demonstrated that when four autistic children were taught manual signs, rate of maladaptive behavior decreased. When Matson and Martin (1979) used a social learning package to increase vocational behavior, they found that the intervention also decreased socially undesirable work behaviors. Finally, Bornstein, Bach, Miles, McFall, Friman, and Lyons (1980) found that a social skills training program was effective in modifying both positive and negative interpersonal behaviors. Thus, although more research is warranted in this area, an interdependent relationship appears to exist between social skills and maladaptive behaviors. That is, as desirable social skills are acquired and reinforced, undesirable behaviors have been shown to decrease.

Summary

Intervention procedures used to control severe behavior problems predominantly have incorporated aversive procedures. Consequences such as punishment, physical restraint, time-out, and overcorrection have generally been successful in reducing rates of maladaptive behaviors (Mulick & Schroeder, 1980; Schroeder, Mulick, & Schroeder, 1979). The use of aversive procedures, however, has not gone without criticism. For example, Rollings, Baumeister, and Baumeister (1977) found that an overcorrection procedure applied to head weaving resulted in increased collateral stereotypic and emotional responses (e.g., self-pinching, self-scratching, complex finger manipulations, screaming). "Emotional" responses and increases in untreated disruptive behaviors have also been reported by others as a function of aversive procedures (Pendergrass, 1972; Sajwaj, Twardosz, & Burke, 1972).

In addition to the unintended side effects of overcorrection procedures, Rollings *et al.* (1977) also found that there was a lack of generalization in decreased stereotypic movements across settings, and further, that the suppression effects were not maintained 6 months later. The lack of maintenance effects for punishment procedures, particularly applied to self-injurious behavior, has also been reported by Frankel and Simmons (1976).

Other reasons for questioning the use of aversive procedures to control severe behavior problems include moral and ethical ones. Many states (e.g., Minnesota) have established such elaborate rules and procedures that must be followed to utilize aversive techniques that these procedures are almost becoming impractical (Tarpley & Schroeder, 1979). For these reasons, there is legitimate cause for concern over the use of aversive procedures. However, a question remains over whether other types of procedures can be found to successfully suppress maladaptive behaviors.

This section has shown that behavior interrelationships exist within the repertoires of mentally retarded persons and that many of their maladaptive behaviors are functionally related to their adaptive behaviors. A number of studies have demonstrated that as more adaptive skills are acquired, rates of maladaptive behaviors decline. For the most part, it appears that adaptive behaviors that are topographically incompatible with maladaptive behaviors will have the greatest suppression effects. Similar conclusions regarding the importance of teaching adaptive behaviors and noting the concomitant effects on maladaptive behaviors has been discussed by Bijou (1982).

> Results have shown repeatedly that individual problem behavior is most effectively reduced when the primary treatment emphasis is on contingencies that strengthen desirable behavior and secondary emphasis is on contingencies that weaken undesirable behavior. (p. 261)

Although assessment of behavior interrelationships is seen as an important part of designing habilitation programs, these behaviors cannot be viewed in isolation from the effects of setting. If teaching adaptive skills can have multiple positive effects (i.e., to decrease maladaptive behaviors), then specifying the type of adaptive skills to be taught, particularly for community integration, is critical.

Setting Variables: Implications for Habilitation Programs

The concept of *setting* or *context* is central to ecological theory. For Barker (1968), behavior and setting were viewed interdependently, and particular patterns of behavior were reliably associated with particular physical, social, and cultural contexts. Thus, even though different individuals may enter and leave contexts, different contexts dictate fairly normative behavior. For example, most people in libraries read quietly, whereas most people at bowling alleys bowl and talk loudly; yet the people at bowling alleys know to change their behavior once they enter libraries, and vice versa.

If the goal of habilitation programs is community integration, then community contexts need to be carefully assessed to discover *ecological congruencies* (Thurman, 1977). According to Thurman, ecological congruence occurs when an individual's behavior is in harmony with the social norms of the environmental context. With mentally retarded persons, *ecological incongruence* often occurs because they display behaviors that vary considerably from established social norms or they lack the particular skills necessary to function or perform adequately in different contexts. When ecological incongruencies occur, then either the behavior of the mentally retarded person will need to be changed, or the environmental context in which the deviant or incompetent behavior occurs will need to be altered. Little research with the mentally retarded has been conducted on changing the environmental context to achieve ecological congruence; more research has been conducted on changing the individual's deviant or incompetent behavior.

Thurman (1977) stated that ecological congruence has two positive benefits: "(a) the individual's expression of this maximum competence and (b) the acceptance of him with his individual differences" (p. 332). This is in keeping with Rusch *et al.*'s (1985) definition of community integration. Thurman also stressed that congruence does not always imply "normal" but that it should be viewed as "maximal adaptation to the environment" (p. 332). That is, environmental contexts or settings define a spectrum of behavioral responses, via social norms or functional behaviors required within those contexts, that are accepted and/or tolerated.

It should be the goal of professionals providing habilitation programs for mentally retarded clients, particularly those with severe behavior disorders, to

1. consider habilitation programs within an ecobehavioral framework;
2. assess environmental contexts to determine those behaviors necessary for functioning within those contexts and those behaviors that are "valued by society";
3. determine if ecological incongruity will occur if mentally retarded persons enter into those contexts;
4. determine the spectrum of behaviors tolerated within those contexts; and
5. engineer ecological congruence by changing the environmental context or the behavior of mentally retarded persons.

The following section describes methodology, referred to as *social validation*, that can be used to establish habilitation goals and also evaluate the results of habilitation efforts in attaining select goals. Readers are referred to Jones and Risley (Chapter 7) for a discussion on engineering ecological congruence by changing the environmental context. Even though social validation methodology is not fully developed, we believe that this methodology can aid service providers who are responsible for establishing habilitation programs in determining the spectrum

of behaviors that are needed to function in different contexts and that
are "valued" by society.

Social Validation: "Fitting" Mentally Retarded Individuals into Community Settings

A methodology has been developing that assists in identifying the
focus of habilitation based upon societal input (Kazdin, 1977; Kazdin &
Matson, 1981; VanHouten, 1979; Wolf, 1978). *Social validation*, as this
methodology is termed, refers to procedures used to determine the social
acceptability of habilitation programs and contains two important components. The first component addresses the focus of habilitation, whereas
the second component focuses upon the acceptability of behavior change
magnitude.

Kazdin (1977) suggested two procedures to evaluate social validity,
which are referred to as *social comparison* and *subjective evaluation*. The
method of social comparison refers to comparing an individual's behavior before and after habilitation with similar behavior of nonhandicapped
persons (e.g., shoppers in a department store). The habilitation program
is acceptable when, after treatment, the *range of competence* of the mentally
retarded individual is indistinguishable from that of target nonhandicapped persons. With the method of subjective evaluation, the mentally
retarded individual's behavior is evaluated by significant others (i.e.,
persons who have an interest in the habilitation outcomes, such as parents and employers) in order to demonstrate that they view behavior
change resulting from the habilitation program as significant (i.e., it has
meaningfully influenced the mentally retarded person's life). The primary difference between the two procedures is that social comparison
relies upon observation of identical behavior of mentally retarded individuals and nonhandicapped persons. Subjective evaluation usually
entails ratings or rankings.

Identifying the Focus of Habilitation

Identifying the focus of habilitation programs has obvious importance for mentally retarded persons with severe behavior disorders.
Behavior has social implications and influences social acceptability. Habilitation programs strive to enhance the behavioral repertoire of mentally
retarded individuals by teaching them a variety of adaptive behaviors
(e.g., mobility skills, domestic skills, self-care, money management, time
management, telephone skills, and social skills). Equally obvious is the

need to eliminate gross behavioral deficits or excesses, including forms of bizarre or self-destructive behaviors. However, behavior problems vary across individuals and settings, and they must, therefore, be identified at the local level and in the individual case (Rusch *et al.*, 1985). Social validation methodology helps to identify an individual's problem as a way to remove obstacles to enhancing community acceptance and achieving ecological congruence. Examples of research utilizing social validation methodology to identify the focus of habilitation follow.

Social Comparison. The method of social comparison identifies standards for community acceptance. For example, Nutter and Reid (1978) utilized social comparison in teaching five institutionalized, severely mentally retarded women how to select their clothing to coincide with popular fashion. Appearance is clearly important for community participation and acceptance. These women were taught to select color-coordinated clothing in accordance with popular fashion based upon a local, community standard. Normative data were obtained through *direct observation* of over 600 nonhandicapped women who resided in the local community. Typical combinations of clothing and the garments worn were recorded in a variety of settings such as in a local shopping mall and in a restaurant. The habilitation program, which included modeling, instruction, practice, praise, and feedback, was successful in teaching popular color-coordination skills. Moreover, although habiliation began with a puzzle with which the mentally retarded women combined or interchanged clothes, a follow-up from 7 to 14 weeks indicated that popular dressing skills generalized and maintained with actual clothing. In another study, O'Brien and Azrin (1972b) used the mean number of mealtime errors made by nonhandicapped patrons in a restaurant to serve as a standard to evaluate mealtime instruction with mentally retarded clients in an institution. Both of these studies represent examples suggesting the usefulness of assessing representative others in natural environments, which provides critical information regarding the focus of habilitation in present and future community settings.

Subjective Evaluations. Subjective evaluations are similarly useful when determining the focus of habilitation. *Opinions* are solicted from persons capable of making meaningful decisions about a mentally retarded person's behavior due to their relationship to the person (e.g., a relative) or their professional expertise (e.g., an employer). An excellent example of this methodology in the area of vocational habilitation has been achieved by Mithaug and his colleagues (Johnson & Mithaug, 1978; Mithaug & Hagmeier, 1978; Mithaug & Hanawalt, 1978; Mithaug, Hagmeier, Haring, 1977; Mithaug, Mar, Stewart, & McCalmon, 1980). This program of research sought to determine the skills severely mentally retarded students should acquire to gain entrance into sheltered workshops. Initial efforts by Mithaug *et al.* (1977) were devoted to conceptualizing the framework for prevocational training activities and job placement in the community. The resulting model suggested 10 steps in the prevocational paradigm, including surveying potential job placements in the community, selecting probable placements, assessing job requisites for vocational placement, and assessing student competencies based upon the validated job requisites. Based upon expert opinion, a pool of questions directed toward such skill areas as endurance/attention, social interactions, behavior (problems), personal hygiene, and productivity were developed (i.e., potential employers were asked to recommend skills and criterion levels of performance). Mithaug and Hagmeier (1978) then surveyed administrative and supervisory personnel in several sheltered workshops throughout the Pacific Northwest and Kansas (Johnson & Mithaug, 1978) to identify skills critical for entry into sheltered workshops. Specific questions were posed to assess the exact skills and criterion levels of skill performance. Finally, Mithaug, Mar, and Stewart (1978) developed the *Prevocational Assessment and Curriculum Guide*, based upon the results of Mithaug's research program, which has since been shown to discriminate among moderately, severely, and profoundly mentally retarded persons placed in work activity versus sheltered workshop programs (Mithaug *et al.*, 1980). Employers representing service (Rusch, Schutz, & Agran, 1982) and light industrial (Schutz, 1984) occupations also have been surveyed to identify specific requisite skills and the proficiency range of skill performance necessary for mentally retarded persons to obtain entry into competitive employment.

In addition to the efforts of Mithaug and his colleagues, Rusch *et al.* (1982), and Schutz (1984), social validation methodology has been used to assess the acceptance of habilitation procedures. Schutz, Rusch, and Lamson (1979) sought to determine the effectiveness of two alternative employer-selected supervisory procedures applied to the verbally abusive behavior of three moderately mentally retarded adults. A warning and 1-day suspension were identified as the procedures a potential employer used when employees were verbally abusive or socially inappropriate. After the use of warnings alone, these investigators applied 1-day suspensions in combination with warnings. The use of a 1-day suspension had an immediate impact on the inappropriate behavior of each of the three potential employees. This study exemplifies Rogers-Warren's (1977) suggestion to determine the contingencies to be found in the eventual placement setting for use among target individuals. These studies represent exemplars using subjective evaluation procedures to socially validate acceptable community behaviors and training procedures.

Assessing the Effects of Habilitation

Social validation methodology is also valuable for assessing intervention effectiveness to ascertain magnitude of habilitation (i.e., the clinical significance) by determining whether mentally retarded persons' everyday functioning has been enhanced. As with identification of habilitation focus, the assessment of habilitation effects is achieved primarily through social comparison and subjective evaluation.

Social Comparison. Azrin and Armstrong (1973) used social comparison data to verify the effectiveness of an habilitation program designed to teach appropriate eating. Severely mentally retarded residents of a state institution, when eating, were reported to use inappropriate utensils, throw and spill food, steal food from each other, and eat food previously spilled on the floor. The habilitation program, which incorporated reinforcement, manual guidance, positive practice, and other techniques, proved useful in eliminating inappropriate eating relative to baseline for each resident and a control group of residents receiving routine staff-supervised training. Normative data for social comparison were collected on ward staff eating behavior. These normative data indicated that residents' eating behavior after habilitation was indistinguishable from that of institution staff. Social comparison analysis led to validation of the clinical importance of the eating program.

Subjective Evaluations. As subjective evaluations are of value in determining the focus of habilitation, they are also useful in determining whether habilitation results are of sufficient magnitude to alter significant others' opinions of target mentally retarded individuals' behavior. Rusch, Weithers, Menchetti, and Schutz (1980) utilized subjective evaluation to assess the effectiveness of a habilitation program designed to reduce conversational, topic repetitions of a moderately mentally retarded client employed in a nonsheltered, competitive employment setting. Rusch *et al.* (1980) consulted supervisors and co-workers in this setting to ascertain troublesome behavior that required change. Supervisors and co-workers indicated that the target employee repeated topics excessively during conversations. Consequently, these co-workers were provided preinstruction on how to use instruction, feedback, and mild social censure as a consequence when this employee repeated a topic. During the intervention, direct measures obtained by trained observers showed that the habilitation program was effective in markedly reducing repetitions (social comparison). However, co-workers indicated that they believed that topical repeats had not been reduced (subjective evaluation), which was in contradiction to the direct measures. Thus, it appeared that treatment effects were not sufficiently large to influence co-workers' ratings.

"Consumer" satisfaction questionnaries were given to a variety of individuals (e.g., living unit staff, administrators, members of the local National Association for Retarded Citizens) in a study reported by VanBiervliet, Spangler, and Marshall (1981). These "significant others" watched video tapes of mentally retarded persons eating family style (i.e., passing food around a table) versus institutional style (i.e., picking up food-filled trays). In this study, mealtime language increased as a result of the meals being served family style. Social validation measures also suggested that family-style procedures were preferred by consumers. These studies indicate how subjective evaluations have been used to judge the acceptability of habilitation programs.

Summary

Although social validation was introduced over 15 years ago (Baer *et al.*, 1968), its use has lagged far behind the expectations of applied habilitation researchers (cf. Wolf, 1978), particularly as it relates to mentally retarded clients with severe behavior disorders. The delay in actual use and development may be related to the fact that what is considered socially important is based upon the expectations of others, and that efforts to measure expectations reliably have lagged behind the measurement of overt behavior. Social criteria, which are based upon expectations, require that habilitation programs be clinically important for the individual and valued by society. Social validation extends beyond examination of traditional skills training as the criterion for acceptability because it identifies therapeutic criteria by experimental means. Clinical significance is difficult to establish unless significant others or the mentally retarded individuals themselves determine "acceptable behavior." Social validation ensures that intervention priorities (i.e., the focus of habilitation and the effectiveness of habilitation) are not arbitrarily or stipulatively circumscribed. This methodology ensures a consensually valid impact upon individual functioning.

Summary and Future Research Directions

The primary thesis of this chapter is that mentally retarded individuals with severe behavior problems should be involved in habilitation programs that are oriented toward community integration and considered within an ecobehavioral framework. An ecobehavioral framework implies that behavior can be influenced by both intrapersonal and setting variables. Further, both sets of variables, and their effect on each other, need to be considered in order to maximize the success of habilitation.

The importance of considering behavior interrelationships was discussed. Research was presented showing that functional relationships exist between maladaptive and adaptive behaviors and that as adaptive skills are acquired, rates of maladaptive behaviors often decline. Because habilitation programs should teach adaptive behaviors that enable mentally retarded clients to fit into community settings, the selection of adaptive skills to be taught appears critical.

The importance of setting variables, particularly those that refer to the spectrum of behaviors that are valued by society, was also discussed. Social validation was presented as a procedure to use to identify habilitation goals and to evaluate the results of habilitation efforts. Two types of social validation were reviewed: (a) social comparison, which refers to comparing mentally retarded individuals' behavior before and after habilitation with identical behavior of nonhandicapped persons; and (b) subjective evaluation, which refers to soliciting the opinions of significant others regarding habilitation program validity.

Intervention procedures designed to suppress severe behavior problems need to be judged according to the degree and rate of suppression (Schroeder, Mulick, & Schroeder, 1979), durability of suppression (Schroeder et al., 1979), and generalization of suppression. Few if any of these issues have been adequately studied with respect to habilitation programming. More research is needed that directly compares the effectiveness of aversive techniques with techniques that teach habilitative responses that directly compete with maladaptive behaviors. Also, whether the acquisition of adaptive behaviors leads to generalization and maintenance of suppression effects has been largely unexplored. In addition, the best way to select keystone behaviors (i.e., those behaviors that have the possibility of altering entire classes of behaviors) is unknown. Voeltz and Evans (1982) suggested multiple response monitoring and social validation as two methods to employ.

In addition, there are several other unanswered questions. For example, type of adaptive behavior taught (i.e., functional versus nonfunctional, community relevant versus not community relevant) may influence rate of suppression as well as generalization and maintenance of suppression of behavior problems. Also, skills and behaviors that are valued by society in different settings (e.g., residential, recreation, and employment) are unknown. Further, the range of competence that society will tolerate poses interesting and answerable topics for advanced study. The answers to these and similar questions will ensure that successful habilitation programs are designed for mentally retarded persons with severe behavior disorders.

References

Azrin, N. H., & Armstrong, P. M. (1973). The "mini-meal"—A method for teaching eating skills to the profoundly retarded. *Mental Retardation, 11,* 9–13.
Azrin, N. H., Kaplan, J. J., & Foxx, R. M. (1973). Autism reversal: Eliminating stereotyped self-stimulation of retarded individuals. *American Journal of Mental Deficiency, 78,* 241–248.
Baer, D. M., Wolf, M. M., & Risley, T. R. (1968). Some current dimensions of applied behavior analysis. *Journal of Applied Behavior Analysis, 1,* 91–97.
Barker, R. G. (1968). *Ecological psychology.* Stanford: Stanford University Press.
Bates, Paul. (1980). The effectiveness of interpersonal skills training on the social skill acquisition of moderately and mildly retarded adults. *Journal of Applied Behavior Analysis, 13,* 237–248.
Bellamy, G. T., Peterson, L., & Close, D. (1975). Habilitation of the severely and profoundly retarded: Illustrations of competence. *Education and Training of the Mentally Retarded, 10,* 174–186.
Bellamy, T., & Buttars, U. L. (1975). Teaching trainable level retarded subjects to count money: Toward personal independence through academic instruction. *Education and Training of the Mentally Retarded, 10,* 18–26.
Berkson, G., & Landesman-Dwyer, S. (1977). Behavioral research on severe and profound mental retardation (1955–1974). *American Journal of Mental Deficiency, 81,* 428–454.
Berkson, G., & Romer, D. (1980). Social ecology of supervised communal facilities for mentally disabled adults: An introduction. *American Journal of Mental Deficiency, 85,* 219–228.
Bijou, S. W. (1982). Waves of the future in the educational intervention of developmental disabilities. *Analysis and Intervention in Developmental Disabilities, 2,* 253–267.
Bornstein, P. H., Bach, P. J., McFall, M. E., Friman, P. C., & Lyons, P. D. (1980). Application of a social skills training program in the modification of interpersonal deficits among retarded adults: A clinical replication. *Journal of Applied Behavior Analysis, 13,* 171–176.
Brooks, P. H., & Baumeister, A. A. (1977). A plea for consideration of ecological validity in experimental psychology of mental retardation: A guest editorial. *American Journal of Mental Deficiency, 81,* 407–416.
Brunswik, E. (1955). Representative design and probablistic theory in a functional psychology. *Psychological Review, 62,* 193–217.
Carr, E. G., Newsom, C. D., & Binkoff, J. A. (1980). Escape as a factor in the aggressive behavior of two retarded children. *Journal of Applied Behavior Analysis, 13,* 101–117.
Casey, L. O. (1978). Development of communicative behavior in autistic children: A parent program using manual signs. *Journal of Autism and Childhood Schizophrenia, 8,* 45–59.
Certo, N. (1983). Characteristics of educational services. In M. E. Snell (Ed.), *Systematic instruction of the moderately and severely handicapped* (2nd ed., pp. 2–15). Columbus: Charles E. Merrill.

Chadsey-Rusch, J. G. (1985). Community integration and mental retardation: The eco-behavioral approach to service provision and assessment. In R. H. Bruininks & K. C. Lakin (Eds.), *Living and learning in the least restrictive environment* (pp. 245–260). Baltimore: Paul H. Brookes.

Close, D. W., Irvin, L. K., Prehm, H. J., & Taylor, V. E. (1978). Systematic correction procedures in vocational-skill training of severely retarded individuals. *American Journal of Mental Deficiency, 83,* 270–275.

Connis, R. T., & Rusch, F. R. (1980). Programming maintenance through sequential withdrawal of social contingencies. *Behavior Research of Severe Developmental Disabilities, 1,* 249–260.

Eyman, R., O'Connor, G., Tarjan, G., & Justice, R. (1972). Factors determining residential placement of mentally retarded children. *American Journal of Mental Deficiency, 76,* 692–698.

Flavell, J. E. (1973). Reduction of stereotypies by reinforcement of toy play. *Mental Retardation, 6,* 1–14.

Frankel, F., & Simmons, J. Q. (1976). Self-injurious behavior in schizophrenic and retarded children. *American Journal of Mental Deficiency, 80,* 512–522.

Garcia, E. (1974). The training and generalization of a conversational speech form in nonverbal retardates. *Journal of Applied Behavior Analysis, 7,* 137–194.

Haywood, H. C., Meyers, C. E., & Switzky, H. N. (1982). Mental retardation. *Annual Review of Psychology, 33,* 309–342.

Hill, B., & Bruininks, R. (1981). *Physical and behavioral characteristics and maladaptive behavior of mentally retarded people in residential facilities: Project Report 12.* Minneapolis: University of Minnesota.

Horner, R. (1980). The effects of an environmental "enrichment" program on the behavior of institutionalized profoundly retarded children. *Journal of Applied Behavior Analysis, 13,* 473–491.

Horner, R., & Keilitz, F. (1975). Training mentally retarded adolescents to brush their teeth. *Journal of Applied Behavior Analysis, 8,* 301–309.

Irvin, L. K. (1976). General utility of easy to hard discrimination training procedures with the severely retarded. *Education and Training of the Mentally Retarded, 11,* 247–250.

Jackson, G. M., Johnson, C. R., Ackron, G. S., & Crowley, R. (1975). Food satiation as a procedure to decelerate vomiting. *American Journal of Mental Deficiency, 80,* 223–227.

Johnson, J. L., & Mithaug, D. E. (1978). A replication of sheltered workshop entry requirements. *AAESPH Review, 3,* 116–122.

Kazdin, A. E. (1977). Assessing the clinical or applied importance of behavior change through social validation. *Behavior Modification, 1,* 427–452.

Kazdin, A. E., & Matson, J. L. (1981). Social validation in mental retardation. *Applied Research in Mental Retardation, 2,* 39–53.

Martin, J. E., Rusch, F. R., James, V. L., Decker, P. J., & Trtol, K. A. (1982). The use of picture cues to establish self-control in the preparation of complex meals by mentally retarded adults. *Applied Research in Mental Retardation, 3(21),* 105–119.

Matson, J. L. (1980). A controlled group study of pedestrain skill training for the mentally retarded. *Behavior Research and Therapy, 18,* 97–106.

Matson, J. L., & Martin, J. E. (1979). A social learning approach to vocational training of the severely retarded. *Journal of Mental Deficiency Research, 23,* 9–16.

Mithaug, D. E. (1978). Case study in training generalized instruction-following responses to preposition–noun combinations in a severely retarded young adult. *AAESPH Review, 3,* 230–245.

Mithaug, D. E., & Hagmeier, L. D. (1978). The development of procedures to assess pre-vocational competencies of severely handicapped young adults. *AAESPH Review*, 3, 94–115.

Mithaug, D. E., & Hanawalt, D. A. (1978). The validation of procedures to assess pre-vocational task preferences in retarded adults. *Journal of Applied Behavior Analysis*, 11, 153–162.

Mithaug, D. E., Hagmeier, L. D., & Haring, N. G. (1977). The relationship between training activities and job placement in vocational education of the severely and profoundly handicapped. *AAESPH Review*, 2, 89–109.

Mithaug, D. E., Mar, D. K., & Stewart, J. E. (1978). *Prevocational assessment and curriculum guide*. Seattle: Exceptional Education.

Mithaug, D., Mar, D., Stewart, J., & McCalmon, D. (1980). Assessing prevocational com-petencies of profoundly, severely, and moderately retarded persons. *Journal of the Association for the Severely Handicapped*, 5, 270–284.

Mulick, J. A., & Schroeder, S. R. (1980). Research relating to management of antisocial behavior in mentally retarded persons. *The Psychological Record*, 30, 397–417.

Mulick, J. A., Hoyt, R., Rojahn, J., & Schroeder, S. R. (1978). Reduction of a "nervous habit" in a profoundly retarded youth by increasing toy play. *Journal of Behavior Therapy and Experimental Psychiatry*, 9, 381–385.

Nutter, D., & Reid, D. H. (1978). Teaching retarded women a clothing selection skill using community norms. *Journal of Applied Behavior Analysis*, 11, 475–487.

O'Brien, F., & Azrin, N. H. (1972a). Symptom reduction by functional displacement in a token economy: A case study. *Journal of Behavior Therapy and Experimental Psychiatry*, 3, 205–207.

O'Brien, F., & Azrin, N. H. (1972b). Developing proper mealtime behaviors of the insti-tutionalized retarded. *Journal of Applied Behavior Analysis*, 5, 389–399.

Pendergrass, V. E. (1972). Timeout from positive reinforcement following persistent, high-rate behavior in retardates. *Journal of Applied Behavior Analysis*, 5, 85–91.

Rogers-Warren, A. (1977). Planned change: Ecobehaviorally based interventions. In A. Rogers-Warren & S. R. Warren (Eds.), *Ecological perspectives in behavior analysis* (pp. 197–210). University Park Press: Baltimore.

Rogers-Warren, A., & Warren, S. F. (1977). The developing ecobehavioral psychology. In A. Rogers-Warren & S. F. Warren (Eds.), *Ecological perspectives in behavior analysis* (pp. 3–8). Baltimore: University Park Press.

Rollings, J. P., Baumeister, A. A., & Baumeister, A. A. (1977). The use of overcorrection procedures to eliminate the stereotyped behaviors of retarded individuals: An anal-ysis of collateral behaviors and generalization of suppressive effects. *Behavior Mod-ification*, 1, 29–46.

Rusch, F. R., & Mithaug, D. E. (1985). Employment education: A systems-analytic ap-proach to transitional competitive programming for the student with severe handi-caps. In K. C. Lakin & R. H. Bruininks (Eds.), *Strategies for achieving community integration of developmentally disabled citizens* (pp. 117–192). Baltimore: Paul H. Brookes.

Rusch, F. R., Weithers, J. A., Menchetti, B. M., & Schutz, R. P. (1980). Social validation of a program to reduce topic repetition in a nonsheltered setting. *Education and Training of the Mentally Retarded*, 15, 208–215.

Rusch, F. R., Schutz, R. P., & Agran, M. (1982). Validating entry-level survival skills for service occupations: Implications for curriculum development. *The Journal of the Association for the Severely Handicapped*, 7, 32–41.

Rusch, F. R., Chadsey-Rusch, J., White, D., & Gifford, J. L. (1985). Programs for severely mentally retarded adults: Perspectives and methodologies. In D. Bricker & J. Filler

(Eds.), *Severe mental retardation: From theory to practice* (pp. 119–140). Lancaster, PA: Lancaster Press.

Sajwaj, T., Twardosz, S., & Burke, M. (1972). Side effects of extinction procedures in a remedial preschool. *Journal of Applied Behavior Analysis, 5,* 163–175.

Schalock, R. L. (1985). Comprehensive community services: A plea for interagency collaboration. In R. H. Bruininks & K. C. Lakin (Eds.), *Living and learning in the least restrictive environment* (pp. 37–63). Baltimore: Paul H. Brookes.

Schalock, R. L., Karan, O. C., & Harper, R. S. (1980). An evaluation-remediation model for serving people with significant handicaps. *Mental Retardation, 18,* 231–233.

Schoggen, P. (1978). Ecological psychology and mental retardation. In G. P. Sackett (Ed.), *Observing behavior: Vol. 1. Theory and applications in mental retardation* (pp. 33–62). Baltimore: University Park Press.

Schroeder, S. R., Rojahn, J., & Mulick, J. A. (1978). Ecobehavioral organization of developmental day care for the chronically self-injurious. *Journal of Pediatric Psychology, 3,* 81–88.

Schroeder, S. R., Mulick, J. A., & Schroeder, C. S. (1979). Management of severe behavior problems of the retarded. In N. R. Ellis (Ed.), *Handbook of Mental Deficiency* (2nd ed., pp. 341–366). Hillsdale, NJ: Erlbaum.

Schroeder, S. R., Schroeder, C. S., Rojahn, J., & Mulick, J. A. (1981). Self-injurious behavior: An analysis of behavior management techniques. In J. L. Matson & J. R. McCartney (Eds.), *Handbook of behavior modification with the mentally retarded* (pp. 61–115). New York: Plenum Press.

Schutz, R. (1984). *The identification of job requisite skills to facilitate the entry of severely handicapped adults into competitive employment settings.* Unpublished doctoral dissertation, University of Illinois, Urbana-Champaign.

Schutz, R. P., Rusch, F. R., & Lamson, D. S. (1979). Evaluation of an employer's procedure to eliminate unacceptable behavior on the job. *Community Services Forum, 1,* 4–5.

Scott, M. (1980). Ecological theory and methods for research in special education. *The Journal of Special Education, 4,* 279–294.

Smith, M., & Meyers, A. (1979). Telephone skills training for retarded adults: Group and individual demonstrations with and without verbal instruction. *American Journal of Mental Deficiency, 83,* 581–587.

Snell, M. E. (1979). Higher functioning residents as language trainers of the mentally retarded. *Education and Training of the Mentally Retarded, 14,* 77–84.

Sowers, J. A., Rusch, F. R., & Hudson, C. (1979). Training a severely retarded young adult to ride the city bus to and from work. *AAESPH Review, 4,* 15–23.

Spears, D., Rusch, F. R., York, R., & Lilly, M. S. (1981). Training independent arrival behaviors to a severely mentally retarded child. *Journal of the Association for the Severely Handicapped, 6,* 40–45.

Talkington, L. W., Hall, S. M., & Altman, R. (1971). Communication deficits and aggression in the mentally retarded. *American Journal of Mental Deficiency, 76,* 235–237.

Tarpley, H. D., & Schroeder, S. R. (1979). Comparison of DRO and DRI on rate of suppression of self-injurious behavior. *American Journal of Mental Deficiency, 84,* 188–194.

Thurman, S. K. (1977). Congruence of behavioral ecologies: A model for special education. *The Journal of Special Education, 11,* 329–333.

VanBiervliet, A., Spangler, P. F., & Marshall, A. (1981). An ecobehavioral examination of a simple strategy for increasing mealtime language in residential facilities. *Journal of Applied Behavior Analysis, 14,* 295–305.

Van Houten, R. (1979). Social validation: The evolution of standards of competency for target behaviors. *Journal of Applied Behavior Analysis, 12*, 581–592.

Voeltz, L. M., & Evans, I. M. (1982). The assessment of behavioral interrelationships in child behavior therapy. *Behavioral Assessment, 4*, 131–165.

Voeltz, L. M., & Evans, I. M. (1983). Educational Validity: Procedures to evaluate outcomes in programs for severely handicapped learners. *The Journal of the Association for the Severely Handicapped, 8*, 3–15.

Vogelsberg, T., & Rusch, F. R. (1979). Training three severely handicapped young adults to walk, look, and cross uncontrolled intersections. *AAESPH Review, 4*, 264–273.

Wahler, R. G. (1975). Some structural aspects of deviant child behavior. *Journal of Applied Behavior Analysis, 8*, 27–42.

Wehman, P., Schutz, R., Renzaglia, A., & Karan, O. (1977). The use of positive practice training in work adjustment with two profoundly retarded adolescents. *Vocational Evaluation and Work Adjustment Bulletin, 14*, 14–22.

Wehman, P., Renzaglia, A., Berry, G., Schutz, R., & Karan, O. (1978). Developing a leisure skill repertoire in severely and profoundly handicapped persons. *American Association for the Education of the Severely and Profoundly Handicapped, 3*, 162–171.

Willems, E. P. (1974). Behavioral technology and behavioral ecology. *Journal of Applied Behavior Analysis, 7*, 151–165.

Willems, E. P. (1977). Steps toward an ecobehavioral technology. In A. Rogers-Warren & S. F. Warren (Eds.), *Ecological perspectives in behavior analysis* (pp. 39–61). Baltimore: University Park Press.

Windle, C. D., Stewart, E., & Brown, S. J. (1961). Reasons for community failure of retarded patients. *American Journal of Mental Deficiency, 66*, 213–217.

Wolf, M. (1978). Social validity: The case for subjective measurement or how applied behavior analysis is finding its heart. *Journal of Applied Behavior Analysis, 11*, 203–214.

Wolfensberger, W. (1972). *The principle of normalization in human services.* Toronto: National Institute on Mental Retardation.

Young, J. A., & Wincze, J. P. (1974). The effects of the reinforcement of compatible and incompatible behaviors on self-injurious and related behaviors of a profoundly retarded female adult. *Behavior Therapy, 5*, 614–623.

Youngberg v. Romeo, 50 U.S.L.W. 4681 (1982).

5

Ecobehavioral Design
Programming for Engagement

MICHAEL L. JONES, JENNIFER LATTIMORE, GARY R. ULICNY
AND TODD R. RISLEY

Introduction

Over a decade ago, *Wyatt V. Stickney* (1972) established the presumed
minimal requirements for a safe and humane living environment for
mentally retarded persons. This class action suit marked the onset of
institutional reform in the United States. Gunzburg and Gunzburg (1979)
offered the following insight into the current state of institutional living
environments:

> The overprotection and oversupport apparent in our institutions is neatly
> camouflaged by providing modern comfort, labour-saving devices, domestic
> staff, canteen facilities, colour television sets, lounges with larger windows,
> colour schemes and soft furnishings—a club atmosphere, relaxing and pleas-
> ant, where people can vegetate in more comfort than in the past with their
> cheerless and cold environments equipped only with the bare essentials.
> (p. 161)

It is fortunate that today, most living environments for mentally
retarded persons provide for basic life support and humane care, so that
issues of health and safety are not as great a concern as in the past. It
is unfortunate, however, that many environments provide little else.
Although the reforms of the 1970s resulted in broad-scale improvements
in physical conditions of residential settings, many environmental features remain unchanged.

MICHAEL L. JONES • Bureau of Child Research, University of Kansas, Lawrence, Kansas
66045.   JENNIFER LATTIMORE and GARY R. ULICNY • Department of Human Development,
University of Kansas, Lawrence, Kansas 66045.   TODD R. RISLEY • Department of Psychology, University of Alaska, Anchorage, Alaska 99508.

In many settings, the emphasis is still on promoting ongoing health care and preventing harm rather than encouraging client development. Opportunities for clients to explore and interact with the environment—behaviors essential for progressive development—are minimized for the sake of client safety and to facilitate staff's ability to provide care and supervision to clients. Socialization with peers and staff is minimal, and interaction between staff and clients, when it does occur, is characterized by staff's performing some activity for clients, rather than encouraging independent behavior or intervening to terminate episodes of undesirable behavior. As a result of this lack of engagement opportunities, clients either spend little or none of their time engaged in appropriate behavior, or worse, they spend their time engaged in disruptive behaviors.

A predominant theme throughout this chapter is the importance of clients' active, appropriate engagement with the environment. Engagement may consist of simply attending to events in the environment, active manipulation and exploration of the environment, or interacting with others in the environment. In whatever form, engagement is important for a number of reasons. First, it is the basis for learning adaptive behavior; adaptation occurs in response to interaction with the environment. Second, appropriate engagement provides a context for teaching. By appropriately consequating client engagement, staff may teach clients to differentiate appropriate from inappropriate behaviors and elaborate on clients' appropriate responding. And third, appropriate engagement is important because it is inversely related to inappropriate engagement. When clients are not engaged in appropriate behavior, they are doing nothing or engaging in undesirable behavior.

This last point may appear overly simplistic, but it is a point worth emphasizing. Too often in treating severe behavior disorders, we focus on undesirable behavior and fail to ask how—if at all—the treatment environment maintains appropriate engagement. It is our position that the best treatment for behavior disorders is to promote appropriate, competing behaviors. These appropriate behaviors are established and maintained by programming an engaging environment. Hence, this chapter focuses on methods for programming a treatment environment that promotes and maintains appropriate engagement. We will begin by discussing ways in which the environment can influence disruptive behavior. We will then describe how to evaluate treatment environments to determine what factors are maintaining appropriate and inappropriate client engagement. Finally, we will describe methods for programming an engaging environment and treating behavior disorders when they do occur in the environment.

Determinants of Behavior Disorders

In his examination of possible etiological factors in self-injurious behavior (SIB), Carr (1977) suggests that SIB and other disruptive behaviors may have multiple and varied causes. Carr presents five causal hypotheses derived from existing theoretical and research literature.

1. *Positive reinforcement hypothesis.* Disruptive behavior is a learned operant behavior maintained by positive social reinforcement. Lovaas and Simmons (1969) examined three hypotheses of the maintenance of SIB by social reinforcement: (a) SIB should decrease if social attention is withheld; (b) SIB should increase if occurrences result in social reinforcement; and (c) SIB should decrease if an aversive stimulus is delivered contingently.

Three severely mentally retarded children with high rates of SIB were exposed to experimental conditions simulating the three hypotheses. Results support the authors' suggestions—reduced rates of SIB were observed in the withdrawal of social reinforcement and punishment conditions, whereas increased SIB was reported when social attention was provided contingent on occurrence of the behavior.

If disruptive behaviors are maintained by social attention, the most logical treatment interventions are those that remove social consequences. The two most frequently cited interventions have been extinction and time-out from positive reinforcement. These interventions have been both effective (Lahey, McNees, & McNees, 1973; Tyler & Brown, 1967; Wolf, Risley, & Mees, 1964) and ineffective (Corte, Wolfe, & Locke, 1971; Duker, 1975; Tate & Baroff, 1966) in reducing disruptive behavior of individuals with mental retardation. Although time-out and extinction alone have, in some cases, eventually proved successful in reducing disruptive behavior, their success can be significantly enhanced when paired with reinforcement of alternative behaviors and overall enriched time-in (AABT Task Force, 1982; Sulzer-Azaroff & Mayer, 1977).

2. *Negative reinforcement hypothesis.* Disruptive behavior is "maintained by the termination of avoidance of an aversive stimulus" (Carr, 1977, p. 805) following occurrence of the behavior. This hypothesis suggests that persons learn to engage in serious disruptive behavior in order to escape or avoid participation in aversive activities. For example, we once worked with a woman who would vigorously poke at her eyes whenever she was faced with instructional demands. Because of the potential harm (detached retina, blindness) of allowing the eye poking to continue, staff had no choice but to discontinue demands.

Several studies support the hypothesis that disruptive behavior may be motivated by escape/avoidance factors. Carr, Newsom, and Binkoff (1976) reported significantly higher frequencies of self-injurious behavior in demand versus free-play settings. The authors also observed significant reductions in SIB when the subject was presented with a "safety signal" correlated with the termination of demands.

Similar research by Favell, McGimsey, Jones, and Cannon (1981) reported that physical restraints may also serve as an escape/avoidance safety signal. Both Carr (1977) and Favell et al. (1981) propose that a viable treatment option may be contingent application of the safety signal upon gradually increasing periods of nonaggression.

3. Self-stimulation hypothesis. Organisms that are placed in environments providing insufficient stimulation may engage in disruptive behaviors to receive sensory stimulation. Barren environments are more conducive to maintaining disruptive behaviors than environments providing opportunities for appropriate engagement (Carr, 1977). Disruptive behaviors typically associated with the self-stimulation hypothesis are those providing high levels of tactile, vestibular, and kinesthetic stimulation (i.e., SIB, stereotyped behaviors). One would not expect this hypothesis to be a maintaining factor in disruptive behaviors such as aggression toward others or aggression toward property. These behaviors are more likely maintained by social reinforcement.

A major problem with studies that attempt to measure the effects of sensory stimulation has been the inability to separate sensory reinforcement effects from social reinforcement effects (Carr, 1977). Horner (1980) evaluated the effects of an enriched environment and an enriched environment plus differential reinforcement of appropriate behavior on the maladaptive behaviors of five profoundly mentally retarded women. Results demonstrated a 20 to 30% increase in adaptive behavior in the enriched environment condition and an additional 20 to 30% increase when the enriched environment was coupled with differential reinforcement of adaptive behavior. These findings suggest that increasing environmental opportunities for stimulation may also increase independent engagement. However, even greater increases in appropriate behavior may occur when an enriched environment is paired with social reinforcement.

4. Organic hypothesis. "Self-injurious behavior is the product of aberrant physiological processes" (Carr, 1977, p. 808). This hypothesis suggests that, in some cases, SIB may be caused by genetic or nongenetic physical processes. However, several studies have reported positive results when using operant strategies to reduce SIB with suspected organic etiology (Anderson & Hermann, 1975; Duker, 1975; Shear, Nyhan,

Kirkman & Stern, 1971). Carr (1977) contends that although organic factors may contribute to the initial development of SIB, the behavior may be maintained by increased attention.

5. *Psychodynamic hypothesis.* Some hypotheses suggest psychodynamic motivations, such as attempts to establish body reality or to trace ego boundaries, are causes of disruptive behavior. Carr dismisses psychodynamic hypotheses because of the inability to operationalize the vague constructs involved. He suggests lack of objectivity may account for the paucity of empirical studies testing these hypotheses. There are also insufficient data to suggest that effective interventions can be developed based on these hypotheses (Bachman, 1972).

Carr suggests that, although etiology may vary, disruptive behavior is largely controlled and maintained by environmental contingencies. In designing treatment interventions for disruptive behavior, the etiology of the behavior may not be as important as identifying the environmental variables currently maintaining it. An example of how these variables may be identified is provided in a past study by Iwata, Dorsey, Slifer, Bauman, and Richman (1982). Environmental determinants of self-injurious behavior in mentally retarded children and adolescents were examined. Iwata *et al.* observed subjects' SIB in four experimenter-created analog environments. The four environmental conditions were (a) social disapproval and nonpunitive physical contact contingent on SIB; (b) simulating an escape/avoidance condition by providing a structured academic task and terminating instructional demands contingent on SIB; (c) unstructured play—a no-demand, enriched environment condition with praise and brief physical contact contingent on the absence of self-injury; and (d) alone—simulating an austere environment by placing the subject alone in a barren room. With six of the nine subjects, higher frequencies of SIB were consistently associated with specific environmental conditions. The authors were able to determine if SIB was maintained by social attention, reduced demands, or self-stimulation. In the first two cases, SIB can be controlled by rearranging the consequences of $\colon$ B (e.g., providing social attention contingent upon nonoccurrences of SIB). In the latter case, however, SIB that is self-stimulatory in nature may not be as readily controlled by rearranging the consequences of SIB. Instead, a more stimulating environment appears to be a necessary, if not sufficient (Horner, 1980), condition for controlling the behavior.

We have already noted that the predominant focus of this chapter is programming an engaging environment. With respect to control of behavior disorders, environmental programming for engagement serves two purposes. First, it results in an environment that promotes appropriate engagement and thus reduces the likelihood of inappropriate engagement. Second, an engaging environment improves the effectiveness of social interventions by providing an appropriate context in which to use these interventions. For example, time-out procedures will only be effective if time-in is truly reinforcing to the client.

The example by Iwata *et al.* (1982) also shows how to identify environmental determinants of behavior on an individual basis. Our focus here, however, is on modifying the overall environment to impact behavior of all inhabitants. The concern in these "actuarial" interventions is determining what environmental modifications are warranted to influence a particular global behavior (appropriate engagement in this case) of inhabitants. In the next section, we will describe important considerations and strategies for evaluating the overall quality of the treatment environment to determine what changes may be needed to promote appropriate engagement.

Evaluating the Treatment Environment

The first step toward programming an engaging treatment environment should be assessment of the existing environment to determine its impact on client behavior. Evaluating the environment is important in three respects. It is necessary to determine inadequacies in the existing environment and thus identify the focus of intervention. Data from this evaluation may be used to justify any necessary environmental changes. These data also permit systematic, proactive planning for change rather than reactive change to address crises. Second, evaluation provides a measure of success or failure for interventions attempted to improve the quality of the environment. Preliminary assessment provides a baseline for comparison to postintervention assessment. Third, repeated evaluation and subsequent feedback to program managers are vital to maintain quality.

Various criteria have been proposed for evaluating the quality of environments for people with mental retardation. Ultimately, criteria for evaluating settings should be related to their actual impact on client functioning (Jones, Risley, & Favell, 1983). Assessing the quality of an environment should be based on a functional analysis of behavior within that environment and the extent to which desirable client outcomes are obtained. In designing environments to reduce disruptive behavior, desirable outcomes are increased frequency and variety of appropriate engagement and reduced inappropriate engagement. These outcomes depend upon the engagement opportunities available to clients in the environment. Thus, environmental assessment should focus on evaluating the relationship between clients' engagement and opportunities provided for engagement.

It is important to emphasize that evaluation of the treatment environment must include an assessment of clients' actual behavior in the environment. The quality of engagement opportunities can only be determined by the levels of engagement they produce. For example, a common assumption about environmental quality is that more material and activity availability is better. But this is true only to the extent that the available materials and activities result in more appropriate engagement (i.e., provide an engaging rather than simply enriched environment). Several studies have shown that simply improving material and activity availability may not be sufficient—improved engagement depends upon the engagement potential of the materials and activities provided (Favell & Cannon, 1977; Jones, Favell, Lattimore, & Risley, 1984). Thus, the only way to determine if engagement opportunities are, in fact, engaging is to assess clients' behavior.

Valid measures of environmental-behavior relationships may best be derived from direct observation of behavior in its environmental context. In a past publication (Jones *et al.*, 1983), we advocated use of an *ecobehavioral* assessment strategy to obtain these measures—a strategy that documents ongoing behavior and features of the immediate environment that may influence behavior. We discussed a number of considerations in developing ecobehavioral observation procedures. Our suggestions are summarized later. The reader is referred to the publication cited previously for a more detailed description of ecobehavioral observation strategies.

There are several methodological considerations in assessing environmental-behavior relationships. First the *locus* or reference point may be either environment-centered or person-centered. Environment-centered measures ignore the specific behavior of individuals and focus on the surrounding environment and more global patterns of behavior. Person-centered measures focus on behavior and the individual's interactions with the surrounding environment. We suggest that a person-centered orientation may be more effective in describing the immediate opportunities available for engagement.

A second consideration is for *sampling* environment and behavior. For example, behavior may be recorded as a continuous stream of discrete samples over time. Ongoing behavior and immediate environmental conditions may be accurately assessed by taking periodic time samples. However, two methodological conditions must be met in order to obtain accurate time samples. Time sampling must be relatively instantaneous so that discrete samples rather than multiple episodes of behavior are observed. Thus, behaviors can be quantified by their duration rather than their rate because the proportion of time a behavior is seen during these time-lapse observations corresponds directly to the absolute proportion of time occupied by the behavior. For example, if clients are observed engaging appropriately in activities during 50% of the observations taken, it may be assumed that clients spent 50% of the total time spanned by the observations engaged in appropriate activity. Time samples of behavior must be made with sufficient frequency to minimize sampling error. As with any sampling procedure, the number of samples required to obtain a representative sample will be determined by the heterogeneity of the population; in this case the behavior of the individuals observed. A related issue is the latency between samples of behavior, which should be determined by the relative interest in the sequential nature of behaviors.

A third consideration is *selecting behavioral and environmental variables* to assess. With respect to client behavior, the primary interest is appropriate and inappropriate engagement. Therefore, behavioral variables can be limited to three categories. Samples of clients' behavior may be classified as either appropriate engagement, inappropriate engagement, or nonengagement. Alternatively, an open data system may be preferred, whereby a brief, narrative description of clients' behavior is recorded. This scoring procedure provides a maximum of flexibility and permits observers to assess any situation encountered without resorting to an extensive system of predetermined codes. This flexibility is important because it may be difficult, at best, to determine on an *a priori* basis all of the events (and corresponding codes) that might be encountered. Further, this procedure results in descriptive data that may be coded into any number of different categories after the fact. These archival records may be reanalyzed in a variety of ways without the limitations imposed by an idiosyncratic recording procedure.

There are two environmental variables of primary interest as opportunities for engagement. First, measures of the availability of engaging materials and activities should be taken. This involves assessing their immediate availability to clients during each instantaneous time sample. It is important to document the type of material or activity available as thoroughly as possible, as well as the manner in which it is provided. Based on the record of client behavior during the observation, it is possible to determine exactly which materials and activities are associated with appropriate engagement.

The second environmental variable of primary interest is clients' interactions with staff. Ideally, these interactions should be conducted so they are learning activities for clients and provide maximum opportunities for independent responding. Thus, in addition to noting the frequency of contacts between staff and clients, the specific nature of interactions should be documented. Staff should have pleasant verbal interactions with clients whenever possible (including basic care activities) to promote language development. They should also provide the least possible assistance necessary to engage clients in an ongoing activity. This will encourage independent responding rather than passive participation by the client. Thus, social interactions may be classified along two dimensions: (a) presence or absence of a positive or corrective verbal interaction (i.e., social vs. nonsocial) and (b) presence or absence of an opportunity to respond independently (i.e., assistive vs. custodial interaction).

In addition to data obtained from time-sampling observations, it will be useful to gather information on a number of variables that may control the environmental conditions noted in the observations. This information will be useful in determining the ultimate cause of deficiencies noted in the environment. Additional information about the setting should include personnel policies, staff scheduling, supervisory structure, degree and type of staff training, nature of interactions between departments, flow of responsibility for client treatment, and existing guidelines and procedures for handling disruptive behavior.

Programming an Engaging Environment

Evaluation of the existing treatment environment should identify a number of areas for improvement. Changes to improve the setting should be addressed in a systematic manner and with a clear understanding that resistance to change is inevitable. In this section, we will describe systematic procedures for implementing changes in the treatment environment. Included are guidelines for reducing resistance to change and maintaining improvement in quality over time. Our research in various settings with various populations has led us to adopt several guiding "principles" for programming an engaging treatment environment. These principles apply to the design of both the physical environment and the activities, or program, that will occur in the environment.

Open Environmental Design

The concept of *open environment design* is perhaps foremost among these principles. An open environment has a minimum of visual and physical barriers among activities. Most or all activities are conducted within a single, large area but with clear delineation between activity areas. Ideally, activity areas are designated by changes in floor surface, arrangement of furnishings, and so on to provide clear but unobtrusive boundaries.

The open environmental design has several advantages. Clients can more freely explore the environment and choose from among several available activities. The design also facilitates supervision of both clients and staff and permits easier transition between sequential activities. Finally, the open design provides greater flexibility in use of space. Activity areas may be rearranged as needs change over time. In short, activities shape the space, rather than space shaping activities.

Several potential problems with the open design should be noted. For example, there must be an adequate match between the setting's physical and program characteristics—open physical plan requires an open program design. The difference between a workable open environment and a barren dayroom is determined largely by program design. This is an advantage in one respect because many settings for mentally retarded persons (e.g., institutional dayrooms) are already open in their physical design. An open program may be implemented with few, if any, extensive physical modifications to the setting.

A frequent criticism of open environments is greater potential for distractibility because of increased noise levels and visual distraction. Research in day-care centers has shown that an open environment does not interfere with small group, training, or other activities (e.g., naps) that require minimum distraction (Twardosz, Cataldo, & Risley, 1974). Day-care centers for nondisabled infants and toddlers may arguably be different from settings for mentally retarded persons, but one need only witness feeding time for 20 infants to note the similarities. The same principles and procedures apply. For example, noise levels can be reduced by choosing sound-absorbing furniture, wall, and floor coverings; visual distractability can be minimized by lower ambient lighting and use of spot lighting.

Another frequent criticism of the open design is clients' loss of privacy. In actuality, this may be less of a problem as a result of improved supervision and thus easier detection of privacy violations. Further, we are advocating use of an open environment in designing the *living* space for clients. Open design may not necessarily apply to clients' private quarters. But even in the living area it may be desirable to designate a private or quiet area where clients may take a rest from ongoing activities. This quite space must be used judiciously, however, so that clients do not spend too much time "resting."

Activity Zones

A second guiding principle is the use of *activity zones*. Each zone is a discrete area in which specific activities occur at specific times. We have found activity zones to be the most effective use of space within an open environmental design. As one might expect, the zone approach requires special arrangements of the program as well as physical environment. For example, we have found that assigning staff to supervise specific activity zones rather than groups of clients (i.e., zone vs. man-to-man staffing) results in less "dead time" and more active engagement for both clients and caregivers (LeLaurin & Risley, 1972).

We have also found that it is important to schedule concurrent activity zones whenever possible. Specifically, it is essential to have a centralized holding zone from which clients may move to other activity zones throughout the day. This *central activity area* is always staffed by at least one caregiver and furnished with an abundance of engaging materials. When clients are not involved in other activity zones (e.g., meals, toileting, training, recreation), they remain in the central activity area, where staff circulate to prompt and reinforce appropriate engagement responses.

It is also important, when activity zones are established, that clear boundaries separate concurrent activities. This serves to designate supervision boundaries for staff (i.e., they are responsible for all clients within their zone). Zone boundaries may also be conditioned as discriminative stimuli for clients, signaling the locations in which certain behaviors can and cannot occur (e.g., toileting is only reinforced in the toileting zone).

We have already alluded to several advantages in using activity zones. Dead time may be reduced by scheduling a continuous holding activity to occupy clients between other activities. Rules governing appropriate and inappropriate activity in each zone may be established and their enforcement facilitated by clearly designating zone boundaries. The use of zones may also increase the amount of individualized attention clients receive. When staff are responsible for an entire group of clients, as in the man-to-man technique, they have little or no time to spend with clients individually. With the zone approach, clients typically arrive at each zone singly, so the caregiver can immediately provide individual attention to engage them in the new activity.

Although the zone approach offers several advantages, there are common criticisms. First, proponents of the man-to-man or family-group approach to activity planning argue that it is preferable because more individualized attention can be given to each client according to his or her needs (Crosby, 1976). In reality, there may be less individualized attention with the man-to-man approach because caregivers must continually supervise an entire group of clients. As a result, clients spend much of their time waiting for other members of the group to complete an activity before the next activity can be initiated.

It is also assumed that the man-to-man approach permits closer interpersonal relationships between staff and clients. Presumably, clients are contacted by fewer caregivers, so closer relationships develop and clients receive more consistent care. It should be noted, however, that a particular caregiver, who generally works a 40-hour week, is with clients less than half of the time they are awake. Further, during this time, the caregiver is or should be distributing attention among all clients in the family group. Thus, there is little assurance that clients will receive more consistent care with the man-to-man approach. Alternatively, consistent care can be assured with the zone approach by specifying exactly how staff should conduct zone activities with each client and training all staff to operate the zone accordingly.

A third common concern with the zone approach is maintaining zones and ensuring that clients remain in a designated area, participate in prescribed activities, and so on. We have found this to be a common problem in establishing a zone system, and it may be the major reason the approach is not adopted more readily. However, we have also found that zones can be maintained, if available materials and activities are sufficiently stimulating to maintain clients' interest. The key to maintaining a zone is to ensure that clients' participation is adequately and consistently reinforced either through selection and presentation of reinforcing materials and activities or the use of programmed contingencies.

We will illustrate this point by noting procedures used in operating a central activity zone. First, the central activity zone is furnished with a variety of toys and materials that have been empirically selected because they promote high levels of independent engagement (Favell & Cannon, 1977; Jones, Favell, Lattimore, & Risley, 1984). If clients are ambulatory, materials may be displayed on open shelves to promote independent selection (Montes & Risley, 1975). Clients are encouraged to select and engage in appropriate activity with materials. This may initially require using reinforcement contingencies whereby clients are rewarded (e.g., with edibles and praise) for any approach and contact with materials.

Differential reinforcement may be used to promote client versus staff-initiated engagement. For example, edible reinforcers may be delivered only when clients independently select and play with toys, and social praise may be used to maintain toy play or when a caregiver must initially prompt toy play.

Additional rules may be established for the zone to maintain appropriate engagement and the zone itself. For example, clients may be prevented from taking materials outside of the zone, and inappropriate engagement (e.g., throwing objects) may be consequated by requiring clients to leave the zone temporarily. If materials and activities available in the zone are truly reinforcing, temporary exclusion from the zone may be used as an effective punisher for disruptive behavior.

Assignment of Staff Responsibilities

A third design principle governs the assignment of staff responsibilities within the treatment environment. We have found it most effective to prepare staff as *generalists* who are capable of meeting almost all client needs. The generalist approach to assigning responsibility to caregivers ensures that each caregiver is trained in all multidisciplinary aspects of basic care. This enables smooth and efficient movement from one activity zone to another across the day. In contrast, a specialist approach allows less flexibility in scheduling because paraprofessionals are hired, trained, and supervised by independent disciplines (e.g., physical therapy, occupational therapy, speech and hearing, nursing, special education) to provide a specific type of care. Paraprofessionals (e.g., physical therapy, nursing, or special education aides) are responsible to different supervisors. This makes it difficult to identify any one person responsible for overall services. The actual quality of care received with specialist caregivers depends upon the ability of each separate supervisor to select, train, supervise, and coordinate services without confusing or omitting responsibilities between specialties.

In a generalist approach, multidisciplinary treatment components of care are disseminated through a single responsible supervisor. A generalist approach maximizes accountability for quality of care, allows more flexibility in time and personnel for scheduling services, and provides an on-site supervisor, whereas a specialist approach results in service disruptions when a specialist is unavailable (e.g., sickness or bad weather) or when conflicts arise between specialists' schedules. Finally, the generalist approach enhances implementation and integration of multidisciplinary services across zones because all caregivers are capable of providing all aspects of care.

In the generalist model, professional staff function primarily as consultants. They prescribe services and design specific programs for clients, provide training and follow-up to caregivers, and when more sophisticated treatment is required, provide therapy directly to clients. Thus, they are freed from the responsibility of supervision to practice the skills for which they were trained.

The simplified management structure also serves to buffer caregivers from concurrent demands by various professionals. Input from each discipline is directed to the program supervisor, who, in turn, assigns work responsibilities to caregivers. As a result, greater integration of services is achieved.

Reducing Resistance to Change

One final design "principle" concerns methods for *reducing resistance to change* of the work environment. Resistance may come from management (those who have veto authority over proposed changes) or from those who are directly affected by the proposed changes—direct service staff and professional service providers who are not in a position to veto changes. We assume that most readers of this chapter are either program managers or will be initiating changes under the authority of program managers. Therefore, the major concern here is resistance from those directly affected by change.

In his text on work methods design, Krick (1962) cites 12 common sources of resistance to change among workers affected by change:

1. *Inertia.* A basic tendency to retain the status quo, which may be especially apparent when change is sudden or radical.
2. *Uncertainty about consequences of change.* Even when existing conditions are unsatisfactory, workers may not want to take the risk that change may result in even worse conditions.
3. *Ignorance about the need for or purpose of change.* Unless a clear rationale is provided, many changes may appear to be arbitrary.
4. *Lack of knowledge or understanding about the new methods.* Inadequate orientation to new procedures may arouse suspicion or insecurity.
5. *Perceived loss of content, responsibility, or control of work.* This may be especially true among professional or supervisory staff who may view change as usurping their authority or expertise.

6. *Fear of economic insecurity.* Workers may suspect that changes will result in loss of jobs or at least loss of earnings.
7. *Peer pressure.* Each individual worker's reaction to change will be influenced by what he or she anticipates that the work group as a whole wants.
8. *Disruption of social relationships.* Fear that change may break up a close-knit work group.
9. *Antagonistic attitude toward change agent.* Antagonism may result from attitudes toward change agent personally, the change agent's function, or the entity represented by the change agent (i.e., management).
10. *Introduction of change by an "outsider."* Workers may be suspicious of any change introduced by agents from outside the work group.
11. *No participation in formulation of new methods.* Workers will resent the lack of opportunity to express and protect their interests and have a part in decisions affecting them.
12. *Poor timing or tactless approach in introducing changes.* Resistance may result simply because changes are introduced when worker relations are strained, there is little advance warning, or there is little consideration for workers' interests.

Krick (1962) also suggests a number of strategies for reducing resistance to change. His suggestions, with comments about specific applications, include:

1. *Provide a thorough, convincing rationale for changes.* Results from evaluating the existing treatment environment should be used to support the need for change and the specific changes needed. It is also important to emphasize that changes are being made in the clients' best interests, and this should clearly be the case.
2. *Provide a detailed explanation of the nature of the proposed changes.* Although it may not be possible to provide detailed descriptions of changes at the time they are announced, some explanation of the changes should be provided. The expected consequences of change, in terms of client treatment and staff activities, should also be discussed.
3. *Encourage participation by staff in formulating changes.* At the very least, staff should have an opportunity to discuss the proposed changes and air their concerns. Staff will also be more receptive to changes if they have a sense of ownership of the new methods. Ownership may be instilled by consulting with staff in the

design of new methods and, whenever possible, incorporating their suggestions into the final design. Even if suggested methods are inferior, they may be worth including, if resistance to the overall proposal is reduced in the process. Staff participation will also help explain existing work methods and environmental design and may ensure that all necessary components are incorporated into the modified methods.

4. *Introduce changes in stages, if possible.* If major changes are considered, it is best to implement them in stages, starting with the more acceptable changes first. We have found, for example, that first implementing changes that lessen the workload for staff (e.g., arranging a more efficient physical environment) will reduce resistance to later changes that may actually increase staff's work load.

5. *Introduce changes on a trial basis, if possible.* This will help identify and correct any problems that may have been overlooked initially and will demonstrate that the changes are, indeed, an improvement. It is also important that adequate follow-up occur to ensure that modified methods continue to be effective. Although trials are recommended, it is important to emphasize to staff that some changes will occur (i.e., that previous methods will not be resumed unless they are found to be superior after all).

6. *Use tactful approach in implementing changes.* Above all, avoid undue criticism of workers or existing work methods. Be sure to provide ample advance notice of impending changes. Changes should appear to be proactive solutions to problems rather than reactions to crisis situations.

7. *Announce and introduce changes through direct line of supervision of those affected, if possible.* Supervisory staff will ultimately be responsible for maintaining changes over time. Therefore, it is important to gain their cooperation and support early. Implementation through existing supervisory channels will also reduce resistance to outside intervention.

Steps in Planning Activity Zones

Our experience suggests that it is best to implement changes in one activity at a time but with a minimum of delay between activities. Steps to be followed in programming an activity zone are described later. In the next section, we will explain how to coordinate activities among the various zones once they are operational.

Before proceeding with implementation of the first zone, activities that will occur in the setting should be identified and priorities set for establishing zones in which to conduct them. First, identify those activities that must occur each day. These will be determined, in part, by the purpose and nature of a particular program. For example, residential programs must be more concerned with health care activities, whereas a day treatment program will be concerned more with training activities. Activities will also be determined largely by clients' needs. Programs for clients with severe multiple handicaps may require a greater emphasis on health and medical care. For higher functioning clients, training and other activities to promote independent responding may have greater emphasis. In addition to client-related activities, consideration must also be given to environmental maintenance activities. Time and space must be programmed for housekeeping, material preparation and storage, equipment maintenance, and so forth.

Once activities have been identified, priorities should be set for implementing zones. We have found that setting up a central holding activity—or central activity zone—should usually be the first priority because this activity typically does not exist in most programs and because it will serve as the geographic and organizational hub for all other activities. Second priority typically goes to reprogramming health care activities, followed by training and other special activity zones, and finally, environmental maintenance zones.

Determine Environmental Requirements

The first step in implementing a given activity zone is to *determine the environmental requirements for the activity*. These include physical features of the environment such as (a) floor space; (b) spatial arrangement to maximize client engagement and staff efficiency; (c) delineation of zone boundaries; (d) lighting, acoustic, and ventilation requirements; (e) equipment and material selection; and (f) signage. We have already noted several considerations in establishing boundaries between zones, control of lighting and noise, and material selection and presentation. Additional suggestions for programming the physical environment are provided later.

Floor space requirements will depend on the type of activity, number of occupants in a zone at once, equipment required for the activity, and type of clients served (e.g., clients in wheelchairs may require more or less space for certain activities than ambulatory clients). Floor space for each zone will also be determined by the space available in the setting and the number of zones operating concurrently. The spatial relationship between zones should also be considered in planning floor space for a zone. As noted, the central activity zone should be the geographical center for all other zones, if possible. Zones that operate concurrently in time should be set up in close proximity to each other, if clients will be moving between zones. Figure 1 shows the arrangement of zones during mealtimes in our program for profoundly mentally retarded, multiply handicapped clients (all are in wheelchairs). The diagram shows three concurrent activity zones (central activity, feeding, cleanup, and toothbrushing) and clients' movement (solid line) through the zones. Zones are arranged to facilitate organized movement of clients through the three activities.

Zones should be spatially arranged to maximize clients' independent engagement. Where desirable, zones should be highly accessible so clients can move freely among activities. Independent engagement may also be enhanced by the arrangement of materials and equipment (e.g., displaying toys on open shelves to prompt independent selection). Where appropriate, seating should be arranged to promote social interaction; chairs should be arranged facing each other or clustered around tables

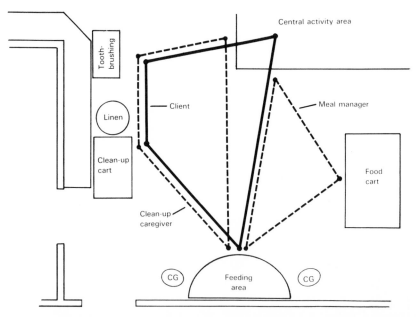

Figure 1. Diagram of concurrent zones during mealtime for nonambulatory, multiply handicapped clients. Solid line indicates movement of client through zones (central activity, feeding, cleanup and toothbrushing). Dotted lines indicate movement of caregivers escorting clients (meal manager delivers client's food tray and escorts client to caregivers in the feeding zone).

rather than lined up side by side or classroom style (Sommer, 1969).

Space should also be arranged to maximize staff efficiency. There are a number of assessment techniques, derived from the field of human factors engineering, for determining the most efficient work setting arrangement. One technique is the trip frequency diagram (Krick, 1962) that can be used to analyze—and reduce—movements between work centers within a zone. The technique involves observing a work activity over a period of time and recording the number of trips made between work centers. Figure 2 presents a trip frequency diagram for the activity of bathing a nonambulatory client. Lines note the path of movement between various work and storage areas. Figure 2a shows the pattern of movements prior to modifying the bathing zone. With the old method, the client was escorted into the bathing zone, lifted from wheelchair to bathing surface, lifted from bathing surface to dressing table after the bath, lifted from dressing table to wheelchair, and escorted out of the zone. After analyzing the existing activity, we modified the bathing surface by stretching a nylon net over the porcelain slab as shown in Figure 3. Because the net does not hold water, staff were then able to conduct the entire bathing activity—undressing, bathing, drying, dressing—on the bathing surface, rather than lift the client to the dressing

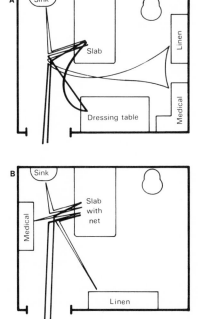

Figure 2. Trip frequency diagrams for caregiver (light lines) and client (bold lines) during bathing routine before (2a) and after (2b) bathing zone is reorganized.

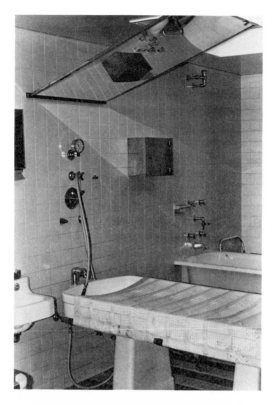

Figure 3. A mesh hammock stretched over the existing procelain slab improves comfort and safety for clients and reduces lifting for staff. Mirror over bathing surface allows clients to observe and participate in bathing.

table. This reduced the number of lifts (by one-third), thus saving staff time, energy, and the risk of back injuries. Eliminating the dressing table also permitted rearrangement of storage space to further reduce movements involved in the activity, as shown in Figure 2b. Finally, use of the net resulted in a more pleasant and safer bathing experience for clients because they did not have to lie on a cold, hard slab with risks of bumped heads and limbs, and the time and energy saved by staff can be devoted to clients.

One final consideration in arranging the physical design of an activity zone is signage to convey necessary treatment information to staff. This is especially important with a generalist staffing approach, where all staff will conduct all activities with all clients. We have found two types of signboards to be effective. One is an *activity board* that lists general and client-specific information explaining how the activity should be conducted. This includes the sequence in which clients will participate in the activity, health and training information, positioning considerations, preferred reinforcers, prosthetic equipment needs, and so on. Typically, the activity boards list all clients down the left-hand side with specific instructions provided beside each client's name. The Master Schedule Board lists in half-hour blocks the scheduled activity for each client. This board should be located over the central activity zone to prompt staff to prepare clients for scheduled activities.

Determine Program Requirements

The second step in implementing an activity zone is to *determine program requirements for the activity*. Specifically, the exact work method and time allocated for conducting the activity should be determined. The work method may be determined by first listing all of the important steps involved in conducting the activity. To accomplish this, we have found it useful to conceptualize each activity as three distinct subroutines, and list the important components of each.

The first subroutine is *set up* for the activity that involves gathering and preparing all necessary equipment, materials, and so forth for the activity. It is important that set-up procedures are completed before the first client enters the zone. This ensures that a caregiver does not have to interrupt the activity or leave a client unattended to locate materials. We have found it useful to complete many of the set-up procedures for an activity a day in advance. Thus, set up for the next day's activity is often the last step in completing the activity. We have also found it useful to arrange all materials for an activity on an activity cart. The cart is brought out to conduct the activity, then restocked and stored for the next day.

The second subroutine is actually *conducting the activity*. All essential steps in conducting the activity are specified in sequential order. Arriving at the optimal sequence of steps involves conducting the activity as desired and making note of each specifiable step. In most cases, there are several correct ways to conduct an activity. Selection of the best alternative should be based on two general criteria: (a) which alternative comes closest to serving the client's best interest (i.e., which results in greatest client engagement); and (b) which alternative is least aversive to staff (i.e., is most likely to be conducted by staff as specified). Of course, these two criteria will often be at odds.

In specifying the method for conducting the activity, it is essential that specific engagement opportunities be included. Two types of opportunities should be specified. First, staff should be instructed to prompt client participation at each step in the activity that involves the client. In bathing, for example, staff should prompt the client to independently complete as much of each step (e.g., undressing, washing, rinsing, drying) as possible. The degree of independence will vary from client to client, but the important point is that independent responding is maximized for each client. Second, specific learning or practice opportunities should be programmed for each client in accordance with his or her habilitation goals. For example, a client who is working on language development should have specific opportunities for language production (e.g., prompting and reinforcing naming of body parts) included as part of the activity.

Finally, procedures should be specified for *cleaning up* after the activity is completed. As noted, it may be most efficient to replenish all materials and make as many preparations as possible for conducting the activity again the next day.

Once the work method has been specified, optimal time requirements for completing the activity should be determined. Knowledge of time requirements is important so that sufficient time can be scheduled for each activity zone. It is also important to ensure that adequate time is spent with each client. Improving efficiency of work methods is not intended to reduce the time needed to complete activities but rather to remove time-wasting aspects of the activity so that more time can be spent prompting client engagement in the activity.

Traditional time-study methods (Krick, 1962) can be used to determine time requirements for each activity. Briefly, these methods involve observing a well-trained caregiver conduct the activity and timing of each subroutine in the activity. Ideally, a time study should be conducted for each client in each activity. Alternatively, representative samples can be taken and an average time requirement calculated for each activity.

Specific Rules for Participation

The third step in programming an activity zone is to *specify the rules for participation in the activity.* As noted earlier, rules are important to maintain appropriate client engagement and to operate the zone in general. Rules for participation also provide staff with an effective, consistent method for dealing with problem behaviors when they occur. These rules are actually specification of social contingencies that should be used to consequate client behavior. In our work with various populations, we have developed several techniques that are effective for maintaining appropriate engagement and dealing with problem behaviors.

Appropriate engagement responses are maintained in three ways. First, positive reinforcement is provided that is contingent upon being engaged. As staff contact clients in a zone, they systematically reinforce clients who are appropriately engaged in the prescribed activity and withhold reinforcement from those who are not engaged. Second, staff use prompting procedures to initiate engagement in those clients who are not participating and to encourage more diverse forms of engagement in those who are participating (e.g., prompt a more elaborate use of a material). And third, staff use incidental teaching procedures (Hart & Risley, 1976) to promote client-initiated learning. The technique involves staff responding to client-initiated interactions by prompting a second, more detailed client response. For example, if a client approaches the caregiver extending a toy as if to prompt a toy-play interaction, the caregiver responds by praising the client for initiating the request and then prompts the client to explain what he or she wants, to name the toy, to show how the toy is used, and so on.

Often, programming a highly reinforcing activity zone is sufficient to control clients' disruptive behavior. It is, nonetheless, important to specify rules for dealing with disruptive behavior should it occur. First, behaviors that will not be permitted in an activity zone should be specified. These should include general behaviors that are not allowed (e.g., inappropriate use of materials, aggression toward other clients) and specific problem behaviors for individual clients (e.g., SIB). That these behaviors must be clearly specified so that all staff who operate the activity zone know the behaviors that should be consistently consequated for each client. This information may be conveyed by signs posted in each zone. The procedure used for dealing with clients' inappropriate engagement is contingent observation (Porterfield, Herbert-Jackson, & Risley, 1976). With this procedure, caregivers respond to each instance of disruptive behavior in the following manner:

1. Interrupt the behavior, briefly describe to the client the form and inappropriateness of the behavior, and briefly explain what would be appropriate behavior in the situation.
2. Escort the client to the periphery of the activity, require him or her to sit, and instruct him or her to observe the appropriate engagement of other clients.
3. Once the client has been watching quietly for a brief period (usually less than 1 minute), the caregiver asks the client if he or she is ready to rejoin the activity and engage in appropriate behavior.
4. When the client returns to the activity, the caregiver makes a point of providing positive attention for the next appropriate engagement response emitted.

The effectiveness of contingent observation, in which the client becomes an observer rather than a participant, relies on a reinforcing setting. Temporary removal of the client from the activity will be effective in reducing problem behavior only if the activity is sufficiently attractive to the client. For some clients, this mild procedure may not be sufficient, even when highly reinforcing activities and materials are available. More aversive procedures such as exclusionary time-out may be required. It cannot be overemphasized, however, that the effectiveness of more aversive procedures also relies on the availability of a reinforcing environment.

Coordination among Zones: Pulling It All Together

Armed with an understanding of our basic principles of environmental design and with guidelines for selecting, prioritizing, and determining requirements of activity zones, the process of developing a comprehensive service system can begin. "Pulling it all together" involves two very important processes: scheduling activity zones and designing staff schedules. Activity zone schedules indicate how many staff are needed to provide services, and staff schedules determine how many services can be provided.

Scheduling Zones

A schedule of activity zones must be developed to ensure that clients move smoothly from one activity to another throughout the day. Further, an activity zone schedule provides information needed to design efficient schedules by determining priority and duration of activities.

The first step in developing an activity zone schedule is to list zones in order of priority. For example, the highest priority activities, such as meals and baths, must be scheduled to occur at or near a specific time and take about the same amount of time to conduct to ensure consistent quality services (Jones *et al.*, 1983). Activities with lower priorities (e.g., environmental maintenance, clerical duties) occur on a more flexible schedule or are scheduled to occur less frequently depending upon staff availability.

The second step in developing an activity schedule is to determine how much time is necessary for setting up, conducting, and cleaning up each zone in order to allow for efficient concurrent and sequential zones. Thus, if it takes 20 minutes for one client to eat lunch (including placing the food and eating utensils on the table, conducting the client to and from the dining area, providing incidental learning activities during the meal, and clearing the table for the next client), 15 minutes to set up the dining area, and 15 minutes to clean up, a meal for 10 clients would take 230 minutes. Some lower priority activities may require a standard amount of time to set up, clean up, and conduct but vary in the total time depending upon the number of clients served. For example, five clients might receive one-to-one skill training sessions in the morning and five in the afternoon. Other activities may be flexible enough to schedule for a given amount of time (e.g., clerical work).

Once priorities and general time constraints (i.e., minimum time per activity, flexibility in when and how often an activity is scheduled) have been established, a graphic representation of zones can be used to help determine sequential and concurrent zones. By placing the list of prioritized activities on one side of a page headed with 30-minute time intervals, as shown in Figure 4, a line can be used to represent the duration of a zone (length of the line) and the number of zones operating concurrently (the number of lines).

Several factors should be considered prior to developing activity schedules. First, there can be only as many activity areas as there are staff. Ideally, each caregiver is responsible for a separate activity area. Individual responsibility increases accountability, lessons probability of staff interacting with staff more frequently than clients, and increases number of activities available to clients. When it is not feasible to assign caregivers to individual activity areas, the area should be designed to enhance caregiver independence. For example, the potential for disruptive behavior during meals or an unreasonably long mealtime may make

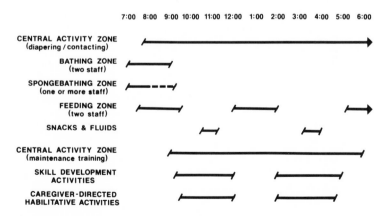

Figure 4. Schedule of activity zones throughout the day. Note that some zones require two caregivers.

it desirable to assign two staff to meal activities. The dining area might be set up to provide two separate geographic areas of staff responsibility while reducing total activity time and increasing client supervision. When geographic separation of caregivers within an area is not possible, caregivers should be assigned to separate responsibilities within the area. Thus, each caregiver is assigned an individual schedule of responsibility for a separate activity, location within an activity, or clearly delineated task within an activity. The final determination of activity schedules is made with the establishment of staff schedules.

Scheduling Caregivers

Once activity zone priorities, time constraints, and minimal staffing requirements per zone are determined, staff schedules can be developed. Individual staff schedules are essential for efficient services and optimal caregiver performance. The most obvious function of scheduling staff is to ensure that all high-priority services are provided. The less apparent functions are to distribute work load evenly among caregivers, rotate caregivers from physically strenuous to less strenuous activities, and make efficient use of down time (i.e., times during which fewer high-priority activities must occur) to conduct activities such as skill training. Without caregiver schedules, supervisors become traffic cops, directing caregivers from one spot to another without knowing if they get there. The quality of services may drop in an attempt to take on more activities than time and numbers permit, or caregivers may wait to be told what to do next. Individual staff schedules increase caregiver responsibility for the quality of their own work and may facilitate independent performance by providing instruction (Quilitch, 1975).

Schedules are developed by assigning each caregiver an activity to manage, a separate geographic region, or job responsibility within an activity. Start with the highest priority, in half-hour blocks of time, and proceed down the list until all staff have been assigned. Peak work times during which multiple high-priority activities such as meals, baths, and dressing are scheduled are typically strenuous. They require a larger number of caregivers to cover necessary activities. What may appear to be barely a sufficient number of caregivers for early activities could result in a surplus later in the day. The strain of peak times can be minimized by rotating staff among activities at naturally occurring breaks (e.g., beginning or end of an activity). Rotations from strenuous to more relaxing activities at hourly intervals will also equalize the work load across caregivers.

A second method of addressing peak times is utilizing part-time staff whenever possible. Part-time staff can supplement the work force during peak times without creating a problem by overstaffing at other times. Part-time staff also require less training because they only need training for activities in which they are scheduled. They are also more easily scheduled because they have no lunch breaks, and so forth. Utilizing part-time caregivers may also be more cost-efficient (i.e., paying for services when services are necessary).

Scheduling is important not only for ensuring client services but also for planning caregiver breaks. Planning and ensuring staff breaks at regular intervals are important to staff morale. Full-time staff should be scheduled for lunch breaks as close as possible to normal meal times, and coffee breaks should be scheduled at approximately 2-hour intervals. It is preferable to schedule caregivers for breaks in groups, leaving one group of caregivers in the living unit to maintain continuous services, while the other group is able to relax with peers. Breaks, like other activities, should take place in a designated area (i.e., outside the living unit) so that caregivers can enjoy an uninterrupted break without distractions from other staff who are working.

Less demanding times of the day can be used to schedule lower priority services such as clerical and housekeeping duties. Many lower priority services are not provided on a daily basis (e.g., charting, staff meetings, program planning conferences), but the alloted time can be used interchangeably among low-priority services. For example, staff meetings might be interchanged with charting and housekeeping, depending on the day of the week or number of available staff. In fact, these lower priority times are ideal for scheduling special activities, such as doctors appointments or trips to the barber/beauty shops, without disrupting basic services.

Arguments against use of standard schedules usually center on two issues: variations in the number of staff present and client schedules. With respect to variations in the number of caregivers, we have found it useful to design a separate schedule for each possible number of staff. Although this may appear to be an unnecessarily trying task, designing different schedules for different numbers of staff prevents the confusion typically associated with unplanned shortages or unorganized extras. Each morning the supervisor can select an appropriate schedule for the day. Caregivers are given a copy of their individual schedule, a copy of caregiver schedule assignments is posted, and the supervisor retains a copy to make needed changes across the day.

With respect to the second argument against staff schedules, daily changes in client schedules, schedules are not inflexible. Rather, they provide the framework for making organized change without hampering the quality of basic services. For example, a supervisor can change the schedule of low-priority activities to accommodate an individual client's doctor appointment without disrupting all client activities.

Maintaining a Quality Environment

Program quality depends upon individual and group staff performance. Caregiver training should be thorough, covering all job responsibilities and activity areas. It should also be effective and result in desired performance. Routine evaluations and feedback on individual caregiver performance and overall program quality will help maintain a quality environment.

Staff Training

Training should be designed around and conducted within the work setting. Many traditional inservice training approaches, such as classroom workshops and lectures, fail to improve the quality of work performance (Gardner, 1972; Quilitch, 1975). Failure is sometimes attributed to lack of positive feedback for desired performance (Ayllon & Azrin, 1968), inability to generalize skills from classroom to work site (Stokes, Baer, & Jackson, 1974), or inappropriate training approach or content (Gilbert, 1982). Training conducted within the work setting improves generalization of skills, addresses feasibility of skill application (i.e., can this skill be applied within the physical and resource constraints of the setting?), and focuses attention on the relevance of training to desired performance. The content and ultimate effectiveness of training should be determined by examining work performance. If training is effective, skill acquisition should be reflected in performance when the environment supports skill application.

Checklists for staff training should be developed that outline content and specify the sequence of procedures for conducting each work activity. Each statement is usually presented in the format of yes and no questions. Answering questions contained within a checklist provides a measure of the process and products of service delivery.

The new employee starts out by reading the checklist for conducting an activity. The supervisor then pairs the trainee with a trained or certified caregiver. The trainee uses the checklist to ask questions and observe the certified caregiver conduct the routine. Once familiar with the steps, the trainee practices conducting the activity, while the certified caregiver observes and provides performance feedback using the checklist. The trainee then conducts the activity for the supervisor. The supervisor provides feedback on all aspects of performance using the checklist and assigns the trainee to reread the procedures if a step is missed, incomplete, or incorrect. This evaluation is repeated until the trainee meets established performance criteria by correctly performing all steps in the activity. The trainee is then certified by the supervisor as capable of conducting the activity independently. Training and certification are conducted in this manner for all zones and responsibilities.

Maintaining Caregiver Performance

Routine monitoring and feedback are essential to maintain consistent high-quality services. Checklists are used to recertify caregivers on each zone of responsibility on a regular basis (e.g., monthly). Feedback is given on both good and bad aspects of performance in order to identify desired behavior and correct deficiencies. Frequent feedback helps maintain a standard of service and ensure that most feedback is positive.

Routine, randomly scheduled observations and feedback not only maintain quality but also provide a systematic method of caregiver evaluations. The need for evaluations that provide the most accurate assessment of work performance has been emphasized in litigation regarding fair methods of employee selection and promotion (Guion, 1974). Checklists can evaluate ongoing performance or process, while caregivers receive feedback to routinely remind them of evaluation content and goals.

Although supervisory monitoring and feedback are essential, checklists may also be used by caregivers to self-monitor work performance (Bacon, Fulton, & Malott, 1982). By checking off completion of each task on a checklist, a caregiver has a visual reminder of what has and has not been done and a public record of completed activities. This public record is especially helpful if an emergency arises that disrupts an activity or requires that a different caregiver take over the routine. The routine can be continued exactly where it was stopped.

Evaluating the consistency of treatment is a necessary prerequisite for determining treatment effectiveness. A record of the frequency of treatment fails to measure how well treatment steps were followed. Individualized treatment across activities and disciplines is easily confused or forgotten. Checklists listing individualized, professionally prescribed treatments may be used for caregiver training and evaluation, self-monitoring, public posting of procedures, and to evaluate consistency of treatment implementation (Lattimore, Stephens, Favell, & Risley, 1984). Once the frequency and consistency of treatment is determined, assessment of treatment effectiveness can be made.

Ensuring Overall Program Quality

In addition to regular monitoring of specific staff performance, global measures of program quality are needed to ensure that essential program features, such as material availability, are maintained. One global measure taken by supervisors in our program is the quality check. Quality check observations are conducted weekly, at random times throughout the day. The supervisor notes (a) the proportion of clients who have materials or activities available; (b) the proportion of clients who are actually engaged in appropriate activities or with materials; (c) the proportion of caregivers in their assigned location, conducting their assigned activity; and (d) the specific behavior of each caregiver (e.g., working with clients, performing nonclient work activities, or off-task). These checks focus the supervisor and staff's attention on essential program components and indicate whether quality standards are being maintained (e.g., whether material availability is consistently high). Quality checks also provide a basis for the supervisor to make adjustments in program procedures (e.g., modify staff schedules) and evaluate their effects. As with all performance checks, staff receive immediate feedback on program quality.

Supervisory monitoring and feedback are critical to program quality. However, it is important to support the internal supervisory procedures with an *external* evaluation process. An external system ensures that the supervisor retains a managerial role, rather than becoming too involved in assisting staff to provide services. Because the supervisor is in close and frequent contact with staff, it is easy to come under their social control. As a result, the supervisor may lose objectivity in evaluating program quality and may be more reluctant to provide feedback to staff, especially if it is negative. These potential problems are eliminated by having an outside consultant who represents, or is, the supervisor's boss, and who is administratively and socially removed from caregivers. The consultant conducts periodic quality checks similar to those performed by the supervisor, thus providing an external evaluation of program quality. This is important because it shows staff that the supervisor is accountable to an external authority to maintain quality standards. The program consultant also assists the supervisor in establishing quality standards, developing program procedures (e.g., developing staff schedules), obtaining additional resources, and working with other professional and support staff.

Conclusion

Throughout this chapter, we have emphasized the importance of an engaging environment to maintain clients' appropriate engagement and, consequently, to control problem behavior. Based on our own research and experience in designing living environments, we have provided a number of suggestions for programming an engaging environment. Inherent in this approach is the premise that behavior is controlled by the environment in which it occurs and may be modified by systematically manipulating environmental determinants.

We are confident that, in many cases, programming an engaging environment will be sufficient to reduce or eliminate disruptive behavior. In all cases, it will be a necessary, if not sufficient, condition for controlling behavior disorders. But more effective interventions will still be required in more intractible cases. Development of more effective treatment techniques and settings requires that we gain a better understanding of the environment's influence on behavior. Better understanding will result only from systematic analyses of environment–behavior relationships—analyses of the sort described here and elsewhere (e.g., Iwata et al., 1982; Jones et al., 1983).

Ideally, data from these analyses will lead to a taxonomy of environmental requirements by behavior disorders. Such a taxonomy would aid in the prescriptive placement of mentally retarded persons in the most suitable treatment environment for their particular type and severity of disability. It should be emphasized, however, that the client's needs will change over time, and features constituting the optimal environment will change accordingly. As clients exhibit more developmentally advanced engagement, the environment must offer more sophisticated—and typically, more demanding—engagement opportunities.

The ultimate goal in programming an engaging environment for people with severe behavior disorders is to eliminate the need for specialized environmental arrangements. Treatment success must be gauged by the ability of these individuals to succeed in the natural environment. The task confronting those who work in treatment settings for mentally retarded persons is to ensure that these settings offer the opportunities necessary to achieve normal functioning. Look around and ask how far you have to go.

ACKNOWLEDGMENTS

The authors are grateful to Mary Ann Cappo and Barbara J. Haile for their assistance in preparation of this manuscript.

References

Anderson, L. T., & Hermann, L. (1975, December). *Lesch–Nyhan disease: A specific learning disability.* Paper presented at the meeting of the Association for the Advancement of Behavior Therapy, San Francisco.

Association for the Advancement of Behavior Therapy Task Force Report. (1982). Treatment of self-injurious behavior. *Behavior Therapy, 13,* 524–554.

Ayllon, T., & Azrin, N. H. (1968). *The token economy: A motivation system for therapy and rehabilitation.* New York: Appleton-Century-Crofts.

Bachman, J. (1972). Self-injurious behavior: A behavioral analysis. *Journal of Abnormal Psychology, 80,* 211–224.

Bacon, D. L., Fulton, B. J., & Malott, R. W. (1982). Improving staff performance through use of task checklists. *Journal of Organizational Behavior Management, 4,* 101–112.

Carr, E. G. (1977). The motivation of self-injurious behavior: A review of some hypotheses. *Psychological Bulletin, 84,* 800–816.

Carr, E. G., Newsom, C. D., & Binkoff, J. A. (1976). Stimulus control of self-destructive behavior in a psychotic child. *Journal of Abnormal Child Psychology, 4,* 139–153.

Corte, H. E., Wolfe, M. M., & Locke, B. J. (1971). A comparison of procedures for eliminating self-injurious behavior of retarded adolescents. *Journal of Applied Behavior Analysis, 4,* 201–213.

Crosby, K. G. (1976). Essentials of active programming. *Mental Retardation, 14*(2), 3–9.

Duker, P. (1975). Behaviour control of self-biting in a Lesch–Nyhan patient. *Journal of Mental Deficiency Research, 19,* 11–19.

Favell, J. E., & Cannon, P. R. (1977). Evaluation of entertainment materials for severely retarded persons. *American Journal of Mental Deficiency, 81*(4), 357–361.

Favell, J. E., McGimsey, J. F., Jones, M. L., & Cannon, P. R. (1981). Physical restraint as positive reinforcement. *American Journal of Mental Deficiency, 85*(4), 425–432.

Gardner, J. M. (1972). Teaching behavior modification skills to nonprofessionals. *Journal of Applied Behavior Analysis, 5,* 517–521.

Gilbert, T. G. (1982). Human incompetence: The autobiography of an educational revolutionist. *Journal of Organizational Behavior Management, 3,* 55–67.

Guion, R. M. (1974). Open a new window: Validities and values in psychological measurement. *American Psychologist, 29,* 287–296.

Gunzburg, H. C., & Gunzburg, A. L. (1979). "Normal" environment with a plus for the mentally retarded. In D. Canter & S. Canter (Eds.), *Designing for therapeutic environments: A review of research* (pp. 159–174). New York: Wiley.

Hart, B. M., & Risley, T. R. (1976). Incidental teaching of language in the preschool. *Journal of Applied Behavior Analysis, 8,* 411–420.

Horner, R. D. (1980). The effects of an environmental "enrichment" program on the behavior of institutionalized profoundly retarded children. *Journal of Applied Behavior Analysis, 13,* 473–491.

Iwata, B., Dorsey, M., Slifer, K., Bauman, K., & Richman, G. (1982). Toward a functional analysis of self-injury. *Analysis and Intervention in Developmental Disabilities, 2,* 3–20.

Jones, M. L., Risley, T. R., & Favell, J. E. (1983). Ecological patterns. In J. Matson & S. Bruening (Eds.), *Assessing the mentally retarded* (pp. 311–334). New York: Grune & Stratton.

Jones, M. L., Favell, J. E., Lattimore, J., & Risley, T. R. (1984). Improving independent leisure activity of nonambulatory multi-handicapped persons through the systematic analysis of leisure materials. *Analysis and Intervention in Developmental Disabilities, 4,* 313–332.

Krick, E. V. (1962). *Methods engineering.* New York: Wiley.

Lahey, B. B., McNees, M. P., & McNees, M. C. (1973). Control of an obscene "verbal tic" through timeout in an elementary school classroom. *Journal of Applied Behavior Analysis, 6,* 101–104.

Lattimore, J., Stephens, T. E., Favell, J. E., & Risley, T. R. (1984). Increasing direct care staff compliance to individualized physical therapy body positioning prescriptions: Prescriptive checklists. *Mental Retardation, 22*(2), 79–84.

LeLaurin, K., & Risley, T. R. (1972). The organization of day-care environments: "Zone" versus "man-to-man" staff assignments. *Journal of Applied Behavior Analysis, 5,* 225–232.

Lovaas, O. I., & Simmons, J. O. (1969). Manipulation of self-destruction in three retarded children. *Journal of Applied Behavior Analysis, 2,* 143–157.

Montes, F., & Risley, T. R. (1975). Evaluating traditional day care practices: An empirical approach. *Child Care Quarterly, 4,* 208–215.

Porterfield, J. K., Herbert-Jackson, E., & Risley, T. R. (1976). Contingent observation: An effective and acceptable procedure for reducing disruptive behaviors of young children in group settings. *Journal of Applied Behavior Analysis, 9,* 55–64.

Quilitch, H. R. (1975). A comparison of three staff-management procedures. *Journal of Applied Behavior Analysis, 8,* 59–66.

Shear, C. S., Nyhan, W. L., Kirkman, B. H., & Stern, J. (1971). Self-mutilative behavior as a feature of the deLange syndrome. *Journal of Pediatrics, 78,* 506–509.

Sommer, R. (1969). *Personal space: The behavioral basis of design.* Englewood Cliffs, NJ: Prentice-Hall.

Stokes, T. F., Baer, D. M., Jackson, R. L. (1974). Programming the generalization of a greeting response in four retarded children. *Journal of Applied Behavior Analysis, 7,* 599–610.

Sulzer-Azaroff, B., & Mayer, G. R. (1977). *Applying behavior-analysis procedures with children and youth.* New York: Holt, Rinehart & Winston.

Tate, B. G., & Baroff, G. S. (1966). Aversive control of self-injurious behavior in a psychotic boy. *Behavior Research and Therapy, 4,* 281–287.

Twardosz, S., Cataldo, M., & Risley,T. (1974). Open environment design for infant and toddler day care. *Journal of Applied Behavior Analysis, 7,* 529–546.

Tyler, V. O., & Brown, G. D. (1967). The use of swift, brief isolation as a group control device for institutionalized delinquents. *Behavior Research and Therapy, 5,* 1–9.

Wolf, M. M., Risley, T. R., & Mees, H. (1964). Application of operant conditioning procedures to the behavior problems of an autistic child. *Behaviour Research and Therapy, 1,* 305–312.

Wyatt v. Stickney, 344 F. Supp. 387, 395–407 (Middle District of Alabama 1972).

6

Assessing and Managing Medical Factors

LINDA FITZPATRICK GOURASH

Introduction

This chapter discusses medical issues related to behavior disorders of
the mentally retarded child or adult. Psychopharmacology (i.e., the use
of behavior-altering drugs, such as neuroleptics, stimulants, axiolytics,
etc.) is not discussed here because this represents a whole area of study
in itself. The present discussion is confined to those issues of medical
diagnosis and treatment that have potential relationships to behavior
and behavior disorders.

Nonmedical professionals who care for patients with behavior disorders, who work with families, who teach in the special education
classroom, or who live with the mentally retarded client in a group home
frequently have questions of a medical nature that, when unanswered,
can interfere with behavior management programming or with the health
of the child. When working with these children or adults, one often
questions: Is there a medical reason why this person vomits, bangs his
head, screams as if in pain, refuses to eat, is incontinent, is somnolent
or hyperactive, unable to sleep? Why is this person intermittently aggressive, inexplicably irritable at times? Does that skin rash have anything
to do with his behavior? How serious is this self-abusive behavior? Is
he likely to injure himself? Has he injured himself? Are his medications
causing any of his behavior problems?

To the physician consultant, some of these questions are virtually
unanswerable; others can be answered with limited confidence whereas

LINDA FITZPATRICK GOURASH • Department of Psychiatry, Western Psychiatric Institute and
Clinic, University of Pittsburgh School of Medicine, Pittsburgh, Pennsylvania 15213.

still others may turn out to be crucial to planning the medical and emotional care of the patient.

The answer often comes in the form of systematically ruling out possibilities. This can be done by reviewing the known pathology of a disorder in question, occasionally identifying it as impossible or highly unlikely. At times, simple, inexpensive laboratory tests can lay some concerns to rest, or they may lead the physician to a more intensive search for pathology. At other times, ruling out medical disorders involves expensive, invasive, or painful procedures, and the physician, in consultation with the parents or the primary caretakers, must make a judgment concerning the relative benefits and risks of such procedures for that patient. The physician's contribution may simply be an assessment as to whether the diagnosis of a given medical condition is clinically important or likely to change the behavioral or medical approaches to treatment of the child.

The Traditional Role of the Physician

The traditional role of the nonpsychiatric physician in assessing the care of the mentally retarded child has included the following.

Identification of Developmental Delay or Mental Retardation. The pediatrician or family practitioner is often the first professional to see a child with any regularity. Early identification of mental retardation has recently been much emphasized and greatly improved due to increased interest in this area in the medical profession. Often the pediatrician identifies the mentally retarded child (or the child with suspected retardation) by assessing development during the regular well-child visits for physical examinations and immunizations. At other times, the family is first to raise the issue of slow development.

Diagnosis and Treatment of Medical Disorders Causing Mental Retardation. Following identification of the child with mental retardation or with suggestive symptoms, the physician seeks an explanatory cause for the developmental delay. This particular task, although well defined, is not a comfortable one for most primary care physicians and equally uncomfortable for pediatricians. This is mainly due to the very large number of disorders, many of them rare, that cause mental retardation as well as the minimal training available to physicians on this subject. Neurologists and developmental pediatricians have more experience in this area. However, it should be remembered that even after a thorough and extensive medical evaluation, a large proportion of mentally retarded persons cannot be given a specific diagnosis of the cause of the mental retardation.

In a few selected disorders, treatment of the specific cause of mental retardation has recently become possible. Most newborns receive blood tests for phenylketonuria (PKU) and hypothyroidism so that treatment can begin early in life. There are several other uncommon but treatable causes for mental retardation. Some states screen for these other, rarer disorders. As further research takes more disorders from the untreatable to treatable categories, the opportunity to provide specific medical intervention and thereby prevent the intellectual deficit will greatly enhance the reward for making a specific diagnosis. Other important reasons for making specific diagnosis include prognostic value, family counseling, genetic counseling, and improved medical management.

Counseling and Referral. Current literature increasingly emphasizes the physician's, especially the pediatrician's, role in advising and counseling the parents of their child's condition, prognosis, and the genetic implications of the diagnosis (Gayton, 1975; Springer & Steel, 1980; Zuckerberg & Snow, 1968). In the past, physician counseling has been highly variable in quality for a number of reasons, not the least of which is the minimal training provided in this area. Many physicians have been too quick to recommend immediate institutionalization of the young mentally retarded child (Kelly & Menolascino, 1976), perhaps reflecting their own uncertainty of how to provide care for children with a mental handicap.

The situation is improving greatly, but parents of older mentally retarded youth often recount a total lack of support from the medical profession during the crucial early years of their child's development (Rubin & Rubin, 1980). Such parents have understandably come to expect little or no benefit from further consultation with physicians.

In recent years, counseling designed to prevent behavior problems is also being recognized as a legitimate role for the primary care physician or nurse practitioner (Fisher & Krajicek, 1974).

Following diagnosis and some counseling with the family, the physician will generally see his or her role as one of providing a referral to community agencies and services that will help the parents to educate and train their handicapped child (Zuckerberg & Snow, 1968). Further medical contact is generally confined to the provision of episodic medical care (e.g., treatment of infections, injuries, seizures, etc.).

The Physician and Behavioral Disorders

No one medical specialty specifically addresses the comprehensive medical care of the mentally retarded patient. Specialists most likely to have some experience or interest in this population are pediatricians, neurologists, psychiatrists, physiatrists (i.e., specialists in physical medicine and rehabilitation), and occasionally internists. Unless the physician has focused his or her practice on the treatment of the retarded patient population, personal clinical experience in any specialty is likely to exist in proportion to the relatively small number of mentally retarded persons in the general population.

Partly as a result of this, there is no cohesive body of literature on the medical problems of the mentally retarded and their relationship to behavior disorders. Clinical experiences are published throughout the literature ranging from dermatological to surgical contributors and are often limited to single-case reports. Some useful studies have been done, however, (Crnic, Sulzbacher, Snow, & Holm, 1980; Nyhan, 1976; Sondheimer & Morris, 1979).

The role of the psychiatrist is somewhat different from other physicians in that the psychiatrist is not likely to be consulted until after a behavior disorder develops. The psychiatrist is singularly accustomed to thinking in terms of behavioral symptoms, but, like the rest of the medical profession, his or her traditional tools of diagnosis and treatment must be modified to meet the needs of the mentally retarded patient. The psychiatrist is the physician most likely to have expertise in the use of the behavior-modifying medications (psychotropic drugs).

The medical consultant may be a member of the treatment team as in a hospital or residential care facility where he or she is in a position to have a precise concept of the severity or nature of the behavior disorder through direct observation and through ongoing reports from other staff. In this setting, the physician has more time to test hypotheses concerning the relationships between medical disorders and behavior problems.

In contrast, the "outside" medical consultant who is approached intermittently by the staff or parents caring for a mentally retarded individual has a much more difficult job. An entire assessment frequently must depend on verbal and written reports of the child's behavior that is often difficult to describe in terms of quality and quantity. In addition, the consultant's own observations of the patient are in a highly artificial environment for that person (i.e., the examining room or the physician's office), a place where the patient perhaps has never been before. For the medical consultant who is not a part of the regular treatment team, the already difficult job of medical diagnosis related to behavior disorders may become nearly impossible.

All this is said in preparation to give the reader an understanding of the consulting physician's approach to the mentally retarded patient.

Each patient is unique, presenting the question: Is *this* medical disorder related to *this* problem behavior in *this* patient?

The scientific method of approaching these clinical problems is more familiar to psychologists than to most physicians in clinical practice because medical therapy is most properly based on data from preexisting, published controlled studies of groups of patients in whom positive results of statistical significance have been obtained. Single-case studies, the use of reversal designs in A-B-A-B format, and so forth (see Chapter 11) are not commonly used by the practicing physician but are frequently necessary in order to test empirically a given hypothesis in an individual patient.

Summary

In summary, then, the physician often obtains very little help from the medical literature concerning the specific problems of the mentally retarded patient. In addition, the physician may have little experience with similar patients in his or her usual practice. Even for the physician who has focused on the care of the mentally retarded patient, it is common to be presented with a patient with a completely new combination of medical and behavioral symptoms with several possible relationships and interactions. Although there are times when it may appear more productive to quit and go play golf, the physician still has much to offer and much to learn from mentally retarded patients.

Medical Factors and Behavior: Multiple Relationships

Any number of possible relationships between medical conditions and behavior can be postulated. In practice, it is helpful to try to define the relationship as accurately as possible; it is also important to keep in mind that several relationships can exist simultaneously and interact (sometimes resulting in a "vicious cycle"). A number of relationships are described later, and examples are given. Such a list by no means describes all the possibilities. The examples are not truly prototypes because some medical disorders and some behavior disorders fall into several categories at the same time. The examples are, therefore, not intended to categorize a particular medical disorder as having only one possible relationship to behavior problems.

For purposes of clarity, the meaning of the words *behavior* and *behavior disorder*, as used presently, must be explained. A behavior is *any* activity (or inactivity) of an individual and may be voluntary or completely involuntary. Some behaviors are psychogenic or voluntary in origin even while there is clearly a causal medical condition (e.g., screaming or aggression while in pain). Other behaviors are strictly involuntary (e.g., convulsive movements during a seizure, urinary incontinence due to a spinal cord tumor). At times, the distinction is difficult to make (e.g., vomiting during an illness or fecal soiling associated with severe constipation). The importance of the distinction is that behaviors that are strictly involuntary symptoms of medical disorders can be expected to cease when medical treatment is complete. Other behaviors may be eliminated without treatment of the medical problems (e.g., a patient may be taught not to be aggressive even if pain is still present). Finally, many behaviors may persist even when the underlying medical cause is eliminated (due to operant or classical conditioning) and behavior therapy is therefore required in addition to medical treatment.

The term *behavior disorder* refers to *voluntary* or psychogenic maladaptive or antisocial behaviors that are *recurrent*. This label generally is not applied to isolated instances of misbehavior or to behaviors that are strictly involuntary physical responses to medical conditions.

Medical Factors Contributing to Behavior Disorders

Medical factors (physical states, pain, certain syndromes, hormone disorders, allergies, drugs, etc.) may have a major or minor contribution to behavior change and behavior disorders. Occasionally, the relationship is simple and clear enough for the medical problem to be considered *causal*. This is, however, the exception, and it is often fruitful clinically to consider a *contributory* role of a medical disorder in relation to behavior change. For instance, a previously aggressive patient may become more aggressive when in physical discomfort.

A medically treatable problem may have an indirect but significant effect on behavior. An example is the patient who practices coprophagia (eating feces). The behavior problem may occur only in the presence of stool incontinence that may be medically treatable. In a personal experience of managing a patient who engaged in the practice of flinging mucus, a chronic, thick nasal discharge from sinusitis provided her with ample ammunition. Following treatment with antibiotics, which eliminated the mucus discharge, she was considerably more popular and more approachable.

Foul body odors are an additional condition that can effectively dissuade staff from implementation of behavior modification programs that require close body contact and, in general, will interfere with good social adjustment. Sources of such odors include the oral pharynx, ear canal, hair, axillae (armpits), vagina, soiled underclothing, and feet. If thorough hygiene has failed to eliminate offensive odors, infections of any of these areas or foreign bodies of the nose, ears, rectum, or vagina should be sought by a physician.

Recognized Contributory or Causal Relationships. Although many medical conditions can have variable effects on behavior, some of these are seen with enough frequency to describe a consistent pattern of response and a recognized relationship. Either an overactive or an underactive thyroid gland can cause major changes in behavior including lethargy, anxiety, even symptoms of psychosis including hallucinations. Such symptoms may be insidious in onset, but once present would not be expected to be intermittent. Other recognized relationships and some syndromes of mental retardation associated with somewhat predictable patterns of behavior are discussed later in this chapter.

Individual or Idiosyncratic Relationships In the clinical setting, our knowledge of known relationships between medical problems and behaviors is quickly exhausted, and the individual's unique responses must be considered, keeping in mind both causal or contributory relationships. Medical problems that do not cause behavior change in normal children may cause significant problems in certain mentally retarded individuals. Earaches, migraine headaches, and menstrual cramps should be considered, for instance, in nonverbal persons with behavior changes.

Behavior Problems Resulting from Medical Therapies. "Prima Nolo Nocere." By far the most common behavior problems in this category are those secondary to drug treatment: oversedation, hyperactivity, or irritability. Such symptoms may be seen with anticonvulsants and major tranquilizers, both used frequently in retarded persons. Less well-appreciated are the behavioral changes sometimes seen with cold preparations (decongestants) that include hyperactivity, irritability, and rarely, hallucinations (Sankey, 1984). Antiasthmatic preparations containing theophylline are reported to be able to cause sleep disturbances, restlessness, irritability, and depressed mood changes (Brumback, Wilson, & Staton, 1984; Furukawa, Shapiro, DuHamel, Weimer, Pierson, & Bierman, 1984).

Corticosteroids in higher doses used to treat severe asthma, arthritis, or other autoimmune diseases can cause psychotic symptoms (Hall & Ropkin, 1979). Numerous other medications have been reported to cause acute and chronic mental disturbances such as delirium, hallucinations, confusion, agitation, and other symptoms (Abramowicz, 1984). The behavioral effects of both the medication prescribed as well as the vehicle in which it is administered (e.g., alcohol) should be considered in patients with unexplained behavioral changes (American Academy of Pediatrics Committee on Drugs, 1984).

Movement disorders (e.g., tardive dyskinesia) may also be mistaken as a behavior disorder rather than being identified as the side effect of certain drug therapy (i.e., neuroleptics). Similar symptoms may also result from rapid drug withdrawal.

In the mentally retarded population, in particular, some behavior problems are associated less directly with medical therapy. Spitting out medications and refusal to take medications, however, are no small problem for the nursing staff or parents. These problems can often be alleviated by a change in the form of the medication to liquid, powder, suppository, or pill, whichever is best tolerated by the patient. In addition, most medications can be mixed safely with a palatable or favorite food such as peanut better, chocolate syrup, applesauce, or honey in order to facilitate their administration. The pharmacist can generally advise on this matter, and with the help of an experienced or imaginative nurse or parent nearly all medications can be administered successfully. Sometimes specific behavior modification programs must be introduced to *teach* the patient to take his or her medication, however.

In the aggressive patient, it should be kept in mind that a number of medical or orthopedic devices can be used as weapons, and it helps to anticipate such problems beforehand. When the aggressive patient has a fracture, especially of the wrist or arm, it may well be expedient to request a soft cast or a plastic cast or to wrap the plaster cast in padding. Aggressive patients may do considerable damage by swinging a plaster cast about. Rather than risk arming an individual who is known to be aggressive with crutches or a cane, a wheelchair may be preferred.

Medical Symptoms Masquerading as Behavior Disorders

As mentioned previously, some medical disorders may result directly in behavioral symptoms that are involuntary. Treatment or cure of the medical problems completely eliminates such behavior. It is, therefore, most gratifying to make a diagnosis in this category. However, a "pure" relationship between physical malady and problem behavior is not common. It seems more frequent that medical conditions merely contribute to increased behavior problems by causing irritability, pain, and so forth. Medical conditions with misleading behavioral symptoms include deafness causing unresponsiveness, gastroesophageal reflux causing vomiting, psychomotor seizures causing any number of unusual

behaviors, or megacolon causing soiling problems. Three of these disorders are discussed in greater detail later in the chapter. Even in this
"clear-cut" relationship, secondary behavior problems are possible. The
child with recurrent vomiting of organic origin may continue to vomit
following medical treatment if he or she has been mistakenly given much
attention for the vomiting. The deaf child may ignore the auditory cues
that he or she receives after being fitted for a hearing device, especially
if others continue to "perform" as they did when compensating for the
child's legitimate handicap.

Diabetes insipidus or diabetes mellitus may both present with frequent drinking of large amounts of fluid, increased urine flow, and
urinary accidents all due to the poor ability of the kidney to concentrate
the urine. The patient may be mistaken as a psychogenic water drinker
or as an enuretic. Both diabetes insipidus and diabetes mellitus are easy
to rule out medically and should be considered when a patient's drinking
and urination habits appear to have changed in the direction of a greater
volume.

Tic disorders can result in repetitive, sometimes obnoxious or
meaningless behaviors such as grunting, winking, sniffing, grimacing,
or touching things repeatedly. If a tic disorder is diagnosed, medical
treatment is often useful (Golden, 1983).

Patients with decreased pain sensation may appear self-abusive
due to a failure to protect their extremities from day-to-day trauma.
Decreased pain sensation does not, of itself, cause self-abuse (Carr, 1977;
Money, Wolff, & Annecillo, 1972). Conditions of complete loss of pain
sensation are extremely uncommon, although parents often believe that
their mentally retarded child is insensitive to pain if he or she does not
cry easily.

Behaviors Masquerading as Medical Disorders

Even more unusual, but equally interesting, are behavior problems
that first appear to be primarily medical in origin. Masturbation can
cause posturing and movements that appear to be convulsive. I have
personally observed an adolescent female lying prone, apparently having a grand mal convulsion or an oculogyric crisis with tonic posturing
and eyes rolled back. It was several minutes before it was clear that the
patient was masturbating. This simulation has been reported elsewhere
in small children, some of whom were even mistakenly placed on anticonvulsants. One diagnostic clue is that the patient resents interruption
of the "seizure" (Snyder, 1972).

Pseudoseizures, a behavioral complex in which a child or adult consciously (feigned) or unconsciously (hysterical) imitates a seizure behavior, are a well-documented phenomenon (Herskowitz & Rosman, 1982), particularly in patients who have a known seizure disorder; pseudoseizures also occur in children who have witnessed seizures. The diagnosis may require special EEG technology in which the electroencephalographic patterns can be recorded continuously while the patient goes about his or her daily activities. Videotaping of the "seizures" while obtaining an EEG recording will clarify the diagnosis. Unfortunately, this technology is not yet widely available; however, studies on documented pseudoseizures do provide clinical descriptions of the phenomenon that are helpful in making the distinction from true seizures (Holmes, Sackellares, McKiernan, Ragland, & Dreifuss, 1980).

In some patients with a number of stereotypic behaviors and staring spells resembling automatisms and lapses of consciousness, the diagnosis of simple self-stimulatory behavior becomes uncertain. EEG telemetry as used for pseudoseizures would be helpful to rule out or to demonstrate psychomotor seizure activity during these movements. Thus far, this technology has not been used in a study of stereotypies in the mentally retarded. A careful clinical trial of an appropriate anticonvulsant, such as carbamazepine, is sometimes justified and fruitful.

Skin changes resulting from hand wringing, picking, chewing, or rubbing the same area repeatedly may stimulate a rash or chronic skin disorder.

The behavior of air swallowing, or aerophagia, has caused clinicians to suspect serious gastrointestinal disease such as malabsorption. Severe aerophagia causing marked abdominal distention, dilatation of the intestines, and even thinning of the abdominal wall musculature is reported (Gauderer, Halpin, & Izant, 1981), but it is unusual. Milder degrees of aerophagia with lesser abdominal distention, abdominal discomfort, or flatus may also raise medical concerns if the behavior of air swallowing is not recognized as the cause. One clue is that the patient is more distended in the latter part of the day and on arising has a flat abdomen.

Behaviors Contributing to Medical Complications

The behaviorally disturbed individual is prone to some medical problems rarely seen in the normal population. Experienced professional caretakers learn to identify and to call to medical attention certain problems typical of the mentally retarded population: self-inflicted skin disorders and eye injuries, foreign bodies in any orifice, serious food refusal, self-induced vomiting, coprophagia, pica, and trichotillomania. It is important to recognize these problems and to institute behavior therapy to interrupt the process and medical therapy if needed to prevent further complications. For instance, trichotillomania, pulling out one's own hair, can be serious if the hair is eaten, because over a period of time hair balls (bezoars) can form and cause life-threatening intestinal obstruction.

Refusal to submit to physical examination can greatly hamper adequate medical care of a mentally retarded person. Many of the problems can be overcome by allowing for the extra amount of time it takes to examine the patient as well as to desensitize the patient to the examining situation (Dahlquist, Gill, Kalfus, Blount, & Boyd, 1984). Occasionally when the examination is medically necessary and cooperation is not possible, general anesthesia must be used.

Some behavior disorders will complicate preexisting medical problems, a relationship familiar to all who work with mentally retarded individuals. The main problem is poor compliance with recommended medical therapies. Mentally retarded patients may have more difficulty understanding and adhering to recommended diets; they may reject medications, refuse dental care, or poorly tolerate recommended bed rest following an injury or other illness. In addition, mentally retarded individuals may reject eyeglasses or hearing aids or break or lose them repeatedly. (Discarded eyeglass frames found in secondhand stores or flea markets are inexpensive and can be used during behavior modification programming while the patient learns not to throw or break the eye glasses.)

This particular category represents a set of medical problems that cannot be treated without intensive behavior therapy. Appropriate and successful behavior modification may be the crucial factor in the medical management of the mentally retarded diabetic, epileptic or asthmatic.

The Relationship between Behavior Therapy and Medical Management: General Principles

In planning an approach to treatment, the preceding relationships, sometimes obvious, sometimes subtle, should be considered. For each patient, the relationships should be defined as specifically as possible. This is valuable so that contributing but not causative medical factors are not overlooked by the physician and so that the relative importance of behavior and medical therapies are fully understood by the treatment team and the family. A pitfall for multidisciplinary teams may be to ascribe too much significance to the medical diagnosis and treatment in relation to behavior problems. Alternatively, in the educational setting, if a physician experienced in the problems of the mentally retarded is not readily available, behavior therapy may be frustrated by a failure to identify an underlying contributory medical problem. In general, when treating *behavior disorders*, it can safely be said that the medical therapy will be an adjunct to the behavior therapy. *Even when the primary cause of a behavior disorder is closely related to an ongoing medical disorder, behavior therapy may remain an important and often primary modality for treatment.* In addition, it is rare for behavior therapy to be contraindicated because there is an underlying or related medical problem. This is especially true for nonaversive behavior therapies. All this is not to say that medical diagnosis and treatment can be overlooked; however, by the time the problem has deteriorated to presenting as a behavior disorder, medical therapy alone is rarely an adequate treatment.

This will hold true even when the behavior disorder is closely linked to a known neurologic abnormality such as a brain lesion, seizure disorder, or drug toxicity. Although *medical therapy should not await the implementation of behavior therapy* in these more serious conditions, behavior therapy need not await the completion of medical therapy unless there is a specific need to delineate exactly which factors are contributing to the problem.

In the situation where the suspected medical problem is minor or highly unlikely, medical diagnosis and therapy may even be deferred while a trial of behavior therapy is instituted. Successful behavior therapy does not necessarily rule out the contributing effect of a medical problem but may reduce the need of expensive or painful medical diagnostic tests that are not indicated for medical reasons alone. The suspicion of allergies or the management of enuresis, as discussed later, illustrate this situation.

There are instances of medical intervention into what appear to be primarily learned behavior disorders. The physician is understandably and rightfully hesitant to resort to such manipulations; however, it is justified in cases where behavior therapy has been unsuccessful or impossible to implement and the behavior disorder is significantly debilitating either to the patient or to his or her caretakers/family. Examples include the use of Tofranil (imipramine) in the enuretic patient, suppositories as an aid to toilet training, and the short-term use of a bedtime sedation in the patient with bedtime refusal. Ideally, when medical treatment is used in such instances, it is done in conjunction with behavior therapy and is gradually withdrawn in support of behavior therapy alone.

Special Problems in the Mentally Retarded Patient

Some medical issues are raised especially frequently among multidisciplinary teams as they exist in the hospital or residential setting serving mentally retarded patients. The discussions that follow are meant to provide practical information and to act as illustrations of the multiple behavioral-medical relationships as they are encountered in clinical practice.

Food Intolerance and Behavior

A number of different hypotheses exist to suggest that behavior problems can be caused or exacerbated by certain foods (Kolata, 1982; Taub, 1975; Taylor, 1979). The issue has received much public attention, and in the clinical setting the question arises frequently, often when other measures at modifying behavior are less than completely successful. This is a complex as well as a controversial issue, but it seems useful for all professionals dealing with behavior disorders to have some appreciation of the diagnostic problems involved.

McCarty and Frick (1983) provide useful distinctions when discussing this topic. *Food intolerances* are defined as any adverse response, immunologic or nonimmunologic, to foods. *Food sensitivity* refers to immune responses to food. The term *food allergy* is reserved to only those immune responses medicated by IgE mechanisms (IgE is the antibody molecule responsible for classic allergic symptoms, e.g., hives, watery eyes, and runny nose).

It is certainly easiest to comprehend a relationship between food and behavior in the child with classic allergic symptoms, congested nose, sneezing, watery eyes, headaches, rashes, itching, and the like, with resulting irritability, chronic fatigue, and behavior problems (Crook, 1975; Rapp, 1979). This group of children is relatively easy to identify, for whom laboratory testing is most likely to be supportive of food or inhalant allergies (e.g., airborne pollen). However, other authors reporting food intolerance/behavioral relationships suggest that classic allergy symptoms may be subtle or absent (Weiss & Kaufman, 1971).

There are case reports in support of food intolerance with or without other allergic symptoms causing behavior disorders (Rapp, 1979; Taub, 1975; Weiss & Kaufman, 1971). Some authors have proposed a direct allergic response in the brain (Campbell, 1973), whereas others have suggested a direct toxic affect of a nonimmunologic nature (Feingold, 1975). Another mechanism to be considered is a behavioral response to gastrointestinal discomfort (cramps) or to migraine headaches caused by-foods (Egger, Wilson, Carter, Turner, & Soothill, 1983).

This is a difficult topic for parents, teachers, or even the nonallergist physician to sort out. Good studies are understandably difficult to design and to carry out, and large groups of mentally retarded children have not been studied with respect to this issue. Studies of nonretarded hyperactive children have demonstrated that food additives are not an important cause of hyperactivity in the majority (Stare, Whelan, & Sheridan, 1980; Taylor, 1979). A single small pilot study in retarded children has also failed to show such a relationship (Thorley, 1984). There may have an adverse affect on a small subset of hyperactive children, however (Stare *et al.*, 1980), but this is not well established. Avoidance of sugar is a common practice carried out by parents, and it is not a bad idea because mentally retarded children have a definite tendency toward tooth decay and obesity. The behavioral benefits are obscure (Gellis, 1983), and empirical studies supporting a positive relationship are nonexistent.

The question remains entirely open, however, as to whether certain foods can cause behavior problems in certain individuals through an idiosyncratic response, either allergic or nonallergic. The parent or other caretakers of a problem patient can find physicians on both sides of the issue with strong opinions. Unfortunately, this is also an area ripe for false promises and charlatanism. Nonetheless, there appear to be enough well-documented and impressive case reports (Campbell, 1973; Hughes, Weinstein, Gott, Binggeli, & Whitaker, 1982; Rapp, 1979; Simeon, O'Malley, Tyrphonas, Graham, Mastronardi, Simeon, & Griffin, 1979; Tryphonas & Trites, 1979; Weiss & Kaufman, 1971) to suggest that it is folly to ignore the possibility.

The offending food can be different for each individual, but it is worth mentioning here that the foods most commonly causing *classic* allergic reactions include milk, chocolate, eggs, wheat, onions, nuts, tomatoes, pork, oranges, corn, shellfish, and oats. These foods are known to be frequent causes of food sensitivities but have not been established as causing *behavioral* symptoms. Nevertheless, it seems reasonable that while looking for culprits these most frequent offenders should be considered first. Foods known to precipitate migraine attacks include cheese and chocolate. Caffeine in large doses can cause irritability and sleeplessness in susceptible persons.

At present, there is no single laboratory test or group of tests to diagnose food intolerance causing behavior problems (Rapp, 1979; Weiss & Kaufman, 1971). IgE responses can be measured using blood tests, but they do not necessarily correlate with behavior symptoms. This poor relationship between laboratory findings and symptomatology also exists in testing for classic food allergy symptoms and is one of the reasons why the issue remains largely unresolved.

The only way to "test" a child for food intolerance is to perform as controlled a study as possible, designing an elimination diet (a diet excluding the suspected offending foods) followed by systematic food challenges looking for a reappearance of symptoms. The person or persons assessing behavior should be blind to the dietary changes. The specifics of how to carry out such a procedure are discussed in several sources (Crook, 1975; Egger *et al.*, 1983; Hughes *et al.*, 1972; McCarty & Frick, 1983).

As more research data in this area become available, it may establish the value of placing more behaviorally disturbed individuals on simplified diets, with few potential protein allergens, for an assessment period in order to establish if some foods are contributing to behavior problems. Until that time, it seems reasonable to be on the lookout for food–behavior relationships and to try an elimination diet and a reversal study with an open-minded skepticism.

Vomiting and Related Symptoms

Recurrent vomiting is a frequent symptom in the mentally retarded population (Cadmen, Richards, & Feldman, 1978) and is one for which both learned and organic causes should be sought. Recurrent vomiting is a disturbing and undesirable symptom with a number of potentially serious complications for the patient. Besides being unpleasant, vomiting represents a health hazard to caretakers who can be exposed to viral hepatitis that is relatively more common in mentally retarded persons, especially those who are institutionalized. Precautions should be taken in cleanup procedures including use of plastic gloves and thorough cleaning of clothes and other items. Screening vomiting patients for the hepatitis carrier state is appropriate.

Some vomiting is self-induced. Disturbed mentally retarded individuals can be observed to gag themselves with fingers or other objects before vomiting. Some patients are able to self-induce vomiting without placing any objects in the throat. Self-induction of vomiting is clearly a behavioral symptom, but it does not exclude the possibility of an underlying organic problem. The patient may be trying to complete an involuntary and uncomfortable regurgitation of gastric contents into the esophagus and has learned that vomiting relieves chest pain or heartburn.

Rumination, the repeated, apparently pleasurable, regurgitation of gastric contents into the mouth where they are chewed, spit out, or reswallowed is a behavioral symptom known to be related to emotional deprivation in both normal and mentally retarded children. However, rumination is seen with increased frequency among the mentally retarded in general (Rast, Johnston, Drum, & Conrin, 1981). Rumination has been successfully treated nonmedically both by nurturing (Wright, 1965; Wright & Menolascino, 1966, 1971) and by mildly aversive methods (Becker, Turner, & Sajwaj, 1978).

Both rumination and vomiting can also be presenting symptoms of gastroesophageal reflux (GER). GER is defined as the abnormally frequent regurgitation of gastric contents into the esophagus. It is often related to anatomic or physiologic abnormalities of the muscular sphincter between the esophagus and the stomach. These abnormalities generally can be demonstrated on X ray with a barium swallow and by other medical tests. Mentally retarded, especially severely retarded, children are predisposed to GER (Sondheimer & Morris, 1979). Among the severely and profoundly mentally retarded, several authors found GER to be the most common cause of vomiting (Byrne, Campbell, Ashcraft, Seibert, & Euler, 1983; Cadman et al., 1978; Sondheimer & Morris, 1979). GER is particularly common in the patient with spasticity or who is non-ambulatory (Byrne et al., 1983) and is reported in mentally retarded adults as well as children (Kumar, 1978).

Gastroesophageal reflux has a number of associated symptoms that may present with or without overt vomiting. Patients may have poor weight gain, recurrent pneumonias, extreme irritability, frequent aspiration and choking, rumination, chronic cough, wheezing, chest pain, abdominal pain, or bloody vomitus (Berquist, 1982).

Sandifer's syndrome, an interesting although rare presentation of GER, has been described in a number of normal children (Bray, Herbst, Johnson, Book, Ziter, & Condon, 1976, 1977; Kinsbourne & Oxon, 1964). The child with Sandifer's syndrome assumes odd postures, often cocking his or her head far to the side or preferring to hang upside down or to hyperextend the trunk. These symptoms are especially seen after meals. Such a presentation of gastroesophageal reflux would be easily misinterpreted in a mentally retarded child (as it has been in normal children) as an emotional or neurologic movement disorder. Sandifer's syndrome also includes hiatus hernia.

Vomiting that appears "clearly learned" or even self-induced vomiting may still have an underlying medical cause. Similarly, a learning component can still be considered in the patient with radiologically proven gastroesophageal reflux. If an individual has received attention and reinforcement for vomiting, then the symptom could become even more frequent and take on an operant pattern in addition to the patient's organic disorder. In short, the distinction may be exceedingly difficult to make between free operant or "behavioral" vomiting and "organic" vomiting when, in fact, the two can exist simultaneously, each perpetuating the other.

Both voluntary and involuntary repeated vomiting can have significant medical complications: malnutrition, pneumonia, esophageal inflammation leading to blood-loss anemia or strictures. The presence or absence of such symptoms may help determine how aggressive the intervention should be. Strongly aversive behavior modification treatments have been used in individuals who are dangerously malnourished from vomiting (Kohlenberg, 1970; Luckey, Watson, & Musick, 1968; Watkins, 1972). Surgical repair of proven GER is now recommended in patients with complications such as those previously mentioned (Byrne, Euler, Ashcraft, Nash, Seibert, & Golladay, 1982; Wilkinson, Dudgeon, & Sondheimer, 1981). Nonsurgical medical therapy, which may be given a trial in milder cases, includes smaller meals, thickened feedings, upright positioning, antacids, and other medications.

Any patient with vomiting or rumination associated with weight loss, poor weight gain, or any other complications severe enough to warrant aversive behavior therapy should be investigated medically for gastroesophageal reflux. Such an investigation should also seek the known complications of recurrent vomiting such as anemia, pneumonia, esophagitis, and so forth. This approach seems warranted even when the symptom appears to be "clearly behavioral" (i.e., learned).

Self-Abuse

Self-inflicted injuries can be misleading in their appearance; the skin's reaction to repeated minor trauma may simulate warts, scabies, dermatitis or other medically caused skin rashes.

Self-biting causes some of the most severe injuries. Some patients are capable of self-amputation of fingers and lips as in Lesch–Nyhan disease. Other patients also destroy not only skin and subcutaneous tissue, but chew down to the muscle layers and underlying tissues, as well. All human bites, particularly of the hand and face, pose a significant infection risk in addition to the traumatic damage.

Some patients direct self-abuse repeatedly to one part of the body. A light bandage or covering over the area sometimes stops the behavior even though the bandage is not mechanically protective. The patient can then be "weaned" from the bandage using fading techniques specific to behavioral programming.

Injury to the eye with development of cataracts, hemorrhage into the eye, or detached retina can result from repeated flicking or poking of the eye or from severe head banging. Change in the appearance of the pupil (shape or color), a wandering eye, or evidence of difficulty seeing should alert caretakers. Clinical experience makes it clear that severe ocular damage resulting in blindness can occur gradually without the process being obvious (Jay, Grant, & Murray, 1982; Noel & Clark, 1982). Shatterproof eyeglasses can sometimes protect from further eye injury in patients taught to tolerate wearing them.

Swallowing foreign bodies is a form of self-abuse seen in mentally retarded and nonretarded disturbed persons. Although pica (eating inedibles) is common in mentally retarded patients, even severely and profoundly retarded patients generally demonstrate good discretion between edibles and nonedibles. Surprisingly, most foreign bodies swallowed cause little or no medical complications (Allen, 1979). Objects as large and ominous as knives, spoons, open safety pins, pencils, and razor blades have been passed naturally without complications (James & Allen-Mersh, 1982). Management of swallowed foreign bodies is, of course, a medical responsibility. Batteries and wristwatch or camera power cells pose a special threat because of the toxic materials in these objects. Removal is required much more urgently than in the case of other objects (Kulig, Rumack, Rumack, Duffy, & Pharm, 1983; Litovitz, 1983).

Foreign bodies lodged by patients in any orifice (e.g., nose, ear, vagina) will often first be identified by a persistent foul odor and occasionally an odiferous or dark discharge. These objects can be very difficult to discover if not suspected and even more difficult to remove, especially in an uncooperative patient. At times general anesthesia is required for safe removal.

Encopresis

Defecation in any location other than the toilet or bedpan is one of the more disturbing and unpleasant symptoms sometimes encountered among mentally retarded persons. Although families may hesitate to bring up this problem, they are thoroughly gratified when it receives professional attention. It can usually be treated quite successfully and is a symptom worth asking about.

Most such behavior is properly called *encopresis* and is defined as repeated, involuntary evacuation of feces into the clothes without apparent organic cause (Bellman, 1966). Cases of deliberate evacuation of feces into a clothes drawer, flowerpot, or wastebasket are uncommon among the mentally retarded and more typical of a psychiatric patient; this behavior is not truly encopresis. Likewise, the incontinent individual with an abnormality of the lower spine, such as severe spina bifida or a deformity of the anorectal region is not considered to have encopresis. Such anatomic and neurologic causes should not be forgotten by the assessing physician; however, they do represent only a small minority of the mentally retarded patients presenting with fecal soiling. Usually these causes are fairly apparent or can be suspected by the known medical history.

The remainder of soiling patients may still represent a somewhat heterogeneous group. Many children with normal IQs have encopresis. The frequency among mentally retarded individuals is much higher and correlates negatively with the IQ (Bellman, 1966). Males outnumber females by about 4 or more to 1 in the normal population, and this male preponderance seems to hold for mentally retarded patients, as well.

Encopresis is nearly always a daytime event in contrast to enuresis (wetting) that is more often nocturnal or both diurnal and nocturnal. Nocturnal encopresis is very unusual. Encopresis and enuresis are often seen in the same patients. Enuresis is a more common problem, however.

Primary or *continuous encopresis* refers to the disorder in individuals who have never been consistently continent for a year or more (Bellman, 1966). *Secondary encopresis* is soiling that appears after 1 or more years of bowel continence. One may suspect faulty bowel training in the former group and chronic constipation with secondary overflow incontinence in the latter, but this relationship is not precise. Both patterns are seen in mentally retarded individuals, whereas secondary encopresis is far more common in the nonretarded population.

It is useful to keep in mind that cerebral palsy patients of all mental ranges, particularly with spasticity of the lower limbs, have a strong tendency to be constipated and to become impacted with feces.

The fact that a patient defecates during a temper tantrum or while being punished does not necessarily prove that the problem is strictly learned and, therefore, nonmedical. The chronically constipated patient with overflow incontinence is capable of defecating either willfully or involuntarily far more easily than is normal. Deliberate defecation into the pants during a temper tantrum is an ability probably reserved for those with a full, dilated rectum and still suggests that the patient is severely constipated or in the habit of retaining routine bowel movements.

Some parents, and other caretakers as well, may believe that soiling is to be expected in the mentally retarded person. An extreme example in my clinical experience was a 9-year-old mentally retarded boy, who presented to an inpatient hospital program with an oversized diaper and his pants legs tied to his ankles with string in order to prevent the feces from dropping out of the bottom of his pants. This youngster was quickly and easily toilet trained by the inpatient staff using standard behavior modification techniques combined with medical management of the patient's mild megacolon. The opinion here is that fecal soiling is not to be tolerated without a valiant effort to eliminate or at least greatly reduce the problem. This is true even for the profoundly mentally retarded or severely autistic individual. In general, if the person can walk, it should be believed he or she can gain bowel control; if the patient cannot walk, it is still worth a serious effort.

Encopresis provides a happy opportunity for collaboration between the physician and the behaviorist. In the chronically constipated patient with overflow incontinence, the medical therapy is indispensable, but success is short-lived without ongoing behavior therapy. In the inadequately trained patient the learned approach offered by behavior modification is primary, but short-term medical intervention, as described later, can aid the process immensely.

Patients with constipation and overflow fecal incontinence (functional megacolon) are chronically full of stool. They often, but not always, have a history of infrequent or hard bowel movements. They can also pass stool of normal consistency, but often parents comment on the very large caliber of the stool (e.g., "How can such a little boy plug up the toilet like that?"). They may have normal bowel movements every day, but this does not exclude a large reservoir of stool in the colon. The colon is chronically dilated (megacolon) and has partially lost muscular tone, contributing to the tendency to retain stool and the loss of the normal urge to defecate. Children with normal IQs with this problem report rather consistently that they did not realize that they were defecating until they felt the stool in their underclothing (Levine, 1975). Presumably this happens also in the mentally retarded individual who is significantly constipated.

In the most severe cases of functional megacolon, the patient may pass stool almost continuously with as many as 12 bowel movements a day and constant fecal smears in the underclothing. On physical examination, the physician can often palpate a large mass of stool in the lower left abdomen that also be demonstrated on X ray.

The patient who appears to have this pattern of stool retention and resulting incontinence can be treated with a combined approach using a bowel cleanout with daily enemas and suppositories for 1 to 2 weeks, followed by the use of mineral oil for 4 to 6 months in order to maintain the colon in a semi-emptied state while muscle tone is regained (Levine & Bakow, 1980). Dietary changes are also recommended (e.g., high-fiber foods, reduced milk intake).

The initial cleanout procedure using enemas and suppositories affords an opportunity to institute intensive behavior modification. Enemas and suppositories cause the patient to have a bowel movement within 10 to 30 minutes of administration. This means that the patient can be kept on or near the toilet so as to insure that the defecation occurs in the right place. The patient is then rewarded with praise, cheers, or other effective reinforcers for this "success." Even the very low-functioning individual may learn the contingencies with this graphic (errorless) demonstration of what is expected of him or her. For the mildly retarded patient, some "demystification" is additionally useful as described by Levine and Bakow (1980). The patient and his or her parents are given an explanation of the soiling problem as being a result of chronic constipation and loss of sensation. Punishment for soiling is eliminated, and, although patients are still responsible for their messes (i.e., they clean up), they are not scolded. Positive reinforcement is given for the successes and may be adjusted according to the IQ and other needs of the patient.

Suppositories (glycerin or bisacodyl 10 mg) and even occasional enemas may be useful in the patient who is not constipated but has a refractory soiling problem for behavioral or social reasons. Short-term use (e.g., several weeks) of these aids has no or few side effects in the healthy individual and does not cause dependency. Especially in the lower functioning individual, the suppository guarantees a "success" and rapid (errorless) association between defecation, toilet, and the sub-sequent praise or food reward. Previously difficult patients have been toilet-trained for stool in 2 weeks using this method, particularly in the hands of enthusiastic and imaginative staff who really know how to celebrate the event of a bowel movement in the toilet.

In bowel training mentally retarded individuals with or without suppositories or other adjuncts, it is useful to take advantage of natural rhythms, remembering that many people defecate shortly after meals as a result of the gastrocolic reflex.

In summary, most mentally retarded patients can become continent for stool regardless of advanced age or low IQ, provided there are not significant physical handicaps interfering with bowel function.

Enuresis

Urinary incontinence can include daytime or nighttime wetting and is a common problem in mentally retarded persons. Nighttime enuresis is quite frequent in children with normal intelligence as well and is often viewed as a developmental maturation problem (Cohen, 1975; Doleys & Dolce, 1982). There are many spontaneous remissions among normal children in support of this idea (Herskowitz & Rosman, 1982). In many severely and profoundly retarded individuals, the symptoms of daytime and nighttime wetting simply represent a failure to be properly toilet trained.

In a few cases, enuresis is not a behavior problem, but a symptom of a medical disorder. A medical condition may be more suspected in certain settings: the appearance of enuresis, especially daytime wetting, in a previously toilet trained individual (Cohen, 1975) or the persistence of enuresis in a moderately or mildly retarded patient in spite of intensive behavior modification training.

Associated symptoms may also point toward a medical diagnosis. Neurologic cause (e.g., spinal cord defect, hydrocephalus, neurodegenerative disease) is suggested by an associated regression or loss in skills, change in gait, staggering, wide-based gait, leg weakness, or spasticity. Simultaneous onset of loss of bowel control may also represent a neurologic symptom.

Urinary tract disease (e.g., infection, obstruction, kidney defects) is suggested by painful voiding, unusual frequency of wetting (day or night), inability to reach the toilet in time in spite of an attempt to do so, constant urinary dribbling, or a weak urinary stream.

Excessive production of urine is seen in diabetes insipidus (due to a hormonal deficiency or a defect in the kidney), diabetes mellitus, and psychogenic water drinking, all of which are associated with an increased intake in fluids in addition to the increase in the frequency of voiding.

Caffeine, alcohol, theophyllines (drugs used to treat asthma or "bronchitis") and some major tranquilizers (thioridizine and haloperidol) can all have an effect increasing the flow of urine (Herskowitz & Rosman, 1982).

Sickle-cell anemia may interfere with the kidney's ability to concentrate urine. Some authors believe bladder irritability due to an allergic response to foods is causative in selected patients (Crook, 1975).

Nocturnal seizures will cause nighttime wetting and are suggested by enuresis in an otherwise continent person with unusual motor activity during sleep and a bitten tongue or sore muscles noticed on awakening (Herskowitz & Rosman, 1982).

A careful medical history seeking these symptoms and conditions, together with a physical examination of the patient, can satisfactorily exclude the vast majority of the previously mentioned conditions. Simple laboratory testing of the urine will identify infection, poorly concentrated urine, or the presence of sugar, protein, or blood in the urine.

Obstructive abnormalities, bladder irritability, small bladder, and food allergies are not as easily excluded. These require more extensive testing, some of which can be rather difficult in an uncooperative patient. It does not seem reasonable to pursue these causes unless the medical history, physical exam, or the laboratory tests, as mentioned, suggest such abnormalities.

Behavior management of wetting does not need to await a full medical investigation when the patient is receiving good ongoing medical care and there is no special reason to suspect illness. Often the social history will indicate that no serious attempts at toilet training have been made previously. It is reasonable to attempt behavior management of the problem first. A change in environment, loss of a favorite caretaker, or a new placement can certainly cause a temporary regression in toileting skills and account for many of the nonmedical cases of secondary enuresis (enuresis occurring in a previously toilet trained individual). Nonetheless, it is a good rule of thumb to consult a physician to determine to what degree the problem needs to be assessed medically.

Patients who are persistently unresponsive to the behavior modification approaches described in the literature (e.g., Azrin & Foxx, 1971; Baumeister & Klosowski, 1965; Edgar, Kohler, & Hardman, 1975; Mahoney, Van Wagenen, & Meyerson, 1971; Rentfrow & Rentfrow, 1969) or who have associated symptoms of concern should certainly be referred for the more extensive medical evaluation. Among persistent enuretics, a medical diagnosis will often not be forthcoming even after radiologic and fibrooptic examinations of the urinary tract.

Treatment, therefore, of the majority of enuretics is with behavior modification. Medical therapy using imipramine (Tofranil) is used frequently with effectiveness in children with normal intelligence (Doleys & Dolce, 1982; Rapoport & Mikkelsen, 1978). Imipramine does not appear to be useful in treating enuresis in mentally retarded adults (Drew, 1967; Fisher, Murray, Walley, & Kiloh, 1963).

Some maneuvers commonly recommended to parents include fluid restriction in the evening and awakening the patient to void during the night. Neither of these approaches is effective in the truly enuretic patient. They take the responsibility for dryness away from the patient, fail to address the basic problem of bladder control, and require an ongoing disruption in the life-style of the patient and his or her parents/caretakers.

Seizures and Behavioral Disorders

Seizures, defined as a "disturbance of movement, sensation, perception, behavior, mood or consciousness due to excessive, disorderly, neuronal discharge" (Hughes, 1980, p. 3) are far more common in the mentally retarded population than in nonretarded individuals. Although the severity of seizures is not related to the severity of mental retardation, the frequency of seizures increases with decreasing IQ, overall affecting about 25% or more of mentally retarded persons (Richardson, Koller, Katz, & McLaren, 1981). Any professional working with mentally retarded patients will want more than a passing knowledge of seizures and seizure disorders. Several summaries may prove useful (Baird, 1983; Balaschak & Mostofsky, 1981; Hughes, 1980). An international classification of seizure types is used by clinicians and researchers but will not be described here (Gastaut, 1970).

Seizures (ictal phenomena, fits, convulsions) are usually classified according to clinical appearance of the seizure with the EEG findings usually secondary in the diagnosis. *Epilepsy* refers to the condition of having recurrent seizures regardless of the cause. It is a threatening word such that many patients and their families do not realize or deny that their seizure disorder is synonymous with epilepsy.

Seizure Disorders

Every possible relationship between a medical disorder and a behavior disorder described in the first part of this chapter is relevant in considering seizures. Three major areas of concern arise with respect to seizures and behavior: *behavior between seizures, behavior during seizures,* and the *behavioral effects of anticonvulsant drugs.*

Behavior between seizures is an issue in the patient with a known diagnosis of epilepsy. The question arises, "Is the seizure disorder related to his behavioral problems?" In these patients, the behavior is distinct in nature from the seizures, but the caretaking staff or family may notice a temporal relationship between convulsions and behavior change. Many individuals experience a prodrome or *aura* prior to their seizures that may be behavioral in nature (e.g., fearfulness, irritability and restlessness). Sometimes these behaviors or sensations can be quite bizarre, but usually they remain typical for any given patient with each seizure (Livingston & Pauli, 1979). Auras generally last only a few minutes before the onset of the seizure, usually a major motor convulsion, and the relationship is generally easy to identify. However, there are patients who experience behavior change for as long as several days prior to a major convulsion (Livingston, 1979). Some patients are increasingly irritable for several days prior to a flurry of convulsions, so much so that parents and caretakers are relieved to see the seizures come.

It also seems evident that some patients experience a general behavioral regression in association with poor seizure control (Herskowitz & Rosman, 1982). Adjustment of anticonvulsant medications is required when seizures are in poor control, but the association between increased seizures and poor behavior does not preclude behavioral treatment, as well. In some patients, imperfect seizure control may be all that is possible without excessive drug toxicity, thereby enhancing the role of behavior modification approaches to controlling oppositional, irritable responding.

Behavioral problems, especially hyperactivity, and psychiatric disturbances including psychoses have been described in patients with seizures arising in the temporal lobe (i.e., temporal lobe epilepsy, partial complex seizures, psychomotor seizures) (Geschwind, Shader, Bear, North, Levin, & Chetham, 1980; Lindsay, Ounsted, & Richards, 1979a, b, c; Pritchard, Lombroso, & McIntyre, 1980; Shukla, Srivastovaa, Katiyar, Joshi, & Mohan, 1979; Stoudemire, Nelson, & Houpt, 1983; Waxman & Geschwind, 1975). This is an interictal phenomenon; that is, the behavior disorder or psychosis is not present simply during seizure activity. It appears to represent a permanent change in the neurologic function of the patient persisting occasionally even after the seizures are well controlled (Geschwind *et al.*, 1980; Stoudemire *et al.*, 1983). If the seizures are subtle, and therefore undiagnosed, behavior change may be the presenting feature.

In some patients with or without a known seizure disorder, a question arises whether certain episodic behaviors represent seizure activity. Those behaviors most commonly questioned include aggression, rage, staring spells, daytime dozing, nighttime sleep disturbances, enuresis, and repetitive eye, hand, or mouth movements that may or may not be self-stimulatory behaviors. The kinds of seizures often in question are absence seizures (petit mal epilepsy) or partial complex seizures (psychomotor epilepsy). It is useful to know that the majority of patients with partial complex seizures have had motor epilepsy as well (Lindsay *et al.*, 1979). True petit mal epilepsy is usually easily diagnosed or ruled out based on EEG findings. This is not true for psychomotor epilepsy, a diagnosis that can be extremely difficult to establish or rule out.

A number of clinical features can be noted during the episode that suggest temporal lobe seizure activity (Delgado-Escueta, Mattson, King, Goldensohn, Speigel, Madsen, Crandall, Dreifuss, & Porter, 1981; Livingston & Pouli, 1979), as follows:

> *Onset*: The onset of abnormal behavior or aggression is generally spontaneous and unprovoked.

> *Duration*: Duration is generally less than 1 minute. Rage or aggression that is sustained much longer is not likely to be seizure activity.

> *Aura*: Prior to the onset of the seizure, the patient may experience nausea, abdominal discomfort, repeated swallowing,

fearfulness, anxiety, or any one of a number of visceral or emotional sensations. Verbal patients may be able to relate this phenomenon. At other times the aura may be manifest by behavior. One of our small patients always ran and buried his head in someone's lap prior to the onset of his seizures.

Automatisms: These are repeated meaningless movements of the hand or mouth during the seizure activity such as lip smacking, tongue movements, grimacing, self-grooming, and so forth; these may be sustained for several seconds at a time. They are an important, often overlooked, clue that there is a temporal lobe epileptic focus.

Stereotypic Behavior: The aggression and destructive behaviors that have been documented to occur during temporal lobe epilepsy are generally simple, stereotypic, and unsustained. They may be directed at an individual and even associated with an angry affect, but they are not complicated or well planned or sustained attacks of aggression. An example is a patient who clawed and bit at our staff during a seizure but when placed on his bed continued to claw and bite at his pillow in a rather meaningless manner. Most such patients are easily restrained (Delgado-Escueta *et al.*, 1981).

Incontinence: Incontinence of stool or urine, particularly in a normally continent patient, is good supportive evidence for seizure activity.

Postictal Drowsiness: The patient may be drowsy or fall asleep following the seizure and return to his or her normal state of alertness several minutes to 24 hours later.

Amnesia: Amnesia for the episode is typical during partial complex seizures (Delgado-Escueta *et al.*, 1981; Livingston & Pauli, 1979), major motor (grand mal), and other nonfocal convulsions.

The diagnosis of seizure disorder is made primarily on the history of clinical features such as those just described. Seizure activity on the electroencephalogram (EEG) is usually supportive rather than diagnostic. It is possible to have a normal encephalographic study in the presence of an obvious seizure disorder, and conversely, many individuals with no history of seizures can show epileptic and other abnormalities on the EEG. It is especially true in temporal lobe epilepsy that a normal EEG does not rule out a seizure disorder because the electroencephalogram is able to detect abnormal activity only in the area of the upper cortex of the brain. Many seizures originate and remain in deeper layers and cannot be detected by the usual techniques. It is for these reasons that the clinical history becomes of paramount importance and remains the primary diagnostic tool in the assessment of possible seizure disorder.

Petit mal epilepsy is a specific term for absence seizures associated with a characteristic EEG pattern of 3 to 3.5 hertz spike and wave changes. The term is too often mistakenly used to describe all nongrand mal seizures, short or medication-aborted grand mals, or staring spells. Petit mal seizures are manifest by staring spells and eye blinking and occasionally by automatisms. They usually last only a few seconds.

Distinguishing among the seizure types is important because the choice of seizure medication is dependent upon the type of seizures present.

Behavioral Complications of Seizure Therapy

In addition to seizure symptoms, epileptic patients are subject to behavioral changes associated with their anticonvulsant medications. The specific behavioral effects of the anticonvulsant medications are poorly studied (Stores, 1978), but some general statements can be made.

Somnolence and lethargy are the most common behavior changes seen with many of the anticonvulsant drugs. They are frequently observed when a patient is first placed on medication and may resolve spontaneously after a few days or several weeks; however, they may be symptoms of toxic blood levels, as well. If these symptoms persist, the seizure medication dosage should be carefully and slowly reduced, and an alternative drug sought if necessary.

Other behavior changes commonly observed with anticonvulsants include hyperactivity, emotional lability, irritability, depression, and aggressive behavior. The barbiturate group of medications, especially phenobarbital, but also Mebaral and Mysoline (which convert in large part to phenobarbital), are particularly capable of causing these effects. Previously existing hyperactivity may not necessarily worsen with the use of phenobarbital, but this is controversial (Livingston, Pruce, Pauli, & Livingston, 1979; Stores, 1978). Irritability, mood changes, depression, euphoria, and psychoses have been attributed to ethosuximide (Zarontin) (Morselli, Pippenger, & Penry, 1983; Stores, 1978) in a minority of patients taking the drug. Acute combativeness, withdrawal, agitation, and even delirium have been reported in a few children in association with carbamazepine (Tegretol) therapy (Silverstein, Parrish, & Johnston,

1982). Behavioral changes have also been reported in association with treatment with clonazepam and trimethadione (Schmidt, D., 1982).

If medication changes are indicated because of behavioral or other side effects, they must be made slowly, even in the face of considerable behavior problems. Rapid reduction of dosage can result in precipitating severe seizures. Before an anticonvulsant can be withdrawn, a second medication is usually introduced in order to provide an adequate protection against seizures.

Patients on seizure medication should have their seizure histories and EEG reviewed periodically because there is a definite tendency for seizure disorders to resolve as patients get older, especially when the seizure disorder was mild initially. This tendency toward improvement is less true for mentally retarded than for nonretarded persons, however (Emerson, D'Souza, Vining, Holden, Mellits, & Freeman, 1981). Still, some patients may be able to remain seizure-free without any medication. This is a tricky clinical decision, however, and should be made only by a physician experienced in seizure management.

Drooling (Sialorrhea)

Drooling is a significant social disability among some mentally retarded persons usually with concomitant cerebral palsy. These patients generally have an abnormality in the motor coordination of their swallowing movements. Most of the difficulty is in the first phase of swallowing during which the contents of the mouth should move from the front of the mouth to the back of the mouth. Reverse tongue thrusting or poorly coordinated tongue, lip, and cheek movements can result in saliva and other mouth contents coming forward and spilling out of the mouth just when a patient is attempting to do the opposite. Some patients, therefore, appear to drool more on the command *swallow*. This could be seen as oppositional behavior when it is not. Although most patients with drooling problems do have cerebral palsy, there can be an occasional patient with drooling with no other evidence of motor impairment. This does not rule out the possibility of an oromotor abnormality.

There are medical complications of drooling in addition to the social stigma: maceration and infection of the skin of the face and neck, hygiene, and odor problems due to constantly wet clothes and the potential transmission of disease.

Therapeutic approaches to severe drooling are many and should be considered in the reverse order of their invasiveness, surgery being a last but important resort. Physical therapy, oral appliances, speech therapy techniques and chin cups have all been used with reported successes (Crysdale, 1980; Haberfellner & Rossiwall, 1977; Harris & Dignam, 1980). Behavior modification procedures are also reported as successful in some patients (Rapp, 1980).

Surgical procedures involve the placement of the salivary ducts to the back of the mouth, removal of salivary glands, or the cutting of the nerves to the salivary glands (Arnold & Gross, 1977; Brody, 1977; Cotton & Richardson, 1981; Crysdale, 1980; Morgan, Hansen, Wells, & Hoopes, 1981; Wilkie & Brody, 1977). In the child with persistent severe drooling, who is unresponsive to less invasive procedures, a consultation with an otolaryngologist or plastic surgeon experienced in one of these procedures may be worthwhile.

Drug therapy for drooling involves medications that reduce the production of saliva. Because of unacceptable side effects, increased dental caries, and the requirement for continuous and prolonged drug therapy, this approach is generally not used (Crysdale, 1980).

Sexual Abuse of the Retarded Person

Very little direct statistical research data are available on sexual abuse of the retarded; however, preliminary studies on sexually abused children suggest that the retarded person is more likely than others to be sexually victimized. With their lesser ability to communicate, witness, or use judgment, this group should unquestionably be considered high risk. Most children who are sexually abused are abused by persons known to them, including natural parents, foster parent, or other surrogate for the parent. Retarded persons are frequently not in the care of their own families and are also in contact with other retarded persons in group homes who may have been abused themselves and are subsequently imitating the behavior. The retarded adolescent or young adult, although sexually mature, has not the social skills or the judgment to dissuade unwanted physical or sexual contacts.

Sexual abuse must be considered as a possible explanation in causes of sudden, unexplained changes in behavior, increase in anxiety, withdrawal, aggression, or refusal to go certain places or to be with certain persons. Masturbation is fairly common among retarded persons, especially males, but more sophisticated sexual behaviors probably require some modeling. Sexually explicit talk or sudden onset of sexual behaviors such as attempting oral-genital or ano-genital contact with another child or adolescent should be considered symptoms of possible sexual victimization by another person.

The discovery of a sexually transmitted disease in a retarded person incapable of sexual consent is extremely strong evidence of sexual victimization. Such diseases include syphilis, gonorrhea, anal warts, chlamydia trachomatis and trichomoniasis, among others (White, Loda, Ingram, & Pearson, 1983).

Obtaining a Medical Opinion

The foregoing discussions of the difficulties in assessing the behavioral and medical components of food intolerances, vomiting, soiling, seizures, and self-abuse illustrate the need for cooperation and much communication between primary caretakers, social workers, psychologists, teachers, parents, and the diagnosing physician. The medical assessment of a retarded patient can be a virtual waste of time if the primary caretakers, parents, and other knowledgeable informants are not present to provide a complete history. This is even more true when the questions concern behavioral symptoms and their relationship to medical problems. Very few such issues can be resolved from even the most thorough physical examination and laboratory testing without a good history. Most laboratory tests should not be done routinely and the decision to obtain X rays, blood tests, or other studies depends heavily on the history and physical findings.

The opinions of primary caretakers and parents concerning causes and precipitants of behavior are also very valuable. Parents, experienced child-care workers and teachers have excellent insights and instincts concerning such relationships.

Often the questions asked by the physician at the initial assessment are not immediately answerable, for instance, in a patient who vomits: How often does he vomit? Before, after or during meals? Does he belch frequently? Does he have loose stools? Do you ever see lip smacking or eye blinking at the times when he vomits? Is he in distress or pain when he vomits? Does he appear relieved by vomiting? Is there a coffee-ground appearing material (blood) in the vomitus? Does he seem to enjoy vomiting? Does he fall asleep after vomiting?

Even very attentive parents may not be able to answer all these questions, but they can then return home and keep a record on the calendar of such occurrences. In short, several visits are often far more productive than one single assessment as the parent/caretaker learns what to watch for and the physician gains a better sense of the symptoms and their severity.

For the child with soiling, information about the frequency, size, odor, and consistency of the stools is extremely useful in the diagnosis.

The presence of smears of stool in underwear is important. Such data are not readily available in the patient who toilets himself or herself much of the time but soils occasionally. Therefore a special effort is necessary to collect this information for the physician.

In the assessment of food allergies and behavior, the caretakers must be prepared to keep a food diary and an accurate behavioral record while the patient's diet is being manipulated. Related symptoms of coughing, snorting, nasal stuffiness, flatulence, loose stools, gastric discomfort, fatigue, and the like should be noted.

In the evaluation for possible seizure disorder, it is especially critical that a good firsthand observer of the seizure be present for the medical history. A written record of observations made immediately after the seizure is a poor, but helpful, substitute. Diagnostic terms such as *automatisms* or "petit mal" should not be used in reporting a possible seizure because these terms constitute a diagnosis and not an observation. These terms are often used inaccurately. Rather, the diagnosing physician should be provided with as complete a *descriptive* history of exactly what occurred during the episode as possible. During the purported seizure the duration of the episode should be timed. Guesses are notoriously inaccurate. The patient's activities before, during, and afterward should be noted, especially noting the presence of automatisms that should be described, incontinence, unusual or rapid eye movements (if a patient's eyes are closed there is never any harm in gently opening them to see the eye movements), skin color (duskiness or cyanosis), responsiveness to voice, and pain. (Pinching an apparently unconscious person is an extremely valuable and acceptable maneuver to ascertain the level of consciousness.) A period of drowsiness following the episode is very significant, and it should be timed as to how long the patient sleeps and how long it is until the patient returns to a normal state of alertness. This information helps the physician decide if the episode was a true seizure or some other phenomenon.

When the question concerns adverse effects of medication, it is necessary to note the duration of treatment, timing of the administration, the dose of the medication, missed or spit-out doses, the time of day that behavior symptoms are noted, frequency of the symptoms, associated symptoms such as dizziness, tremors, drowsiness, dry mouth, unusual movements of the mouth and hands, hyperactivity, gastric distress, and so on.

When using an outside consultant, it is helpful to distinguish between questioning medical problems as *causing* behavior disorders and medical problems *contributing* to behavior disorders. The distinction may make it seem more reasonable to the physician to pursue possible medical factors. Few physicians would be interested in attributing a behavior such as biting people to food intolerances, for instance. But if it is clear that the concern is not merely the biting but that the patient is irritable, tense, and hyperactive when he or she bites, such an investigation may appear far more promising.

Finally, it should be reemphasized that even after a thorough medical history and physical exam with routine laboratory tests, any physician can easily overlook a relationship between behavioral and medical disorders unless the issue is raised by the caretakers, parents, or other advocates of the patient. Mentally retarded patients are dependent on such advocacy; if the question is not raised, it very likely will not be answered. As one of my more benevolent mentors has said, "The only 'stupid' question is the one you don't ask."

Syndromes of Mental Retardation with Recognized Behavioral Features

In the description of syndromes, physicians attempt to identify those features (physical, chemical, clinical, and otherwise) that group patients together as likely to be suffering from a single etiologic defect (i.e., missing enzyme and chromosomal imbalance) (Smith & Jones, 1982; Carter, 1979; Gellis & Feingold, 1968). In syndromes that lack marked physical abnormalities or those with extremely consistent and aberrant behavior, the behavior features are noted from the earliest clinical description. Lesch-Nyhan disease and phenylketonuria are two such disorders. Many syndromes are described in conscientious detail with respect to chemical, physical, or genetic features, but behavioral symptoms are noted or are only mentioned in passing as generic "behavior problems." More precise descriptions are undoubtedly difficult because of the relative rarity of most syndromes, providing only a small number of patients in any one research center. Paradoxically, the behavioral symptoms may be the most significant factors affecting the ongoing well-being and care of the patient.

It is important to note that the majority of mentally retarded individuals do not fit into any one specific syndrome, and even among those who do, the behavior disorders and the medical diagnosis do not generally correlate very well (Philips & Williams, 1975). Finally, it is impressive that even for those syndromes in which specific behavior patterns have been identified as typical, there is still an exceedingly important and complex interplay of environmental as well as medical factors affecting the presentation of the behavior disorder. This tiny minority is nevertheless of great interest because they invite us to formulate and test our hypotheses about the organic mechanisms for behavior disorders.

Several medical syndromes with known behavioral symptoms are described next. They are chosen for discussion because of their relative frequency or because of the certainty of the relationship between the syndrome and specific behavioral problems. Numerous other syndromes are thought to predispose to behavioral disorders, but the patients remain too small in number or inadequately studied to describe specific expected behaviors with much certainty. Except where noted, there are no specific medical treatments for these syndromes, a situation that may change in the next decade.

Lesch-Nyhan Disease

This disorder is a prototype of an organic etiology identified with a specific behavior disorder. Although it is a relatively rare disorder, it is one of the most frequent metabolic diseases causing mental retardation (Nyhan, 1976). The behavior problems are better studied than in virtually any other syndrome of mental retardation.

Lesch-Nyhan disease (Lesch & Nyhan, 1964), is an X-linked recessive disorder of uric acid metabolism caused by the absence of a single enzyme resulting in several metabolic abnormalities. The excess uric acid in the serum at one time was a major cause of morbidity and mortality, causing gout symptoms (arthritis, tophi) and kidney failure with eventual death. Administration of allopurinol promotes uric acid excretion and avoids these complications but has no effect on the neurologic and behavioral symptoms. The disorder is seen only in males who present with severe motor disability (spastic and choreoathetoid cerebral palsy), variable degrees of mental deficiency, and a striking pattern of self-mutilation seen in nearly all such patients. The self-mutilation is more severe and persistent than that seen in any other group of mentally retarded patients; yet, there is no evidence of a sensory deficit (lack of awareness of pain). There patients will begin by chewing their own lips and fingers until there is tissue loss or actual amputation of fingers and lips. They later demonstrate more complex and innovative but equally vicious means of self-mutilation. They appear to have a compulsion to self-mutilate by any means and in addition are aggressive toward caretakers, biting and hitting them whenever they have the opportunity. The patients are fully aware and conscious of their behavior and are sometimes described as "remorseful" (Nyhan, 1976).

Until recently, treatment has been largely dependent on restraints (often, interestingly enough, appreciated by the patients) and removal of the teeth (Anderson, Dancis, & Alpert, 1978).

Lesch-Nyhan disease offers the unusual possibility of specific medical therapy for a behavior disorder (Nyhan, Johnson, Kaufman, & Jones, 1980). Biochemical abnormalities in the neurotransmitters, particularly serotonin, are known to occur in these patients. Several investigators have established that exogenous administration of a serotonin precursor (5-hydroxytryptophan) has benefits in reducing the self-mutilating behavior in these patients (Carr, 1977; Mizuno & Yugari, 1974; Nyhan *et al.*, 1980). Unfortunately, a tolerance for the treatment occurs and only short-lived benefits are possible, thus far.

It is also important to note, however, that a significantly successful behavior therapy for Lesch-Nyhan patients has been described (Anderson *et al.*, 1978) in which patients were found to respond to positive reinforcement for nonself-injurious behaviors. This was in contrast to their failure to respond to aversive treatment for self-mutilation. This is not surprising in the light of the observation that the self-inflicted tissue damage itself causes the patient pain and emotional distress without inhibiting the behavior. Positive reinforcement (in this case contingent attention) for nonself-injurious behaviors appears to be a dramatically useful and an apparently long-lasting therapy for at least some of these patients, allowing for the reduction or elimination of the use of arm restraints and tooth extraction. In addition, the success of the therapy points out the apparent interaction between environment and biochemistry in the etiology of the behavior of this syndrome. Lesch–Nyhan disease is a well-documented example of a disorder illustrating that in spite of biochemical changes and their known relationship (although the mechanism remains unclear) to a specific behavior disorder, behavior therapy remains an essential and useful tool in patient management.

Cornelia de Lange Syndrome

Like Lesch-Nyhan disease, Cornelia de Lange syndrome appears to result in a specific predilection toward severe self-mutilation (Bryson, Sakati, Nyhan, & Fish, 1974; Nyhan, 1976). Patients with Cornelia de Lange syndrome are severely mentally retarded, small in stature, have a low birth weight, distinctive facial features, small hands and feet, and abnormal dermatoglyphics (Bryson *et al.*, 1971). (*Dermatoglyphics* are ridge patterns on the hands and feet that develop prior to 18 weeks' gestation and indicate an abnormality in early prenatal development. Such abnormalities are also seen in chromosome disorders such as Down syndrome.)

Unlike Lesch-Nyhan disease, an underlying cause for the features of Cornelia de Lange syndrome is unknown. A consistant chromosomal abnormality is still sought (Wilson, Hieber, & Schmickel 1978). It affects both males and females and appears to be nonfamilial. These patients, together with Lesch-Nyhan patients, stand out in the severity and nature of their self-injurious behaviors. The tissue loss and self-amputation as seen in these patients is extremely unusual even among those other patients with severe self-injurious behaviors (Nyhan, 1976).

Together Cornelia de Lange and Lesch-Nyhan syndromes stand to broaden our view of the causes for self-injurious behavior.

Phenylketonuria

Phenylketonuria (PKU) represents a prototype of a preventable mental retardation syndrome. If placed on a diet low in phenylalanine shortly after birth, these children have an excellent prognosis for normal development (Kleinman, 1964). Since the early 1960s, the U.S. and many other industrial countries have screened their neonatal populations for phenylketonuria in order to prevent the irreversible brain damage that occurs within the first few months of life.

Untreated individuals are therefore rare among children but are represented in the adult mental retardation population, mostly among the institutionalized. These patients appear to be especially predisposed to behavior problems even when compared with other institutionalized mentally retarded individuals (Paine, 1957). They have been specifically described as dull in their response to their surroundings but also are emotionally labile, given to frequent temper tantrums and to aggressiveness. Severe fright reactions are especially typical. The patients are often in constant motion with numerous stereotypic movements and body rocking. At other times, they are described as catatonic and withdrawn (Wright & Tarjan, 1957). Like congenital rubella syndrome, PKU is sometimes cited as one of the organic etiologies known to cause some of the cases of infantile autism. Although behavioral descriptions vary, most authors seem to agree with the summary that "none could be described as friendly, placid, or happy" (Wright & Tarjan, 1957, p. 407).

Although most clinicians will never encounter such a case, it is interesting to note that rare phenylketonurics, untreated, have normal or borderline intelligence but demonstrate many of the same behavioral symptoms seen in their more severely damaged counterparts: extreme apprehensiveness, emotional outbursts, negativism and dull, expressionless faces (Sutherland, Berry, & Shirkey, 1960). There is evidence that patients treated successfully for phenylketonuria from infancy also have some behavioral symptoms related to the disorder (Schor, 1983).

Low phenylalanine diet therapy instituted after infancy seems to have a demonstrable effect in reducing some of these behavioral and personality traits in phenylketonuric patients even though the neurologic damage is irreversible as is the mental retardation (Hsia, Knox, Quinn, & Paine, 1958; Sutherland et al., 1960).

Down Syndrome (Trisomy-2)

Down syndrome, caused by a duplication of all or part of the 21st chromosome before or at conception, is the syndrome most likely to be familiar to the reader. The level of retardation ranges from profound to mild. The relatively large number of Down syndrome individuals among the mentally retarded population has allowed for the recognition of personality traits definitely related to the condition.

As younger children, they are described as friendly (sometimes overly so) and given to mimicry and mischievousness (Smith & Jones, 1982). Down syndrome patients are strikingly underrepresented in the general referral population of severely behaviorally disturbed retarded children, but significant behavior and emotional problems are still an important part of their symptomatology (Menolascino, 1965). Many problems begin in the second or third decade and have a major impact on family life. Many of these later appearing behavior problems are at least in part easily viewed in a dynamic model. As the Down syndrome child becomes older, his or her family system is changing dramatically. Older siblings leave home, and aging parents begin to prepare for their inability to care for the child indefinitely, possibly by investigating group homes or other institutional arrangements. Like other moderately and mildly retarded individuals, previously well-adjusted Down syndrome persons face significant life stress situations as they realize, perhaps slowly, that their parents will not always be there to care for them.

In later years (fourth and fifth decades) Down syndrome patients are subject to the early development of a dementia (or early senility) essentially indistinguishable from Alzheimer's disease that also affects normal populations (Wisniewski, Howe, Williams, & Wisniewski, 1978). This pattern is clearly an organic phenomenon related to the trisomy-21 condition. The frequency of this complication may approach 100% of Down patients and is highly relevant in the planning for the care of this subgroup of the mentally retarded population (Miniszek, 1983).

Prader-Willi Syndrome

Prader-Willi syndrome is an illustration of a distinctive chain of behavioral and physiologic events contributing to the severe morbidity and even mortality of these patients.

The syndrome, which in at least a portion of cases appears to result from a deletion of chromosome 15 (Ledbetter, Riccardi, Airhart, Strobel, Keenan, & Crawford, 1981), is relatively rare (estimated at 1-2/10,000) (Crnic et al., 1980) but milder cases can go unrecognized. The patients are frequently mentally defective and have marked short stature, obesity, and underdevelopment of the genitalia (Jancar, 1971).

Behavior problems, more frequent with advancing age, are characteristic in their nature and extremely common. The children are docile and quiet but with limited provocation will show temper tantrums and violent behaviors. Depression is also common (Hall & Smith, 1972). Beginning in early childhood they develop severe obesity. The obesity is, in part, related to an eating disorder. These patients are remarkably preoccupied with food; they will sneak and hide food. Gorging is characteristic as is the consumption of sometimes large amounts of rather unusual items such as butter, frozen bread, garbage, and rotten apples (Holm & Pipes, 1976). These behaviors appear to antedate the onset of obesity in these children. The obesity is certainly related to overeating, but in addition there is evidence that these individuals have a physiological need for fewer calories than normal children and are therefore predisposed to obesity on that basis (Crnic et al., 1980).

Morbidity from obesity-related complications is significant in adulthood (Crnic et al., 1980). Crnic et al. have published evidence that suggests that the control of the obesity through early behavior modification of eating habits is possible and seems to improve the prognosis of intellectual development as well. The mechanism for this relationship is certainly not clear at this time.

Psychosocial Dwarfism

This is not a mental retardation syndrome, but the condition is frequently associated with significant developmental delays. The behavioral symptoms associated with the syndrome of psychosocial dwarfism (deprivational dwarfism, psychosocial deprivation) raise a number of important questions regarding the interaction of physiologic and environmental factors in producing a significant behavior disorder. Psychosocial dwarfism as a recognized medical syndrome consists of reversible growth hormone deficiency causing inhibition of growth and short stature. The underlying etiology is a disturbed environment, particularly a disturbed parent–child relationship. The disorder of pituitary hormone production is reversible if the child is removed from the home. There is consequent catchup growth.

In the extreme, these children are found to be inactive, depressed, and withdrawn. Some stereotypic posturing is also described. Abnormal feeding behavior is especially characteristic, and patients may drink extraordinary amounts of fluid, gorge food, horde and hide food, and eat or drink from the garbage or toilet. Rumination is seen in these patients and may contribute at times to poor nutrition (Patton & Gardner, 1962). Endocrine studies have clearly shown a deficiency of growth hormone comparable to that seen in true hypopituitary dwarfs (Money *et al.*, 1972; Patton & Gardner, 1975), with delayed or completely absent pubertal development seen in both syndromes.

Self-injurious behaviors seen in psychosocial dwarfism have some distinctions from those seen in other syndromes. This helps to illustrate the need to consider multiple etiologies when viewing the same behavior in different patients. Like many other self-abusive patients, these children headbang, bite themselves, tear at their nailbeds, and pull out their hair (Money *et al.*, 1972). However, in some of these children there appears to be a less than normal sensitivity to pain. Money *et al.* (1972) described this phenomenon as a failure to recognize pain or pain agnosia. The self-inflicted injuries, as well as dental procedures, physical punishment, and even minor surgery do not elicit the usual crying, complaints, or other behaviors suggesting a pain awareness in some of these patients. Lack of pain awareness is recognized not only through their lack of reaction to self-induced injury but by an abnormal response to accidents. They often seem unwilling to protect themselves from injury, falling without protecting their faces with their hands, for example. This behavior is not typical of most self-abusive patients, nor is it universal among psychosocial dwarfs. It appears to be reversible as is the hypopituitarism and growth deficiency and, like the growth deficiency, can reappear if the children are returned to the original depriving home situation (Money *et al.*, 1972).

The syndrome of psychosocial dwarfism is highly relevant to those caring for the mentally retarded patient. Unfortunately, the relationships are extremely complex and unclear. Severely deprived children demonstrate intellectual and motor retardation in addition to their growth retardation that in some cases, is strikingly reversible when the children enter foster care or are placed in community living arrangements, such as group homes and even a hospital. In other cases, the reversibility is less complete, and the children are left with intellectual deficits, especially language delays (Patton & Gardner, 1975). The question arises, Is this second group of children predisposed to be mentally retarded apart from their deprivation, or are they simply permanently damaged from the prolonged deprivation? Conversely, it seems evident to clinicians working in the field of mental retardation that, for multiple psychological and social reasons, the mentally retarded child tends to be predisposed to child abuse and neglect (Sangrund, Gaines, & Green, 1974). To further complicate the picture, the relatively frequent short stature and self-abuse of mentally retarded patients, with no history of abuse or neglect, causes a significant amount of clinical overlap with the psychosocial deprivation syndrome.

The incidence of full-blown psychosocial dwarfism syndrome is not known. The number of unrecognized cases, especially among the mentally retarded, may be quite significant and might first be suspected based on the behavioral characteristics. A caveat must be issued, however. Although the possibility of psychosocial dwarfism must be considered when the behavioral and physical symptoms suggest it, great harm can be done to the parent and child when this diagnosis is falsely made. The parent of the mentally retarded child must be given the greatest benefit of the doubt; there are some children who will be withdrawn, autistic, delayed, self-abusive, and short-statured in the best, most stimulating home environment. These parents need all the support (and sympathy) that professionals can give them and not additional guilt from suggestions of deprivational dwarfism. In this population, the diagnosis is most easily made when a child is institutionalized or placed in foster care for other reasons and demonstrates a *dramatic* growth spurt together with behavior change. Outside of such a fortuitous setting, the diagnosis must be considered and investigated slowly and carefully based on growth rates, behavior symptoms, family interviews, and selected hormonal studies.

Congenital Rubella Syndrome

Congenital Rubella syndrome was recognized in 1941 by Sir Norman Gregg (Gregg, 1941). The syndrome is the result of neurologic and somatic damage to the fetus occurring when a pregnant woman contracts rubella (German measles) during the first 5 months of pregnancy. The risks and severity of damage increase the earlier in the pregnancy the infection occurs. The last major rubella epidemic in the U.S., in 1964, produced large numbers of multiply handicapped children with neurosensory deafness, congenital heart defects, cataracts, microcephaly, small stature of variable degrees, and mental retardation, usually severe. Most of the affected children, however, were not mentally retarded at all and had only one or two of the previously mentioned defects (Chess, Fernandez, & Korn, 1978). Although congenital rubella still occurs in small epidemics, the widespread use of rubella vaccine now given to children at the age of 18 months in clinics and pediatric offices has prevented epidemics of the scale seen periodically in the past.

Victims of the last major epidemic, now approaching their early 20s, are a well-studied but heterogeneous group. The brain injury is often generalized and nonspecific. Behavior disorders, particularly a behavioral symptom complex essentially identical with infantile autism, are thought to occur more often than in the general population (Chess et al., 1978).

Because the abnormalities of congenital rubella syndrome represent sequellae of neurologic inflammation and tissue damage, there is no medical treatment, and behavioral approaches are appropriate. It should be remembered that significant hearing losses in patients with few other evident abnormalities can be seen in congenital rubella syndrome and should be ruled out in any suspected congenital rubella patient.

Sanfilippo Syndrome

Sanfilippo syndrome is one of the mucopolysaccharide disorders inherited as an autosomal recessive trait. Patients with this disorder, in addition to their physical and biochemical abnormalities, are almost uniformly hyperactive and aggressive (Danks, Campbell, Cartwright, Mayne, Taft, & Wilson, 1972). Patients generally die in the second decade of life (Smith & Jones, 1982).

Klinefelter's Syndrome (XXY Syndrome)

This is a chromosomal abnormality seen in males that is associated with mild retardation or normal functioning and frequent behavior problems. Apparently there are a disporportionate number of children and adults with Klinefelters syndrome among psychiatric referrals (Smith & Jones, 1982), but a direct causal relationship is questioned (Kessler & Moos, 1973).

Fragile X Syndrome

The Fragile X syndrome (Hecht, Hecht, & Glover, 1981; Turner, Daniel, & Frost, 1980) is a chromosomal disorder known to cause moderate retardation in males. These individuals are described as having "litany speech" that is repetitive and narrative. The chromosomal defect may also be responsible for some cases of infantile autism (Fryns, Jacobs, Kleczkowska, & van den Berghe, 1984; Levitas, Hagerman, Braden, Rimland, McBogg, & Matus, 1983).

Rett's Syndrome

Rett's syndrome is a recently recognized disorder of unknown cause affecting only females (Hagsberg, Aicardi, Dias & Ramos, 1983). These patients have an arrest or loss of development in the first 2 years of life progressing to severe dementia, autism, and characteristic behaviors including loss of purposeful use of hands, often frequent hand wringing and unusual breathing patterns including hyperventilation and aerophagia.

Other Syndromes

Some other syndromes noted to have behavior problems include tuberous sclerosis, the 18 p-syndrome (Smith & Jones, 1982), Williams syndrome (Smith & Jones, 1982), XXXX syndrome (females only) (Smith & Jones, 1982), the Ring 20 chromosome abnormality (Herva, Saarinen, & Leikkonen, 1977; Jacobsen, Mikkelsen, & Rosleff, 1973) and Fetal Alcohol syndrome (Council on Scientific Affairs, AMA, 1983).

Summary

The traditional role of the medical physician in the care of the mentally retarded patient has not usually emphasized the elucidation of the complex interactions between medical disorders and behavior disorders. Our knowledge in this area is quite limited.

There are multiple possible relationships between medical disorders and behavior problems. These must be considered and investigated by the treating physician if medically treatable behavior problems are not to be overlooked. Some medical disorders, such as gastroesophageal reflux, seizures, or diabetes may produce symptoms mistaken for behavior problems. Behaviors such as pseudoseizures, psychogenic water drinking, aerophagia, or masturbation can masquerade as medical problems. Behavior problems can cause severe medical complications or interfere with the treatment of existing medical disorders.

Medical syndromes with known behavioral features represent a small minority of patients with behavior disorders but include Lesch–Nyhan disease, Cornelia de Lange syndrome, some chromosomal syndromes, phenylketonuria, Prader-Willi syndrome, and psychosocial dwarfism. Our efforts to understand the biologic and environmental mechanisms of these disorders and their behavior symptoms may lead us to better understanding of behavior disorders in other patients as well.

It is often the nonmedical professional or the parent who first raises the issue of medical factors contributing to a behavior disorder. The medical consultant must depend heavily on clinical history from the primary caretakers before any useful medical diagnostic investigation or intervention can be planned.

It is frequently counterproductive to think too rigidly about behavior problems as being *either* medical *or* psychogenic. Complex interactions are probably the rule rather than the exception; therefore, combined treatment approaches developed through cooperation between medical and behavior experts are ideal.

References

Abramowicz, M. (1984). Drugs that cause psychiatric symptoms. *The Medical Letter on Drugs and Therapeutics, 23,* 1–4.

Allen, T. (1979). Suspected esophageal foreign body—choosing appropriate management. *Journal of the American College of Emergency Physicians, 8,* 101–105.

American Academy of Pediatrics Committee on Drugs. (1984). Ethanol in liquid preparations intended for children. *Pediatrics, 73*(3), 405–407.

Ampola, M. G. (1982). *Metabolic diseases in pediatric practice.* Boston: Little, Brown.

Anderson, L., Dancis, J., & Alpert, M. (1978). Behavioral contingencies and self-mutilation in Lesch–Nyhan disease. *Journal of Consulting and Clinical Psychology, 46,* 529–536.

Arnold, H. G., & Gross, C. W. (1977). Transtympanic neurectomy: A solution to drooling problems. *Developmental Medicine and Child Neurology, 19,* 509–513.

Azrin, N. H., & Foxx, R. M. (1971). A paired method of toilet training the institutionalized retarded. *Journal of Applied Behavior Analysis, 4,* 89–99.

Azrin, N. H., Sneed, T. J., & Foxx, R. M. (1973). Dry bed: A rapid method of eliminating bedwetting (enuresis) of the retarded. *Behavior Research and Therapy, 11,* 427–434.

Baird, H. W. (1979). Convulsive disorders. In W. E. Nelson, V. C. Vaughan, R. J. McKay, & R. E. Behrman (Eds.), *Nelson Textbook of Pediatrics* (11th ed., pp. 1713–1728). Philadelphia: W. B. Saunders.

Balaschak, B. A., & Mostofsky, D. I. (1981). Seizure disorders. In E. J. Mash & L. G. Terdal (Eds.), *Behavioral Assessment of Childhood Disorders* (pp. 601–637). New York: Guilford Press.

Baumeister, A., & Klosowski, R. (1965). An attempt to group toilet train severely retarded patients. *Mental Retardation, 2,* 24–26.

Becker, J. V., Turner, S. M., & Sajwaj, T. E. (1978). Multiple behavioral effects of the use of lemon juice with ruminating toddler-age child. *Behavior Modification, 2,* 267–279.

Bellman, M. (1966). Studies on encopresis. *Acta Paediatrica Scandinavica, 170,* 1–151.

Berquist, W. E. (1982). Gastroesophageal reflux in children: A clinical review. *Pediatric Annals, 11,* 135–142.

Bray, P. F., Herbst, J. J., Johnson, D. G., Book, L. S., Ziter, F. A., & Condon, V. R. (1976). Childhood heartburn mimicking neuropsychiatric disease. *Transactions of the American Neurological Association, 101,* 129–133.

Bray, P. F., Herbst, J. J., Johnson, D. G., Book, L. S., Ziter, F. A., & Condon, V. R. (1977). Childhood gastroesophageal reflux: Neurologic and psychiatric syndromes mimicked. *Journal of the American Medical Association, 237,*1342–1345.

Brody, G. S. (1977). Control of drooling by translocation of parotid duct and extirpation of mandibular gland. *Developmental Medicine and Child Neurology, 19,* 514–517.

Brumback, R. A., Wilson, H., & Staton, R. D. (1984). Behavioral problems in children taking theophylline. *The Lancet, 1,* 958.

Bryson, Y., Sakati, N., Nyhan, W. L., & Fish, C. H. (1971). Self-mutilative behavior in the Cornelia de Lange syndrome. *American Journal of Mental Deficiency, 76,* 319–324.

Bryne, W. J., Campbell, M., Ashcraft, E., Seibert, J. J., & Euler, A. R. (1983). A diagnostic approach to vomiting in severely retarded patients. *American Journal of Diseases of Childhood, 137,* 259–262.

Bryne, W. F., Euler, A. R., Ashcraft, E., Nash, D. G., Seibert, J. J., & Golladay, E. S. (1982). Gastroesophageal reflux in the severely retarded who vomit: Criteria for the results of surgical intervention in twenty-two patients. *Surgery, 91,* 95–98.

Butterworth, T. (1971, June). Dermatologic disorders in institutionalized mental defectives. *Birth Defects: Original Article Series, VII,* 178–183.

Cadman, D., Richards, J., & Feldman, W. (1978). Gastro-esophageal reflux in severely retarded children. *Developmental Medicine and Child Neurology, 20,* 95–98.

Campbell, M. B. (1973). Neurologic manifestations of allergic disease. *Annals of Allergy, 31,* 485–498.

Carr, E. G. (1977). The motivation of self-injurious behavior: A review of some hypotheses. *Psychological Bulletin, 84,* 800–816.

Carter, C. H. (1979). *Handbook of mental retardation syndromes* (3rd ed.). Springfield: Charles C Thomas.

Chess, S., Fernandez, P., & Korn, S. (1978). Behavioral consequences of congenital rubella. *Journal of Pediatrics, 93,* 699–703.

Ciaranello, R. D., Anders, T. F., Barchas, J. D., Berger, P. A., & Cann, H. M. (1976). The use of 5-hydroxytryptophan in a child with Lesch-Nyhan syndrome. *Child Psychiatry and Human Development, 7,* 127–133.

Cohen, M. W. (1975). Enuresis. *Pediatric Clinics of North America, 22,* 545–560.

Conners, D. K., Goyette, C. H., Southwick, D. A., Lees, J. M., & Andruionis, P. A. (1976). Food additives and hyperkinesis: A controlled double-blind experiment. *Pediatrics, 58,* 154–166.

Cotton, R. T., & Richardson, M. A. (1981). The effect of submandibular duct rerouting in the treatment of sialorrhea in children. *Otolaryngology and Head and Neck Surgery, 89,* 535–541.

Council on Scientific Affairs. (1983). Fetal effects of maternal alcohol use. *Journal of the American Medical Association, 249,* 2517–2521.

Crnic, K. A., Sulzbacher, S., Snow, J., & Holm, V. A. (1980). Preventing mental retardation associated with gross obesity in the Prader-Willi syndrome. *Pediatrics, 66,* 797–789.

Crook, W. G. (1975). Food allergy—the great masquerader. *Pediatric Clinics of North America, 22*, 227–238.

Crysdale, W. S. (1980). The drooling patient: Evaluation and current surgical options. *The Laryngoscope, 90*, 775–783.

Dahlquist, L. M., Gil, K. M., Kalfus, G. R., Blount, R. L., & Boyd, M. S. (1984). Enhancing an autistic girl's cooperation with gynecologic examinations. *Clinical Pediatrics, 23*, 203.

Danks, D. M., Campbell, P. E., Cartwright, E., Mayne, V., Taft, L. I., & Wilson, R. G. (1972). The Sanfilippo syndrome: Clinical, biochemical, radiological, haematological and pathological features of nine cases. *Austrian Paediatric Journal, 8*, 174–186.

Delgado-Escueta, A. V., Mattson, R. H., King, L., Goldensohn, E. S., Spiegel, H., Madsen, J., Crandall P., Dreifuss, F., & Porter, R. J. (1981). The nature of aggression during epileptic seizures. *New England Journal of Medicine, 305*, 711–716.

Doleys, D., & Dolce, J. (1982). Toilet training and enuresis. *Pediatric Clinics of North America, 29*, 297–314.

Drew, L. R. H. (1967). Drug control of incontinence in adult mental defectives. *Medical Journal of Australia, 2*, 206–207.

Edgar, C. L., Kohler, H. F., & Hardman, S. (1975). A new method for toilet training developmentally disabled children. *Perceptual and Motor Skills, 41*, 63–69.

Egger, J., Wilson, J., Carter, C. M., Turner, M. W., & Soothill, J. F. (1983). Is migraine food allergy? *The Lancet, 2*, 865–869.

Emerson, R., D'Souza, B., Vining, E., Holden, K. P., Mellits, E., & Freeman, J. (1981). Stopping medication in children with epilepsy. *New England Journal of Medicine, 304*, 1125–1129.

Feingold, B. B. (1975). Hyperkinesis and learning disabilities linked to artificial food flavors and colors. *American Journal of Nursing, 75*, 797.

Feldman, W. (1979). Gastroesophageal reflux in retarded children. *Journal of Pediatrics, 94*, 850–851.

Firth, C. D., Johnstone, E. C., Joseph, M. H., Powell, R. J., & Watts, R. W. E. (1976). Double-blind clinical trial of 5-hydroxytryptophan in a case of Lesch-Nyhan syndrome. *Journal of Neurology, Neurosurgery and Psychiatry, 39*, 656–662.

Fischer, H. L., & Krajicek, M. J. (1974). Sexual development of the moderately retarded child: How can the pediatrician be helpful? *Clinical Pediatrics, 13*, 79–83.

Fisher, G. W., Murray, F., Walley, M. R., & Kiloh, L. G. (1963). A controlled trial of imipramine in the treatment of nocturnal enuresis in mentally subnormal patients. *American Journal of Mental Deficiency, 67*, 536–538.

Fryns, J. P., Jacobs, J., Kleczkowska, A., & van den Berghe, H. (1984). The psychological profile of the Fragile X syndrome. *Clinical Genetics, 25*, 131–134.

Furukawa, C. T., Shapiro, G. G., DuHamel, T., Weimer, L., Pierson, W. E., & Bierman, C. W. (1984). Learning and behaviour problems associated with theophylline therapy (Letters to the editor). *The Lancet, 1*, 621.

Gastaut, H. (1970). Clinical and electroencephalographical classification of epileptic seizures. *Epilepsia, 11*, 102–113.

Gauderer, M. W. L., Halpin, T. C., & Izant, R. J. (1981). Pathologic childhood aerophagia: A recognizable clinical entity. *Journal of Pediatric Surgery, 16*, 301–305.

Gayton, W. F. (1975). Management problems of mentally retarded children and their families. *Pediatric Clinics of North America, 22*, 562–570.

Gellis, S. (1983). Food and human behavior. *Pediatric Notes, 7*, 1.

Gellis, S., & Feingold, M. (1968). *Atlas of Mental retardation syndromes: Visual diagnosis of facies and physical findings.* Washington, DC: U.S. Government Printing Office.

Geschwind, N., Shader, R. I., Bear, D., North, B., Levin, K., & Chetham, D. (1980). Behavioral changes with temporal lobe epilepsy: Assessment and treatment. *Journal of Clinical Psychiatry, 41,* 89–95.

Giles, D. K., & Wolf, M. M. (1966). Toilet training institutionalized severe retardates: An application of operant behavior modification techniques. *American Journal of Mental Deficiency, 70,* 766–767.

Golden, G. S. (1983). Tics in childhood. *Pediatric Clinics, 12,* 821–824.

Gregg, N. (1941). Congenital cataract following German measles in the mother. *Transcript of the Ophthalmologic Society of Australia, 3,* 35.

Haberfellner, H., & Rossiwall, B. (1977). Treatment of oral sensorimotor disorders in cerebralpalsied children: Preliminary report. *Developmental Medicine and Child Neurology, 19,* 350–352.

Hagberg, B., Aicardi, J., Dias, K. & Ramos, O. (1983). A progressive syndrome of autism, dementia, ataxia, and loss of purposeful hand use in girls: Rett's syndrome: Report of 35 cases. *Annals of Neurology, 14,* 471–479.

Hall, B. D., & Smith, D. W. (1972). Prader-Willi syndrome. *The Journal of Pediatrics, 81,* 286–293.

Hall, R. C., Popkin, M. K., Devaul, R. A., Faillace, L. A., & Stickney, S. K. (1978). Physical illness presenting as psychiatric disease. *Archives of General Psychiatry 35(11),* 1315–1320.

Harnsberger, J. K., Corey, J. J., Johnson, D. G., & Herbst, J. J. (1983). Long-term follow-up of surgery for gastroesophageal reflux in infants and children. *Journal of Pediatrics, 102,* 505–508.

Harris, M. M., & Dignam, P. F. (1980). A nonsurgical method of reducing drooling in cerebralpalsied children. *Developmental Medicine in Child Neurology, 22,* 293–299.

Hecht, F., Hecht, B. K., & Glover, T. W. (1981). Fragile sites and X-linked retardation. *Hospital Practice, 16,* 81–88.

Herskowitz, J., & Rosman, N. P. (1982). *Pediatrics, neurology and psychiatry—Common ground.* New York: Macmillan.

Herva, R., Saarinen, I., & Leikkonen, L. (1977). The r(20) syndrome. *Journal of Medical Genetics, 14,* 281–283.

Holm, V. A., & Pipes, P. L. (1976). Food and children with Prader-Willi syndrome. *American Journal of Diseases of Childhood, 130,* 1063–1067.

Holmes, G. L., Sackellares, J. C., & McKiernan, J., Ragland, M., & Dreifuss, F. E. (1980). Evaluation of childhood pseudoseizures using EEG telemetry and video tape monitoring. *The Journal of Pediatrics, 97,* 554–558.

Horwitz, A. L. (1979). The mucopolysaccharidoses: Clinical and biochemical correlations. *American Journal of Mental Deficiency, 84,* 113–123.

Hsia, D. Y.-Y., Knox, W. E., Quinn, K. V., & Paine, R. S. (1958). A one year, controlled study of the effect of low-phenylalanine diet on phenylketonuria. *Pediatrics, 21,* 178–179.

Hughes, E. C., Oettinger, L., Johnson, F., & Gottschalk, G. H. (1979). Case report: A chemically defined diet in diagnosis and management of food sensitivity in minimal brain dysfunction. *Annals of Allergy, 42,* 174–176.

Hughes, E. C., Weinstein, R. C., Gott, P. S., Binggeli, R., & Whitaker, K. L. (1982). Food sensitivity in attention deficit disorder with hyperactivity (ADD/HA): A procedure for differential diagnosis. *Annals of Allergy, 49,* 276–279.

Hughes, J. R. (1980). Epilepsy: A medical overview. In B. P. Hermann (Ed.), *A multidisciplinary handbook of epilepsy* (pp. 3–35). Springfield: Charles C Thomas.

Jacobsen, P., Mikkelsen, M., & Rosleff, F. (1973). A ring chromosome, diagnosed by quinacrine flourescence as no. 9, in a mentally retarded girl. *Clinical Genetics, 4,* 434–441.

James, A. H., & Allen-Mersh, T. G. (1982). Recognition and management of patients who repeatedly swallow foreign bodies. *Journal of Royal Society of Medicine, 75,* 107–110.

Jancar, J. (1971). Prader-Willi syndrome (hypotonia, obesity, hypogonadism, growth and mental retardation). *Journal of Mental Deficiency Research, 15,* 20–29.

Jay, J. L., Grant, S., & Murray, S. B. (1982). Keratoconjuctivitis artefacta. *British Journal of Ophthalmology, 66,* 781–785.

Juul, J., & Dupont, A. (1967). Prader-Willi syndrome. *Journal of Mental Deficiency Research, 11,* 12–22.

Kelly, N. K., & Menolascino, F. J. (1976). Physician's awareness and attitudes toward the retarded. Part II. *Nebraska Medical Journal, 61,* 4–6.

Kessler, S., & Moos, R. H. (1973). Behavioral manifestations of chromosomal abnormalities. *Hospital Practice, 8,* 131–137.

Kinsbourne, M., & Oxon, D. M. (1964). Hiatus hernia with contortion of the neck. *The Lancet, 1,* 1058–1061.

Kleinman, D. S. (1964). Phenylketonuria: A review of some deficits in our information. *Pediatrics, 33,* 123–124.

Kohlenberg, R. J. (1970). The punishment of persistent vomiting: A case study. *Journal of Applied Behavior Analysis, 3,* 241–245.

Kolata, G. (1982). Food affects human behavior. *Science, 218,* 1209–1210.

Kulig, K., Rumack, C. M., Rumak, B. H., & Durry, J. P. (1983). Disk battery ingestion: Elevated urine mercury levels and enema removal of battery fragments. *Journal of the American Medical Association, 18,* 2505–2506.

Kumar, B. B. (1978). Gastroesophageal reflux in mentally retarded adults. *Journal of the American Medical Association, 240,* 346.

Ledbetter, D. H., Riccardi, V. M., Airhart, S. D., Strobel, R. J., Keenan, B. S., & Crawford, J. D. (1981). Deletions of chromosome 15 as a cause of the Prader-Willi syndrome. *Medical Intelligence, 304,* 325–329.

Lemke, H. (1974). Self-abusive behavior in the mentally retarded. *The American Journal of Occupational Therapy, 28,* 94–98.

Lesch, M., & Nyhan, W. L. (1964). A familial disorder of uric acid metabolism and central nervous system function. *American Journal of Medicine, 36,* 561.

Levine, M. (1975). Children with encopresis: A descriptive analysis. *Pediatrics, 56,* 412–416.

Levine, M. D. (1982). Encopresis: Its potentiation, evaluation and alleviation. *Pediatric Clinics of North America, 29,* 2.

Levitas, A., Hagerman, R., Braden, M., Rimland, B., McBogg, P., & Matus, I. (1983). Autism and the Fragile X syndrome. *Journal of Developmental and Behavioral Pediatrics, 4*(3), 151.

Lindsay, J., Ounsted, C., & Richards, P. (1979a). Long-term outcome in children with temporal lobe seizures. I: Social outcome and childhood factors. *Developmental Medicine and Child Neurology, 21,* 258–298.

Lindsay, J., Ounsted, C., & Richards P. (1979b). Long-term outcome in children with temporal lobe seizures. II: Marriage, parenthood and sexual indifference. *Developmental Medicine and Child Neurology, 21,* 433–440.

Lindsay, J., Ounsted, C., & Richards, P. (1979c). Long-term outcome in children with temporal lobe seizures. III: Psychiatric aspects in childhood and adult life. *Developmental Medicine and Child Neurology, 21,* 630–636.

Litovitz, T. L. (1983). Button battery ingestions. A review of 56 cases. *Journal of the American Medical Association, 249,* 2495–2500.

Livingston, S., & Pauli, L. L. (1979). Diagnosis of epilepsy. *Pediatric Annals, 8,* 40–76.

Livingston, S., Pruce, I., Pauli, L., & Livingston, H. (1979). Managing side effects of antiepileptic drugs. *Pediatric Annals,* 261/97–266/102.

Luckey, R. E., Watson, C. M., & Musick, J. K. (1968). Aversive conditioning as a means of inhibiting vomiting and rumination. *American Journal of Mental Deficiency, 73,* 139–142.

MacWilliams, P., Lee, J. M., & Moojin, R. O. (1974). Gnaw warts. *Southern Medical Journal, 67,* 643–644.

Mahoney, K., Van Wagenen, R. K., & Meyerson, L. (1971). Toilet training of normal and retarded children. *Journal of Applied Behavior Analysis, 4,* 173–181.

Mattes, J. A., & Gittelman, R. (1981). Effects of artificial food colorings in children with hyperactive symptoms. *Archives of General Psychiatry, 38,* 714.

McCarty, E. P., & Frick, O. L. (1983). Food sensitivity: Keys to diagnosis, *The Journal of Pediatrics, 102,* 645–652.

Menolascino, F. J. (1965). Psychiatric aspects of mongolism. *American Association on Mental Deficiency, 70,* 653.

Miniszek, N. A. (1983). Development of Alzheimer disease in Down's syndrome individuals. *American Journal of Mental Deficiency, 87,* 377.

Mizuno, T., & Yugari, R. (1974, April). Self-mutilation in Lesch-Nyhan syndrome (Letter to the editor). *The Lancet,* 761.

Money, J., Wolff, G., & Annecillo, C. (1972). Pain agnosia and self-injury in the syndrome of reversible somatotropin deficiency (psychosocial dwarfism). *Journal of Autism and Childhood Schizophrenia, 2,* 127–139.

Morgan, R. F., Hansen, F. C., Wells, J. H., & Hoopes, J. E. (1981, June). The treatment of drooling in the child with cerebral palsy. *MD State Medical Journal,* pp. 79–80.

Morselli, P., Pippinger, C., & Penry, J. (1983). *Antiepiletic drug therapy in pediatrics.* New York: Raven Press.

Mostofsky, D. I., & Balaschak, B. A. (1977). Psychobiological control of seizures. *Psychological Bulletin, 84,* 723–750.

Noel, L. P., & Clarke, W. N. (1982). Self-inflicted ocular injuries in children. *American Journal of Ophthalmology, 94,* 630–633.

Nyhan, W. L. (1976). Behavior in the Lesch-Nyhan syndrome. *Journal of Autism and Childhood Schizophrenia, 6,* 235–252.

Nyhan, W. L., Johnson, H. G., Kaufman, K. A., & Jones, K. L. (1980). Serotonergic approaches to the modification of behavior in the Lesch-Nyhan syndrome. *Applied Research in Mental Retardation, 1,* 25–40.

Ounsted, C. (1969). Aggression and epilepsy rage in children with temporal lobe epilepsy. *Journal of Psychosomatic Research, 13,* 327–342.

Paine, R. S. (1957). The variability in manifestations of untreated patients with phenylketonuria (phenylpyruvic aciduria). *Pediatrics, 20,* 290–301.

Parraga, H. C., Simonds, J. F., & Butterfield, P.T. (1982). Iatrogenic behavioral and psychiatric symptoms in children with partial complex seizures. *Developmental and Behavioral Pediatrics, 3,* 25–28.

Patton, R. G., & Gardner, L. I. (1962). Influence of family environment on growth: The syndrome of "maternal deprivation." *Pediatrics, 30,* 957.

Patton, R. G., & Gardner, L. I. (1975). Deprivation dwarfism (psychosocial deprivation): Disordered family environment as cause of so-called idiopathic hypopituitarism. In L. I. Gardner (Ed.), *Endocrine and genetic diseases of childhood and adolescence* (2nd ed., pp. 85–98) Philadelphia: W. B. Saunders.

Pearson, P. H. (1968). The physician's role in diagnosis and management of the mentally retarded. *Pediatric Clinics of North America, 15,* 835–859.

Philips, R., & Williams, N. (1975). Psychopathology and mental retardation: A study of

100 mentally retarded children: I. Psychopathology. *American Journal of Psychiatry, 132*, 1265–1271.

Pritchard, P. B., Lombroso, C. T., & McIntyre, M. (1980). Psychological complications of temporal lobe epilepsy. *Neurology, 30*, 227–232.

Rapoport, J. L., & Ferguson, H. B. (1981). Biological validation of the hyperkinetic syndrome. *Developmental Medicine and Child Neurology, 23*, 667–682.

Rapoport, J. L., & Mikkelsen, E. J. (1978). Antidepressants. In J. S. Werry (Ed.), *Pediatric Psychopharmacology: The use of behavior modifying drugs in children* (pp. 208–233). New York: Brunner/Mazel.

Rapp, D. (1980). Drool Control: Long-term follow-up. *Developmental Medicine and Child Neurology, 22*, 448–453.

Rapp, D. J. (1979). Food allergy treatment for hyperkinesis. *Journal of Learning Disabilities, 12*, 42–50.

Rast, J., Johnston, J. M., Drum, C., & Conrin, J. (1981). The relation of food quantity to rumination behavior. *Journal of Applied Behavior Analysis, 14*, 121–130.

Rentfrow, R. K., & Rentfrow, D. K. (1969). Studies related to toilet training of the mentally retarded. *American Journal of Occupational Therapy, 23*, 425–426.

Richardson, S. A., Koller, H., Katz, M., & McLaren, J. (1981). A functional classification of seizures and its distribution in a mentally retarded population. *American Journal of Mental Deficiency, 85*, 457–466.

Rubin, A. L., & Rubin, R. L. (1980). The effects of physician counseling technique on parent reactions to mental retardation diagnosis. *Child Psychiatry and Human Development, 10*, 213–229.

Rumack, B. H., & Rumack, C. M. (1983). Disk battery ingestion. *Journal of the American Medical Association, 249*, 2509–2511.

Sandgrund, A., Gaines, R. W., & Green, A. H. (1974). *American Journal of Mental Deficiency, 79*, 327–330.

Sankey, R. J., Nunn, A. J., & Sills, J. A. (1984). Visual hallucinations in children receiving decongestants. *British Medical Journal, 288*, 1369.

Schmidt, D., & Seldon, L. (1982). *Adverse effects of antiepileptic drugs* (pp. 117, 153). New York: Raven Press.

Schor, D. P. (1983). PKU and temperament: Rating children three through seven years old in PKU families. *Child Development, 22*(12), 807–811.

Shukla, G. D., Srivastava, O. N., Katiyar, B. C., Joshi, V., & Mohan, P. K. (1979). Psychiatric manifestations in temporal lobe epilepsy: A controlled study. *British Journal of Psychiatry, 135*, 411–417.

Silverstein, F. S., Parrish, M. A., & Johnston, M. V. (1982). Adverse behavioral reactions in children treated with carbamazepine (Tegretol). *The Journal of Pediatrics, 101*, 785–787.

Simeon, J., O'Malley, M., Tryphonas, H., Graham, D., Mastronardi, M., Simeon, S., & Griffin, J. (1979). Cromolyn DSG effects in hyperkinetic and psychotic children with allergies. *Annals of Allergy, 42*, 343–347.

Smith, D. W., & Jones, K. L. (1982). *Recognizable patterns of human malformation—Genetic, embryonic and clinical aspects*. Philadelphia: W. B. Saunders.

Snyder, C. H. (1972). Conditions that simulate epilepsy in children. *Clinical Pediatrics, 11*, 487–491.

Sondheimer, J. M., & Morris, B. A. (1979). Gastroesophageal reflux among severely retarded children. *Journal of Pediatrics, 94*, 710–714.

Spencer, D. A. (1968, September). Prader-Willi syndrome (Letter to the editor). *The Lancet*, 571.

Springer, A., & Steele, M. W. (1980). Effects of physicians' early parental counseling on rearing of Down syndrome children. *American Journal of Mental Deficiency, 85*, 1–5.

Stare, F. J., Whelan, E. M., & Sheridan, M. (1980). Diet and hyperactivity: Is there a relationship? *Pediatrics, 66,* 521–525.

Stores, G. (1978). Antiepileptics (anticonvulsants). In J. S. Werry (Ed.), *Pediatric psychopharmacology: The use of behavior modifying drugs in children* (pp. 274–315). New York: Brunner/Mazel.

Stoudemire, A., Nelson, A., & Houpt, J. L. (1983). Interictal schizophrenia-like psychoses in temporal lobe epilepsy. *Psychosomatics, 24,* 331–339.

Sutherland, B. S., Berry, H. K., & Shirkey, H. C. (1960). A syndrome of phenylketonuria with normal intelligence and behavior disturbances. *The Journal of Pediatrics, 57,* 521–525.

Taub, S. J. (1975). Allergies may lead to minimal brain dysfunction in children. *The Eye, Ear, Nose and Throat Monthly, 54,* 72–73.

Taylor, E. (1979). Annotation—Food additives, allergy and hyperkinesis. *Journal of Child Psychology and Psychiatry, 20,* 357–363.

Thorley, G. (1984). Pilot study to assess behavioural and cognitive effects of artificial food colours in a group of retarded children. *Developmental Medicine & Child Neurology, 26,* 56–61.

Tryphonas, H., & Trites, R. (1979). Food allergy in children with hyperactivity, learning disabilities and/or minimal brain dysfunction. *Annals of Allergy, 42,* 22–27.

Turner, G., Daniel, A., & Frost, M. (1980). X-linked mental retardation, macro-orchidism, and X q 27 fragile site. *Journal of Pediatrics, 96,* 837–841.

Watkins, J. T. (1972). Treatment of chronic vomiting and extreme emaciation by an aversive stimulus: Case study. *Psychological Reports, 31,* 803–805.

Waxman, S. G., & Geschwind, N. (1975). The interictal behavior syndrome of temporal lobe epilepsy. *Archives of General Psychiatry, 32,* 1580–1586.

Weiss, J. M., & Kaufman, H. S. (1971). A subtle organic component in some cases of mental illness: A preliminary report of cases. *Archives of General Psychiatry, 25,* 74–78.

White, S. T., Loda, F. A., Ingram, D. L., & Pearson, A. (1983). Sexually transmitted diseases in sexually abused children. *Pediatrics, 72(1),* 16–21.

Wilkie, T. F., & Brody, G. S. (1977). The surgical treatment of drooling: A ten-year review. *Plastic and Reconstructive Surgery, 6,* 791–798.

Wilkinson, J. D., Dudgeon, D. L., & Sondheimer, J. M. (1981). A comparison of medical and surgical treatment of gastroesophageal reflux in severely retarded children. *The Journal of Pediatrics, 99,* 202–205.

Wilson, G. N., Heiber, V. C., & Schmickel, R. D. (1978). The association of chromosome 3 duplication and the Cornelia de Lange syndrome. *The Journal of Pediatrics, 93,* 783–788.

Wisniewski, K., Howe, J., Williams, D. G., & Wisniewski, H. M. (1978). Precocious aging and dementia in patients with Down's syndrome. *Biological Psychiatry, 13,* 619–627.

Wright, M. M. (1965). Loving care alleviates rumination in mentally retarded child. *Hospital Topics, 43,* 97–107.

Wright, M., & Menolascino, F. J. (1966). Nurturant nursing of mentally retarded ruminators. *American Journal of Mental Deficiency, 71,* 451–459.

Wright, M., & Menolascino, F. J. (1971). Nurturant nursing of mentally retarded ruminators. In F. J. Menolascino (Ed.), *Psychiatric aspects of the diagnosis and treatment of mental retardation* (pp. 228–240). Seattle: Special Child Publications.

Wright, S. W., & Tarjan, G. (1957). Phenylketonuria. *AMA Journal of Diseases of Children, 93,* 405–419.

Zuckerberg, H. D., & Snow, G. R. (1968). What do parents expect from the physician? *Pediatric Clinics of North America, 15,* 861–871.

7

Counseling and Psychotherapy

Introduction

A psychodynamic approach to the treatment of behavior disorders in
the mentally retarded population has had to justify itself over several
decades. The history of this topic is replete with claims and counter-
claims. Some authors (e.g., Clark, 1933), considering mental retardation
as an example of the regression to the fetal stage, view clients as potentially capable of responding to psychoanalytic therapy. Others (e.g.,
Rogers, 1942) consider counseling only effective for individuals of average or superior intelligence. These are extreme views, however, and
over the past few years a consensus appears to be emerging. The essence
of this viewpoint is that, although psychodynamic principles can be
applied successfully to an individual with virtually any IQ, the applicability of a traditional psychotherapeutic approach is limited by a number of factors. These factors include not only the severity of the mental
retardation but also the nature and quality of the severe behavior disorder that the individual may be exhibiting. The second point leads to
the necessity of understanding not only psychodynamic factors but also
neurophysiological, neurochemical, and sociocultural vectors that
underlie the behavior disorder of the mentally retarded individual. A
comprehensive diagnostic formulation of the individual under consideration is, therefore, predicated. The comprehensive management of the
severely disordered mentally retarded individual will require a com-
posite of approaches by individuals from many disciplines, all working
together as a team. Counselors or psychotherapists working within the
framework of psychodynamic principles will need to understand the
theoretical bases of their co-workers and integrate their approaches with

EDWARD J. NUFFIELD • Department of Psychiatry, Western Psychiatric Institute and Clinic,
and University of Pittsburgh School of Medicine, Pittsburgh, Pennsylvania 15213.

those of others in order to avoid dissonance among the team members and confusion in the structuring of a comprehensive treatment plan.

Definitions of Counseling and Psychotherapy

Although counseling and psychotherapy are obviously two separate terms, an examination of the content of their definitions indicates much overlap. Preference for one term or another relates more to the institutional basis of the agent (i.e., the counselor or psychotherapist), rather than to the actual operation. It is apparent that counselors are drawn largely from the nonmedical section of the helping professions, whereas psychotherapists are largely, though not entirely, drawn from the medical part of that profession. Clinical psychologists, however, are as likely to be psychotherapists as counselors. To complicate matters further, Hinsie and Campbell (1970) define counseling as a type of psychotherapy of the supportive or reeducative variety, thereby deposing counseling to a subcategory of psychotherapy. Blurring the distinction further, Snyder (1947) also speaks of psychotherapeutic counseling, which he defines as

> a face-to-face relationship in which a psychologically trained individual is consciously attempting by verbal means to assist another person to modify emotional attitudes that are socially maladjustive and in which the subject is relatively aware of the personality organization through which he going. (p. 298)

There has been a general notion abroad (e.g., Western Europe) that psychotherapy, as compared to counseling, cuts more deeply and may go on for a longer period of time, but no hard and fast distinction between the two can be drawn along those two parameters.

Counseling is sometimes seen to be overlapping with what can be called *guidance*. Trotzer (1977), speaking in the context of groups, describes group guidance, group counseling, and group psychotherapy as existing in a continuum. Nevertheless, the distinction between group guidance and group counseling is much sharper than that between group counseling and group psychotherapy. In the case of group guidance, one is considering an essentially didactic process where the relationship between the provider of guidance and the recipient is of little consequence. Thus, in schools, group guidance is used to tell the students what the adults think that the youngsters should know about themselves. Guidance, as a form of intervention, deals with individuals who are not only not sick in a clinical sense but who have not manifested any problems either of an intrapersonal or interpersonal kind. On the other hand, counseling

deals with individuals who are in themselve not considered clinically ill
but who have already begun to experience certain problems that interfere
with their lives. The distinction between having problems and being
clinically ill is not a very easy one to maintain. Clearly, it depends on
the context in which the difficulty occurs rather than the severity of the
issue. As Trotzer (1977) points out, individuals who are in psychotherapy
are considered not normal in some respects (i.e., they are sick; they are
emotionally disturbed; they have deep neurotic conflicts or engage in
some deviant behavior).

A number of general definitions of psychotherapy confine the subject to individual psychotherapy (Close, 1966) or else exclude nonverbal
methods (Shoben, 1953). Others (English & English, 1958) tend to be
overinclusive, allowing for any method or technique that is psychological
(i.e., does not involve physical methods) as qualifying for the designation of psychotherapy. Other authors have attempted to apply definitions of psychotherapy to the mentally retarded population. Cowen
(1955) specifies two essential ingredients: (a) an individual who is seeking help; and (b) the establishment of a relationship between the therapist and the client. Cowen concluded that "the essence of therapy is
the response of the client to another person" (p. 521). Certain qualities
in the counselor or therapist become particularly important when one
considers the reactions to this specific population. Warmth, sensitivity,
understanding, empathy, and spontaneity are mentioned by a number
of writers (Cowen, 1955; Rogers, 1951, 1961; Trotzer, 1977; Truax &
Mitchell, 1971).

A need to include nonverbal techniques in any definition of psychotherapy with the mentally retarded has been felt by Bialer (1967). He
defines psychotherapy as a systematic utilization of psychological techniques without confining these techniques to verbal ones. He also stresses
the close interpersonal relationship between the therapist and the clients
of this method. Szymanski (1980) provides a comprehensive and systematic definition as follows:

> Psychotherapy is a treatment procedure performed by a trained mental health
> professional through the application of psychologically based verbal and
> nonverbal means within the context of a relationship with the patient or
> client and with definite goals of improving the patient's coping abilities and/
> or ameliorating psychopathological symptoms. (p. 132)

This definition would also serve as a definition of counseling if one
substituted problems of daily living for psychopathological symptoms.
By distinguishing the individual's status as either a client or a patient,
one also tends to define the process as either counseling or psychotherapy. The question of the subject's insight does not seem to be a very

useful distinguishing mark between the two processes. Both clients and patients are usually aware that they have either problems or symptoms but have little idea of the source and origin of these, and this is the main reason why they seek help. There seems to be little usefulness in focusing on the unconscious fantasies of mentally retarded individuals although, no doubt, they do exist within this population. Any of the varieties of traditional psychotherapy with the general population (i.e., the whole spectrum ranging from insight therapy via relation therapy to supportive therapy) has some place with the mentally retarded. Nevertheless, the major emphasis will be toward the supportive end of that spectrum.

The author's preference is for the following definition:

> *Psychotherapy is the formalized exchange between one or more therapists and one or more patients or clients for the purpose of attaining a defined clinical goal. It is an event that can be described in terms of structure, process, and content.*

The formalized nature of the exchange excludes random or casual contact between the therapist and patient and specifies institutional sanction for the procedure. A certain therapeutic contract between the parties involved is also implied by this definition. There is insistence on some plan to the exercise and an indication that a goal lies at the endpoint, the goal having something to do with the amelioration of a client's or patient's position. An agreed-upon framework of place and time within which psychotherapy takes place give meaning to the term *structure*. Process and content of psychotherapy or counseling can be clearly separated and will be described as such later on. This definition is designed to encompass all the essential ingredients of counseling and psychotherapy.

Context of Counseling and Psychotherapy

A comprehensive description of the various contexts of counseling and psychotherapy would involve a historical review of the various facilities within which the mentally retarded population has found itself over the decades and the centuries (Kanner, 1964). A brief history of psychotherapy for the mentally retarded appears elsewhere (Nuffield, 1983). It suffices to say that formal counseling or psychotherapy for the mentally retarded can only be considered when these treatment methods were invented by the modern mental health and child guidance movements. During the second quarter of the 20th century, the practice of psychoanalytic therapy became prominent, and this approach also spread to the treatment of mentally retarded individuals, especially children, nearly all of whom were found in institutional settings (Ackerman & Menninger, 1936; Chidester, 1934; Chidester & Menninger, 1936).

The contexts within which the mentally retarded individual exists can be dichotomized into community and institutional settings. The latter vary considerably in terms of their being closed or relatively open in relation to the outside community. A state-run hospital or school is generally seen as a closed society clearly demarcated from the surrounding community. On the other hand, there are group homes of various sizes that are so much a part of general society that they are considered community-living arrangements. Nevertheless, the client or patient resides in a facility that provides its own discrete social network. If the residential facility is a large one, the individual psychological environment will be constituted by some part or section within which the patient is embedded. Such a division may be constructed specifically in order to enhance the success of a psychotherapeutic or counseling program.

Thus, Fine and Dawson (1965) described a separate psychiatric program in a state hospital. Here a part of the total institutional population was separated out in order to create a climate particularly favorable for progress in psychotherapy. Balthazar and Stevens (1975) have also pointed out that some institutions have attempted to create a therapeutic milieu in at least part of their total area. Traditionally, however, large residential facilities have been considered as providing an unsatisfactory climate for counseling and psychotherapy (Wiest, 1955). With the expectations that deinstitutionalization and the breaking up of large clusters of mentally retarded individuals in state institutions will continue, a consideration of the effect of such milieus on the process of counseling and psychotherapy becomes less and less important. On the other hand, the varieties and complexities of community settings are likely to increase. Community-living arrangements are of varying sizes and quality and can be classified as being either familylike or not familylike. Naturally, this distinction is not a hard and fast one. It is easy to see how a configuration of 2 house parents living with 3 mentally retarded clients can mimic a nuclear family. Larger group homes, however, with perhaps 8 or 10 clients and a larger number of staff can resemble a more extended family configuration. Additionally, the mentally retarded individual in such a setting often has members of his or her natural family maintaining contact with him or her. Depending on the background of past experiences with such family members, they may be viewed as either being objects of primary attachment or else uncle, aunt, or cousin surrogates. The psychological matrix within which such an individual operates is, indeed, a very complex one.

The corresponding contextual consideration relates to the counselor or therapist who may be connected in various ways to the facility or the context within which the mentally retarded individual is living. If client or patient lives with the natural family and the counselor or therapist is a freestanding agent, then the relationship is an almost completely independent one. At the other extreme, the therapist or counselor may be employed by the agency that takes complete responsibility for the mentally retarded person. In that case, clinical and administrative vectors may intersect and interfere with each other. This issue has been described in detail in state institutions. Thus, Thorne (1948), in describing his work at the Brandon State School (VT), considered that the administrative position the therapist held enhanced his therapeutic effectiveness. Such a happy convergence may not always be in effect, and most clinicians seek to divorce themselves for administrative responsibilities vis-à-vis those clients or patients whom they actively treating. Small community-based residential facilities are likely to call in counselors or therapists from the outside, just as they use outside consultants for establishing behavior modification regimes. The "outside" therapist can feel relatively unhampered in setting up treatment objectives. On the other hand, the average-sized mental retardation service, which is part of the community mental health center, will have difficulty in having separate individuals carry out case management and counseling activities. If these factors are carried out by separate individuals, these two are likely to be still connected to each other because of a common employer. A counselor who is a freestanding agent such as a private practitioner will have a contract with the caretaking agency for carrying out counseling, but more usually the counselor will be part of an organization that is intimately connected with the care of the mentally retarded individual. The therapist will, therefore, be an "insider."

The structural aspects of the counselor–client or psychotherapist–patient relationship are important in that they influence the primary attitude with which the carrying out of counseling or therapy is approached. These basic attitudes are what are sometimes carelessly called *countertransference issues*. More accurately, however, what one is considering is the biased and prejudicial ideas that the counselor or therapist brings along before actually approaching the client or patient. Distorted viewpoints may lead the counselor or therapist into different directions: unrealistic enthusiasm, a messianic complex, the setting of excessively high goals; or cynicism, nihilism, pessimism, and inadequate investment in the process of therapy. Historically, it is the latter attitudes that have been considered prevalent among professionals dealing with the mentally retarded (Walker, 1977). Apart from the individual counselor or therapist's attitudes and prejudices, however, different settings also tend to stimulate or dampen enthusiasm for counseling or therapy of mentally retarded individuals or groups of such.

Goals and Objectives of Counseling and Psychotherapy

In classifying the therapeutic goals for a given individual, these have usually been dichotomized as short-term goals versus long-term goals. When considering the whole universe of the treated population, however, it is more useful to speak of general goals, as against specific goals, that apply to some sections of that population only.

The general goals of counseling and psychotherapy for the mentally retarded population can be described simply as the achievement of a state in the treated individual whereby he or she can function optimally, taking into account the basic limitations that exceptional cognitive development imposes on them. Naturally, these limitations can be viewed differently depending on one's viewpoint as regards the basic nature of mental retardation, both in an individual and in the population as a whole. The majority of experts will agree presently that there are genetic and biochemical determinants that set a limit to the individual's performance in the intellectual sphere and that this will probably also set a ceiling to emotional and social functioning, because intellect, affect, and social performance are intimately interwoven. Although this overall objective fits the general population, one has to be much more particular when it comes to specific individuals in outlining both the endpoint or objective of a given treatment program, as well as noting certain intermediate steps that may have to be undertaken. There are some intermediate points on the way, the arrival at which constitutes the attaining of a short-term or intermediate goal.

The practical outcome of counseling or psychotherapy is, of course, a situation whereby such treatment will no longer be required. What must be the client's or patient's state for this conclusion to be reached in a convincing manner? At this point, we assume that the clients or patients have had some difficulties, problems, or symptoms that inhibited their progress along developmental lines. If the situation is conceptualized in terms of problems or difficulties, then the answer lies in the solution of those problems. If it is conceptualized in terms of symptoms, then symptom removal is the goal as far as that individual is concerned.

Irrespective of whether a given manifestation is designated as a problem or as a symptom, it may take one of three forms. It can either be appreciated by the subject alone, or it can be noted by his or her close associates, or both. To complicate matters further, the intensity with which the problem or symptom is felt by either party can vary along a continuum. Furthermore, different aspects of the problem may be focused upon by the various parties. Thus, clients or patients may feel that their closest relatives are rejecting them and that they are therefore unhappy. Family members, however, may feel that the problem resides in the mentally retarded persons' unsavory and repulsive personal habits. Obviously those two aspects are related to each other. The resolution of interpersonal conflicts is often a major goal of counseling or psychotherapy, and it may be approached through individual treatment modalities as well as through conjoint methods. This, of course, also applies to the nonretarded population who have similar problems or symptoms.

There are some problems and issues that, although they are not confined to the mentally retarded population, tend to be more prevalent among them than in the rest of society. These are as follows: (a) a particular feeling of suspiciousness toward outsiders; (b) a lack of self-confidence and feeling of self-worth; (c) an inclination to avoid responsibility for one's actions; and (d) general clumsiness in interpersonal relationships, not only with nonretarded individuals, but also within their own peer group. The fact that a considerable number of the adult mentally retarded presently seen in the community have spent significant periods of time in institutions gives them a common background and tends to bias those professionals who make decisions about counseling or psychotherapy in the direction of recommending or actually employing group methods. Irrespective of the structure of methods employed, however, one can see a certain homogeneity in the problems or symptoms that mentally retarded individuals present when being considered for some psychological intervention. Another problem area which leads to specific goal setting is that of impulse control. This tends to be stressed particularly with mentally retarded children (e.g., Leland & Smith, 1965). There is a trend in the direction of emphasizing the more superficial aspects of the mentally retarded individual's social functioning. This is described by Balthazer and Stevens (1975, p. 6) as "attaining an improvement in personality and adaptive behavior so that when the opportunity arises for acceptance and approval by others the retarded individual gains increased feelings of worth and satisfaction."

This emphasis is predicated on the supposition that the mentally retarded person has somewhat reduced capacity for inquiry and self-reflection. Some authors (e.g., Jakab, 1970) do place some emphasis on

the affective side of the patient or client. Thus, Jakab stressed the importance of the accumulation of positive affective experiences such as love,
gratification, and acceptance. Szymanski (1980) implied that the attainment of some insight is not impossible in mentally retarded individuals.
Patients can make a better inventory of their strengths and limitations
and therefore gain a more realistic expectation of what they are capable
of. Szymanski also mentioned conflict resolution particularly in the areas
of dependency and guilt. Better appreciation of the mentally retarded
client's emotions is also seen as one of the goals. Obviously the lower
functioning intellectually the mentally retarded person is, the more difficult and the less realistic it will be to expect attainment of such goals.

A summary of the experience of counselors and psychotherapists
in terms of the goals and objectives that they set goes as follows: (a) getting
the client or patient to a position where he or she is finding better
acceptance by the people he or she relates with; (b) helping him or her
to act more independently and more maturely; and (c) obtaining for him
or her a feeling of greater self-worth. The first two are objective phenomena; the third is a subjective one. Obviously those three factors are
closely interrelated, and progress toward one of these goals is likely to
carry progress toward the other two. There is, however, a tendency to
focus on the external or objective aspects of the individuals' functioning
and to concentrate efforts in those areas.

Description of Psychotherapy and Counseling with Children

It was recognized quite early in the history of psychotherapy that
a psychotherapeutic approach to disturbed children involves the medium
of play in the majority of cases. Some older latency-aged children can
be approached successfully through purely verbal methods, but, in the
majority of the child population a therapeutic approach employs techniques that utilize play materials. This is even more true in the case of
mentally retarded children whose cognitive development, by definition,
lags behind that of the nonretarded population of the same chronological
age. The pace at which mentally retarded children pass through the
various stages of play hierarchy (i.e., solitary play/parallel play/coop-
erative play/competitive play) is slower in the retarded child than in
nonretarded age-mates. There are qualitative differences as well (Weiner
& Weiner, 1974). The transition from parallel play to cooperative play
appears to be a particularly difficult step for some mentally retarded
children to take. Additionally, Capobianco and Cole (1960) found that

mentally retarded children were slower than nonretarded children of the same mental age in making this transition.

Many of the objectives of preschool nursery education of mentally retarded children pertain to the development of play skills (i.e., the ability to handle toylike material in an investigative and constructive manner). Play therapy, or rather psychotherapy through play methods, presupposes that a child has some rudimentary play skills. Another prerequisite is that the child should have some potentiality at least for relating to another human being, in this case the therapist. The establishment of a positive relationship between the therapist and the child is a fundamental ingredient of any process of psychotherapy. Indeed, a number of therapists, particularly those with a psychoanalytic orientation, consider the choice of play materials to be of minor importance. Thus, Mundy (1957), working with a group of young children, some of whom were quite severely retarded, found that the use of the therapist's body was of greater help than an assortment of inanimate materials. She operated from the point of view that the children whom she was treating had suffered from severe degrees of maternal deprivation, and she saw the essence of her therapy as "scientific mothering."

Similarly, Davidson (1975) focused very much on the child–therapist relationship. The therapeutic props used were in line with the child's developmental stage and, in the case material quoted, the client was at a level of oral needs. Hence, the materials supplied related to that stage of development. On the other hand, Smith, McKinnon, and Kessler (1976) used a greater variety of materials appropriate to varying developmental levels. Both Mundy (1957) and Davidson (1975) used interpretations and literal reflections very freely. Their techniques would appear to derive from the principles laid down by Melanie Klein (1932) and illustrated by Schwartz (1979). Klein felt that play was actually a regressive move and regretted holding the first session in the playroom. She also mentioned the importance of limit setting, a point that is made by a number of basic authorities on play therapy (Axline, 1957; Ginott, 1976; Moustakas, 1953).

There are a number of media that can potentially facilitate the communication between child and therapist and the establishment of a relationship between the two. In this group of subjects one medium stands out, namely that of art; so much so, that art therapy has become a subspecialty of its own. Drawing and finger painting have, of course, been used by play therapists who might not claim to be specifically art therapists or have any particular expertise in the understanding of the artistic value of the child's productions. Freeman (1936) described drawing as an aid to communicating with children who had difficulty expressing themselves and discussed the usefulness of this technique. The way that the tactile experiences and the experience of color stimulated fantasies and facilitated personal associations was described by Kadis (1951). In some cases, art materials can be used by one therapist and three-dimensional toys by a second therapist. The synergistic effects of this approach have been described by Roth and Barrett (1980). A multimedia approach combining art, dance, and music therapy was illustrated by Cantalapiedra, DeWeerdt, and Frederick (1977). All these contributions indicate that there is a need for flexibility in approaching a mentally retarded child who may be difficult to reach through traditional methods.

A useful approach in differentiating between methods and materials was provided by LeLand and Smith (1965). These authors have provided a fourfold classification of play therapists using the parameters of structure, methods, and materials. The four possibilities are unstructured methods with unstructured materials (U-U), unstructured methods with structured materials (U-S), structured methods with unstructured materials (S-U), and structured methods with structured materials (S-S). Unstructured materials are necessarily primitive and can be formed, bent, twisted, or shaped in various ways. Examples are water, sand, pipe cleaners, pieces of string, beads, scraps of wood, and wooden blocks. On the other hand, structured materials are obviously those that already represent something very specific, such as family figures and furniture in a doll house. The question of structuring the approach relates somewhat to that of limit setting. There is clearly a continuum between the most passive and permissive therapeutic stance and the most directive and constrictive one. Many play therapists fall somewhere in the middle, allowing much freedom of expression and playing a nondirective role for much of the time while setting certain limits, such as those that refer to the prohibition of aggression toward the therapist, self-injury, and the destruction of physical objects.

A very structured approach with structured material indicates that the process may be an educational and not a therapeutic one in that the goal of the exercise is more the creation of a product rather than the resolution of some emotional or behavioral symptom. It can be pointed out, however, that this distinction, although theoretically elegant, is not a practical one in individual cases. Thus, the achievement of an art object may enhance the sense of worth and the self-image of the child. Many of the benefits of individual play therapy derive from the positive feedback that the therapist can genuinely and sincerely supply the child with. This leads to a cyclic movement whereby the actions of child and therapist continually reinforce and enhance each other.

The grouping of mentally retarded children for purposes of therapy has been described more often than experiences with individual therapy in that population. When these children become aggregated in settings such as institutions, community residences, and hospitals or schools, it is natural to attempt to treat them in numbers rather than one at a time. The establishment of such a therapeutic group may not be an easy matter. Some of the guidelines may be derived from the group psychotherapy literature (e.g., the need for group balance) (see Slavson & Schiffer, 1975). These authors exclude mentally deficient children from consideration of group psychotherapy. Nevertheless, group techniques have been used widely in treating mentally retarded children, particularly in institutions. One of the pioneers of this approach was Cotzin (1948). He used psychodramatic techniques as an important vehicle for getting therapy started. Clearly one of the important considerations in selecting members for a group is the question of cognitive levels. Although a certain range is permissible and may be useful, too wide a disparity in cognitive functioning may prove to be antitherapeutic. The principle of balancing children who act out with others or are inhibited and anxious has considerable validity when a higher functioning group of children is considered. The lower functioning the group, the less this becomes a consideration.

Just as there are a number of different cognitive levels in the potential pool of children to be treated, so there are different clusters of goals and objectives. In the lowest functioning children, the main goal is to facilitate and enhance a process of socialization or peer relationship development. In the higher group, the goals have to do much more with impulse control, improvement of interpersonal relationships, and a sense of greater self-worth.

The most primitive form of group play therapy is what has been described as *peer play therapy*. The conceptual basis for this approach has been derived from the work of Birnbaum (1974) and Fuller (1977) who have developed a technique of pairing nonretarded children who have somewhat complementary emotional problems in a dyadic form of therapy. The complementarity of the treated children provides the essential rationale for this approach. In order to transpose this concept to substantially mentally retarded children, different techniques must be fashioned. This form of therapy, which is intermediate between individual and group methods, consists of a therapist's guiding and shaping each child through the activity of interacting with a peer, using a variety of tools or props that are conducive to cooperative play. The activity may be quite simple such as rolling a ball toward the other child and receiving it back, or it may be more complex such as using a toy doctor's kit on another child. This type of intervention lies at the borderlands of therapy because it can be described as a very fundamental form of social skills training as well as a form of group play therapy. The technique is potentially expandable to be applied to more than two children at a time,

although experience teaches that the number of children a single therapist can handle is strictly limited in this population. A need for close
monitoring of the flow of communication between the clients entails a
relatively low ceiling to the size of the group. Over the decades of
experience with groups of mentally retarded children the need for structure and direction has become somewhat crystallized. Thus, Newcomer
and Morrison (1974) have described a difference between *directive* and
nondirective therapy and pointed to the greater usefulness of the former.

With older latency-aged children, who have some facility with verbal expressions, so-called verbal or discussion groups are often helpful.
As a rule, the therapist needs to set clear limits as well as providing
input in terms of choosing certain themes for the child patients to consider. The children themselves have considerable difficulty in setting an
agenda that is likely to be fruitful. The content of such verbal therapies
deals with family relationships, peer relationships, reaction to authority,
understanding one's feelings, and self-managing one's impulses, among
others.

Group counseling methods shade off into group guidance programs, and some of these are targeted to enhance the self-image of the
participant in the group. These interventions have generally been carried
out in a school setting. Deblassie and Lebsock (1979) have described
particular techniques for helping subgroups of handicapped children in
a school setting in an attempt to prepare these youngsters for some
vocational future. Group counseling techniques will naturally play a
larger part in the treatment of adolescents and adults than in the management and assistance for children.

Psychotherapy and Counseling with Adolescents and Adults

Although the themes and matters of content are generally different
between these two age groups (i.e., adolescents and adults), the process
and overall structure of treatment tend to be similar; hence, treatment
of these two groups of individuals can be described together. The fairly
large body of literature on this topic divides itself between those authors
who describe individual methods as against those who favor group
methods.

One of the earliest contributions to the literature on individual
counseling with mentally retarded adults comes from Thorne and Dolan
(1953). These authors employed individual counseling in the protective
atmosphere of a state institution. Although they attribute considerable
importance to the context of the counseling process, they also indicate
a preference for nondirective methods and a very supportive stance on

the part of the counselor. Much of the early literature dealt with psycho-therapy and counseling carried out in institutional settings (see Stacey, DeMartino, & Sarason, 1957).

There has been much reluctance to engage mentally retarded individuals in psychotherapeutic or counseling procedures. This opposition has been traditionally attributed to the influence of psychoanalytic theory and the work of Carl Rogers in client-centered counseling (Rogers, 1942, 1951). With increasing motivation toward psychotherapeutic work with such individuals as chronic schizophrenics and borderline personalities, such resistances appear to be diminishing. The work of Jakab (1970) and Szymanski (1980) is particularly important in this area. Nevertheless, this type of intervention is still rarely applied, and pleas have been made recently for its wider application (Selan, 1979; Walker, 1977).

The project of individual psychotherapy or counseling of a patient or client may be undertaken by that individual's case manager or by an outside consultant. In the former case the therapist needs to differentiate clearly between the process of case management, on the one hand, and that of counseling and psychotherapy, on the other. One of the main distinctions is that the latter has a finite goal, a point in time when the process will come to an end, whereas, case management, just by its very nature, is interminable. The broad goals of counseling and psychother-apy are to help individuals understand themselves better, to realize their assets, as well as their limitations, and to understand better the environment with which they have to cope, particularly in the area of inter-personal relationships. Thus, counseling and psychotherapy run parallel with what is often described as *social skills training*, the broad objectives of which are to render mentally retarded individuals more palatable to their environment. The theories behind counseling and psychotherapy conceptualize the person at greater depth, however, and lay more stress on the individual's feelings about himself or herself. Obviously, there is a dynamic link between feelings of self-worth and behavior toward others.

A well-structured series of psychotherapeutic or counseling ses-sions will tend to go through a number of distinct phases. The initial or warmup phase may occupy a considerable period of time particularly if the client or patient is undermotivated. This relative lack of motivation is not the sole prerogative of the mentally retarded population but is quite widespread among individuals who have been engaged in some form of psychotherapy. During this initial phase, the two participants get to know each other and feel each other out. It is at this stage that the counselor or therapist should be able to decide whether or not to work with this client or patient. The mentally retarded individual is not in as good a position to break off an endeavor that may ultimately prove to be sterile. The middle phase is the main working period of the therapy. It is at this stage that specific issues will be discussed. Inevitably one of the issues will be the fact that the individual is mentally retarded and thereby different from most others. On this subject one may encounter much resistance and denial that is the case with all handicapped individuals, whatever their deficit. Another issue that emerges frequently is that of dependency and difficult and complicated family relationships. The mentally retarded individual is likely to be the object of attitudes on the part of family members that tend to lower self-esteem, encourage feelings of helplessness, and induce patterns of undue dependency on others that are often long-standing. Although it may be possible to directly target the attitude of others and make some realignment in them, this is often not feasible in the case of adults and of adolescents. The objective then becomes the attainment of the client's better adaptation to such persistent and unchangeable influences on the part of significant others. As the patient experiences the therapist's confidence in the abilities that the patient can demonstrate and as some measure of identification with the therapist begins to form, the patient may begin to develop some immunity against the devaluing opinion of critical others. This influential process, as well as the process of identification with the therapist, naturally takes a considerable time. Identification with the therapist, which plays a considerably beneficial role in many cases, is particularly difficult for the mentally retarded individual to achieve.

It is customary to speak of a third or termination phase of the therapeutic process. This may have been planned from the outset, but, in a number of cases, it is thrust upon the participants due to some extraneous or adventitious factor such as the geographic move by either the therapist or the patient. The general expectation is that, once termination has been announced, there will be some slippage in terms of the patient's adjustment, and some symptoms may resurface. The sense of being abandoned and rejected becomes particularly poignant in those mentally retarded individuals who have been institutionalized in early life and who have spent considerable time away from their objects of primary attachment. Depending on how much progress has been made during the working phase of the treatment, some degree of emancipation from the therapeutic process is usually possible by pointing to the patient's attainment of a degree of autonomy and independence. Obviously, there are some individuals who will need to be referred for further therapy with another therapist. However, counseling or therapy should always be conceptualized as eventually reaching a point of termination.

Because verbal exchange may not be the preferred vehicle of communication between therapist and patient, certain adjunctive therapies have been described using such media as art, music, movement, dance, and the like. These media are specifically useful with individuals who lack verbal facility but who are capable of expression through other channels. The medium of art is particularly relevant in intensifying and concretizing the therapist–patient relationship. Other media such as dance, movement, and music are more appropriate as vehicles for group therapy. Several authors (Espenak, 1981; Kunkle-Miller, 1978) clearly distinguish between the therapeutic and educational uses of these clinical tools. Self-expression, a vehicle for communication, and the ultimate increase in self-confidence are the main assets that these methods contain within themselves. In terms of art, there are possibilities of bridging gaps between the patient and family members. Espenak (1981) has illustrated this at some length. Naturally the acquisition of a particular skill will always be conducive to some improvement in the individual's self-esteem. Cassity (1977) has described using a specific guitar technique in the context of individual therapy. A certain therapeutic ingredient stems from the positive feedback that the therapist provides the patient that not only enhances the latter's positive feelings about himself but also cements the therapist—patient relationship. In the case of movement therapy, as described by Shuman-Carpenter (1977), a particular aspect of the patient's self-image is enhanced, namely the positive experience of body image. The value of all these specific experiences is enhanced by the fact that they occur within the context of a positive one-to-one relationship.

Group Methods with Adolescents and Adults

From the very beginning of psychotherapeutic endeavors with the mentally retarded, there has been a clear preference for group over individual methods. Two main reasons account for this bias. First, it is obvious that a group approach is more suitable when one has to deal with a considerable number of patients or clients. Second, adolescent and adult mentally retarded have often had similar past experiences in being subjected to comparable negative environmental influences so that their grouping together in therapy is a natural consequence. Thus, Davis and Shapiro (1979) found that their clients, though living in the community, suffered from isolation. After a fairly long warmup period of about 3 months, individual group members began to show an interest in each other, and a spirit of cohesion became evident in the group.

Group counseling can be seen as a process that lies intermediate between group guidance and group psychotherapy (Trotzer, 1977). One of the chief distinctions is that group counseling deals with the here and now, whereas, group psychotherapy tends to explore the past of the individuals. If one considers that the mentally retarded person has difficulty in reflecting upon the past but is faced frequently with very serious problems of present adjustment, it becomes apparent that the bulk of the reported literature falls into the area of group counseling. However, it should not be implied that individuals who are receiving counseling are less seriously disturbed than those whose management is described as psychotherapy. The literature indeed seems to use the terms *group counseling* and *group psychotherapy* almost indiscriminately.

One of these earliest descriptions of group psychotherapy with mentally retarded adolescents was the work of Cotzin (1948). Having a group of mildly retarded adolescent boys as the subjects of the therapy, Cotzin relied mainly on psychodramatic techniques, using such devices as mock courtroom trials in order to produce participation by the group members. The use of various activities such as group games, the practice of simple parliamentary procedures such as reading of minutes and payment of dues, and the like was also described by Michal-Smith, Gottsegen, and Gottsegen (1955). Role playing was also the essential technique in the group conducted by Lavalli and Levine (1954). Sternlicht (1964, 1966) paid particular attention to techniques when dealing with mentally retarded adolescents. Foremost among these techniques was engaging the strongest member of the group in Indian arm wrestling in order to establish the group leader's position of superiority or command. He also described the "silent insult" technique as one efficacious way of establishing some movement in the group. Crenshaw (1976) used such techniques as role-playing scenes and structured group exercises that are common in encounter groups. Weinstock (1979) found that simple discussion was ineffective and used a number of simple board games, checkers, cards, and small crafts projects to get movement in the group. On the other hand, Moore (1981), dealing with a slightly smaller group, found that the introduction of balls, puppets, and "play-doh" simply led to the group members' being more interested in talking and that they could then be encouraged to discuss their feelings. Verbal instructions, discrimination training, role playing, and discussion were the techniques used by Lee (1977). Positive feedback, such as social praise, as a form of positive reinforcement is a common behavioral measure applied in the course of group counseling or group psychotherapy. Combinations of activities and verbal methods were demonstrated by the work of Norman (1977) and Hynes and Young (1976).

Some early workers (Ringelheim & Polatsek, 1957; Vail, 1955) had difficulty in obtaining any progress with nondirective methods. Snyder and Sechrest (1959) prescribed a role for the therapist that was that of a guiding, manipulating leader who was sometimes didactic. The need for planning and for introducing concrete material was stressed. Much, however, depends on the composition of the group of clients; the lower the mental age of the membership the greater the need for positive leadership, guidance, and structure. Most workers in the field tend to select the subjects along a fairly narrow range of mental capacity. Welch and Sigman (1980) stressed the importance of considering the mental rather than chronological age of the selected individual. On the other hand, a certain variety of problems, ages, and issues could be an advantage to get the group moving.

The process of group therapy has usually been described as a triphasic one, with an introductory or testing-out stage, a main working stage, and a final termination stage. Szymanski and Rosefsky (1980) have described an additional second stage that they characterize by the development of a power struggle with members either among themselves or with a group leader. This can better be described as a subphase of the initial or testing-out stage. As Yalom (1970) points out, the phases of group development are not often well demarcated and tend to overlap. Competition and power struggles tend to coexist with the phase of cohesiveness. Progression and regression may succeed themselves rapidly and repeatedly.

A distinction in terms of group process can be made between *open* and *closed* groups. The open group tends to go on and on and may be the appropriate one in closed settings such as institutions, residences, and hospital wards. Closed groups are more likely to be used with ambulatory clients in open settings such as outpatient clinics. In open groups, there is a continual coming and going of members so that beginning and termination phases occur intermittently, depending on the turnover of group members, and this may preoccupy the working of the group entirely. Closed groups, therefore, offer easier descriptive possibilities and hence are more frequently found in the literature. They have more of a life of their own and stand out more clearly against the milieu in which patients or clients find themselves.

An item on which there is no general agreement is the optimum size for the therapy groups of mentally retarded adolescents and adults. Szymanski and Rosefsky (1980) recommend the traditional number of six to eight group members. When confronted with seriously disturbed adolescents, this may well be too large a number. In such instances a group composed of four adolescents appears to be more reasonable. The problem with using a larger group is that one or more clients may well be left out. Using too small a number runs the risk of too little interaction between group members and too much one-to-one interaction between the therapist or counselor and an individual member. Another variant is whether one or two group therapists is employed. Recommendations for two group leaders are often made on the basis that it is useful to have one male and one female professional person leading a given group, especially if this group is composed of members of both sexes. Such a structure becomes particularly desirable if one is planning some role playing and modeling of behavior for the group members. When the issue is one of grave difficulty in relating to the opposite sex, this type of group structure is particularly appropriate.

The issues that are now customarily addressed in group therapy or group counseling with mentally retarded individuals are manifold. They cover all the topics that one can encounter with a nonretarded population, such as emancipation from parents and family, establishment of relationships with the opposite sex, establishment of career goals, adjusting to changes in the work place or in the family's life cycle, issues of retirement, acculturation, and so forth. However, there are some specific concerns that will be encountered with the mentally retarded population, and these naturally pertain to the fact that this group of individuals is different from the rest of the population and has been demarcated from it strictly in the past. Due to a very extensive and effective deinstitutionalization movement there are now many adult mentally retarded living in the general community. Many of these individuals have spent lengthy periods of time in institutions under segregated circumstances. Often they have established substantial emotional ties to their peers in the former living situation that have now been disrupted but for which they seek some form of replacement or restitution. Participation in a group with their peers often forms the first stage of such a restitution process. In counseling or treating such a group of individuals, one must be extremely sensitive to the peculiar nature of the group members' past emotional experiences and the difficulties that such members encounter in forming new relationships with those of their peers who have never been institutionalized. Some members will exhibit a helpless dependency in the group, and others will practice adamant denial. These defenses need to be understood for what they are and be dealt with as tactfully as possible.

The groups dealing with mentally retarded adolescents and adults tend to employ directive or even confrontational methods, and the goals are clearly in matters of behavior change, better current adjustment, and better social performance, rather than in concentrating on achieving any new insight in the subjects. The most common yardstick for change in the direction of improvement is whether the group member has become more acceptable to his or her contemporaries by the time that the counseling or therapy has been concluded. Such changes are not easy to measure.

Results of Counseling and Psychotherapy and a Critique of Outcome Studies

The difficulties of assessing the outcome of psychotherapy generally have been discussed extensively (Bergin & Lamberg, 1978; Heinrichs & Carpenter, 1981). The problems are manifold, but the chief ones are the fuzzy and poor description of the therapeutic process, the inadequate description of the context, the failure to describe intercurrent events that may be important, and the lack of objective outcome measures that are meaningful and that can be considered to be empirically valid. Nevertheless, there is a growing consensus that psychotherapy is reasonably effective in certain problems of maladjustment and emotional conflict (Meltzoff & Kornreich, 1970). Gunzberg (1974), in reviewing outcome studies in the mentally retarded population, complained about the lack of follow-up in the description of therapeutic work. Jakab (1970) considered the problem of measuring change and recommended a behavior rating scale (i.e., Devereaux Behavior Rating Scale), as well as psychological testing concerning cognitive functioning. Objective observational rating scales in which information is supplied by relatives or family members are also recommended. Craft (1965) used the Stott Social Adjustment Guide, the MMPI, and the Porteus Maze Test. Johnson (1953) used a cognitive measure, the Raven's Progressive Matrices, and compared it with the Stanford-Binet scores to predict success. She found the former more useful. The earliest work relied much on tests of cognitive functioning. Chidester and Menninger (1936) reported that in a single case the IQ increased from 62 to 90. Similarly, Axline (1949) found a range from 15 to 26 points of improvement in IQ in a treated group of mentally retarded children. A much more impressionistic finding was produced by Thorne (1948), who simply rated the treated population as improved (45), unchanged (15), and worse (7). Similarly, Cotzin (1948) categorized outcome simply as "good," "fair," or "poor." However, he did gather follow-up data 1 year after his cessation of treatment. Fisher and Wolfson (1953) found no change in IQ but reported 8 out of 12 subjects substantially improved. Ringelheim and Polatsek (1957) reported mixed results. In a small private group of 7 individuals only 2 improved substantially, 3 were unchanged, and 2 were evidently worse.

Albini and Dinitz (1965) used a comparison group of untreated subjects, but the two groups were not well matched. Academic achievement and attitudes toward parents as well as parents' attitudes toward the subjects and the frequency of parents' visits were the dependent variables. No difference was found between the treated and the comparison groups. Subotnik and Callahan (1959) used a control period rather than a control group. Comparing their subjects on behavior ratings and anxiety measures before treatment, at the beginning of treatment, at the end of treatment, and 8 weeks after the conclusion of treatment, they found no significant difference between the changes during treated and untreated time periods.

Snyder and Sechrest (1959) constructed a placebo group who had contact in the form of some nondirected therapy offered without support or encouragement, as well as a treated group who were greatly encouraged and received much positive input. A second control group was simply not treated at all. The positively encouraged group of subjects had fewer violations on the ward than the placebo and the no-treatment group. Dealing with a similar group of delinquent adolescent boys who were also mentally retarded, Yonge and O'Connor (1954) also found significant differences. The experimental group was greatly superior to the control group on an attitude checklist and a workshop behavior rating scale. However, a double blind design was not feasible. A similar design was used by Humes, Adamczyk, and Myco (1969) who provided group counseling for adolescent boys and girls in an ambulatory setting. These workers used a more extensive battery of outcome measures including a test of personality and a number of measures estimating self-concept. They also included two sociometric measures. There were significantly favorable changes in the experimental group on the personality test as well as on the behavior rating scales; however, the self-concept measures showed no significant difference between the experimental and control groups. Hayes (1977) attempted to compare the outcome in 20 mentally retarded adolescents with the outcome of 20 adolescents of average or above-average intelligence. Careful matching of various behavior problems, length of treatment, socioeconomic status, and family constellation was achieved. The dependent measure was outcome as rated by the individual therapist. Interestingly enough, there was a slight difference in favor of the mentally retarded group.

Gorlow, Butler, Einig, and Smith (1963) attempted to estimate the effectiveness of group therapy in 38 young adults in an institutional setting. They had a control group of 31 individuals who received no group therapy. Unfortunately, they omitted from selection the most suitable subjects who were on a summer vacation at the time and not surprisingly attained negative results. Schachter, Myer, and Loomis (1962) compared the effect of psychotherapy with mentally retarded children as against therapy with psychotic children. The mentally retarded group made greater gains than the psychotic group. Unfortunately, the types of psychotherapies were not equivalent because three of the mentally retarded had individual therapy and three had group therapy, whereas all the psychotic children had group therapy.

A different design was employed by Mundy (1957) who treated 15 severely and profoundly retarded children in a London hospital over a period of 9 to 12 months. She compared this group with 10 children matched for age, neurological involvement, and IQ, who were left untreated. Results found that the treated group gained 9 IQ points and the untreated group only 2. However, improvement in social adjustment was much more impressive in the treated group. Mundy then used another small group of children and compared their progress during an untreated period with that during a treated period. The results of this study were spectacular because during the treated period the children gained an average increase in IQ of 22 points. Newcomer and Morrison (1974) used the Denver Developmental Screening Test to gauge the effect of individual play therapy as compared to group therapy stimulation. They found no difference between the individually and group-treated children, both of whom improved, whereas a group of controls made no gains. In an extension of this work, Morrison and Newcomer (1975) used the same screening test as a dependent measure in order to compare directive group therapy with nondirective group therapy. Unfortunately the groups were not well matched so that no conclusions could be drawn from their negative findings.

Knapczyk and Yoppi (1975) used measures of a play hierarchy of solitary-to-parallel-to-cooperative-to-competitive play. In an attempt to assess the efficacy of teaching children to play together they found that cooperative play appeared earlier than competitive play that became more prominent during a second treatment phase. Strain (1975) used an observational measure that focused on social play in children, in order to assess the effects of sociodramatic play activities with severely retarded 4-year-olds. This essentially behavioral or training method produced clearly positive results using a systematic return to a baseline phase after the first and second intervention periods. Ohwaki (1976) demonstrated significant increases in human figure drawings in 19 adult mentally retarded individuals who had dance therapy over 25 sessions. Schweisheimer and Walberg (1976) used a battery of measures including a general self-concept scale. A control group was used, and there was an overall trend toward improvement in the treated group. The results produced by Lee (1977) were particularly striking. Measurements used before and after a 10-week period of group counseling included the AAMD Adaptive Behavior Scale, some sociometric measures, and the Peabody Picture Vocabulary Test. The sociometric test showed the greatest change in the direction of improvement.

Dolly and Page (1981) measured the changes produced by a period of reality therapy with 20 mentally retarded adolescents. The chief objective measure of change was the TMR Performance Profile that is an adaptive behavior scale. They had a comparison group of 19 individuals who showed no change over a period of 2 years, whereas, the experimental group gained significantly. These positive results were in contrast to the lack of improvement that had been found by Zapf (1976) using similar methodology. Moore (1981) attempted to assess developmental progress as a result of group therapy with 6 clients. He also used the Devereaux Elementary School Behavior Rating Scale before the first session and after the last group session. Although there was considerable increase in the size of the drawn human figure that would indicate improved self-esteem, no firm conclusions can be drawn from this study in the absence of a comparison group. Finally, Sherwood (1980), using peers as therapists following the work of Strain, found significant differences depending on whether same-age or younger age therapists were used.

In summary, it can be seen that although the quality of much of the outcome research in the area of psychotherapy and counseling with mentally retarded individuals is not high, a number of the contributors do provide some evidence of the efficacy of this mode of treatment for certain mentally retarded individuals under specific conditions.

Summary and Conclusions

The experience of a number of clinicians indicates that counseling and psychotherapy for the mentally retarded are carried out very widely, more so than can be gleaned from a perusal of the literature, which is fairly sparse on those topics. Since the establishment of a network of mental health/mental retardation centers around the country, it is to be expected that much supportive work will be carried out with mentally retarded individuals residing in the community. Because much of this is not of an exciting nature, it is not too surprising that it is not written about to a great extent. When it comes to dealing with the severe behavior disorders and serious mental illnesses of the mentally retarded, psychotherapeutic methods are overshadowed by those involving behavioral (operant) techniques and psychopharmacological interventions. The relative verbal inexpressiveness of the mentally retarded patients remains a stumbling block for anything like *furor psychotherapeuticus*.

However, if one abandons total reliance on verbal methods, it is possible to engage even seriously disturbed mentally retarded individuals in a therapeutic transaction. The use of what may be described as kinetic rather than linguistic techniques is of considerable value. In the case of children, therapists have known for many decades that they must engage in action as well as in words. An active therapist has an advantage over a passive one in the treatment of this group of individuals. An understanding and recognition of developmental levels is also useful and will assist in achieving successful engagement with the client or patient. Both directive and nondirective strategies have a place in the psychological management of the mentally retarded individuals. A decision in this regard will be made largely on the basis of the therapist's temperament and preference. It is easy to underestimate the mentally retarded individual's perceptiveness and capacity for emotional growth. A theme encountered again and again consists of the fact that the mentally retarded client or patient is a member of a minority group (i.e., the patient tagged as an outsider in the universe of average persons). This is a pertinent factor and accounts for much maladjustment. To help bridge the gap between this outsider and the rest of the community remains one of the chief goals of counseling and psychotherapy with retarded individuals.

Finally, there is an ongoing need to validate the effects of psychotherapy through experimental methods. There are reliable methods of measuring behavioral changes through time-sampled observations and behavior rating scales; often their clinical significance is suspect. Kazdin and Matson (1981) have described validation procedures that consist of social comparison, that is, comparing treated mentally retarded with their "normal" peers, and subjective evaluation, which is actually intersubjective evaluation, consisting of having "blind" observers rate subjects before and after treatment. Much more work needs to be done along these lines before the pursuit of psychotherapy of the mentally retarded overcomes the skepticism and resistance of mental health practitioners.

References

Ackerman, N. W., & Menninger, C. F. (1936). Treatment techniques for mental retardation in a school for personality disorders in children. *American Journal of Orthopsychiatry, 6*, 294–312.

Albini, J. L., & Dinitz, S. (1965). Psychotherapy with disturbed and defective children: An evaluation of changes in behavior and attitudes. *American Journal of Mental Deficiency, 69,* 560.

Axline, V. (1949). Mental deficiency—Symptom or disease. *Journal of Consulting Psychology, 13,* 313–327.

Axline, V. (1957). *Play therapy.* Boston: Houghton Mifflin.

Balthazar, E. E., & Stevens, H. A. (1975). *The emotionally disturbed, mentally retarded: A historical and contemporary perspective.* Englewood Cliffs, NJ: Prentice Hall.

Bergin, A. E., & Lambert, M. J. (1978). The evaluation of therapeutic outcomes. In S. L. Barfield & A. E. Bergin (Eds.), *Handbook of psychotherapy and behavior change* (pp. 139–180). New York: Wiley.

Bialer, I. (1967). Psychotherapy and other adjustment techniques with the mentally retarded. In A. A. Baumeister (Eds.), *Mental retardation, appraisal, education and rehabilitation* (pp. 138–180). Chicago: Aldine.

Birnbaum, M. K. (1974). Peer–pair psychotherapy: A new approach to withdrawn children. *Journal of Clinical Child Psychology, 2,* 13–20.

Cantalapiedra, M. A., DeWeerdt, C., & Frederick, F. (1977). Le role psychotherapique de l'educateur dans un extemat póur jeunés enfánts. *Revue de Neuropsychiatrie Infantile, 25,* 787–811.

Capobianco, R. J., & Cole, D. A. (1960). Social behavior of mentally retarded children. *American Journal of Mental Deficiency, 64,* 638–651.

Cassity, M. D. (1977). Nontraditional guitar techniques for the educable and trainable mentally retarded residents in music therapy activities. *Journal of Music Therapy, 14,* 39–42.

Chidester, L. (1934). Therapeutic results with mentally retarded children. *American Journal of Orthopsychiatry, 4,* 464–472.

Chidester, L., & Menninger, K. A. (1936). The application of psychoanalytic methods to the study of mental retardation. *American Journal of Orthopsychiatry, 6,* 616–625.

Clark, L. P. (1933). *The nature and treatment of amentia.* London: Bailliere, Tindall and Cox.

Close, H. T. (1966). Psychotherapy. *Voices, 2,* 124.

Cotzin, M. (1948). Group therapy with mentally defective problem boys. *American Journal of Mental Deficiency, 53,* 268–283.

Cowen, E. L. (1955). Psychotherapy and play techniques with the exceptional child. In W. H. Cruikshank (Ed.), *Psychology of exceptional children and youth* (1st ed., pp. 343–375). Englewood Cliffs, NJ: Prentice-Hall.

Craft, M. (1965). *Ten studies into psychopathic personality.* Bristol: John Wright and Sons.

Crenshaw, D. A. (1976). Teaching adaptive interpersonal behavior: Group techniques in residential treatment. *Child Care Quarterly, 5,* 211–220.

Davidson, C. D. (1975). Psychotherapy with mentally handicapped children in a day school. *Psychotherapy: Theory, Research and Practice, 12,* 13–21.

Davis, K. R., & Shapiro, L. J. (1979). Exploring group process as a means of reaching the mentally retarded. *Social Casework, 60,* 330–337.

Deblassie, R. R., & Lebsock, M. S. (1979). Counselling with handicapped children. *Elementary School Guidance and Counselling, 13,* 199–206.

Dolly, J. P., & Page, D. P. (1981). Reality therapy with institutionalized emotionally disturbed mentally retarded adolescents. *Journal for Special Educators, 17,* 225–232.

English, H. G., & English, A. C. (1958). *A comprehensive dictionary of psychological and psychoanalytic terms.* New York: Longmans, Green and Co.

Espenak, L. (1981). *Dance therapy, therapy and application.* Springfield, IL: Charles C Thomas.

Fine, R. H., & Dawson, J. C. (1965). A therapy program for the mildly retarded adolescent. *American Journal of Mental Deficiency, 69,* 23–30.

Fisher, L., & Wolfson, I. (1953). Group therapy of mental defectives. *American Journal of Mental Deficiency, 57,* 463–476.

Freeman, M. (1936). Drawing as a psychotherapeutic intermedium. *American Journal of Mental Deficiency, 41,* 182–187.

Fuller, J. S. (1977). Duotherapy: A potential treatment of choice for latency children. *Journal of the American Academy of Child Psychology, 16,* 469–477.

Ginott, H. G. (1976). Therapeutic intervention in child treatment. In C. Schaeffer (Ed.), *Therapeutic use of child's play* (pp. 279–290). New York: Jason Aronson.

Gorlow, L., Butler, A., Einig, K. G., & Smith, J. A. (1963). An appraisal of self-attitudes and behavior following group psychotherapy with retarded young adults. *American Journal of Mental Deficiency, 67,* 893–898.

Hayes, M. (1977). The responsiveness of mentally retarded children to psychotherapy. *Smith College Studies in Social Work, 47,* 112–153.

Heinrichs, D. W., & Carpenter, W. T. (1981). The efficacy of individual psychotherapy: A perspective and review emphasizing controlled outcome studies. In S. Arieti (Ed.), *American handbook of psychiatry* (pp. 586–613). New York: Basic Books.

Hinsie, L. E., & Campbell, R. J. (1970). *Psychiatric dictionary* (4th ed.). New York and London: Oxford University Press.

Humes, C. W., Adamczyk, J. S., & Myco, R. W. (1969). A school study of group counselling with educable retarded adolescents. *American Journal of Mental Deficiency, 74,* 191–195.

Hynes, J., & Young, J. (1976). Adolescent group for mentally retarded persons. *Education and Training for the Mentally Retarded, 11,* 226–231.

Jakab, I. (1970). Psychotherapy of the mentally retarded child. In N. Bernstein (Ed.), *Diminished people* (pp. 223–261). Boston: Little, Brown.

Johnson, E. (1953). The clinical use of Raven's progressive matrices to appraise potential for progress in play therapy: A study of institutionalized and educationally retarded children. *American Journal of Orthopsychiatry, 23,* 391–398.

Kadis, O. L. (1951, May). *The use of fingerpainting in psychotherapy with mentally retarded children.* Paper presented at the 75th Annual Meeting of the American Association in Mental Deficiency, New York.

Kanner, L. (1964). *A history of the care and study of the feebleminded.* Springfield, IL: Charles C Thomas.

Kazdin, A. E., & Matson, J. L. (1981). Social validation in mental retardation. *Applied Research in Mental Retardation, 2,* 39–54.

Klein, M. (1932). *The psychoanalysis of children.* London: Hogarth Press.

Knapczyk, D. R., & Yoppi, J. D. (1975). Development of cooperative and competitive play resources in developmentally disabled children. *American Journal of Mental Deficiency, 80,* 245–255.

Kunkle-Miller, C. (1978). Art therapy with mentally retarded adults. *Art Psychotherapy, 5,* 123–133.

Lavalli, A., & Levine, M. (1954). Social and guidance needs of mentally handicapped adolescents as revealed through sociodrama. *American Journal of Mental Deficiency, 58,* 544–552.

Lee, D. Y. (1977). Evaluation of a group counselling program designed to enhance social adjustment of mentally retarded adults. *Journal of Counselling Psychology, 24,* 318–323.

Leland, H., & Smith, D. (1965). Unstructured material in play therapy for emotionally disturbed, brain damaged mentally retarded children. *American Journal of Mental Deficiency, 66,* 621–627.

Meltzhoff, J., & Kornreich, M. (1970). *Research in psychotherapy*. New York: Atherton Press.

Michal-Smith, H., Gottsegen, M., & Gottsegen, G. (1955). A group therapy technique for mental retardates. *International Journal of Group Psychotherapy, 5*, 84–90.

Moore, C. L. (1981). Activity group failure: Verbal group therapy success in a special education program. *International Journal of Group Psychotherapy, 31*, 223–231.

Morrison, T. L., & Newcomer, B. L. (1975). Effects of directive vs. nondirective play therapy with institutionalized mentally retarded children. *American Journal of Mental Deficiency, 79*, 666–669.

Moustakas, C. (1953). *Children in play therapy*. New York: McGraw-Hill.

Mundy, L. (1957). Therapy with physically and mentally handicapped children in a mental deficiency hospital. *Journal of Clinical Psychology, 13*, 3–9.

Newcomer, R. B., & Morrison, T. L. (1974). Play therapy with institutionalized mentally retarded children. *American Journal of Mental Deficiency, 78*, 727–733.

Norman, M. I. (1977). A counseling program for TMR students. *School Counselor, 24*, 274–277.

Nuffield, E. J. (1983). Psychotherapy for the retarded. In J. L. Matson & J. A. Mulick (Eds.), *Handbook of mental retardation* (pp. 351–368). New York: Pergamon Press.

Ringelheim, D., & Polatsek, I. (1957). Group therapy with a male defective group (a preliminary study). *American Journal of Mental Deficiency, 62*, 157–162.

Rogers, C. R. (1942). *Counseling and psychotherapy*. Boston: Houghton Mifflin.

Rogers, C. R. (1951). *Client-centered therapy*. Boston: Houghton Mifflin.

Rogers, C. R. (1961). *On becoming a person*. Boston: Houghton Mifflin.

Roth, E. A., & Barrett, R. P. (1980). Parallels in art and play therapy with a disturbed retarded boy. *The Arts in Psychotherapy, 7*, 19–26.

Schachter, F. F., Myer, L. R., & Loomis, E. A. (1962). Childhood schizophrenia and mental retardation: Differential diagnosis after one year of psychotherapy. *American Journal of Orthopsychiatry, 32*, 584–594.

Schwartz, C. (1979). The application of psychoanalytic theory to the treatment of the mentally retarded child. *Psychoanalytic Review, 66*, 133–141.

Schweisheimer, W., & Walberg, H. J. (1976). A peer counseling experiment: High school students as small-group leaders. *Journal of Counselling Psychology, 23*, 398–401.

Selan, B. H. (1979). Psychotherapy with the mentally retarded. *Social Work, 24*, 263.

Sherwood, S. (1980). *Play psychotherapy with socially maladaptive mentally retarded children using same age and younger age peers as therapists*. Unpublished doctoral dissertation, Ohio State University, Columbus.

Shoben, E. J. (1953). Some observations on psychotherapy and the learning process. In O. H. Mowrer (Ed.), *Psychotherapy: Theory and research* (p. 125). New York: Ronald Press.

Shuman-Carpenter, B. (1977). The effects of two methods of therapy on the body language of emotionally disturbed, retarded female adolescents (Doctoral dissertation, University of Michigan). *Dissertation Abstracts International, 38*.

Slavson, S. R., & Schiffer, M. (1975). *Group therapies for children: A textbook*. New York: International Universities Press.

Smith, E., McKinnon, R., & Kessler, J. W. (1976). Psychotherapy with mentally retarded children. *Psychoanalytic Study of Children, 31*, 493–514.

Snyder, R., & Sechrest, L. (1959). An experimental study of directive group therapy with defective delinquents. *American Journal of Mental Deficiency, 64*, 117–123.

Snyder, W. V. (1947). The present status of psychotherapeutic counselling. *Psychological Bulletin, 44*, 297–386.

Stacey, C. L., DeMartino, M. F., & Sarason, S. B. (1957). *Couseling and psychotherapy with the mentally retarded.* Glencoe, IL: Free Press.

Sternlicht, M. (1964). Establishing an initial relationship in group psychotherapy with delinquent retarded male adolescents. *American Journal of Mental Deficiency, 69,* 39–41.

Sternlicht, M. (1966). Treatment approaches to delinquent retardates. *International Journal of Group Psychotherapy, 16,* 91–93.

Strain, P. S. (1975). Increasing social play of severely retarded preschoolers with socio-dramatic activities. *Mental Retardation, 13,* 7–9.

Subotnik, L., & Callahan, R. J. (1959). A pilot study in short-term play therapy with institutionalized educable mentally retarded boys. *American Journal of Mental Deficiency, 63,* 730–735.

Szymanski, L. S. (1980). Individual psychotherapy with retarded persons. In L. S. Szymanski & P. E. Tanguay (Eds.), *Emotional disorders of mentally retarded persons* (pp. 131–147). Baltimore: University Park Press.

Szymanski, L. S., & Rosefsky, Q. B. (1980). Group psychotherapy with retarded persons. In L. S. Szymanski & P. E. Tanguay (Eds.), *Emotional disorders of mentally retarded persons* (pp. 173–194). Baltimore: University Park Press.

Thorne, F. C. (1948). Counselling and psychotherapy with mental defectives. *American Journal of Mental Deficiency, 52,* 263–271.

Thorne, F. C., & Dolan, K. M. (1953). The role of counselling in a placement program for mentally retarded females. *Journal of Clinical Psychology, 9,* 110–113.

Trotzer, J. P. (1977). *The counselor and the group: Integrating theory, training and practice.* Monterey, CA: Brooks/Cole.

Truax, C. B., & Mitchel, K. M. (1971). Research on certain therapist interpersonal skills in relation to process and outcome. In A. E. Bergin & S. L. Garfield (Eds.), *Handbook of psychotherapy and behavior change* (pp. 346–369). New York: Wiley.

Vail, D. J. (1955). An unsuccessful experiment in group therapy. *American Journal of Mental Deficiency, 60,* 144–151.

Walker, P. W. (1977). Premarital counselling for the developmentally disabled. *Social Casework, 58,* 475–479.

Weiner, E. A., & Weiner, B. J. (1974). Differentiation of retarded and normal children through toy-play analysis. *Multivariate Behavioral Research, 9,* 245–252.

Weinstock, A. (1979). Group treatment of characterologically damaged, developmentally disabled adolescents in a residential treatment center. *International Journal of Group Psychotherapy, 29,* 369–381.

Welch, V. O., & Sigman, M. (1980). Group psychotherapy with mildly retarded, emotionally disturbed adolescents. *Journal of Clinical Child Psychology, 8,* 209–212.

Wiest, G. (1955). Psychotherapy with the mentally retarded. *American Journal of Mental Deficiency, 59,* 640–644.

Yalom, I. D. (1970). *The theory and practice of group psychotherapy.* New York: Basic Books.

Yonge, K. A., & O'Connor, N. (1954). Measurable effects of group psychotherapy with defective delinquents. *Journal of Mental Science, 100,* 944–952.

Zapf, R. F. (1976, September). Group therapy with retarded adults: A reality therapy approach. *Dissertation Abstracts International, 37*(3A), 1418.

8

Parent and Family Training

KAREN S. BUDD AND PAMELA L. FABRY

Introduction

Professionals who work with handicapped children and their families appear to share an implicit assumption that strengthening the family is an important part of habilation (Simeonsson & Simeonsson, 1981). This assumption is based on a recognition that, even in families of healthy, well-functioning children, child rearing is a challenging and stressful process. For families with a handicapped child, the problems associated with child rearing are magnified. Not all families of handicapped children want or need professional help, and for us to presume otherwise is to ignore the enormous variability among individuals. However, for many of these families, the demands of caretaking call for increased knowledge, resources, and support. Thus the question for professionals frequently is not *if* but rather *how* best to assist families in dealing with the specialized situation created by a handicapped child.

This chapter approaches parent and family training from a pragmatic standpoint by addressing the question: What can I as a practitioner do to foster healthy functioning in families of mentally retarded children? Because the focus of this volume is on handicapped individuals with severe behavior disorders, our chapter pays special attention to family services related to seriously deviant or antisocial behavior in mentally retarded children. Behavior problems such as persistent noncompliance, aggressiveness, and self-stimulation or repeated resistance to acquiring and practicing basic self-care skills present burdens beyond the child's delayed development. This chapter examines the ways such problems affect the family and suggests services that can help the family to manage deviant behavior patterns.

KAREN S. BUDD and PAMELA L. FABRY • Meyer Children's Rehabilitation Institute, University of Nebraska Medical Center, Omaha, Nebraska 68105.

Most professionals have limited time available for direct services to families, so assistance often involves helping them obtain access to existing community resources along with providing selective training or counseling. To be of assistance, professionals need to be sensitive to the demands and stresses facing families of mentally retarded children, knowledgeable about available community resources, and skilled in evaluating and serving individual family needs. Accordingly, following sections of this chapter discuss the impact of a handicapped child on the family, commonly existing community services for families, methods of assessing family needs, and intervention strategies related to selected behavior problems. Although it is recognized that the effects of handicapping conditions on the family are lifelong, this chapter concentrates primarily on services during the child's preadolescent years.

Impact of a Handicapped Child on the Family

A Family Systems Perspective

As persons without handicapped family members, we often are at a disadvantage in understanding the impact of a handicapped child on family life. Because our contacts are limited to the clinic, school, or occasional home visits, we do not experience many of the situations in which handicapping conditions are manifested. Paul and Porter (1981) illustrated the broad impact on the family in the following description:

> We are talking about a child who may be a constant disruptive force at mealtime, with food that can never stay on the plate or be successfully negotiated into the child's mouth, or with drinks that are constantly spilled no matter how clean the tablecloth or who has come to dinner. We may be speaking about a child who has a high energy level and is constantly seeking the parent's help or attention in some way. Many of the children who have severe physical, learning, and/or behavior problems also have limited social skills. Consequently, these children have great difficulty in getting along with other children, whether siblings, children in the neighborhood, children of friends, or children at church or at school. Privacy for parents is virtually impossible, in many instances, and it is usually difficult for parents to find a sitter in whom they can have full confidence in order to enjoy a brief respite. We may be speaking of a child whose physical health is such that the parents live in a constant state of tension and fear. Many of these children are a source of great sadness to parents who hurt inside when their child must always be excluded from the games other children play. Some severely handicapped children have behavior so bizarre and uncontrollable that the parents live in a state of terror and feel forced to compromise their own sensibilities. In some instances these children are viewed by their parents and siblings as being in charge of family life and holding the reins on the pleasure and joy of the family. (pp. 8–9)

Paul and Porter's description highlights the continuous demands for guidance, attention, and planning of even routine activities along with the emotional wellspring of fear, sadness, and anger likely to be experienced by families with a handicapped child. Many of these same characteristics were observed by Turnbull and her associates (Skrtic, Summers, Brotherson, & Turnbull, 1984; Turnbull, Summers, & Brotherson, 1984) in their systems analysis of the family. Through extensive case studies, they identified nine functions performed by families and ways these functions can be altered due to a handicapped person, as described next.

According to Turnbull et al., the economic function of the family may be affected due to increased medical, educational, and therapeutic costs together with the increased time required to provide care—time that might have been spent on economically productive pursuits. Greater demands are placed on the family's physical care function to provide safety, protection, and mobility for the handicapped child. Opportunities for rest and recuperation may be restricted due to difficulties in obtaining respite care or lack of accessibility to recreational facilities by handicapped individuals. The area of socialization can be affected by lack of time or opportunity for social interaction and embarrassment over stares and inappropriate public reactions. The function of self-identity, by which family members develop a sense of their place in the community and a feeling of self-worth, can be affected by feelings of guilt, shame, overidentification with the handicapped individual or unrealistic expectations of nonhandicapped siblings. Chronic feelings of jealousy, resentment, or frustration triggered by the handicapped child and lack of privacy for parents and siblings can disrupt the function of providing affection or engender a reverse pattern of overprotection. The guidance function, by which family members provide feedback to one another to solve day-to-day problems, may be overtaxed by the extensive supervision needs of the handicapped child. Similarly, there are increased demands on the education function of the family, both to teach the handicapped child and to enhance family members' skills in care and management. The vocational function, by which families provide an understanding of work responsibilities and assist in career development, can be affected by specialized needs for vocational training and potential difficulties in obtaining employment for the handicapped person.

The systems framework employed by Turnbull and her colleagues illustrates the diverse and far-reaching impact of a handicapped child on the family, not just in areas that directly involve the handicapped child but also in other areas of spouse, sibling, and extrafamily functioning. The breadth of potential impact implies that professionals working with handicapped children and their families need to anticipate an equally broad scope of service needs. Possible service areas include those directed toward the child (e.g., medical care, education, transportation, and specialized training opportunities), the parents (e.g., emotional support, advocacy, training in behavior management and teaching skills, respite care, and time management), siblings (e.g., social support and training in behavior management), and the family (e.g., economic assistance, genetic counseling, and problem-solving and communication training). Although the array of possible services exceeds what most individual therapists or organizations could provide, an awareness of the diverse needs families present is important to effective planning, referral, and provision of services. Professionals can then help families to identify priorities for services based on the individual family situation.

Chronicity of Family Needs over Time

Another general concern facing families relates to changes in needs over time. Traditionally, it was assumed that families of handicapped children went through a predictable sequence of emotional stages in adjusting to a mentally retarded child. Although the specific categorization of stages varied across authors, the pattern was thought to be characterized by initial feelings of shock and despair, followed by denial and guilt, and then progressing to acceptance and adjustment (Parks, 1977; Wolfensberger, 1967). Such a view implies that mental health professionals should identify the stages families are in, help them work through the stages, and discontinue services at the conclusion of the adjustment process.

However, the notion of time-bound stages of adjustment has been questioned by several authors (Olshansky, 1962; Searl, 1978), leading to an alternative view that families go through chronic periods of adjustment across the life span of the handicapped child. The latter view is supported by research (Wikler, Wasow, & Hatfield, 1981) indicating that parents of handicapped children perceive themselves to have recurrent periods of intense sorrow and stress. These difficult periods may cluster around specific life events that create stress for all families (e.g., moving, job changes, a child leaving home, or a death in the family) or at developmental change points when the handicapped child's delays are emphasized (e.g., the child's failure to begin walking or talking at the expected age, entry into school, or the point at which a younger sibling surpasses the handicapped child developmentally). At these stressful periods, families may need assistance in making the transition between existing patterns of family functioning and altered patterns required of the new life circumstances (Foster, Berger, & McLean, 1981; Skrtic *et al.*, 1984).

An awareness of the chronicity of family needs over time implies that professionals should provide a continuum of services for families at different developmental points. At initial diagnosis, families are most in need of emotional support and information regarding the nature and extent of the handicapping condition. Later, parents may seek assistance on techniques for care and management, but their specific educational needs vary widely as children grow older. As an infant, care, feeding, and environmental stimulation are a focus. By the time the infant becomes a toddler, parents need to begin setting goals of expected behavior and implementing specific procedures to teach the child. Self-feeding, dressing, play, and toileting are areas for which the family is largely responsible. As a preschooler, the child often requires supplemental training at home in preacademic skills, attending, and following instructions. Target behaviors and management techniques change as the child continues to develop. The developmental milestones that provide a guide to parents of nonhandicapped children on expectations for their children are not appropriate for handicapped children (Cerreto, 1981), so parents may need assistance in determining appropriate expectations. At some points, economic or time management concerns may exceed educational needs, and renewed emotional support may be called for as life transitions occur.

Assumptions Regarding the Value of Professional Intervention

Given the diverse and changing needs families present at different points in time, there is a tendency by professionals to assume that the more assistance we provide to families the better. Similarly, it often is presumed that the more involved family members become in accommodating the needs of the handicapped child, the healthier it is for the family. For example, in our enthusiasm to help a family, we might recommend that the parents join a local advocacy organization, enroll in behavior management training, participate in developing the child's educational plan at school, work with the child daily at home to enhance development, send the nonhandicapped children to a siblings workshop, and so on. However, the impact of such a high level of involvement may actually be detrimental for some families. As Foster *et al.* (1981) pointed out, a heavy investment by a parent in a handicapped child can lead to exhaustion and depression for that parent, anger and resistance by other family members whose needs are neglected, and stressful relationships between the parent and handicapped child due to overly intense interactions. They noted that families who choose not to participate in recommended services often are viewed as resistant and experience feelings of guilt at the implication that they are not acting in the best interests of the child. Rather than assuming that more parent or family involvement is better, Foster *et al.* argued that services should be viewed in terms of their impact on overall family functioning.

Winton and Turnbull (1981) addressed the issue of family involvement by assessing parents' perspectives on their role within preschool educational programs for handicapped children. They found that an important factor to parents in choosing and evaluating programs is the relief from full-time caretaking responsibilities provided by enrolling their children in a preschool program. They also found that, although parents often selected preschool programs based on the availability of parent involvement activities, most parents preferred informal contacts with teachers on their child's progress to formal parent training or counseling activities. Based on their findings, Winton and Turnbull stressed the importance of informal ties with families as a legitimate means of involvement at some times.

Existence of Behavior Problems

Another concern facing some families of handicapped children relates to the prevalence of severe behavior problems. Schroeder, Mulick, and Schroeder (1979), in their review of management techniques for severe behavior problems in mentally retarded persons, defined "severe" behavioral disturbances as "having consequences which are correlated with tissue damage requiring medical treatment or which result in exclusion from social and educational programs appropriate to one's adaptive level" (p. 342). This chapter employs a similar definition, with specific attention to behaviors in the home environment that restrict or alter family activities because of the deviant nature of the behaviors. Examples of behavior problems include physical aggression, temper tantrums, self-injury, stereotypic responses (e.g., hand flapping, rocking, bizarre noises), persistent noncompliance, destructiveness, and running away, as well as failure to acquire or practice self-help skills such as toileting, dressing, and eating that are within the child's developmental capabilities.

The likelihood that mentally retarded children will display behavior problems appears to be higher than for nonretarded children. In their review of epidemiological studies, Schroeder *et al.* (1979) reported prevalence rates for behavioral disturbances (not necessarily severe) of 20 to 40% for retarded persons compared to around 5% for the general population. From these findings, they proposed that intellectual retardation may be a predisposing factor for other behavior problems, although they noted that the variables influencing the likelihood of behavior problems are not well understood. Possible variables include genetic or neurological anomalies, environmental history, and atypical operant levels and reinforcement values for specific behaviors.

Although the causes of serious behavior problems in retarded children are not clear, there is little argument about the distressing effects of deviant behavior patterns on the family. Parents with whom we have worked often report feeling discouraged, exhausted, or emotionally distant from their child as a result of contending perpetually with disruptive and oppositional behavior. Not surprisingly, these psychological reactions can undermine parents' attempts to modify the behavior problems, as indicated by the less successful outcomes of behavioral parent training programs with parents reporting depression at the outset of training (Griest & Wells, 1983). Professionals also have commented on the negative self-perceptions held by family members, who interpret the handicapped child's deviant behavior as an indication of their own inadequacy as caretakers (Heifetz, 1977; Paul & Porter, 1981). Without a normative reference for developmental or behavioral expectations, families are at risk to demand too much or too little of the retarded child and to lack confidence and consistency in their own disciplinary practices.

Thus, the existence of serious behavior problems appears to magnify further the impact of the developmentally delayed child on numerous areas of family functioning. To manage such behaviors and teach more adaptive skills requires persistent attention, patience, and consistency in daily interactions despite receiving less affection and responsiveness back from the child. Likewise, professionals need to be especially sensitive to the caretaking and emotional demands on family members and assist them in establishing reasonable goals and priorities.

Commonly Existing Community Services

As a first step in strengthening families of handicapped children, it is essential to know what services are currently available in the community. In the past decade, services for handicapped individuals have developed and expanded at a rapid rate (Loop & Hitzing, 1980; Newman, 1983). Triggered by the deinstitutionalization movement, the Education for all Handicapped Children Act (P.L. 94-142, 1975), and heightened sensitivity to the legal and human rights of handicapped persons, communities have become increasingly active in offering services to handicapped persons.

Parental involvement is regarded as so fundamental a component in programs for handicapped children that it was mandated by federal legislation in the Education for All Handicapped Children Act. However, despite the prevailing opinion that parental involvement has been a positive factor in terms of the child's performance, parental satisfaction, and program effectiveness, most agencies have focused on direct services to the child and have placed little emphasis on developing services for families. The number and availability of family-centered services have lagged seriously behind educational and residential programs for children. Home-based services receive less than 1% of the total federal expenditure in the area of health and social services (Loop & Hitzing, 1980). The present section of this chapter addresses ways professionals can assist families in using existing services, provides an overview of referral networks, and describes model community programs.

Locating Services

When a family with a handicapped child first decides to look for services, a number of obstacles may interfere with their search. As services have not been well integrated, different programs have different priorities and mandates. Cost to the families and geographic stipulations may also be complicating factors. Perhaps the most confusing issue in looking for services involves parents not knowing what services they need and not knowing how to label the services they are seeking. Rubin and Quinn-Curran (1983) identified three steps that a parent must go through to gain access to services. First, parents need to identify their own needs. Second, they need to translate their needs into the appropriate service label. Third, they need to contact the appropriate agency that delivers the service.

In matching families to community services, several issues can be addressed. The daily demands of child care should be discussed as well as the nature and extent of the child's handicap, in order to determine how well the family is coping with the child's needs and what services might be of help. Inquiring about parental expectations for the child and family might also reveal additional service needs. When parents first recognize that their child has special needs, most have little information about the range of available services in education, medicine, psychology, social work, law, employment, housing, and recreation. The federal Education for All Handicapped Children Act and the Rehabilitation Act of 1973, section 504, have educational, employment, and transportation provisions that might be applicable to a family. Information about these acts should be disseminated to parents. Two useful handbooks for parents and professionals are Cutler's *Unraveling the Special Education Maze: An Action Guide for Parents* (1981) and *Parents—You're a Part of the Team* (Leise, 1980).

Information and Advocacy Networks

In response to the need for family services, over 200 local programs for families of handicapped children have been developed. The availability of any program varies depending on the community and on local initiatives for its survival (Loop & Hitzing, 1980). Several national organizations have been developed to provide information and referral. The National Information Center for Handicapped Children and Youth and the Office for Handicapped Individuals are two of several organizations that help information flow between individuals who offer services and those who desire services. Table 1 includes a listing of national resources that can be contacted to identify existing community resources for handicapped children and their families.

It is likely that in some areas, especially rural areas, few resources have been developed. There also is a deficiency of services for specific minority populations (Perske, 1978). If parents or professionals within an area encounter families who would benefit from supportive services, these individuals might conduct a needs assessment to address the issue of developing community services. Many times, local chapters of the Association for Retarded Citizens have been a place where community members have met to plan the expansion of services.

Because obtaining appropriate services for handicapped children often is an uphill battle, several programs have gone beyond national information networks to provide families with direct assistance in locating local resources. One of these programs is the South Bronx Community Services Team (Assael & Waldstein, 1982). This model program locates and synthesizes available services for parents of retarded children in the Bronx, New York. The Parents as Professional Coordinators (Assael & Waldstein, 1982) in Orange County, California, is another model program that conducts intensive training for parents, after which they become official program coordinators for their child.

Family Support Services

Many articles and books written by and for parents of retarded children (e.g., DeMyer, 1979; Featherstone, 1980; Park, 1967) have emphasized the emotional and social benefits obtained from talking to

Table 1. National Information Centers

American Civil Liberties Union 132 West 43rd Street New York, NY 10036	National Easter Seal Society 2023 West Ogden Avenue Chicago, IL 60612
American Genetics Association 818 18th Street, N.W. Washington, DC 20036	National Rehabilitation Association 633 S. Washington Street Alexandria, VA 22314

Coordinating Council for Handicapped
  Children
220 South Street, Room 412
Chicago, IL 60604
	Office for Handicapped Individuals
	U.S. Department of Health and Human
	  Services
	200 Independence Avenue, S.W.
	Washington, DC 20201

Council for Exceptional Children 1920 Association Drive Reston, VA 22091	Office of Rehabilitation Services U.S. Department of Education 400 Maryland Avenue, S.W. Washington, DC 20202

Developmental Disabilities Office
U.S. Department of Health and Human
  Services
200 Independence Avenue, S.W.
Room 338E
Washington, DC 20201
	President's Committee on Employment of
	  the Handicapped
	Washington, DC 20010

Human Resources Center I. U. Willets Road Albertson, NY 11507	President's Committee on Mental Retardation Washington, DC 20201
Library of Congress Division for the Blind and Physically Handicapped 1291 Taylor Street, N.W. Washington, DC 20542	Special Education Programs U.S. Department of Education 400 Maryland Avenue, S.W. Washington, DC 20202

Note. Write to these agencies for information about all handicapping conditions. Specify exactly what information is needed. Listing obtained from fact sheets developed from the National Information Center for Handicapped Children and Youth, P.O. Box 1492, Washington, DC 20013.

and regularly meeting with other parents who have retarded children. The Pilot Parents Program (Porter, 1978) is an organization with chapters throughout the United States whose purpose is to bring together experienced parents of handicapped children with parents who were recently informed of their child's handicap. The program matches a new family with an experienced family and arranges an initial meeting. The two families continue to meet according to the schedules and needs of the families. The local chapter of the Association for Retarded Children (ARC) is another organization where parents can meet with other parents who have handicapped children and where support might be obtained on a long-term basis.

Whereas Pilot Parents and ARC's provide support and assistance to any parent of a disabled child, a number of organizations serve only families with children who have specific disabilities. United Cerebral Palsy, the Association for Children with Learning Disabilities, the Spina Bifida Association, and the National Society for Children and Adults with Autism are examples of organizations that have been developed around a particular disability. A more complete listing of organizations with specialized information about a child's handicap is provided in Table 2. Although many of these organizations offer services other than parent support, the support aspect of the program should be considered in planning overall services for a family.

There are many benefits to using the support component of already existing organizations. Unlike individual therapists, many of these organizations are comprised in part of other parents who have a lifelong commitment to adjusting to living with a handicapped individual. Low cost to families is another benefit of these programs. Professionals working with families of handicapped children might find transferring emotional support from the therapist to a parent support group as an effective, practical way to deal with the need for long-term emotional support for families and to avoid creating an unhealthy dependence on the professional (Heifetz, 1977).

Parent Education and Training Services

Besides emotional support, there are many issues that often need to be addressed when a handicapped individual resides with the family. For example, the family of a child with medical problems will need training in medical aspects relating to the disability. Parents with a non-ambulatory child face practical issues related to care, such as obtaining wheelchair ramps and adaptive equipment. Families are likely to encounter difficulties finding trained baby-sitters and respite services. Parents of nonhandicapped children obtain information about child rearing from their families or friends. Parents of handicapped individuals, however, are likely to need assistance because of the unique needs of their handicapped child.

Whereas emotional support programs have begun to organize at a national level, parent education is an area where there has been little continuity of services (Loop & Hitzing, 1980). Parent educational services may be available within a community, but the focus of training, the orientation of the service provider, and the cost to the family varies. Community mental health centers, child guidance clinics, University

Table 2. National Organizations for Specific Handicaps

Alexander Graham Bell Association for
the Deaf
3417 Volta Place, N.W.
Washington, DC   20007

American Coalition of Citizens with
Disabilities
1200 15th Street, N.W.
Washington, DC   20036

American Council for the Blind
1211 Connecticut Avenue, N.W.
Suite 506
Washington, DC   20036

American Federation for the Blind
15 West 16th Street
New York, NY   10011

American Speech-Language-Hearing
Association
10801 Rockville Pike
Rockville, MD   20852

Association for Children & Adults with
Learning Disabilities
4156 Library Road
Pittsburgh, PA   15234

Association for Persons with Severe
Handicaps
7010 Roosevelt Way, N.E.
Seattle, WA   98115

Association for Retarded Citizens
National Headquarters
P.O. Box 6109
2501 Avenue J
Arlington, TX   76011

Association for the Care of Children's
Health
3615 Wisconsin Avenue
Washington, DC   20016

Council for Exceptional Children
1920 Association Drive
Reston, VA   22091

Down's Syndrome Congress
1640 West Roosevelt Road
Chicago, IL   60608

Epislepsy Foundation of America
4351 Garden City Drive, Suite 406
Landover, MD   20785

Goodwill Industries of America
9200 Wisconsin Avenue, N.W.
Bethesda, MD   20814

March of Dimes Birth Defects Foundation
1275 Mamaroneck Avenue
White Plains, NY   10605

Mental Health Association
1800 North Kent Street
Arlington, VA   22209

National Association of the Deaf
814 Thayer Avenue
Silver Spring, MD   20910

National Easter Seal Society
2023 West Ogden Avenue
Chicago, IL   60612

National Society for Children & Adults
with Autism
1234 Massachusetts Avenue, N.W.
Suite 1017
Washington, DC   20005

National Spinal Cord Injury Association
369 Elliot Street
Newton Upper Falls, MA   02164

Spina Bifida Association of America
343 South Dearborn Street
Suite 319
Chicago, IL   60604

United Cerebral Palsy Association
666 East 34th Street
New York, NY   10016

Affiliated Programs, public schools, hospitals, the Visiting Nurses Association, and university special education or psychology departments are likely places to inquire about training.

A number of programs have been developed on regional levels to provide parents with educational services. One model program that has addressed the educational needs of parents is the Regional Intervention Program (RIP) (Ora, 1971; Strain, Steele, Ellis, & Timm, 1982). Started in Tennessee and in operation since 1969, this program trains parents in behavior management skills to use with their disabled and behaviorally impaired children. The program charges no fees because of a unique pay-back system. New parents are required to make a 1-year commitment to learning parent skills and a 6-month commitment to teaching other parents. Available throughout Tennessee, this program has recently been expanding to other parts of the country as well.

The Portage Project (Shearer & Loftin, 1984; Shearer & Shearer, 1972) is another model program that focuses on early parent involvement in children's educational development. Originally funded by local school districts in south central Wisconsin in cooperation with the Wisconsin Department of Public Instruction, the program provides a home teacher each week to help parents assess the child's skill level in five developmental areas and to provide technical assistance with home-based programs. Replications of the Portage Project model have been developed in numerous communities across the country and in several foreign countries.

The Home-Aid Resource (Perske & Perske, 1981) in Olympia, Washington, is another regional education program for families of mentally retarded persons. This program provides an impressive array of in-home resources for families including respite care, therapy services, program skill development, and government subsidized parent-to-parent contacts. Regional offices also offer other services including case management, individual program planning, vocational training, and recreational services.

The Down's Syndrome Infant–Parent Program (Perske & Perske, 1981) in Eugene, Oregon, is another educationally oriented program that teaches parents to be in-home educators to their children. This program offers several services such as teaching parents developmental milestones of normal children, helping parents discover how routine activities can be broken down into sequential steps for learning, showing parents specific ways they can teach their child, and keeping accurate records of a child's improvement. As with parent support groups, mental health workers should survey the array of possible educational services to determine if parents would benefit from the programs that are already available.

In addition to the model programs described previously, many University Affiliated Facilities (UAF) offer educational and treatment services to families (U.S. Government Printing Office, 1976). For example, the Meyer Children's Rehabilitation Institute at the University of Nebraska Medical Center is one of 45 UAF's receiving federal funds to systematically address the manpower needs for care of the nation's mentally retarded citizens. The institute, which includes nine disciplines, provides evaluation and therapy for developmentally disabled children, youth, and adults as well as their families. Referrals are received from private physicians, public and volunteer agencies, the university clinics, or parents. Services include family therapy, behavior management training, and support programs, as well as recreational and educational activities for handicapped children and their siblings.

As the number of services for families increases, continuity and referral between programs will continue to pose challenges for service workers and parents alike. Professionals who are aware of available community services can provide assistance to families in obtaining the most appropriate services.

Assessment and Planning for Behavioral Intervention

When a handicapped child exhibits serious behavior problems, there is a high likelihood that the family will at some point seek assistance in dealing with the behaviors. The request may occur before the family is fully aware that a disability exists, shortly after learning of the diagnosis of a handicapping condition, or later when the family experiences new difficulties in managing particular behaviors. Because the family will have very different needs at different points in the child's development, individualized assessment is pivotal to planning appropriate intervention. The field of behavioral assessment (Cone & Hawkins, 1977; Haynes, 1978) has developed in response to a need by behavioral therapists to determine effective strategies for planning individualized interventions.

This section of the chapter discusses an approach for assessing family needs and planning intervention based on a five-stage model of behavioral assessment described by Gordon and his colleagues (Gordon & Davidson, 1981; Keefe, Kopel, & Gordon, 1978). Their model consists of five steps: (a) problem identification; (b) measurement and functional analysis; (c) matching treatment to client; (d) assessment of ongoing therapy; and (e) evaluation of therapy. As discussed earlier, assessment of the family's needs for behavioral intervention should be carried out in the context of a comprehensive view of the demands facing the family and the priorities established by the family. Several resources (Gurman & Kniskern, 1981; Turnbull *et al.*, 1984) have provided guidelines for assessing overall family functioning from a systems perspective. The current section focuses on more in-depth evaluation and planning regarding behavioral intervention. Although the behavioral assessment model is applied here to planning family treatment of the handicapped child's behavior problems, it would also be useful when other interventions (e.g., marital therapy, child self-control training, or relaxation training) are being considered.

Problem Identification

The initial task of behavioral assessment is to pinpoint the presenting problems and the likely controlling variables for these behaviors in the natural environment. This task usually begins with a clinical interview of the child's primary caretakers (the parents and, when possible, older siblings or extended family members closely involved with the child). Often the interview is supplemented with information from behavioral checklists, informal observation of family members interacting with the target child, and/or a brief interview directly with the child (Atkeson & Forehand, 1981; Evans & Nelson, 1977). The goal of this stage of assessment is to define the major behavioral concerns facing the family, determine the response characteristics, and identify common antecedents and consequences related to the behaviors.

It is not uncommon for family members to have difficulty in pinpointing the child's problems (Gordon & Davidson, 1981). Often, complaints are stated in global terms (e.g., "she's so demanding" or "he has a negative attitude"), or problems are merely implied in parents' remarks ("I feel exhausted by the time breakfast is over" or "we can't go out alone anymore because we can't trust Martin with a baby-sitter"). Thus, the interview proceeds from these general concerns to helping parents specify behavioral referents. Through the interview, the therapist attempts to obtain a behavioral description of each major problem, its frequency, and severity, as well as a tentative formulation of the events leading up to and following the problem. Questions about the history of the problem, when it is most likely to occur, how long it lasts, and what typically happens to deal with it are helpful to illuminate response characteristics and possible controlling variables.

It is important to keep in mind that information obtained from a clinical interview represents the family members' perceptions of the problems and may not accurately reflect reality. Still, these comments provide a rich base of information for becoming familiar with the child and the family's view of the problems. The interview can be enhanced by the administration of behavioral checklists such as the Child Behavior Checklist (Achenbach & Edelbrock, 1981, 1983), the Eyberg Behavior Inventory (Robinson, Eyberg, & Ross, 1980), or the Walker Problem Behavior Checklist (Walker, 1976). Checklists sometimes reveal concerns that would otherwise be overlooked or omitted in an interview, and they provide a referent group for comparison purposes (Gordon & Davidson, 1981). However, few behavioral inventories are designed specifically for handicapped children, and thus the norms and behavioral categories listed may not be fully appropriate. For families with severely retarded children, an adaptive behavior inventory such as the AAMD Adaptive Behavior Scale (Lambert, 1981), the Alpern Boll Developmental Profile (Alpern, Boll, & Shearer, 1980), or the revised Vineland Adaptive Behavior Scales (Sparrow, Balla, & Cicchetti, 1984) would provide useful information.

Besides the clinical interview and behavioral checklists, informal observation of family interactions can help to confirm or elaborate upon problem identification. By observing the level and frequency of parental instructions to the child, responses to the child's interruptions or misbehavior, attention paid to the handicapped child in comparison to nonhandicapped siblings, evidence of affection or animosity, and social interchanges around appropriate behavior, the therapist can gain an idea of how well the family's verbal report fits with ongoing behavior. Discrepancies can be noted for further exploration during later sessions, or clarification can be sought through questioning in the interview such as, "Is Martha's behavior here typical of how things go at home?" or "I noticed you picked Chad up when he came over to you or cried during our talk today—is that how you often respond when he does that?"

When children have appropriate language skills, they can be interviewed to determine their own view of the problems and to identify possible reinforcers. In our experience, this interview often is accomplished most effectively by visiting with the child alone for a few minutes after the family interview has been completed. If other key individuals are identified as central to the behavioral difficulties (for example, relatives who spend a lot of time with the child, school personnel, or a baby-sitter), obtaining information from them also assists in gaining a comprehensive understanding of the presenting problems. Parents usually are open to allowing the therapist to contact these individuals when it is requested as a part of the assessment process.

After obtaining initial information through an interview, checklists, and observation, the therapist selects the primary target behaviors for treatment. There is no empirically based rationale for determining which of several problematic behaviors should be the focus of intervention or in what order training should proceed. Several programs have taught parents to modify undesired behaviors before attempting to teach new skills. It has been recommended that self-stimulation, self-injury, and stereotypic behaviors be given priority over other behaviors because they are potentially dangerous to the child and might interfere with learning other behaviors (Lovaas, Koegel, Simmons, & Long, 1973; Lovaas & Newsom, 1976). Some therapists have begun training with target behaviors for which they assume parent intervention will be successful (Gardner, 1976), and the importance of taking parent priorities into account has been advocated as a way to produce greater parent cooperation (Altman & Mira, 1983).

Measurement and Functional Analysis

Once the target behaviors have been identified, the second stage of behavioral assessment is the measurement of child responses and determination of functional variables related to the responses. As Gordon and Davidson (1981) caution, measurement and functional analysis are vital components of the behavioral approach that should be applied to every clinical case, not just those designated as research. This stage provides a baseline level of child behavior from which to assess change following intervention, as well as documentation of family members' behaviors and other environmental events that relate to the behavior.

Family members usually participate directly in the measurement process by observing and recording behaviors at home. Often parents are asked to keep daily records on one to three target behaviors by monitoring the frequency of each behavior, its duration, or specific characteristics of the behavior. Responses can be recorded throughout the day if they are infrequent or for a prespecified time if they occur many times each day. To provide more information about the controlling variables, family members can be instructed to record behaviors in a three-term contingency table by denoting the events that precede the problem behavior (antecedents), a description of what the child does (behavior), and the events that follow the behavior (consequences). One to 2 weeks of baseline records usually are sufficient for planning intervention strategies.

Data collection by family members provides a measure of the pre-treatment level of target behaviors, but the accuracy of the data varies greatly depending on the explicitness of the behavior, the convenience of the recording system, and the vigilence of the observer. Accuracy can be improved by using a written definition of the behaviors, shortening the recording intervals, arranging periodic reliability observations, and providing preliminary training in recording procedures. However, in spite of likely inaccuracies in the data, having family members participate in the measurement process serves an important clinical function. By observing and recording behaviors in an objective format, family members become more aware of the actual levels and patterns of child behaviors and of the relationship between their own behavior and the target responses of concern. In this way, measurement contributes directly to functional analysis and intervention planning.

Despite our endorsement of data collection by family members whenever feasible, there are times when it might not be appropriate. When a parent's ability to track behavior is in question, when the family is under much stress, or when motivation is low, requiring data collection could promote faking of records or dropout from the program. In these cases, the therapist might delay asking parents to keep records until later in the training programs or substitute written records with periodic telephone contacts to obtain an informal report of the child's behavior.

To supplement parents' behavioral records, it is desirable to obtain objective measures of family interactions by a nonparticipant observer whenever feasible. In research-oriented parent training programs, these measures are collected during clinic or home observations by trained staff using a standardized, reliable coding system (Reid, 1978; Wahler, House, & Stambaugh, 1976). Although sophisticated data collection is not practical for most applied settings, we have found that simplified observation systems can be developed for use in clinical evaluation of parent training (Budd & Fabry, 1984; Budd, Riner, & Brockman, 1983). We developed a structured observation system for recording specific parent and child behaviors that frequently were the focus of our intervention programs with families of preschool children. By collecting measures of parent–child interactions on a standardized instrument, we can evaluate the effectiveness of treatment and compare interventions across families. Other therapists (Atkeson & Forehand, 1981) also have found structured observation procedures helpful in clinical behavioral assessment of families, although care must be taken to employ a coding system appropriate to the age, developmental level, and presenting problems of the target child referred within the family.

When formal observational procedures are not practical, therapists can gain useful clinical information by periodically observing family interactions informally and recording ongoing behaviors. These observations can take place in the clinic when necessary, although home visits provide a more realistic picture of family functioning and often alert the therapist to environmental conditions that need to be dealt with in order to make intervention effective.

One final point relating to measurement in behavioral treatment concerns the practical value of data collection for families of handicapped, behaviorally disruptive children. Because a defining feature of these children is that they emit numerous inappropriate behaviors, there usually is no difficulty in finding responses to record. The fact that these children will, in many cases, continue to display some undesirable or atypical behavior on a long-term basis suggests that data collection will be useful for helping to decipher when treatment has produced meaningful change. In order to document progress on desired behaviors, the recording categories will need to be broken down into small steps or include approximations toward target behaviors (cf. Adubato, Adams, & Budd, 1981).

Matching Treatment to Client

Once the presenting problems have been identified, and measurement and functional analysis are underway, the next stage of behavioral assessment is to design the intervention procedures to be taught to the family. Because behaviorally oriented treatment is rooted in basic principles of human behavior, the choice of intervention techniques begins by analyzing the antecedent and consequent events for target behaviors, identifying possible treatment strategies, and deciding on the one approach that appears to be best suited to the individual family (see Dangel & Polster, 1984, for a compendium of behavioral treatment programs for families). This stage requires a careful integration of information regarding the skills and motivation of the caretakers, the range of treatment procedures applicable to the target behaviors, and the ways to approach the family to make the intervention most likely to succeed in the particular case. Each of these issues is considered later.

An initial question to be addressed is whether the family situation is amenable to behavioral intervention at this time—that is, whether there is a reasonable chance that the family can and will carry out a treatment program to modify the child's behavior. Although there are no clear-cut rules for determining treatment feasibility, factors to consider include family members' statements of willingness to participate in training sessions, the physical health and energy level of the family, evidence of cooperation among family members, and existing skills in child management. As discussed previously, families of handicapped children have differing priorities and responsiveness to services over time, and we must not assume that all families are ready for behavioral intervention simply because they present themselves to us for an initial interview. If they are responding to the hints of others that they "need" help or are seriously considering institutionalizing the handicapped child when they inquire about services, families may have a hidden agenda to see treatment fail in order to justify their own views of the problem (Gordon & Davidson, 1981).

A second issue to consider in matching treatment to the family is the range of options for modifying the target behaviors. As discussed in the following section on intervention strategies, several different techniques have been shown successful for treating the behaviors displayed by handicapped children. Some techniques rely on arranging reinforcing consequences, some on applying punishing consequences, some on altering the antecedent events or structuring the environment to change the opportunities for a behavior, some on reprogramming behavioral patterns through explicit teaching procedures, and some on combinations of the preceding strategies. Within any technique, the specific stimuli selected for modification also can vary. For example, a reinforcement program to strengthen compliance with parental instructions might employ verbal approval, hugs and affective physical contact, stickers or stars on a chart, access to preferred activities, food, or money as reinforcers.

The choice of which treatment procedures to use with a family rests on the therapist's judgment of what would be most effective, given what is known about the child's preferences, the history of the problem and previous attempts to deal with it, and what family members appear capable and willing to do in order to change the behavior. Immediate, tangible consequences may be necessary with low-functioning children, whereas social contingencies would be more acceptable and normalizing for higher functioning children. Families who are indulgent and non-demanding of the handicapped child would benefit from learning to apply effective disciplinary procedures, whereas emphasis on positive techniques would be more appropriate for families with existing negative interaction patterns. Often the selection of treatment techniques follows logically from the pretreatment records collected by the family, which provide for analysis of specific efforts tried by family members and discussion of likely options with the family. Although at present the selection of treatment procedures is based more on clinical guesswork than on science (Willems, 1974), therapists who tailor interventions to individual families are likely to meet with greater success and cooperation from families than those who apply a routine intervention package to all cases.

A third consideration in matching treatment to the client is the approach to be taken in introducing particular behavioral strategies to the family. Training can occur in the clinic or at home, with only one or two family members or the entire family, through didactic or experiential methods, on an intensive or nonintensive schedule, by teaching general principles first, or proceeding directly to specific behavior problems, and so forth. Some research is available to guide these decisions (cf. O'Dell, 1985); however, due to the wide variety among families, child needs, and available options in service programs, therapists again are faced with evaluating what is reasonable and likely to be successful for the individual family.

Therapists also need to judge how and when to introduce behavioral terminology and combinations of behavioral techniques. Inundating a family with a complex behavioral program is likely to be met with confusion or noncompliance. We have found that introducing new procedures gradually over several sessions is best both for the parents and the child. A progressive introduction of new procedures also gives the therapist feedback about the appropriateness and effectiveness of the intervention.

Ongoing Assessment and Evaluation of Therapy

The two remaining stages of behavioral assessment concern continued application of the measurement and analytic procedures throughout the process of family treatment. As Haynes (1978) and others have discussed, assessment and intervention are interdependent in a behavioral approach, with the course of intervention determined by the effectiveness of initial treatment procedures and by additional information regarding possible controlling variables. In this way, ongoing assessment allows for self-correction and self-evaluation within the intervention program. The methods of assessment that were used during the initial phases of evaluation and treatment are readministered at various points during intervention, and new assessment procedures are introduced as treatment goals shift. After treatment has been terminated, periodic reassessment provides the therapist with a yardstick for determining maintenance of intervention gains and need for additional treatment.

Strategies for Behavioral Intervention

Once the need and direction for behavioral intervention have been clarified, family training can begin. A considerable body of research over the past two decades has shown that parents can modify many important child responses through behavioral intervention (see reviews by Gordon

& Davidson, 1981; Graziano, 1977; O'Dell, 1985). Although much of this research has focused on families of normally developing children, a substantial proportion has dealt with mentally retarded, autistic, or brain-damaged children, as reviewed in a comprehensive publication by Altman and Mira (1983). A broad range of problem behaviors has been addressed including noncompliance, tantrums, sleep disturbances, high activity rates, aggression, self-injury, and stereotypic behaviors. In addition to managing inappropriate behaviors, parents of developmentally disabled children have learned to teach specific skills including toileting, feeding, social interaction, speech, and motor performance.

Behavior therapists have used a variety of approaches to teach parents behavior management skills. Often, texts are provided such as Patterson and Gullion (1968), Patterson (1971), Krumboltz and Krumboltz (1972), Morris (1976), Christophersen (1977), or Baker, Brightman, Heifetz, and Murphy (1976a). Group or individual instruction, telephone calls, clinic visits, and home visits have been employed. Interested readers are referred to the parent training reviews cited previously for more information about the methods for teaching family members behavioral techniques.

The present section has been organized into a discussion of behavior excesses and behavior deficits. Selected inappropriate responses and basic adaptive skills that often are the focus of intervention programs with mentally retarded children are described, along with a review of treatment procedures applicable to the home setting.

Behavior Excesses

Behavior excesses refer to those maladaptive behaviors that are targeted for reduction. As noted earlier, a number of studies have documented the association between behavior problems and retardation (cf. Schroeder, Mulick, & Schroeder, 1979). Although the reason for this association is unclear, families who keep their developmentally disabled child at home will be likely to need assistance in managing the child's behavior.

Noncompliance. Noncompliance has been perceived as the most significant behavior problem experienced by parents of mentally retarded children (Tavormina, Henggeler, & Gayton, 1976) and parents of nonhandicapped children (Forehand, 1977) alike. The term *noncompliance* usually refers to the failure or refusal to complete an instruction given by another person. Violation of rules such as destroying property, jumping on furniture, and inappropriate play also are subsumed under noncompliance. The frequency of the problem and its implications for later adjustment problems if left untreated indicate the need to develop treatment procedures for this particular problem.

Johansson (1971) noted that noncompliance is a term that can include almost any type of deviant behavior. With a few exceptions (e.g., Budd, Green, & Baer, 1976), research with developmentally disabled children and their families has not specifically addressed noncompliance as a target behavior. Decreasing noncompliance or increasing compliance has instead been included as one of several goals of treatment, as in studies to reduce aggression and disruptive behavior (Gardner, Cole, Berry, & Nowinski, 1983), increase conversational skills (Arnold, Sturgis, & Forehand, 1977), eliminate inappropriate verbalizations (Pinkston & Herbert-Jackson, 1975), and enhance cooperative play behaviors (O'Leary, O'Leary, & Becker, 1967). Noncompliance also has been addressed in several studies that have focused on teaching parents basic behavior management skills. Mash and Terdal (1973), for example, taught mothers of mentally retarded children about effective play behaviors and about behavior management skills to increase compliance, self-help, and communication skills. Parents who participated in the program increased their interaction and praise, whereas children showed greater compliance. In one sense, the majority of studies dealing with appropriate or inappropriate behavior have addressed the issue of noncompliance.

The technology for training parents to treat noncompliance has received attention both in research and in clinical reports. The literature has included both handicapped and nonhandicapped populations, and the procedures taught to parents are very similar. A book by Forehand and McMahon (1981) provided a detailed description of a treatment program designed to teach parents to modify their children's noncompliant and other deviant behavior. Although this program does not specifically address the special needs of parents with handicapped children, the procedures described in the book are relevant to this population as well.

Based on a parenting program developed by Hanf and Kling (1973) at the University of Oregon Medical School, Forehand and McMahon's program makes use of a controlled learning environment to teach parents to change maladaptive interactions between parents and children. Sessions are held with individual families in a clinical setting, and discrete parenting skills are taught in a systematic manner. Parents practice the skills in the clinic, receiving feedback from therapists. New skills are added when parents have demonstrated mastery of previous skills. The treatment itself is comprised of two parts. The first deals with teaching parents to reinforce appropriate behavior, and the second deals with teaching instruction giving and time-out. Forehand and McMahon's program for treating child noncompliance has undergone a considerable amount of applied research (McMahon & Forehand, 1984) and is widely respected as a model treatment program.

Self-Stimulation and Self-Injury. It is not unusual for retarded and autistic individuals to display a number of aberrant behaviors, some of which are directed toward themselves. Self-stimulation includes several excessive and bizarre behaviors such as arm flapping, spinning, rocking, grimacing, gesturing, giggling, and screaming. These patterns often are very persistent and interfere with therapeutic attempts to teach the child (Koegel & Covert, 1972). Self-injurious behavior is a more severe form of self-stimulation and includes head banging, hair pulling, eye gouging, and repetitive scratching. The incidence of self-injury is reported to range from 8 to 17% in institutionalized retarded clients (Augustine & Cipani, 1982; Schroeder, Schroeder, Smith, & Dalldorf, 1978; Smeets, 1971). Self-injurious behavior is not only physically damaging, but it often excludes the individual from other educational or social activities because of treatment priorities, chemical restraints, or physical restraints.

Self-stimulation is aversive to others and can interfere with social interactions at home. Paradoxically, the process of self-stimulation and self-inflicted pain appears to have a reinforcing value for the handicapped individual, which may be further strengthened by the reactions of caretakers. The child might be considered to be confused or distressed, and a well-meaning caretaker may attempt to meet the behavior with comfort, reassurance, and decreased demands on the child. Unfortunately, this type of intervention can be harmful, as loving adults have inadvertently reinforced self-destructive behavior (Lovaas, 1982). It would seem that one of the first goals of parent education would be to teach family members that protecting, soothing, and caring reactions to self-stimulatory or self-injurious behaviors are not beneficial and may in fact be deleterious to the child's habilitation.

Before examining some of the procedures that have been used to reduce self-stimulation and self-injury, consideration should be given to whether the behavior does in fact interfere with learning or pose harm. In some cases, self-directed behavior can be reduced by actively promoting and reinforcing alternative positive responses. Favell, McGimsey, and Schell's (1982) finding that self-injury was reduced by giving individuals access to toys, which provided sensory stimulation topographically similar to self-injury, highlights a need to closely examine and modify the external environment before intervening on the child's behavior.

The problem of self-stimulatory behavior in mentally retarded persons has been discussed extensively in literature reviews (Carr, 1977; Johnson & Baumeister, 1978). The greatest success has been found using methods based on operant conditioning principles; however, some mixed findings have been noted with almost all interventions. Differential reinforcement of incompatible behaviors, extinction, time-out, and overcorrection have been effective in some instances but not in others, whereas interventions based on contingent aversive stimulation have been consistently effective (Iwata, Dorsey, Slifer, Bauman, & Richman, 1982).

The role of parents in treating self-stimulatory or self-injurious behaviors has not been extensively addressed. Mild self-injury or non-harmful self-stimulation seems to be within the realm of parent intervention. Hanley, Perelman, and Homan (1979) taught a parent to decrease violent hand and arm waving using time-out and differential reinforcement of other behavior. Barnard, Christophersen, and Wolf (1976) taught a mother to decrease self-injurious behavior using an overcorrection procedure. Several studies have involved parents in applying procedures found to be effective in a clinic situation. Merbaum (1973) taught a parent to use shock to extend treatment effects for self-injurious behavior from home to school, and Cook, Altman, Shaw, and Blaylock (1978) taught a parent to use lemon juice to achieve generalization of treatment for public masturbation. There have been few, if any, research studies involving parents as primary treatment agents for a child's serious self-injury. Lovaas (1982) expressed concern that only a small proportion of institutional staff are qualified to treat serious self-injury, and this same concern may apply to family members. When harmful self-directed behaviors are exhibited, it would be judicious to obtain immediate professional treatment before proceeding with family intervention.

Aggressive and Disruptive Behaviors. Educators in residential training programs rank aggression and disruption by mentally retarded students as among the most difficult behaviors to manage (Wehman & McLaughlin, 1979). They have been identified as a major reason parents initiate institutionalization (Thorsheim & Bruininks, 1979) and as a reason for unsuccessful community placements (Heal, Sigelman, & Switzky, 1978). Because aggressive and disruptive behaviors are a prevalent problem among the mentally retarded, it is likely that families with handicapped children will need training in this area.

Aggressive behavior can take a variety of forms, such as physical attacks on another person, destruction or theft of property, or verbal abuse. *Disruptive behavior* is a broad term that can refer to excessive talking, bizarre noises, getting into another person's things, interrupting others, and repeatedly demanding attention. Both aggression and disruption are similar in upsetting the routine of the family, drawing attention to the individual, and being maintained by the reactions the behaviors promote in others (see Bandura, 1973; Zillmann, 1979, for reviews).

Among the many theories that attempt to explain aggression, there is a large body of research to indicate that the behavior is learned (Fehrenbach & Thelan, 1982).

The behavioral literature includes many examples of parents effectively changing children's aggressive or disruptive behaviors (Christophersen & Sykes, 1979; O'Leary *et al.*, 1967; Patterson, Reid, Jones, & Conger, 1975). Treatment procedures have been diverse and have included positive reinforcement strategies such as differential reinforcement of other behaviors and contingency contracting as well as decelerating procedures such as extinction, time-out, response cost, punishment, and overcorrection (see Fehrenbach & Thelan, 1982, for further information about the use of each procedure). The specific procedures taught to parents are likely to vary according to the age and functioning level of the child and the motivation of the parents. As Patterson and Fleischman (1979) indicated, the success of any treatment is, in part, a function of the parents' ability to modify their habitual pattern of responding to the child's coercive behavior.

Other Inappropriate Behaviors. Besides the excess behaviors previously mentioned, there are a number of undesirable responses that have been observed in mentally retarded children. Pica, the consumption of nonfood items, has been estimated to occur in 25% of institutionalized mentally retarded adults (Danford & Huber, 1982). Persons practicing pica are at risk for nutritional problems, gastrointestional obstructions, and lead intoxication. Although pica has been treated primarily in institutional environments, it could be modified in the home as well (see Albin, 1977; Danford & Huber, 1982 for reviews). Chronic ruminative vomiting, another problematic behavior, is estimated to occur in 10% of mentally retarded individuals (Ball, Hendricksen, & Clayton, 1974). The loss of large amounts of ingested food may cause malnutrition, dehydration, gastrointestinal upset, and lowered resistance to disease (see Davis & Cuvo, 1980, for a review). Stealing can also be a problem for families of the retarded (Azrin & Wesolowski, 1974), as unintentionally or intentionally taking others' belongings is a disruptive emotional issue for many families. Although most of the research about these and other specialized deviant behaviors of mentally retarded individuals has been conducted in institutional settings, treatment procedures could be taught to family members for use at home as well.

Behavior Deficits

In addition to modifying behavior problems, parents of developmentally disabled children have been trained to teach a variety of new skills. The relevance of educating family members in the area of self-help skills was indicated in a survey by Sparling, Lowman, Lewis, and Bartel (cited in Altman & Mira, 1983). Their findings showed that parents were interested in receiving assistance in promoting the child's learning and development once the health of the child and the functioning of the family were assured. Parents surveyed by Lance and Koch (1973) prioritized toileting, eating, and dressing as the most important self-help skills. Several programs have been developed to give parents a comprehensive behavioral repertoire for training new skills in the home (Baker, Brightman, Heifetz, & Murphy, 1976b; Ramey, Collier, Sparling, Loda, Campbell, Ingram, & Finkelstein, 1976; Revill & Blunden, 1979; Shearer & Shearer, 1976). Strategies for training family members to foster specific adaptive skills are reviewed next.

Toilet Training. Of all self-help behaviors, independent toileting is among the most important to be taught to the developmentally delayed child. As the child grows older, incontinence can cause serious social problems as well as being a disruptive factor at home and school. Many community programs require independent toileting as a criterion for entry into services. Toileting can also be one of the more difficult self-care skills to teach because the elimination of waste is learner controlled. Few research studies have addressed the extent to which parents can teach independent toileting to their developmentally disabled child, but some written materials (Baker, Brightman, Heifetz, & Murphy, 1977; Foxx & Azrin, 1973) for parents focus directly on toilet training retarded children.

In planning interventions for toileting, physiological and psychological signs should be taken into account to determine whether a child is ready for instruction. Physiological readiness includes being aware of being wet or soiled and a pattern of having intervals of at least 1½ hours between elimination times. Psychological readiness factors include the ability to follow simple instructions, sit in a chair for 5 minutes, and independently pull pants up and down. If a child is unable to complete the readiness behaviors, parents should first concentrate on teaching these skills before attempting toilet training. One aspect of training that should be emphasized to parents is that it will involve a long-term and consistent effort from the family. Six months to 1 year is not an unusual amount of time for achieving continence with a handicapped child.

Before beginning any toilet training, parents should keep records of elimination for 1 to 2 weeks or until a fairly consistent pattern is witnessed. After this baseline, the method of toilet training can proceed in several directions. Baker *et al.* (1977) recommended beginning with bowel training because bowel movements are more systematic and occur less frequently. These authors suggested that parents take their children to the toilet at scheduled times. Foxx and Azrin (1973) proposed intensive training (8 hours a day) over several days until toileting is mastered. They also recommended using cotton briefs with moisture-detecting snaps inserted in the crotch area, urine alerts, and frequent consumption of fluids during the training period. Other authorities (e.g., Christophersen, 1977) have cautioned parents against the scheduling method of toilet training, in favor of having the child perform all self-help skills independently and sit on the potty chair for many times each day for short periods. The latter approach has been useful for families of non-handicapped children, but no research has demonstrated its feasibility for developmentally disabled children. Probably the most commonly accepted procedure for toilet training retarded children is to begin with training urination by having the child sit on the toilet for short periods of time when she or he is likely to urinate (Mori & Masters, 1980; Morris, 1976).

An integral part of a toilet training program is using rewards such as parental attention and praise, snacks, and favorite games and toys. Initially, rewards should be used for small steps such as sitting on the toilet. Later, rewards can be used for successful elimination; when a child consistently eliminates in the toilet, praise alone can be used to support a child's efforts.

Eating and Dressing. Eating and dressing are two other self-help skills of frequent concern to parents of handicapped children. Whereas these skills usually are acquired with little formal training in nonhandicapped children, some mentally retarded children do not demonstrate independent eating and dressing even when the skills are within their capabilities. One reason for the lack of emergence probably relates to a history of having other family members do many things for handicapped children as a time-saving measure. Thereafter it becomes difficult to recognize when a child's motor coordination and instruction-following abilities have advanced to independent self-care capabilities. Also the child may resist parents' attempts to encourage independent skill performance by remaining passive or noncompliant to parent requests. Adubato et al. (1981) showed that the parents of a severely to profounded retarded 6-year-old boy could learn to teach independent dressing, eating, and toy use through a systematic behavioral program. Other studies also have reported successful outcomes with parents as self-care skill teachers (Fowler, Johnson, Whitman, & Zukotynski, 1978; Heifetz, 1977).

The process of teaching independent eating skills can be broken down into a number of subskills including swallowing, holding food in the mouth, chewing, finger feeding, drinking from a cup, eating with a spoon, eating with a fork, cutting with a knife, pouring liquids, serving food, eating in a group, and passing foods. Independent eating typically is achieved by nonhandicapped children by around age 3. Eating skills are learned sequentially and should be taught to the developmentally disabled child one skill at a time. In general, a backward chaining procedure is useful, by which the parent guides the child through the entire chain of behaviors and begins to reduce the physical assistance at the end of the chain of behaviors. In a drinking program, for example, the parent would place his or her hand over the child's hand and release the child's hand when a sip had been taken and the cup was nearly to the table. Resistence or inappropriate behaviors should be treated in a routine manner, and care should be taken to avoid scolding or showing anger. As with any skill training program, praise and adult attention should be given for small steps of progress. Baker and his colleagues (1976b) addressed independent drinking, eating with a fork, and eating with a spoon in their *Early Self-Help Skills* manual designed for parents. Mori and Masters (1980) covered many additional skills and may be useful in addressing problems with children who have oral-motor problems or physical handicaps.

Independent dressing also can be divided into many subskills, based on the type of clothing and whether it is being put on or taken off. A recommended order for teaching dressing skills is as follows: removing socks, removing underwear and pants, removing pullover shirts and dresses, removing jackets and sweaters, removing shoes, unbuttoning, unzipping, putting on socks, putting on underwear and pants, putting on pullover shirts and dresses, putting on shoes, putting on coats or sweaters, buttoning, zipping, fastening and unfastening a belt, lacing shoes, and tying shoes. Completely independent dressing with nonretarded individuals usually is not achieved until age 5 or 6. Many hours of practice often are needed to teach a handicapped child.

As is the case when teaching independent eating, a backward chaining procedure is most widely used to teach both dressing and undressing. The use of oversized clothing can facilitate the learning process, especially with children who have poor motor control. When mastery has been achieved, parents can gradually reduce the size of clothing until the size of the child has been reached. Task analysis and teaching procedures for dressing skills are available in the Baker *et al.* (1976b) and Mori and Masters (1980) publications.

Social Skills. Many handicapped children have social skills deficiencies that result in rejection by their nonhandicapped peers (Gresham, 1981). Some children may have difficulty due to organic deficiencies, whereas others appear slow or awkward, making them subject to abuse or ridicule by other children. The cycle of rejection and retaliation can exacerbate the initial problem of not being skillful in relating to others. The construct of *social competence* has been difficult to define, due to the complexity of skills involved and the variety of behaviors considered appropriate in different situations. Foster and Ritchey (1979) suggested that social competence be defined as those responses occurring in a specific situation to maximize the probability of positive effects.

Many different behaviors have been taught in social skills programs, including eye contact, greeting, inviting others to join an activity, offering assistance, and sharing materials (Combs & Slaby, 1977). Although most programs to teach social skills to handicapped children have been designed for a school setting using teachers or peers as change agents (see Gresham, 1981; Strain & Fox, 1981, for reviews), a few studies have taught parents to change their child's social behaviors. Arnold *et al.* (1977) taught a mother of a retarded adolescent girl to improve her daughter's conversational skills, and Matson (1981) trained mothers how to overcome their retarded daughters' fearfulness in response to strangers. Powell, Salzberg, Rule, Levy, and Itzkowitz (1985) showed that parents could learn to effectively increase play interactions between their handicapped children and nonhandicapped siblings.

Few programs are available thus far for teaching parents to enhance children's social skills (Budd, 1985). Because of the complexity of skills involved and the fact that social interactions occur in many different settings, parents may have difficulty in helping their children learn appropriate social behaviors. However, considering that parents have been successful in training many other adaptive behaviors and that handicapped children often will need special assistance in learning and refining acceptable social skills, parent involvement could be very valuable. Several potential approaches to including parents in social skills training programs are discussed by Budd (1985).

Summary

This chapter has discussed several issues likely to arise when working with families of mentally retarded children displaying severe behavior problems. Our approach has been problem oriented and pragmatic, in order to help practitioners recognize the demands and stresses facing the family, locate potential community services, assess family needs, and provide behavioral intervention. The existence of a handicapped child can exert a broad impact on all aspects of family functioning. The chronicity of problems at different developmental points and changing family needs over time imply that professionals should anticipate a broad continuum of potential services. Rather than assuming that particular family needs predominate across families, individualized evaluation and planning are essential in order to match families to appropriate services.

As a result of the deinstitutionalization movement and normalization efforts, a greater proportion of mentally retarded children are remaining with their families now than was the case in past years. Community services for handicapped children have grown accordingly, but many gaps and inadequacies still exist. Management of deviant behaviors remains one of the ongoing concerns of families, calling for programs to train parents and other key family members in behavioral intervention strategies. Because systematic training programs for families are not prevalent in most communities, the responsibility for providing behavioral intervention often falls to practitioners in outpatient settings who work with mentally retarded children.

Although the assessment and treatment techniques discussed in this chapter relate primarily to the initial training of family members, there is reason to expect that periodic retraining or refinement of intervention skills will be needed in most families. This is not surprising, given that the behavioral difficulties presented by handicapped children change over time and require somewhat different treatment methods. However, the need for retraining also reflects the well-documented limitations in maintenance and generalization of behavioral treatment outcomes (Forehand & Atkeson, 1977; Stokes & Baer, 1977). Rather than assuming that any family interventions have a lasting impact, it is realistic to expect that follow-up checks and occasional supplemental training will be the norm.

This chapter has focused mainly on the needs of families during the handicapped child's early years; however, families encounter a serious lack of services once formal educational programs have been completed. Little assistance currently is available for families in dealing with problems relating to the handicapped individual's adolescent adjustment, vocational training, transition to living outside the family, and the challenges of adult life. Intervention programs for mentally retarded individuals and their families are needed that span the entire developmental spectrum, from assisting parents in the care of handicapped children, to serving handicapped children as they grow into adolescence and adulthood, and to helping those mentally retarded adults who themselves become parents in caring for their own children (Greenspan & Budd, in press). Skill training and support to the family in the child's early years will provide a firm foundation for meeting the developing issues of the handicapped individual throughout the life span.

References

Achenbach, T. M., & Edelbrock, C. S. (1981). Behavioral problems and competencies reported by parents of normal and disturbed children aged 4 through 16. *Monographs of the Society for Research in Child Development, 46,* (Serial No. 188).

Achenbach, T. M., & Edelbrock, C. S. (1983). *Manual for the Child Behavior Checklist and Revised Child Behavior Profile.* (Available from T. M. Achenbach, Department of Psychiatry, University of Vermont, Burlington, VT 05401).

Adubato, S. A., Adams, M. K., & Budd, K. S. (1981). Teaching a parent to train a spouse in child management techniques. *Journal of Applied Behavior Analysis, 14,* 193–205.

Albin, J. (1977). The treatment of pica (scavenging) behavior in the retarded: A critical analysis and complications for research. *Mental Retardation, 15,* 14–18.

Alpern, G., Boll, T., & Shearer, M. (1980). *Alpern Boll Developmental Profile II.* Aspen, CO: Psychological Development Publications.

Altman, K., & Mira, M. (1983). Training parents of developmentally disabled children. In J. L. Matson & F. Andrasik (Eds.), *Treatment issues and innovations in mental retardation* (pp. 303–371). New York: Plenum Press.

Arnold, S., Sturgis, E., & Forehand, R. (1977). Teaching a parent to teach communication skills: A case study. *Behavior Modification, 1,* 259–276.

Assael, D., & Waldstein, D. (1982). *Handicapped children's early education programs.* Washington, DC: United States Department of Education.

Atkeson, B. M., & Forehand, R. (1981). Conduct disorders. In E. J. Mash & L. G. Terdal (Eds.), *Behavioral assessment of childhood disorders* (pp. 185–219). New York: Guilford Press.

Augustine, A., & Cipani, E. (1982). Treating self-injurious behavior: Initial effects, maintenance and acceptability of treatment. *Child and Family Behavior Therapy, 4,* 53–67.

Azrin, N. H., & Wesolowski, M. D. (1974). Theft reversal: An overcorrection procedure for eliminating stealing by retarded persons. *Journal of Applied Behavior Analysis, 7,* 577–581.

Baker, B. L., Brightman, A. J., Heifetz, L. J., & Murphy, D. M. (1976a). *Behavior problems.* Champaign, IL: Research Press.

Baker, B. L., Brightman, A. J., Heifetz, L. J., & Murphy, D. M. (1976b). *Steps to independence: A skills training series for children with special needs.* Champaign, IL: Research Press.

Baker, B. L., Brightman, A. J., Heifetz, L. J., & Murphy, D. M. (1977). *Toilet training.* Champaign, IL: Research Press.

Ball, T. S., Hendricksen, H., & Clayton, J. A. (1974). A special feeding technique for chronic regurgitation. *American Journal of Mental Deficiency, 78,* 486–493.

Bandura, A. (1973). *Aggression: A social learning analysis.* Englewood Cliffs, NJ: Prentice-Hall.

Barnard, J. D., Christophersen, E. R., & Wolf, M. M. (1976). Parent-mediated treatment of children's self-injurious behavior using overcorrection. *Journal of Pediatric Psychology, 1,* 56–61.

Budd, K. S. (1985). Parents as mediators in social skills training of children. In L. L'Abate & M. Milan (Eds.), *Handbook of social skills training and research* (pp. 245–262). New York: Wiley.

Budd, K. S., & Fabry, P. L. (1984). Behavioral assessment in applied parent training: Use of a structured observation system. In R. F. Dangel & R. A. Polster (Eds.), *Parent training: Foundations of research and practice* (pp. 417–442). New York: Guilford Press.

Budd, K. S., Green, D. R., & Baer, D. M. (1976). An analysis of multiple misplaced parental social contingencies. *Journal of Applied Behavior Analysis, 9,* 459–470.

Budd, K. S., Riner, L. S., & Brockman, M. P. (1983). A structured observation system for clinical evaluation of parent training. *Behavioral Assessment, 5,* 373–393.

Carr, E. G. (1977). The motivation of self-injurious behavior: A review of some hypotheses. *Psychological Bulletin, 84,* 800–816.

Cerreto, M. C. (1981). Parental influences on the socialization of mentally retarded children. *Advances in Special Education, 3,* 83–111.

Christophersen, E. R. (1977). *Little people.* Lawrence, KS: H & H Enterprises.

Christophersen, E. R., & Sykes, B. W. (1979). An intensive, home-based family training program for developmentally delayed children. In L. A. Hammerlynck (Ed.), *Behavioral systems for the developmentally disabled: Vol. I. School and family environments.* New York: Brunner/Mazel.

Combs, M. L., & Slaby, D. A. (1977). Social-skills training with children. In B. B. Lahey & A. E. Kazdin (Eds.), *Advances in clinical child psychology* (Vol. 1, pp. 161–201). New York: Plenum Press.

Cone, J. D., & Hawkins, R. P. (1977). *Behavioral assessment: New directions in clinical psychology.* New York: Brunner/Mazel.

Cook, J. W., Altman, K., Shaw, J., & Blaylock, M. (1978). Case histories and shorter communications: Use of contingent lemon juice to eliminate public masturbation by a severely retarded boy. *Behaviour Research and Therapy, 16,* 131–134.

Cutler, B. (1981). *Unraveling the speical education maze: An action guide for parents.* Champaign, IL: Research Press.

Danford, D. E., & Huber, A. M. (1982). Pica among mentally retarded adults. *American Journal of Mental Deficiency, 87,* 141–146.

Dangel, R. F., & Polster, R. A. (Eds.). (1984). *Parent training: Foundations of research and practice.* New York: Guilford Press.

Davis, P. K., & Cuvo, A. J. (1980). Chronic vomiting and rumination in intellectually normal and retarded individuals: Review and evaluation of behavioral research. *Behavior Research of Severe Developmental Disabilities, 1,* 31–59.

DeMyer, M. K. (1979). *Parents and children in autism.* New York: Wiley.

Evans, I. M., & Nelson, R. O. (1977). Assessment of child behavior problems. In A. R. Ciminero, K. S. Calhoun, & H. E. Adams (Eds.), *Handbook of behavioral assessment* (pp. 603–681). New York: Wiley.

Favell, J. E., McGimsey, J. F., & Schell, R. M. (1982). Treatment of self-injury by providing alternate sensory activities. *Analysis and Intervention in Developmental Disabilities, 2,* 83–104.

Featherstone, H. (1980). *A difference in the family.* New York: Basic Books.

Fehrenbach, P. A., & Thelen, M. H. (1982). Aggressive disorders. *Behavior Modification, 6,* 465–498.

Forehand, R. (1977). Child noncompliance to parental requests: Behavior analysis and treatment. In M. Hersen, R. M. Eisler, & P. M. Miller (Eds.), *Progress in behavior modification* (Vol. 5, pp. 111–147). New York: Academic Press.

Forehand, R. L., & Atkeson, B. M. (1977). Generality of treatment effects with parents as therapists: A review of assessment and implementation procedures. *Behavior Therapy, 8,* 575–593.

Forehand, R. L., & McMahon, R. J. (1981). *Helping the noncompliant child.* New York: Guilford Press.

Foster, M., Berger, M., & McLean, M. (1981). Rethinking a good idea: A reassessment of parent involvement. *Topics in Early Childhood Special Education, 1*(3), 55–65.

Foster, S. L., & Ritchey, W. L. (1979). Issues in the assessment of social competence in children. *Journal of Applied Behavior Analysis, 12,* 625–638.

Fowler, S. A., Johnson, M. R., Whitman, T. L., & Zukotynski, G. (1978). Teaching a parent in the home to train self-help skills and increase compliance in her profoundly retarded adult daughter. *AAESPH Review, 13*(3), 151–161.

Foxx, R. M., & Azrin, N. H. (1973). *Toilet training the retarded*. Champaign, IL: Research Press.

Gardner, J. M. (1976). Training parents as behavior modifiers. In S. Yen & R. W. McIntire (Eds.), *Teaching behavior modification*. Kalamazoo, MI: Behaviordelia.

Gardner, W. I., Cole, C. L., Berry, D. L., & Nowinski, J. M. (1983). Reduction of disruptive behaviors in mentally retarded adults. *Behavior Modification, 7*, 76–96.

Gordon, S. B., & Davidson, N. (1981). Behavioral parent training. In A. S. Gurman & D. P. Kniskern (Eds.), *Handbook of family therapy* (pp. 517–555). New York: Brunner/Mazel.

Graziano, A. M. (1977). Parents as behavior therapists. In M. Hersen, R. M. Eisler, & P. M. Miller (Eds.), *Progress in behavior modification* (Vol. 4, pp. 251–298). New York: Academic Press.

Greenspan, S., & Budd, K. S. (in press). Research on mentally retarded parents. In J. J. Gallagher & P. Vietze (Eds.), *Families of handicapped persons: Current research, treatment, and policy issues*. Baltimore, MD: Paul Brookes.

Gresham, F. M. (1981). Social skills training with handicapped children: A review. *Review of Educational Research, 51*, 139–176.

Griest, D. L., & Wells, K. C. (1983). Behavioral family therapy with conduct disorders in children. *Behavior Therapy, 14*, 37–53.

Gurman, A. S., & Kniskern, D. P. (Eds.). (1981). *Handbook of family therapy*. New York: Brunner/Mazel.

Hanf, C., & Kling, J. (1973). *Facilitating parent–child interaction: A two-stage training model*. Unpublished manuscript, University of Oregon Medical School.

Hanley, E. M., Perelman, P. F., & Homan, C. I. (1979). Parental management of a child's self-stimulation behavior through the use of timeout and DRO. *Education and Treatment of Children, 2*, 305–310.

Haynes, S. N. (1978). *Principles of behavioral assessment*. New York: Gardner Press.

Heal, L. W., Sigelman, C. K., & Switzky, H. N. (1978). Research on community residential alternatives for the mentally retarded. In N. R. Ellis (Ed.), *International review of research in mental retardation* (Vol. 9). New York: Academic Press.

Heifetz, L. J. (1977). Professional preciousness and the evolution of parent training strategies. In P. Mittler (Ed.), *Research to practice in mental retardation: Vol. 1. Care and intervention* (pp. 205–212). Baltimore: University Park Press.

Iwata, B. A., Dorsey, M. F., Slifer, K. J., Bauman, K. E., & Richman, G. S. (1982). Toward a functional analysis of self-injury. *Analysis and Intervention in Developmental Disabilities, 2*, 3–20.

Johansson, S. (1971). *Compliance and noncompliance in young children*. Unpublished doctoral dissertation, University of Oregon.

Johnson, W.L., & Baumeister, A. (1978). Self-injurious behavior: A review and analysis of methodological details of published studies. *Behavior Modification, 2*, 465–484.

Keefe, F. J., Kopel, S. A., & Gordon, S. B. (1978). *A practical guide to behavioral assessment*. New York: Springer.

Koegel, R. L., & Covert, A. (1972). The relationship of self-stimulation to learning in autistic children. *Journal of Applied Behavior Analysis, 5*, 381–387.

Krumboltz, J. D., & Krumboltz, H. B. (1972). *Changing children's behavior*. Englewood Cliffs, NJ: Prentice-Hall.

Lambert, N. (1981). *Diagnostic and technical manual for the AAMD Adaptive Behavior Scale* (school ed.). Monterey, CA: Publishers Test Service.

Lance, W. D., & Koch, A. C. (1973). Parents as teachers: Self-help skills for young handicapped children. *Mental Retardation, 11,* 3–4.

Leise, C. J. (1980). *Parents—You're a part of the team.* Omaha, NE: Meyer Children's Rehabilitation Institute, University of Nebraska Medical Center.

Loop, B., & Hitzing, W. (1980). Family resource services and support systems for families of handicapped children. In J. A. Stark (Ed.), *Family resource systems.* Omaha, NE: Meyer Children's Rehabilitation Institute, University of Nebraska Medical Center.

Lovaas, O. I. (1982). Comments on self-destructive behaviors. *Analysis and Intervention in Developmental Disabilities, 2,* 115–124.

Lovaas, O. I., & Newsom, C. D. (1976). Behavior modification with psychotic children. In H. Leitenberg (Ed.), *Handbook of behavior modification and therapy.* Englewood Cliffs, NJ: Prentice-Hall.

Lovaas, O. I., Koegel, R., Simmons, J. Q., & Long, J. S. (1973). Some generalization and follow-up measures on autistic children in behavior therapy. *Journal of Applied Behavior Analysis, 6,* 131–166.

Mash, E. J., & Terdal, L. (1973). Modification of mother–child interactions: Playing with children. *Mental Retardation, 11,* 44–49.

Matson, J. L. (1981). Assessment and treatment of clinical fears in mentally retarded children. *Journal of Applied Behavior Analysis, 14,* 287–294.

McMahon, R. J., & Forehand, R. (1984). Parent training for the noncompliant child: Treatment outcome, generalization, and adjunctive therapy procedures. In R. F. Dangel & R. A. Polster (Eds.), *Parent training: Foundations of research and practice* (pp. 298–328). New York: Guilford Press.

Merbaum, M. (1973). The modification of self-destructive behavior by a mother-therapist using aversive stimulation. *Behavior Therapy, 4,* 442–447.

Mori, A. A., & Masters, L. F. (1980). *Teaching the severely mentally retarded.* Germantown, MD: Aspen Publications.

Morris, R. J. (1976). *Behavior modification with children: A systematic guide.* Cambridge, MA: Winthrop.

Newman, J. (1983). Handicapped persons and their families: Philosophical, historical, and legislative perspectives. In M. Seligman (Ed.), *The family with a handicapped child: Understanding and treatment* (pp. 3–25). New York: Grune & Stratton.

O'Dell, S. L. (1985). Progress in parent training. In M. Hersen, R. M. Eisler, & P. M. Miller (Eds.), *Progress in behavior modification* (Vol. 19, pp. 57–108). New York: Academic Press.

O'Leary, K. D., O'Leary, S., & Becker, W. C. (1967). Modification of a deviant sibling interaction pattern in the home. *Behaviour Research and Therapy, 5,* 113–120.

Olshansky, S. (1962). Chronic sorrow: A response to having a mentally defective child. *Social Casework, 18,* 190–193.

Ora, J. P. (1971). *Instruction pamphlet for parents of oppositional children.* Nashville, TN: George Peabody College for Teachers. (ERIC Document Reproduction Service No. ED 070 220)

Park, C. C. (1967). *The siege.* Boston: Little, Brown.

Parks, R. (1977). Parental reactions to the birth of a handicapped child. *Health and Social Work, 2,* 52–66.

Patterson, G. R. (1971). *Families: Applications of social learning to family life.* Champaign, IL: Research Press.

Patterson, G. R., & Fleischman, M. J. (1979). Maintenance of treatment effects: Some considerations concerning family systems and follow-up data. *Behavior Therapy, 10,* 168–185.

Patterson, G. R., & Guillion, M. (1968). *Living with children: New methods for parents and teachers.* Champaign, IL: Research Press.

Patterson, G. R., Reid, J. B., Jones, R. R., & Conger, R. E. (1975). *A social learning approach to family intervention: Vol. 1. Families with aggressive children.* Eugene, OR: Castalia.

Paul, J. L., & Porter, P. B. (1981). Parents of handicapped children. In J. L. Paul (Ed.), *Understanding and working with parents of children with special needs* (pp. 1–22). New York: Holt, Rinehart & Winston.

Perske, R. (1978). *Mental retardation: The leading edge.* Washington, DC: U.S. Government Printing Office.

Perske, R., & Perske, M. (1981). *Hope for the families.* Nashville, TN: Abingdon Press.

Pinkston, E. M., & Herbert-Jackson, E. W. (1975). Modification of irrelevant and bizarre verbal behavior using parents as therapists. *Social Service Review, 49,* 46–63.

Porter, F. (1978). *The Pilot Parent Program: A design for developing a program for parents of handicapped children.* (Available from GOARC, 3610 Dodge St., Omaha, NE, 68183)

Powell, T. H., Salzberg, C. L., Rule, S., Levy, S., & Itzkowitz, J. S. (1985). Teaching mentally retarded children to play with their siblings using parents as trainers. *Education and Treatment of Children, 6,* 343–362.

Ramey, C. T., Collier, A. M., Sparling, J. J., Loda, F. A., Campbell, F. A., Ingram, D. L., & Finkelstein, N. W. (1976). The Carolina Abecedarian Project: A longitudinal and multidisciplinary approach to the prevention of developmental retardation. In T. D. Tjossem (Ed.), *Intervention strategies for high risk infants and young children.* Baltimore: University Park Press.

Reid, J. B. (Ed.). (1978). *A social learning approach to family intervention: Vol. 1. Observation in home settings.* Eugene, OR: Castalia.

Revill, S., & Blunden, R. (1979). A home training service for preschool developmentally handicapped children. *Behavior Research and Therapy, 17,* 207–214.

Robinson, E. A., Eyberg, S. M., & Ross, A. W. (1980). The standardization of an inventory of child conduct problem behaviors. *Journal of Clinical Child Psychology, 9*(1), 22–29.

Rubin, S., & Quinn-Curran, N. (1983). Lost, then found: Parents' journey through the community service maze. In M. Seligman (Ed.), *The family with a handicapped child: Understanding and treatment* (pp. 63–94). New York: Grune & Stratton.

Schroeder, S. R., Schroeder, C. S., Smith, R., & Dalldorf, J. (1978). Prevalence of self-injurious behavior in a large state facility for the retarded: A three year follow-up study. *Journand of Autism and Childhood Schizophrenia, 8,* 261–269.

Schroeder, S. R., Mulick, J. A., & Schroeder, C. S. (1979). Management of severe behavior problems of the retarded. In N. R. Ellis (Ed.), *Handbook of mental deficiency, psychological theory, and research* (rev. ed., pp. 341–366). Hillsdale, NJ: Erlbaum.

Searl, S. J. (1978). Stages of parent reaction. *The Exceptional Parent, 8,* 23–27.

Shearer, D. E., & Loftin, C. R. (1984). The Portage Project: Teaching parents to teach their preschool children in the home. In R. F. Dangel & R. A. Polster (Eds.), *Parent training: Foundations of research and practice* (pp. 93–126). New York: Guilford Press.

Shearer, M., & Shearer, D. (1972). The Portage Project: A model for early childhood education. *Exceptional Children, 36,* 172–178.

Shearer, D., & Shearer, M. (1976). The Portage Project: A model for early childhood intervention. In T. Tjossem (Ed.), *Intervention strategies for high-risk infants and young children.* Baltimore: University Park Press.

Simeonsson, R. J., & Simeonsson, N. E. (1981). Parenting handicapped children: Psychological aspects. In J. L. Paul (Ed.), *Understanding and working with parents of children with special needs* (pp. 51–88). New York: Holt, Rinehart & Winston.

Skrtic, T. M., Summers, J. A., Brotherson, M. J., & Turnbull, A. P. (1984). Severely handicapped children and their brothers and sisters. In J. Blacher (Ed.), *Severely handicapped young children and their families: Research in review* (pp. 215–246). Orlando: Academic Press.

Smeets, P. M. (1971). Some characteristics of mental defectives displaying self-mutilation behavior. *Training School Bulletin, 68*, 131–135.

Sparrow, S. S., Balla, D. A., & Cicchetti, D. V. (1984). *Vineland Adaptive Behavior Scales.* Circle Pines, MN: American Guidance Service.

Stokes, T. F., & Baer, D. M. (1977). An implicit technology of generalization. *Journal of Applied Behavior Analysis, 10*, 349–367.

Strain, P. S., & Fox, J. J. (1981). Peer social initiations and the modification of social withdrawal: A review and future perspective. *Journal of Pediatric Psychology, 6*, 417–433.

Strain, P. S., Steele, P., Ellis, T., & Timm, M. A. (1982). Long-term effects of oppositional child treatment with mothers as therapists and therapist trainers. *Journal of Applied Behavior Analysis, 15*, 163–169.

Tavormina, J. B., Henggeler, S. W., & Gayton, W. F. (1976). Age trends in parental assessments of behavior problems of their retarded children. *Mental Retardation, 14*, 38–39.

Thorsheim, M. J., & Bruininks, R. H. (1979). *Admission and readmission of mentally retarded people to residential facilities.* Minneapolis: University of Minnesota, Department of Psychoeducational Studies.

Turnbull, A. P., Summers, J. A., & Brotherson, M. J. (1984). *Family systems theory: A guide for research and intervention.* (Available from University of Kansas, Research and Training Center on Independent Living, Lawrence, KS)

U.S. Government Printing Office. (1976). *The role of higher education in mental retardation and other developmental disabilities.* Washington, DC: Author.

Wahler, R. G., House, A. E., & Stambaugh, E. E. (1976). *Ecological assessment of child problem behavior.* New York: Pergamon Press.

Walker, H. M. (1976). *Walker Problem Behavior Identification Checklist Manual.* Los Angeles: Western Psychological Services.

Wehman, P., & McLaughlin, P. J. (1979). Teachers' perceptions of behavior problems with severely and profoundly handicapped students. *Mental Retardation, 17*, 20–21.

Wikler, L., Wasow, M., & Hatfield, E. (1981). Chronic sorrow revisited: Parent vs. professional depiction of the adjustment of parents of mentally retarded children. *American Journal of Orthopsychiatry, 51*(1), 63–70.

Willems, E. P. (1974). Behavioral technology and behavioral ecology. *Journal of Applied Behavior Analysis, 7*, 151–165.

Winton, P. J., & Turnbull, A. P. (1981). Parent involvement as viewed by parents of preschool handicapped children. *Topics in Early Childhood Special Education, 1*(3), 11–19.

Wolfensberger, W. (1967). Counseling parents of the retarded. In A. A. Baumeister (Ed.), *Mental retardation, appraisal, education and rehabilitation.* Chicago: Aldine.

Zillmann, D. (1979). *Hostility and aggression.* Hillsdale, NJ: Erlbaum.

9

Teacher and School Personnel Training

MARY MARGARET KERR

Introduction

This chapter offers a discussion of issues in training teachers and other school personnel to work with severely behaviorally disordered/mentally retarded students. *School personnel* may include classroom teachers, paraprofessionals, preservice or student teachers, school psychologists, and a host of other staff members (e.g., principals, counselors, speech and language specialists). This discussion, however, will be limited to the former group of professionals. The *school* may refer to a regular public school in which a few self-contained classes for the severely handicapped operate, or a special public, private, or parochial school devoted entirely to the education of the handicapped. A group of classrooms may also be located on the grounds of a public or private residential institution.

Training for school personnel may be designated as inservice or preservice. Inservice refers to seminars, workshops, supervision, and consultation offered to professionals and paraprofessionals already employed by a school. Preservice training activities, on the other hand, include college courses, workshops, practica, student teaching rotations, and volunteer orientation programs—all designed to prepare an individual for future service in the schools. This chapter, moreover, emphasizes competency-based and field-based personnel preparation approaches. Elam (1971) defined *competency-based teacher education*, or CBTE, as a program in which trainees are required to demonstrate empirically validated teaching skills and to produce pupil change as a result. Performance objectives and criteria are outlined in advance, and an emphasis is placed on demonstrated products (Semmel & Semmel, 1976). *Field-based* programs, similar in many dimensions to competency-based,

MARY MARGARET KERR • Department of Psychiatry, Western Psychiatric Institute and Clinic, University of Pittsburgh School of Medicine, Pittsburgh, Pennsylvania 15213.

emphasize the importance of applying instructional practices in the classroom. As defined by Nelson (1978),

> Field-based teacher education refers to a broad based range of training curricula and activities. The focal point of these activities, however, is upon the trainee's execution of professional skills in a professional milieu, rather than in a laboratory, clinic or other contrived situation. It is also characteristic of field-based programs that field experiences are an integral part of training activities throughout the training program, as opposed to those occurring primarily toward the end of training. (pp. 3–4)

In contrast to CBTE and field-based models, a more traditional approach to school personnel training might consist of didactic lectures, infrequent pencil-and-paper assessments, and limited classroom experiences.

Continuing with this introduction to the emphases and accompanying terminology of this chapter, the reader is directed to the outline of topics covered in the remainder of the chapter. First follows a brief history of school personnel training issues in severely behaviorally disordered/mentally retarded. With this review as background, the discussion turns to specialized training needs in (a) assessment and planning, (b) teaching and behavior management, (c) progress monitoring, and (d) related professional areas.

Historical Issues (Pre-1975)

Prior to the passage of Public Law 94-142 (the Education for All Handicapped Children's Act, 1975), training programs in severe behavioral disorders and mental retardation addressed somewhat different topics from those listed in college syllabuses today. Personnel preparation, in fact, had a different handicapped population as its focus because the severely and profoundly handicapped individuals served in today's schools were not—prior to 1975—taught by special educators. Rather, many spent their lives in residential placements, receiving no special education services (Snell, Taylor, & Thompson, 1978; Spence, 1978). The fact that personnel training programs addressed a different and much less severely handicapped population remains a major issue for inservice consultants and supervisors of personnel trained prior to 1975. These psychologists, teachers, and support service persons most likely were trained for work with mildly or moderately handicapped individuals— not the nonverbal, self-injurious or self-stimulatory students who joined public education after 1975. Yet these inadequately prepared school personnel now find themselves called upon to work with a "new" population of severely behaviorally disordered/retarded students.

The *categorical design* of teacher training programs in the recent past places a second obstacle in the path of those who train school personnel. Most teachers preparing for work with the "emotionally disturbed" (the term used most often during the 1960s and 1970s to describe students with behavior problems) expected to teach mildly handicapped students who met the following criteria:

1. An inability to learn *which cannot be explained by intellectual, sensory, or health factors*.
2. An inability to build or maintain satisfactory interpersonal relationships with peers and teachers.
3. Inappropriate types of behavior or feelings under normal conditions.
4. A general, pervasive mood of unhappiness or depression.
5. A tendency to develop physical symptoms, pain, or fears associated with personal or school problems. (Bower, 1969, p. 20)

The University of California at Los Angeles, in fact, was one of the first training programs in the country to address the special—and cross-categorical—needs of the severely behaviorally disordered. It did so under a third disability category: schizophrenia, or autism (see Hewett, 1964; Lovaas, 1966; Lovaas, Koegel, Simmons, & Long, 1973).

While teachers of the emotionally disturbed prepared to teach pupils as described by Bower (1969) and others, the future instructors of the mentally retarded went about their training in a nearly mutually exclusive manner. Academics (e.g., arithmetic and reading) were replaced in their curriculum by self-care skills and other courses designed to meet the needs of students described as

having subaverage general intellectual functioning existing concurrently with deficits in adaptive behavior and manifested during the developmental period, which adversely affects a child's educational performance. (*Federal Register*, 1977, pp. 42478–42479)

These historically separate and categorical tracks in special education personnel preparation still are significant forces in preservice and inservice training. Many, if not most, of today's special educators lack adequate training in dual handicaps. In fact, many teacher training programs persist in mutually exclusive routes for behavior disorders and mental retardation, a concept reinforced by categorical certification programs in certain states. A retiring teacher whose training focused solely on the mentally retarded summed up her dilemma aptly: "It took me a long time to realize that severely and profoundly retarded students could be oppositional brats, *too!*"

The specialized issues of teacher training programs prior to 1975 were in many instances just a reflection of the young special education field in general. Special education classroom practices for the emotionally disturbed, for example, emerged for the first time after 1960. And not until the passage of P.L. 88-164 in 1963 were federal funds allocated for personnel preparation in the specialty of emotionally disturbed (Kauffman, 1981). Reports of behavior modification in classroom settings appeared for the first time as recently as 1968. Moreover, three national organizations whose mission is to disseminate information on "best practices" to professionals and parents of the severely handicapped were established only in the decade immediately preceding P.L. 94-142: The Association for the Severely Handicapped in 1974, Council for Children with Behavioral Disorders in 1964, and the National Society for Autistic Children in 1965 (Kauffman, 1981).

In summary, present-day training of school personnel to meet the needs of severely behaviorally disordered/mentally retarded students has its roots in the very recent past and continues to be influenced by three major forces: categorical and separate training tracks, preparation focused on the moderately and mildly handicapped, and the inevitable delay in information transmitted from a still infant research field to training programs for school personnel.

Historical Issues (Post-1975)

In November 1975, Congress enacted the Education for All Handicapped Children Act, commonly known as Public Law 94-142 (P.L. 94-142, sec. 601c). A comprehensive review of the Education for All Handicapped Children Act is beyond the scope of this chapter (see Bateman & Herr, 1981; Martin, 1979, for discussion). Nevertheless, a brief review of its major tenets may help the reader to understand the influence exerted on school personnel training efforts. These six major principles include:

1. *Zero reject.* Under this principle, *all* handicapped children between ages 3 and 21 are provided a free, appropriate, public education, unless contradicted by state laws (applicable only to ages 3 to 5 and 18 to 21). The law also mandated that the previously unserved (e.g., severely behaviorally disordered/mentally retarded) and those most severely handicapped in each category receive federal funding priority. This resulted in widespread deinstitutionalization.

2. *Nondiscriminatory evaluation.* Prior to special education placement, each child must receive a full evaluation of his or her strengths and weaknesses. (This process and its impact on personnel training are

described in the next section.) Upon evaluation, each special education student is assigned a disability label. "Emotionally disturbed" and "mentally retarded" follow the definitions cited earlier. "Autism," classified as a health impairment, is "manifested by severe communication and other developmental and educational problems" (*Federal Register*, 1981, pp. 3865–3866).

3. *Individualized education programs (IEPs)*. This document is the focus of mandatory IEP meetings, in which parent involvement is mandated. The IEP serves as a "communication vehicle, . . . a commitment of resources," "a management tool, . . . a compliance/monitoring document, . . . and . . . an evaluation device" (*Federal Register*, 1981, p. 5462).

4. *Least restrictive environment (LRE)*. This controversial principle requires that handicapped students, to the maximum extent appropriate, be educated with nonhandicapped students. The popular term, *mainstreaming*, while never appearing in the legal definition of LRE, has a similar connotation.

5. *Due process*. This component may be considered "a system of checks and balances concerning the identification, evaluation, and provision of services regarding handicapped students" (Turnbull, Strickland, & Brantley, 1982, p. 10).

6. *Parental participation*. Reflected in all of the principles is the right of parents to participate in educational decisions.

References to this legislation as "the Employment for All Special Educators Act" are not entirely inaccurate. In fact, the passage of P.L. 94-142 made a tremendous impact on both inservice and preservice training (Nelson, 1978). This impact is illustrated by an excerpt from the "Comprehensive System of Personnel Development" section of P.L. 94-142:

> Each annual program plan must include a description of programs and procedures for the development and implementation of a comprehensive system of personnel development which includes:
>
> a. The inservice training of general and special educational instructional, related services, and support personnel;
>
> b. Procedures to insure that all personnel necessary to carry out the purposes of the Act are qualified (as defined in 121a.12 of Subpart A) and that activities sufficient to carry out this personnel development plan are scheduled; and
>
> c. Effective procedures for acquiring and disseminating to teachers and administrators of programs for handicapped children significant information derived from educational research, demonstration, and similar projects, and for adopting, where appropriate, promising educational practices and materials developed through those projects. (*Federal Register*, 1977 p. 42492)

Furthermore, the Personnel Development Plan submitted by the state educational agency extended to include paraprofessionals, parents, surrogate parents, and volunteers; and federal funds for training these other personnel have been allocated (*Federal Register*, 1977, p. 42493).

The remainder of the chapter highlights current school personnel training issues in assessment and planning, implementation, progress monitoring, and related professional topics. The first three areas were chosen because they reflect the customary chronological sequence of events for school personnel. The fourth topic allows a discussion of often-overlooked professional concerns such as liability and burnout.

Issues in Assessment and Planning

Assessment

What is meant by assessment? According to P.L. 94-142, an assessment, or evaluation, for special education placement must meet strict criteria:

> (a) Tests and other evaluation materials:
> (1) Are provided and administered in the child's native language or other mode of communication, unless it is clearly not feasible to do so;
> (2) Have been validated for the specific purpose for which they are used;
> (3) Are administered by trained personnel in conformance with the instructions provided by their producer;
> (b) Tests and other evaluation materials include those tailored to assess specific areas of educational need and not merely those which are designed to provide a single general intelligence quotient.
> (c) Tests are selected and administered so as to ensure that when a test is administered to a child with impaired sensory, manual, or speaking skills, the test results accurately reflect the child's aptitude or achivement level or whatever other factors the test purports to measure, rather than reflecting the child's impaired sensory, manual, or speaking skills (except where those skills are the factors which the test purports to measure);
> (d) No single procedure is used as the sole criterion for determining an appropriate educational program for a child; and
> (e) The evaluation is made by a multidisciplinary team or group of persons, including at least one teacher or other specialist with knowledge in the area of suspected disability.
> (f) The child is assessed in all areas related to the suspected disability, including, where appropriate, health, vision, hearing, social and emotional status, general intelligence, academic performance, communicative status, and motor abilities. (Turnbull, Strickland, & Brantley, 1982, p. 4)

This section alone has reformed assessment practices throughout the country. Moreover, the criteria take on special and often complex meanings when applied to severely behaviorally disordered/mentally retarded students.

The provision of testing in a student's own mode of communication suggests that school psychologists (often the key staff in a special education evaluation) should be trained in manual communication. Furthermore, the traditional verbally dominated format of many standardized measures renders them impractical for use with nonverbal individuals. If a pupil is physically handicapped or sensor-impaired, then additional modifications are necessary (Dubose, Langley, & Stagg, 1979). A review of tests for the severely handicapped revealed few that met this criterion (Dubose et al., 1979). Once modifications are made in the traditional format of an instrument, it still may fail to meet the second criterion—validity. Few if any tests have been validated with severely behaviorally disordered/mentally retarded individuals because of the low incidence of this dual handicap (Dubose et al., 1979). Moreover, modifications made by school personnel to enhance the utility of an evaluation material may violate the third guideline: that a test be administered according to its manual.

For behaviorally disordered/mentally retarded individuals, the well-intended mandate to ensure that the test results do not reflect solely on the child's impairment and exclude his or her strengths may be impossible to achieve. The very nature of these students' behavior problems (e.g., attention deficits, overselectivity, self-stimulation, aggressive behavior toward the examiner, and/or destruction of the test items) may distort the test results. In response to this likelihood, many examiners resort to an attribution of "untestable," abbreviating or terminating altogether their efforts to assess an individual's strengths and weaknesses.

The last three criteria (d, e, and f) underscore the importance of multidisciplinary collaboration. The separate, categorical training programs cited earlier may directly contradict this attempt to unite disciplines in the assessment process. The premise of multidisciplinary teams (or "M-teams," as they are called) implies that trainees in school psychology, mental retardation, behavior disorders, speech and language, physical therapy and education, psychiatry, and regular education study together and share the complexities of diagnostic questions. Yet this innovative training has been slow to develop into a reality. Cross-disciplinary diagnostic and planning work are especially important for behaviorally disordered/mentally retarded individuals whose remedial programs will derive inevitably from research that includes psychopharmacology, behavior modification and therapy, learning theory, special education, and vocational education.

A further, albeit unspecified, issue in assessing severely behaviorally disordered/mentally retarded individuals rests in the need for excellent applied behavior analysis skills. These skills contribute to a level of assessment that may be critical to a student's educational success, or— more dramatically—to continued health, as in the case of analyzing self-injurious behaviors. One might argue that self-injurious behaviors are outside the purview of school personnel, yet these behaviors take place in school settings and usually prevent learning (Schroeder, Schroeder, Rojahn, & Mulick, 1981). The successful treatment of self-injury, and of many of the problems that characterize severe behavior disorders and mental retardation, depends on a careful scrutiny of the situational contexts of the behaviors. Yet many textbooks for school personnel training offer only cursory information on this topic (see Kerr & Nelson, Chapter 8, 1983, for discussion).

Subsumed under applied behavior analysis is the important skill of direct observational measurement. Any direct observation, moreover, is based on a concise, incontrovertible definition of the target behavior(s). For school personnel working with individuals who engage in bizarre and/or low-rate, problem behaviors, standard problem behavior checklists do not suffice as measures of these often high-rate and complex actions. Instead, psychologists and educators must develop their own target behavior statements, incorporate them into a reliable direct observational recording system, and collect—or train someone else to collect— representative, daily samples of the behavior for analysis. This complex activity raises another issue for personnel preparation: competence in reading and applying information from research reports, the best source of information on such data systems.

Summary. The assessment competencies required of school personnel today range from fluency in a second language (e.g., manual communication) to critical reading of professional journals. Recommendations for preservice and inservice programs include:

1. competency-based training in specialized formal assessment of low-incidence handicaps, with an emphasis on test adaptation, motivated assessment, and criterion-referenced, diagnostic teaching trials;

2. participation (by contributing test data) in field testing efforts to validate standardized measures with low-incidence handicapped populations;

3. field-based training with the severely handicapped that emphasizes one's role in a multidisciplinary evaluation team;

4. careful training in applied behavior analysis, with extensive opportunities to *apply* these principles to severe behavior problems (e.g., self-stimulation, self-injury); and,

5. multiple opportunities to read and discuss assessment procedures cited in research publications, accompanied by an increased emphasis on data-based assessment practices in textbooks (e.g., Kerr & Nelson, 1983; Snell, 1983) and field-based coursework.

Planning

The assessment skills required of today's school personnel make an essential contribution to the development of a satisfactory Individualized Education Program (IEP), the core document mandated under P.L. 94-142. To illustrate the application of assessment and planning skills, Figure 1 represents an IEP for a severely behaviorally disordered/mentally retarded student.

INDIVIDUAL EDUCATION PROGRAM: TOTAL SERVICE PLAN

Child's Name *Jenny Payton*

School *Mondale School*

Date of Program Entry *9/16/83*

Summary of
Present Levels of Performance

Jenny was identified as severely MR/BD, never interacting with others and involved in stereotypic behavior (hand waving)

Prioritized Long-Term Goals

1. *Jenny will participate in sharing toys at school*
2. *Jenny will not hand wave during school activities*
3. _____

Short-Term Objectives	Evaluation	Educational and/or Support Services	Person(s) Responsible	Percent of Time	Beg. and Ending Date	Review Date
1. *Jenny will not wave or stare at hands during 15 minutes of sharing toys at school.*	*through direct observation (daily)*	*cooperative toys will be available for activity. Teacher will reinforce Jenny for sharing toys.*	*1. teacher 2. student, Jenny 3. peers at school*	*20% of intervals observed*	*9/16/83 - 11/14/83*	*6/6/84*

Percent of Time in Regular Classroom
20%

Placement Recommendation

Committee Members Present

Ralph Jernigan, Principal
Peggy Gibbs, School Consultant
Bonnie Jamison, Teacher
Joe and Mary Payton, Parents

Dates of Meeting *11/21/82; 12/6/82.*

Figure 1. Individualized education program.

As manifested in Figure 1, an IEP includes:

1. a documentation of the student's current level of educational performance;
2. annual goals or the attainments expected by the end of the school year;
3. short-term objectives, stated in instructional terms, which are the intermediate steps leading to the mastery of annual goals;
4. Documentation of the particular special education and related services that will be provided to the child;
5. an indication of the extent of time a child will participate in the regular education program;
6. projected dates for initiating services and the anticipated duration of services; and,
7. appropriate objective criteria, evaluation procedures, and schedules for determining mastery of short-term objectives, at least on an annual basis. (Turnbull *et al.*, 1982, p. 5)

Teaching school personnel to write comprehensive and well-articulated IEPs is a major issue for supervisors and consultants. For whereas P.L. 94-142 was enacted in 1975, states were not required to provide full educational opportunities to the full age range of children until September of 1980. Therefore, the development of Individualized Education Programs (and compliance with other provisions of the regulations) is a relatively new skill for special educators. Revent findings suggest that, despite the obvious importance of clearly defined educational objectives, special educators often lack adequate, behaviorally stated plans (Gable, Hendrickson, & Young, 1983; Whitney & Striefel, 1981). In the following paragraphs, issues in training school personnel to develop Individualized Education Programs are discussed.

The first requirement of an IEP is a documentation of the student's current performance level. This summary of the previous special education evaluation is intended as an overview, or preface, to the instructional objectives that follow. Accordingly, the validity of subsequent instructional objectives largely depends on whether an adequate educational evaluation has taken place. A recurring problem in the development of IEPs is the failure to establish continuity of personnel between assessment and educational program development. In other words, the evaluation team may or may not be adequately represented in the IEP conference. This problem appears especially acute in the case of behaviorally disordered students, whose major evaluation may take place in a psychiatrist's office, whereas the IEP meeting takes place in a school setting, often without the evaluating psychiatrist present. To circumvent this problem, school personnel should be well acquainted with evaluation procedures that precede the development of an IEP, particularly when those evaluation procedures take place outside the school system.

The second component of an IEP is a statement of annual goals. "Annual" implies 9-month school year, although 12-month school programs may be instituted for severely behaviorally disordered/mentally retarded students. For such students, annual goals should reflect the extended educational term. The content of annual goals represents a major problem in the training of school personnel. Many teachers rely on commercial materials for the development of annual goals and short-term objectives (the third requirement of an IEP). Yet the majority of commercially available materials may be ill-suited to the assessment and instructional needs of severely handicapped learners (Stowitscheck, Gable, & Hendrickson, 1980). Furthermore, school personnel working with the severely behaviorally disordered/mentally retarded may have little or no experience in targeting severe problems for intervention, particularly if they received their professional training sometime ago. For example, this author has often reviewed Individualized Education Programs that fail to recognize self-injurious, aggressive, or self-stimulatory behaviors as intervention priorities.

Documentation of special education and related services is the fourth requirement of an IEP. Special mental health services are a source of continuing controversy, with many school systems hesitant to provide financial support for the psychiatric help needed by severely behaviorally disordered students (Turnbull *et al.*, 1982).

Timelines are the concern of the fifth and sixth components of the IEP. The IEP must specify the extent of time a child will participate in the regular education program—not always an issue for persons working with very severely handicapped students—and dates for initiating and terminating services.

The final component of each IEP consists of objective criteria and evaluation procedures for determining mastery of the previously delineated short-term objectives. This author has reviewed few IEPs that adequately met the criteria for evaluation. Rather, many IEP objectives conclude with the criteria, "80% of the time" (a nebulous statement of mastery), and determine accomplishment of objectives "by teacher judgment." School systems reluctant to use more efficient (e.g., computerized) techniques for writing IEPs inadvertently may encourage teachers to abbreviate objectives and criteria (e.g., resort to the extensive use of ditto marks). (A young autistic boy, attending his own IEP conference early in this author's teaching career, saw ditto marks and commented to the chairperson of the IEP conference, "Look! A little bird has left tiny footprints up and down my IEP!") School personnel should be trained to develop appropriate objective statements for the programs within their school system, to enter and retrieve these statements through an easily accessed computer program, and to review these statements on an annual basis. In summary, "even though teaching to specific objectives leads to substantially greater gains than use of non-behaviorally specified objectives (e.g., Snell & Smith, 1978) . . . many teachers have not incorporated this competency into their planning and teaching repertoires" (Gable *et al.*, 1983, p. 12).

Issues specific to helping school personnel plan for severely behaviorally disordered/mentally retarded students include:

1. the establishment of effective information-sharing between evaluators and IEP developers;
2. extensive practice in producing pertinent target behaviors, meaningful mastery criteria, and evaluation procedures;
3. resolution of the controversy regarding funds for mental health related services; and,
4. Training in more efficient ways to store, retrieve, and review annual and short-term objectives.

Once annual and short-term goals are produced, school personnel can begin the dual tasks of teaching and managing behaviors. These topics shape the discussion that follows.

Issues in Teaching and Behavior Management

Three major intervention areas constitute this section: environmental, adult-mediated, and peer-mediated. Within each designation, school personnel training plays a major role.

Environmental Interventions

The first consideration in analyzing a school or classroom environment is its safety. Personnel who work with severely behaviorally disordered/mentally retarded students must concern themselves with the unpredictable nature of their students' interactions with the environment. For example, aggressive students may destroy materials and equipment, whereas self-injurious individuals may harm themselves with items available in the setting (see Kerr & Nelson, 1983, for discussion). The arrangement of an instructional setting may prevent harmful behaviors (e.g., aggression) from ever occurring (Nolley, Breuning, & Staub, 1982).

Related to this concern for safety is the need for all school personnel to undergo training in routine (for those working with the health impaired) and emergency medical care. McCubbin (1983) highlighted this new area of responsibility for teachers:

> Schools are facing medical concerns beyond their routine scope of expertise. Teachers are handling seizures and intermittent clean catheterization as well as chicken pox and skinned knees. Many schools do not have a full-time nurse, so the immediate responsibility for emergencies is shifted to the teacher. As handicapped students attend school regularly, the teacher becomes a critical observer of behaviors that may be the first indications of serious medical problems. (p. 148)

(McCubbin, 1983, and Oettinger & Coleman, 1981, offer excellent suggestions for managing the medical problems of handicapped students.)

A second training problem, often reflected in the multiple settings of the severely handicapped student's school program, is the generalization of learned skills across these settings (Lovaas, *et al.*, 1973; Norsworthy & Sievers, 1980). Specific attributes of the setting or task may require modification, as in the case of some autistic individuals whose learning is characterized by stimulus overselectivity (Etzel & LeBlanc, 1979) or stimulus preference in stereotypic behavior patterns (Rincover, 1978; Rincover, Cook, Peoples, & Packard, 1979). Norsworthy and Sievers (1980) commented on the training issues involved in environmental modifications for autistic individuals:

> Teachers must be very familiar with these methods before they can use them effectively. It is often time consuming to use them and there is no guarantee that the child will learn to respond to relevant features within a given stimulus dimension, nor that the learned performance will generalize. (p. 209)

The severely handicapped student's schedule, an often overlooked aspect of the environment, has been cited by a number of researchers as an important factor in teaching new skills (Carr, Newsom, & Binkoff, 1976; Dunlap & Koegel, 1980; Schroeder & Humphrey, 1977). Coursework should introduce school personnel to topics such as stimulus variation and analysis of task demands. Finally, teachers should learn how best to select and present instructional materials, by reading about and applying such practices as selecting play materials that promote social cooperation (Strain & Kerr, 1981), designing response-reinforcer tasks (Bittle & Hake, 1975), and planning longitudinal curriculum sequences for vocational preparation (Bellamy, Wilson, Adler, & Clarke, 1980).

Adult-Mediated Interventions

Most Individualized Education Programs for handicapped students rely on an adult as the primary teacher or behavior change agent. Indeed, an adult takes responsibility for the environmental changes mentioned in the previous section. To discuss all of the adult-directed teaching and behavior management practices that should be included in personnel preparation programs for the severely handicapped is beyond the scope of a single chapter. Readers who are interested in pursuing this topic in more depth should consult Snell (1983) and Kerr and Nelson (1983). This section will serve only to highlight specialized issues in teaching and in managing the problem behavior of severely behaviorally disordered/mentally retarded students.

The importance of competency-based and field-based educational experiences cannot be overestimated for those preparing to teach the severely handicapped (Snell, *et al.*, 1978). The topics that should be included in preservice personnel preparation are as extensive and varied as the chapters in this volume. Figure 2 displays one teacher trainer's summary of the skills required in systematic instruction for the severely handicapped (Snell, 1983). This chart, representing an applied behavior analysis approach to systematic instruction, reflects the numerous program revisions that must occur if instruction is to be most effective. Note the emphasis on maintenance and generalization of learned skills, as well as the inclusion of data collection and graphing skills, which will be discussed in the next section.

In addition to training teachers and other school personnel to carry out systematic instruction, inservice and preservice trainers must be cognizant of the special problems raised by the severely behaviorally disordered/mentally retarded. First, as Figure 1 reflects, teachers must be trained to use highly sophisticated planning strategies and must be made aware of the importance of data-based program modifications (Deno & Mirkin, 1978). Second, inservice supervisors must be sensitive to the additional time required in planning and making program modifications, and teacher schedules should be modified accordingly. Third, classroom teachers engaged in intensive behavior management programs (e.g., overcorrection, DRO) should be allocated additional staff to assist in these programs or to supervise other ongoing classroom activities (Kerr & Nelson, 1983). Fourth is the need for expert consultation to teachers (Favell, 1981). In addition to analyzing problem behaviors, planning often-complex interventions and program modifications, and evaluating the effects of these daily programs, consultants should play a major role in programs that employ aversive procedures (e.g., overcorrection, seclusionary time-out).

Peer-Mediated Interventions

A recent body of literature (see Strain, 1981) offers new teaching and behavior management programs to school personnel working with the severely handicapped. These peer-mediated interventions rely on classmates of the target child to serve as tutors or behavior change

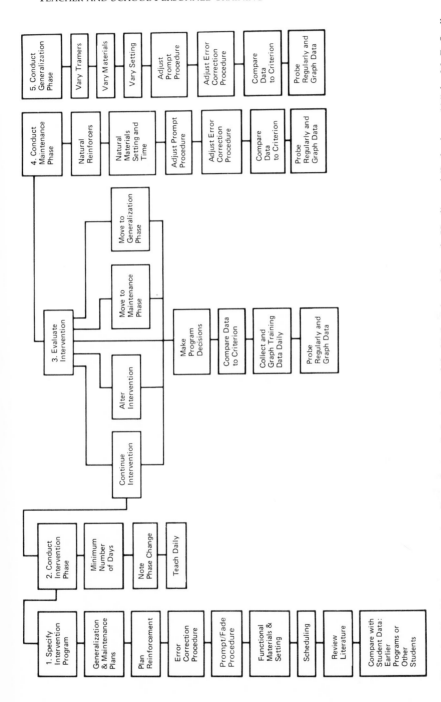

Figure 2. Teaching competencies. From *Systematic Instruction of the Moderately and Severely Handicapped* (2nd ed., p. 114) by M. E. Snell, 1983, Columbus, OH: Charles E. Merrill. Copyright 1983 by Charles E. Merrill. Reprinted by permission.

agents. In their review of peer imitation training, Peck, Cooke, and Apolloni (1981) described several studies utilizing peers as trainers for severely handicapped persons (e.g., Berkowitz, 1968; Mansdorf, 1977; Talkington & Altman, 1973; and Whalen & Henker, 1969). These studies addressed the important classroom skills of motor responses, compliance to directions, and language.

Cooke and his colleagues (Apolloni, Cooke, & Cooke, 1977; Cooke, Cooke, & Apolloni, 1978; Peck, Apolloni, Cooke, & Raver, 1978) have developed a systematic line of research with direct applications to school settings. Their procedure, Peer Imitation Training (PIT), addresses the needs of severely handicapped children in preschools. Peer models (usually the nonhandicapped) have taught severely handicapped students to engage in appropriate toy use and to initiate social interactions with others in a generalization setting.

In work that is also classroom applicable, Strain and his colleagues (Strain, Kerr, & Ragland, 1981) have utilized classroom peers to improve the social interactions of severely behaviorally disordered students of school age. This procedure, known as Peer Social Initiation, relies on a handicapped or nonhandicapped peer to make social bids to the target student(s). The peer trainer also uses commonly cited teaching procedures such as prompting, verbal and gestural feedback, and can even learn to modify the play environment to render it more conducive to positive interactions (Ragland, Kerr, & Strain, 1978).

Peer Imitation Training and Peer Social Initiation are only two examples of the new peer-mediated interventions available to school personnel. Both have been validated empirically in school settings and accordingly have much to offer teachers who wish to increase the available opportunities for individualized instruction. For school personnel whose concern is the integration of handicapped children into least restrictive environments, the strategies are quite promising (Cooke *et al.*, 1978). Others may find the peer-mediated approach helpful in ameliorating the behavioral problems of institutionalized child and adults (see Dy, Strain, Fullerton, & Stowitschek, 1981). Inservice trainers should arrange didactic experiences for school personnel to learn about peer-mediated interventions, and preservice teachers should include this new technology in course and fieldwork.

Summary

In summary, the scope of training for school personnel is increasing as more seriously handicapped students enroll in classroom experiences. Special aspects of preparing school personnel to teach the severely behaviorally disordered/mentally retarded include:

1. training in identifying environmental arrangements and items that are unsafe;

2. certification in emergency medical procedures and coursework in routine medical procedures;

3. field-based training in the promotion of generalized learning through environmental modifications (e.g., alterations in schedule, stimulus variation);

4. provision for the resources needed by classroom teachers engaged in complex sequences of systematic instruction (i.e., planning time, additional classroom personnel, and consultants);

5. competency-based training, applied through fieldwork, in peer-mediated programming; and,

6. at least basic training in related areas (e.g., psychopharmacological intervention, school law, stimulus control procedures, vocational training, and self-defense).

Issues in Progress Monitoring

Closely allied with issues in assessment (see earlier discussion) are progress-monitoring activities, perhaps the least popular training topic for school personnel, who may claim:

> "I don't have enough time to collect data—I have to teach";
> "Collecting data doesn't help me teach"; or
> "I don't get any support or reinforcement for data collection." (Kerr & Nelson, 1983, pp. 30–31)

Often these statements of resistance reflect pitfalls in data collection that make progress monitoring cumbersome and irrelevant. These include:

1. trying to take data on every behavior;

2. collecting data on low-priority or nonessential behaviors (e.g., collecting data on both off-task and on-task intervals, monitoring skills that have already been learned and generalized); and

3. not responding to data that are collected (see Kerr & Nelson, 1983).

Many of these problems could be remediated through preservice training in which trainees are taught more appropriate data collection procedures and priorities. Such training, moreover, is greatly enhanced by intensive, long-term (e.g., two semester) applications of the new skills in classroom settings.

Inservice supervisors may find the suggestions of Deno and Mirkin (1978) useful in overcoming common issues in progress monitoring. Their recommendations are displayed in Table 1.

Table 1. Two × Two Contingency Table of Possible Agreements and
Disagreements of Two Observers and the Occurrence (O) or
Nonoccurrence (NO) of an Event

		Observer 2	
		O	NO
Observer 1	O	A	B
	NO	C	D

Summary. School personnel who serve the severely behaviorally disordered/mentally retarded must learn the assessment skills highlighted in an earlier section, as well as progress-monitoring strategies. In most instances, assessment will overlap with progress monitoring. That is, assessment for the severely handicapped should be direct and continuous—not pre- and posttests (Kerr & Nelson, 1983). Competence in applied behavior analysis allows school personnel to monitor interventions carefully and continuously, and to make thoughtful program changes when warranted. This ongoing evaluation is an essential component of the IEP.

Related Professional Issues

School personnel face numerous professional issues as they prepare to handle the complex and often distressing problems of severely behaviorally disordered/mentally retarded individuals. For many of their responsibilities, school personnel have not been well prepared. This seems certainly the case in the implementation of punishment, or aversive, programs that make many demands on classroom and support personnel. Clearly stated guidelines for using aversive or punishment programs are essential. Moreover, this author recommends that student-teacher supervisors guard against the involvement of trainees in high-risk programs such as the application of aversives. Practicing teachers should be taught the proper measures for obtaining approval for punishment programs and should be encouraged to protect themselves with professional liability insurance (usually obtainable through professional organizations).

Another safety measure for school personnel working with unpredictable, behaviorally disordered students is training in self-defense and physical management of combative students. This controversial topic has received little attention in school personnel textbooks, but workshops are available to educators throughout the country (Nolley, Breuning, & Staub, 1982). Supervisors must insure that such training emphasizes *prevention* of aggression, rather than focusing exclusively on physical restraint.

The importance of knowledge in routine and emergency medicine has been highlighted as has information on the many psychopharmacological treatments in which school personnel are asked to participate (see Miksic, 1983, for discussion).

The overarching legal principles of P.L. 94-142 exert a major influence on school personnel; accordingly, anyone who works in special education must be very familiar with this important legislation and its regulations. School personnel are often called to due process hearings, where testimony is requested according to legalistic guidelines. Some preparation for this experience is warranted.

Finally, school personnel who spend most of their professional lives with severely behaviorally disordered/mentally retarded students are at risk for stress and burnout. *Burnout*, defined by Maslach (1978, p. 56), is "emotional exhaustion resulting from the stress of interpersonal contact." Regrettably, little empirical evidence on the prevention and management of burnout is available for school supervisors. Nevertheless, all who work in the stressful environment created by demanding, dually handicapped students should be offered ways to reduce their stress. Weiskopf (1980) suggested that teachers (a) set realistic goals for themselves and students, (b) delegate work when possible, (c) avoid professional isolation, (d) break up direct contact with students through team teaching, and the like, and (e) engage in stimulating intellectual and physical activities away from the job.

Concluding Remarks

The field of special education for the severely handicapped has been rearranged dramatically in the few years since the passage of the Education for All Handicapped Children's Act. Training that once might have prepared personnel quite adequately for classrooms of severely behaviorally disordered or mentally retarded children has fallen far short of the goals of P.L. 94-142. Supervisors and college professors face a tremendous challenge, as outlined in each section of this chapter, to accommodate the multiple special needs of the severely handicapped and their teachers. Field-based training based on repeated practice of thoughtfully delineated compentencies will provide a foundation for today's future teachers. For those in the inservice arena, new skills as well as new attitudes (see Walker & Rankin, 1982) are mandated. Although the law states that every *child*, regardless of his or her handicap, shall receive a free, appropriate, special education, let us not forget that school personnel also have a right to a special education—beginning at the preservice level and continuing through competent inservice, until their last day in the classroom.

References

Apolloni, T., Cooke, S. A., & Cooke, T. P. (1977). Establishing a nonretarded peer as a behavioral model for retarded toddlers. *Perceptual and Motor Skills, 44*, 231–241.

Bateman, B., & Herr, C. (1981). Law and special education. In J. M. Kauffman & D. P. Hallahan (Eds.), *Handbook of special education*. Englewood Cliffs, NJ: Prentice-Hall.

Bellamy, G. T., Wilson, D. J., Adler, E., & Clarke, J. Y. (1980). A strategy for programming vocational skills for severely handicapped youth. *Exceptional Education Quarterly, 1*, 85–98.

Berkowitz, S. (1968). *Acquisition and maintenance of generalized imitative repertoires of profound retardates with retarded peers functioning as models and reinforcing agents*. Unpublished doctoral dissertation, University of Maryland.

Bittle, R., & Hake, D. F. (1975). A multielement design model for component analysis and cross-setting assessment of a treatment package. *Behavior Therapy, 8*, 906–914.

Bower, E. M. (1969). *Early identification of emotionally handicapped children in school* (2nd ed.). Springfield, IL: Charles C Thomas.

Carr, E. G., Newsom, C. D., & Binkoff, J. A. (1976). Stimulus control of self-destructive behavior in a psychotic child. *Journal of Abnormal Child Psychology, 4*, 139–152.

Cooke, S. A., Cooke, T. P., & Apolloni, T. (1978). Developing nonretarded toddlers as verbal models for retarded classmates. *Child Study Journal, 8*, 1–8.

Deno, S. L., & Mirkin, P. K. (1978). *Data-based program modification: A manual*. Reston, VA: Council for Exceptional Children.

Dubose, R. F., Langley, M. B., & Stagg, V. (1979). Assessment of multihandicapped children. In E. Meyer, G. Vergason, & R. Whelan (Eds.), *Instructional planning for exceptional children*. Denver: Love Publishing Co.

Dunlap, G., & Koegel, R. L. (1980). Motivation of autistic children through stimulus variation. *Journal of Applied Behavior Analysis, 13*, 619–627.

Dy, E. B., Strain, P. S., Fullerton, A., & Stowitschek, J. (1981). Training institutionalized, elderly mentally retarded persons as intervention agents for socially isolate peers. *Analysis and Intervention in Developmental Disabilities, 1*, 199–215.

Elam, S. (1971). *Performance-based teacher education*. Washington, DC: American Association of Colleges for Teacher Education.

Etzel, B., & LeBlanc, J. (1979). The simplest treatment alternative: The law of parsimony applied to choosing appropriate instructional control and errorless-learning procedures for the difficult-to-teach child. *Journal of Autism and Developmental Disorders, 9*, 361–382.

Favell, J. (1981). *The treatment of self-injurious behavior*. New York: American Association for Behavior Therapy.

Federal Register. (1977, January 23). Washington, DC: U.S. Government Printing Office.

Federal Register. (1981, January 19). Washington, DC: U.S. Government Printing Office.

Gable, R.A., Hendrickson, J. M., & Young, C. C. (1983). *Teacher behavior in classes for the mentally retarded and multiply handicapped: A comparative analysis.* Unpublished manuscript, University of Pittsburgh School of Medicine.

Hewett, F. M. (1964). Teaching reading to an autistic boy through operant conditioning. *The Reading Teacher, 18,* 613–618.

Kauffman, J. M. (1981). *Characteristics of children's behavioral disorders.* Columbus, OH: Charles E. Merrill.

Kerr, M. M., & Nelson, C. M. (1983). *Strategies for managing behavior problems in the classroom.* Columbus, OH: Charles E. Merrill.

Lovaas, O. I. (1966). A program for the establishment of speech in psychotic children. In J. K. Wing (Ed.), *Early childhood autism: Clinical, educational, and social aspects.* New York: Pergamon Press.

Lovaas, O. I., Koegel, R. L., Simmons, J. Q., & Long, J. S. (1973). Some generalizations and follow-up measures on autistic children in behavior therapy. *Journal of Applied Behavior Analysis, 6,* 131–166.

Mansdorf, I. J. (1977). Rapid token training of an institution ward using modeling. *Mental Retardation, 15,* 37–39.

Martin, R. (1979). Legal issues in special education. In D. Cullinan & M. H. Epstein (Eds.), *Special education for adolescents: Issues and perspectives* (pp. 305–329). Columbus, OH: Charles H. Merrill.

Maslach, C. (1978). Job burnout: How people cope. *Public Welfare, 36,* 56–58.

McCubbin, T. (1983). Routine and emergency medical procedures. In M. E. Snell (Ed.), *Systematic instruction of the moderately and severely handicapped.* Columbus, OH: Charles E. Merrill.

Miksic, S. (1983). Drug abuse and drug therapy. In M. M. Kerr & C. M. Nelson (Eds.), *Strategies for managing behavior problems in the classroom.* Columbus, OH: Charles E. Merrill.

Nelson, C. M. (1978). Field-based special education teacher training and the university: Mismatch or match made in heaven? In C. M. Nelson (Ed.), *Field-based teacher training: Applications in special education* (pp. 3–25). Minneapolis: Advanced Institute for Trainers of Teachers for Seriously Emotionally Disturbed Children and Youth, Department of Psychoeducational Studies, University of Minnesota.

Nolley, D., Bruening, S. E., & Staub, R. W. (1982). *Physical management.* Unpublished manuscript, University of Pittsburgh School of Medicine.

Norsworthy, K., & Sievers, P. (1980). The teacher's perspective: The struggle to provide quality education to autistic children. In B. Wilcox & A. Thompson (Eds.), *Critical issues in educating autistic children and youth.* Washington, DC: United States Department of Education.

Oettinger, L., Jr., & Coleman, J. (1981). Emergency medical procedures. In J. M. Kauffman & D. Hallahan (Eds.), *Handbook of special education* (pp. 767–782). Englewood Cliffs, NJ: Prentice-Hall.

Peck, C. A., Apolloni, T., Cooke, T. P., & Raver, S. A. (1978). Teaching retarded preschoolers to initiate the free-play behavior of nonretarded classmates: Trained and generalized effects. *Journal of Special Education, 12,* 195–207.

Peck, C. A., Cooke, T. P., & Apolloni, T. (1981). Utilization of peer imitation in therapeutic and instructional contexts. In P. S. Strain (Ed.), *The utilization of classroom peers as behavior change agents.* New York: Plenum Press.

Ragland, E. U., Kerr, M. M., & Strain, P. S. (1978). Effects of peer social initiations on the behavior of withdrawn autistic children. *Behavior Modification, 2,* 565–578.

Rincover, A. (1978). Sensory extinction: A procedure for eliminating self-stimulatory behavior in developmentally disabled children. *Journal of Abnormal Child Psychology, 6,* 299–310.

Rincover, A., Cook, R., Peoples, A., & Packard, D. (1979). Sensory extinction and sensory reinforcement principles for programming multiple adaptive behavior change. *Journal of Applied Behavior Analysis, 12,* 221–233.

Schroeder, S. R., & Humphrey, R. H. (1977). *Environmental context effects and contingent restraint time-out of self-injurious behavior in a deaf-blind profoundly retarded woman.* Paper presented at the 101st Annual Meetings of the American Association on Mental Deficiency, New Orleans.

Schroeder, S. R., Schroeder, C. S., Rojahn, J., & Mulick, J. A. (1981). Self-injurious behavior: An analysis of behavior management techniques. In J. L. Matson & J. R. McCartney (Eds.), *Handbook of behavior modification with the mentally retarded* (pp. 61–115). New York: Plenum Press.

Semmel, M. I., & Semmel, D. (1976). Competency-based teacher education: An overview. *Behavioral Disorders: Journal of the Council for Children with Behavioral Disorders, 2,* 69–82.

Smith, D. D., & Snell, M. E. (1978). Classroom management and instructional planning. In M. E. Snell (Ed.), *Systematic instruction of the moderately and severely handicapped.* Columbus, OH: Charles E. Merrill.

Snell, M. E. (1983). *Systematic instruction of the moderately and severely handicapped* (2nd ed.). Columbus, OH: Charles E. Merrill.

Snell, M. E., Taylor, K. G., & Thompson, M. S. (1978). The active response inservice model: A method of providing inservice to educators of the severely handicapped. In C. M. Nelson (Ed.), *Field-based teacher training: Applications in special education* (pp. 41–66). Minneapolis: Advanced Institute for Trainers of Teachers for Seriously Emotionally Disturbed Children and Youth, Department of Psychoeducational Studies, University of Minnesota.

Spence, J. (1978). Clinical educator: A direction in training for seriously emotionally disturbed children. In C. M. Nelson (Ed.), *Field-based teacher training: Applications in special education* (pp. 27–39). Minneapolis: Advanced Institute for Trainers of Teachers for Seriously Emotionally Disturbed Children and Youth, Department of Psychoeducational Studies, University of Minnesota.

Stowitschek, J. J., Gable, R. A., & Hendrickson, J. M. (1980). *Instructional materials for exceptional children: Selection, management, and evaluation.* Germantown, MD: Aspen Systems.

Strain, P. S. (1980). Social behavior programming with severely emotionally disturbed and autistic children. In B. Wilcox & A. Thompson (Eds.), *Critical issues in educating autistic children and youth* (pp. 179–206). Washington, DC: Bureau of Education for the Handicapped.

Strain, P.S., & Kerr, M. M. (1981). Modifying children's social withdrawal: Issues in assessment and clinical intervention. In M. Hersen, R. Eisler, & P. Miller (Eds.), *Progress in behavior modification* (Vol. 11, pp. 203–242). New York: Academic Press.

Strain, P. S., Kerr, M. M., & Ragland, E. U. (1979). Effects of peer-mediated social initiations and prompting/reinforcement procedures on the social behavior of autistic children. *Journal of Autism and Developmental Disorders, 9,* 41–54.

Talkington, L. W., & Altman, R. (1973). Effects of film-mediated aggressive and affectual models on behavior. *American Journal of Mental Deficiency, 77,* 420–425.

Turnbull, A. P., Strickland, B. B., & Brantley, J. C. (1982). *Developing and implementing individualized education programs.* Columbus, OH: Charles E. Merrill.

Walker, H. M., & Rankin, R. (1982). Assessing the behavioral expectations and demands of less restrictive settings: Instruments, ecological assessment procedures and out-comes. *School Psychology Review, 2,* 115–124.

Whalen, C. K., & Henker, B. A. (1969). Creating therapeutic pyramids using mentally retarded patients. *American Journal of Mental Deficiency, 74,* 331–337.

Whitney, R., & Striefel, S. (1981). Functionality and generalization in training the severely and profoundly handicapped. *Journal of Special Education Technology, 4,* 33–39.

10

Direct Care Staff Training

DENNIS H. REID AND MAUREEN M. SCHEPIS

Introduction

A major component in the treatment of severe behavior disorders of mentally retarded persons is providing effective services within institutional settings. Institutions have been a principal service provider for mentally retarded individuals in the United States since the mid 1800s (Maloney & Ward, 1979) and are likely to continue to be a significant source of service and training. As an example of the role of institutions in service provision, a recent estimate indicates that well over 125,000 persons reside in public residential facilities for the mentally retarded (Scheerenberger, 1982). Subsequently, if a large segment of the mentally retarded population is to have immediate access to treatment for severe behavior disorders when such treatment is needed, then appropriate therapeutic procedures will need to be provided within institutional environments.

The need for effective treatment of severe behavior disorders in institutions is actually more paramount today than in past years because of prevailing service philosophies and practices. For example, as a result of the national emphasis on deinstitutionalization during the 1970s and early 1980s, many mentally retarded individuals with less serious behavior problems have been discharged from state institutions and/or are no longer admitted to institutional facilities (see Eyman & Borthwick, 1980, for a discussion). As a result, a higher percentage of those mentally retarded individuals who currently live in institutions exhibit severe behavior disorders. Similarly, a major reason for current admissions of mentally retarded individuals to institutions is the presence of serious behavior problems (Repp & Deitz, 1979a). Institutional populations also are becoming more restricted to the severely and profoundly mentally retarded in contrast to the mildly and moderately mentally retarded (Scheerenberger, 1982). The former population usually displays a higher

DENNIS H. REID and MAUREEN M. SCHEPIS • Western Carolina Center, Morganton, North Carolina 28655.

incidence of severe behavior disorders than their less seriously retarded peers (Eyman & Call, 1977; Jacobson, 1982).

If the treatment that is needed for severe behavior disorders of the institutionalized mentally retarded is to occur, then the implementation of that treatment must effectively involve the direct care staff members of the institutions. Whether referred to as attendants, nurses' aides, health care technicians, or a variety of other personnel classifications, those institutional staff members who provide the day-to-day, basic resident services are very integral in the total care and training of institutionalized persons. More specifically, direct care staff typically represent the largest component of an institution's total working population, spend the most amount of time with residents (Bensberg & Barnett, 1966), and are typically charged with the most comprehensive set of resident care and training responsibilities of all institutional staff (see Whitman, Scibak, & Reid, 1983, for an overview of attendant work duties). Given such an influential role in the lives of institutionalized mentally retarded persons, it becomes apparent that comprehensive and effective treatment of severe behavior disorders in institutions is heavily dependent upon proficient performance of direct care personnel.

The purpose of this chapter is to discuss the training of institutional direct care staff and the related management of their work performance as it relates to the treatment of severe behavior disorders of institutionalized mentally retarded persons. Throughout the chapter we will focus on staff programs that have a behavioral orientation (Baer, Wolf, & Risley, 1968), or that have been evaluated from a behavioral point of view because that is our own professional orientation. Also, behavioral approaches have become rather dominant in the institutional staff training and management literature since the early 1960s. Following a discussion of the need for staff training, an overview of the history of behavioral research on institutional staff training will be presented. Using the information presented in the first two sections as the groundwork, practical suggestions will then be discussed for practitioners charged with training direct care staff for working with mentally retarded persons with severe behavior disorders. Within the suggestions for practitioners will be references to areas that warrant the attention of investigators for future research.

Reasons for Training Direct Care Staff in Treatment Procedures for Severe Behavior Disorders

The preceding comments briefly indicated the general need to train direct care staff in the treatment of severe disorders of the mentally retarded. Basically, our rationale for such training was that (a) there is a relatively high incidence of persons with severe behavior disorders in institutions for the mentally retarded; and (b) attendants have more involvement with institutionalized persons than any other group of institutional staff. This section more specifically describes why direct care personnel need training in certain skills if severe behavior disorders among institutionalized mentally retarded populations are to be remediated. Four main reasons for the need for effective staff training will be discussed.

Lack of Preparation for Assigned Job Responsibilities

It has been well recognized that persons who are hired into institutional direct care positions usually have no formal preparation for that type of job (Marshall & Marks, 1981; Whitman, Scibak, & Reid, 1983). The lack of formal training prior to becoming an attendant pertains to almost every aspect of assigned responsibilities but can be most detrimental for the completion of those duties that involve relatively technical and/or complex tasks. One performance area that often involves a number of technical skills is the implementation of certain behavior management procedures with residents who exhibit behavior problems. For instance, reinforcing successively lower rates of maladaptive client behavior can be effective in improving problem behaviors of residents but also involves a number of rather precise actions of staff members such as determining the appropriate rate of behavior to reinforce, when to change the criterion rate, and so forth. Clearly, it is unreasonable to expect individuals with no background in behavior modification to effectively carry out complex behavior change strategies that professionals conduct only after having received years of formal education pertaining to those types of treatment approaches. As a result, direct care staff need effective orientation and/or inservice training programs in the application of behavior management procedures.

Prevention of Inadvertent Deleterious Effects of Staff Activities on Resident Behavior Disorders

Due to the frequent contact attendants have with residents, what these staff do in response to resident problem behaviors can actually serve to make the problems worse if staff do not use appropriate interaction paradigms. For example, a relatively frequent dilemma for institutional personnel is how to interact with a resident who is crying or screaming. A common reaction is to nurture the client such as holding or rocking him or her. However, if the resident does not show any signs of physical distress, this approach may be contraindicated. By overly attending to the crying or screaming, staff may be reinforcing this behavior and in essence teaching the resident that crying or screaming is an effective way to get attention. In approaching this situation more appropriately from a behavioral viewpoint, staff might attend to the resident when the resident is seeking attention in a more acceptable way such as talking or manual signing. Also, staff may insure that there is no physical need (i.e., an injury of the resident that may be evoking the crying or screaming) and then ignore the outbursts. Unfortunately, a common situation in institutions is that staff often not only attend in a positive manner to screaming or crying, but they do not attend to more appropriate language behaviors of residents. This type of interaction pattern sets the occasion for behavior problems of residents to increase in seriousness as well as for decreasing the likelihood of desired social skills development. Hence, training programs are needed to train staff in therapeutic interaction patterns for their frequent encounters with resident behavior problems in order to avoid the establishment of environments that encourage maladaptive behavior.

Therapeutic Utilization of Staff's Knowledge about Residents

Because direct care personnel spend a large amount of time with residents, they are in an excellent position to be aware of individual resident preferences and response tendencies. This type of information can be useful to professional staff who are responsible for developing resident treatment programs. The information may, for example, relate to what time of day a resident is usually most acceptable to particular types of programming such as before or after lunch or nap. For instance, a staff member who works daily with a resident on a self-feeding training program may notice that the resident does not appear to be hungry at certain training times and tends to become aggressive at these times (i.e., hitting, kicking the trainer). In this situation the staff might suggest that the program be scheduled at alternate times when the client has more of an appetite, thus decreasing the likelihood of aggression by the resident as an escape-from-training maneuver.

Generally, if the information that staff possess about residents is to be useful programmatically, then the staff are going to need specific training to know what type of information is most relevant in this respect and how to best collect and describe this information. For example, training in methods of data collection regarding resident compliance to staff requests across various types of situations could be useful in developing a treatment procedure for a severe behavior disorder. Similarly, training in methods to observe and determine likely reinforcing stimuli to use in programs with certain residents would be helpful.

Currently, participation of direct care personnel in the development of treatment programs by providing useful information as just exemplified is mandated by regulatory standards for institutions (e.g., ACMRDD, 1978). However, based on our experience, in actuality very few front-line staff are trained to provide relevant information, nor are they seriously involved in program development regarding the treatment of behavior disorders. Hence, training staff in these types of skills would have the advantage from a management and administrative standpoint of assisting facilities in being in true compliance with regulatory guidelines. Additionally, some research in institutional staff management suggests that active involvement of staff in supervisory strategies that relate to their activities with residents are better received by staff than those strategies in which staff are not involved (Burgio, Whitman, & Reid, 1983).

Low Frequencies of Therapeutic Staff–Resident Interactions

The final reason to be discussed regarding the need for effective training of staff relates to one of the most frequently reported problem areas in institutions in terms of efficacious services, or lack thereof— very low frequencies of staff interactions with residents during unstructured periods in the daily institutional routine. Numerous studies have indicated that when residents are in their institutional living areas and no formal training or basic care is scheduled, which continues to represent a significant portion of the day in many institutions, staff spend very little time directly interacting with residents (e.g., Dailey, Allen, Chinsky, & Veit, 1977; Warren & Mondy, 1971). That is, although staff have frequent contact with residents as noted earlier, the contact is usually when staff are assisting residents in self-care routines or performing basic care activities for residents. When there is no basic care need that requires staff to interact with residents, then there is often no alternative interaction such as general, social exchanges. Also, as we suggested previously and others have discussed in more detail (Blindert, 1975; Burgio et al., 1983), when staff do interact with residents the attention is often contingent on maladaptive resident behaviors. Again, such a situation may serve to make resident behavior problems worse by reinforcing inappropriate behaviors. Additionally, the lack of more desirable interactions fails to take advantage of opportunities to reinforce acceptable behavior patterns that are incompatible with inappropriate behaviors. In contrast, if staff are appropriately trained in therapeutic interaction patterns, then some inappropriate resident behaviors could become less frequent, and residents would engage in more desirable activities during the day.

The possibilities for attendants to use their daily contacts with residents in a therapeutic manner have recently been emphasized through successful applications of incidental teaching techniques. Briefly, incidental teaching involves using naturally occurring interactions between clients and caregivers to train specific skills to clients such as functional language (Hart & Risley, 1980). Incidental teaching strategies have been successful in increasing appropriate verbalizations among mentally retarded persons during institutional mealtimes (Halle, Marshall, & Spradlin, 1979) and in increasing manual signing interactions during less structured times in the residents' living area (Schepis, Reid, Fitzgerald, Faw, van den Pol, & Welty, 1982). The importance of using incidental teaching strategies for increasing resident language skills in regard to the treatment of behavior disorders becomes quite apparent when considering data that suggest that improvement in language skills can result in decreased aggression/disruption of developmentally disabled persons (Casey, 1978).

Historical Overview of Research on Training Institutional Staff to Manage Severe Behavior Disorders

In order to best discuss the most proficient ways of meeting the training needs of institutional staff as described in the preceding section, a brief review of what we have learned from applied research on staff training programs will be presented. Basically, the professional literature on methods of assisting institutional staff to manage resident behavior disorders has been embodied in research related to training more general behavior modification skills to staff. That is, most of the research has focused on the management of behavior disorders as only one aspect of a more comprehensive use of behavioral procedures with mentally retarded persons. For example, many early programs were designed to train staff in methods of teaching self-help skills to residents, as well as for dealing with resident behavior problems. Hence, an overview of the research on staff training programs related specifically to the treatment of severe behavior disorders can best be provided by looking at the development of behavioral staff training regimes in general. Because behavioral research on institutional staff training has been reviewed and/ or discussed in a number of previous reports (e.g., Gardner, 1973; Miller

& Lewin, 1980; Whitman, *et al.*, 1983), only a brief summary will be presented here.

Initially, the main concern of behaviorally oriented staff programs was to demonstrate methods of training staff, primarily direct care personnel, to use behavior modification procedures to teach basic skills to institutional residents. These programs focused on teaching a general knowledge (i.e., verbal skills) of principles of behavior change (reinforcement, satiation, etc.) to staff as well as effective application of the principles while working with clients (i.e., performance skills). A variety of training strategies have been used in programs with attendants including lecture formats (Gardner, 1972), modeling (Watson, Gardner, & Sanders, 1971), role playing (Gardner, 1972), structured practice with videotaped feedback (Bricker, Morgan, & Grabowski, 1972) and programmed instruction (Bassinger, Ferguson, Watson, & Wyant, 1971). The results of research that evaluated these programs demonstrated that institutional staff could acquire and apply specific behavior modification teaching skills as a result of well-specified, highly structured staff development programs.

Despite the relative success of the early staff training programs, these endeavors suffered from a major shortcoming from a clinical point of view. Specifically, the staff training programs of the 1960s and early 1970s showed only that institutional staff could acquire verbal and/or behavior modification teaching strategies within a classroom-type environment. The programs did not demonstrate that following an in-service activity in behavior modification, staff would improve their day-to-day performance in the regular work setting (typically being a residential cottage or ward). Because it is the performance of staff during their usual work routine that is generally the basis for needing to conduct staff training in the first place, if such performance is not shown to have been altered as a result of the training, then the ultimate utility of the in-service program is questionable.

Because of the importance of the day-to-day job performance of attendants, particularly their interactions with residents during training sessions as well as during less structured social-type situations, researchers in the mid-1970s began looking at the impact of staff training programs in behavior modification on the daily job activities of staff. A somewhat surprising and rather discouraging result of this research was that frequently the staff training programs did not significantly affect daily job performance (Greene, Willis, Levy, & Bailey, 1978; Iwata, Bailey, Brown, Foshee, & Alpern, 1976; Montegar, Reid, Madsen, & Ewell, 1977; Quilitch, 1975). As discussed elsewhere (Whitman *et al.*, 1983), the failure of the staff training programs in this respect was due basically to the lack of generalization of behavior changes from the staff development setting to the daily work site. Furthermore, if generalization did occur, the improved performances did not maintain over time in the workplace.

Due to the results of the staff research in the mid- to late 1970s as just summarized, recent investigations have focused more heavily on directly changing staff job performance in the normal work setting. Usually this latter group of investigations is referred to as research on *staff management* in contrast to the earlier work on *staff training*. Actually, these two descriptors have been used inconsistently to refer to a variety of staff-related programs and a point of clarification is in order. The term *staff training* is probably best used to refer to those programs that have as their main focus the teaching of new skills to staff (e.g., teaching staff appropriate use of extinction strategies with resident behavior problems). In contrast, *staff management* is more appropriately used when referring to programs designed to alter the manner in which staff apply previously acquired skills. For example, staff management practices are typically concerned with how often staff engage in a particular work activity and whether staff engage in that activity at the desired time and in the appropriate places. Throughout this chapter we will use these two terms in the manner as just described, although our dichotomization is by no means universal. We recommend differential reference to *staff training* versus *staff management* programs because the respective acquisition of new work skills and the changing of day-by-day work activities of institutional staff can represent different problems for researchers and staff supervisors, often requiring different behavior change strategies for resolution.

Once behaviorally oriented investigators began to focus on changing the work performance of institutional staff in the daily job situation, a wide variety of staff managment procedures were developed, evaluated, and reported in the professional literature. Again, because these procedures have been described in previous reviews (see also Prue, Frederiksen, & Bacon, 1978; Reid & Whitman, 1983), only a brief overview will be provided here, and the interested reader is referred to earlier reports. In general, the behavioral staff management practices that have been reported as being effective can be categorized according to whether they represent *antecedent procedures, consequence procedures, self-management* or *participative management procedures,* or *multifaceted procedures* (Reid & Whitman, 1983; Whitman *et al.,* 1983).

The first category of behavioral staff management interventions, *antecedent procedures,* refers to steps taken prior to the occurrence of certain staff performances with the purpose being to improve the probability that the performances do, in fact, occur. For example, Korabek, Reid, Page, Albrecht, and Fitzgerald (1979) used the antecedent procedures of supervisor modeling (supervisor demonstrations of desired staff behavior) and written prompts (information describing what staff should do posted on the work unit wall) in a staff management program. These procedures were used by Korabek et al. to increase the frequency with which attendant staff positioned nonambulatory, profoundly mentally retarded residents in therapeutic resting positions in accordance with physical therapy prescriptions. Additional examples of the types of antecedent procedures that have been investigated in institutional settings and performance areas they have been used with are presented in Table 1. Overall, with some notable exceptions (e.g., Gladstone & Spencer, 1977), antecedent interventions have not been very effective in consistently improving institutional staff performance, although these interventions do help set the occasion for consequence procedures to be effective (see Reid & Whitman, 1983; Whitman et al., 1983, for further discussion).

By far the most frequently investigated type of behavioral procedure used in staff management has been the provision of certain consequences following specified staff behaviors in order to change the frequency with which those behaviors occur. Although a few reports of *consequence procedures* have attempted to decrease undesirable job performances by using presumably negative consequences such as reduction in pay (Gardner, 1970) and threat of job loss (Repp & Deitz, 1979b), the vast majority of studies have focused on increasing desirable work behaviors by providing presumably positive consequences following those performances. Consequence systems designed to positively reinforce work behaviors have included tangible items such as money (Pommer & Streedbeck, 1974), less tangible events or activities such as highly preferred schedules of days off from work (Reid, Schuh-Wear, & Brannon, 1978), and statements from a supervisor indicating explicit approval of previous work (Montegar et al., 1977) or objective feedback regarding various parameters of the work (Brown, Willis, & Reid, 1981). Table 2 provides additional examples of procedures that have involved a positive reinforcement approach to improving staff performance.

Typically, the consequence procedures have been quite effective in improving targeted areas of staff performance. The most frequently reported consequence intervention with apparent efficacy in this respect has been the use of performance feedback. Feedback has been an effective intervention within a variety of implementation formats including

Table 1. *Examples of Antecedent Procedures Used in Research with Institutional Staff*

General procedure	Description	Reference
Instructions	Written instructions regarding attendance criteria provided individually to staff persons	Shoemaker & Reid, 1980
	Written instructions with pictorial representation on a chart publicly posted in the work unit	Fielding, Errickson, & Bettin, 1971
	Written job description publicly posted in the work unit	Pommer & Streedbeck, 1974
	Vocal instructions during in-service training activity	Quilitch, 1975; Greene, Willis, Levy, & Bailey, 1978; Montegar, Reid, Madsen, & Ewell, 1977
Increased job structure	"Duty cards" specifying behaviors, times, and locations of job responsibilities	Sneed & Bible, 1979
	Assignments specifying behaviors and clients to be involved as part of job responsibilities	Iwata, Bailey, Brown, Foshee, & Alpern, 1976
	Specification of behaviors, times, and locations of job responsibilities publicly posted in work unit	Quilitch, 1975
Modeling	Repeated supervisory demonstrations in the work unit of providing praise statements to residents contingent on appropriate behaviors during training	Gladstone & Spencer, 1977

Note. From *Behavior Modification with the Severely and Profoundly Retarded: Research and Application* by T. S. Whitman, J. W. Scibak, and D. H. Reid, 1983; p. 339. Copyright 1983 by Academic Press. Reprinted by permission.

Table 2. *Types of Consequences Used in Positive Reinforcement Programs with Institutional Staff Performance*

Consequence[a]	Reference
Publicly posted feedback	Greene, Willis, Levy & Bailey, 1978
Supervisor vocal praise	Brown, Willis, & Reid, 1981
Rearrangement of days off from work	Iwata, Bailey, Brown, Foshee, & Alpern, 1976
Money	Pomerleau, Bobrove, & Smith, 1973
Relief time from certain job duties	Shoemaker & Reid, 1980
Commercial trading stamps	Bricker, Morgan, & Grabowski, 1972
Written feedback and praise via memoranda	Shoemaker & Reid, 1980
Preferred activities with residents	Seys & Duker, 1978
Supervisor vocal feedback	Brown, Willis, & Reid, 1981
Publicly posted praise	Korabek, Reid & Ivancic, 1981

[a]The particular consequence listed does not necessarily represent the only management procedure used in each study.

written notices in which the feedback is publicly posted in the staff work area (Greene *et al.*, 1978), written memoranda that are presented privately to individual staff members (Shoemaker & Reid, 1980), and verbal statements in which the feedback is spoken privately to staff persons (Brown *et al.*, 1981). In addition to procedural efficacy, feedback procedures seem to be more cost-efficient than many of the other consequence approaches in that they rely on resources that are usually indigenous to the normal work setting. However, it should also be noted that the investigations on feedback programs, as well as consequence applications in general, have been criticized for affecting only restricted areas of staff performance and for not completely analyzing their effective program components (Reid & Whitman, 1983).

The third category of behavioral staff management procedures, *self-management* or *participative management* strategies, represents an area that has long been of interest in industrial organizations (McCormick & Ilgen, 1980) but only recently has received attention from behavioral researchers/practitioners in institutional settings. However, whereas participative management approaches in industrial psychology applications have involved procedures based on a variety of theoretical orientations (McCormick & Ilgen, 1980), we are referring specifically to the use of behavioral self-control strategies by staff to improve their own work performance. Several self-control procedures, although not necessarily labeled as such, recently have been used in conjunction with supervisory-controlled antecedent and consequence programs in institutions with staff, including self-recording (Andrasik, McNamara, & Abbott, 1978;

Korabek, Reid, & Ivancic, 1981; Seys & Duker, 1978) and goal setting (Seys & Duker, 1978). A smaller number of management programs have relied more exclusively on self-control procedures such as self-recording (Burg, Reid, & Lattimore, 1979) and self-recording plus goal setting, self-evaluation, and self-reinforcement (Burgio *et al.*, 1983) to increase desired work behaviors of attendants such as interactions with residents. Also, self-recording and self-evaluation (Kissel, Whitman, & Reid, 1983) methods have appeared useful in *maintaining* desired levels of certain staff behaviors such as proficiency in training self-help skills to residents once the skills are initially acquired by staff.

Generally, we view self-management strategies as not involving total self-control by staff members in regard to their work performance. Rather, these procedures allow staff to be more explicitly involved with supervisors in the management of their work activities than what typically happens in institutional management practices (see Burgio *et al.*, 1983, for more discussion on varying degrees of self-control versus supervisory control in staff management). Based on the research just noted, these procedures appear to be an effective approach to institutional staff management. Perhaps just as important, behavioral self-management systems potentially can be very well received by staff persons relative to procedures with more supervisory control (Burgio *et al.*, 1983). However, considerably more research with self-control programs in institutional staff management is needed before definitive conclusions are warranted regarding the effectiveness and acceptability of these programs.

The final category of behavioral management programs consists of *multifaceted procedures*. These approaches are designed to include a large number of different behavioral techniques that are combined into one overall management system as opposed to focusing on one or a few behavioral procedures. The intent of these programs is to provide a maximally powerful behavior change strategy (Reid & Whitman, 1983; Whitman *et al.*, 1983). The focus on multifaceted systems with a behavioral orientation has occurred relatively recently in the applied research literature, and results to date offer support for their effectiveness in institutional staff management (e.g., Fabry & Reid, 1978; Korabek *et al.*, 1981; Shoemaker & Reid, 1980).

An example of the variety of procedures used in the multifaceted programs is reflected in the staff management approach used by Ivancic, Reid, Iwata, Faw, and Page (1981) to increase attendants' language-training activities during institutional care routines with profoundly handicapped children. The Ivancic *et al.* program included (a) a 10- to 40-minute instructional session; (b) antecedent prompting procedures involving vocal and written instructions as well as supervisory modeling; and (c) consequence components consisting of vocal and publicly posted written feedback along with supervisor praise. The basic rationale of the Ivancic *et al.* system was to increase the probability of changing staff behavior by including a large number of specific procedures that had previously been effective in improving staff performance. Hence, as opposed to management programs that are dependent on only one behavior change component to produce the desired effect, the Ivancic *et al.* program was established such that if one component was ineffective the system could still work because one or more of the other program components could have the intended effect.

Suggestions for the Practitioner for Training/Managing Staff for Treating Severe Behavior Disorders

Our suggestions for practitioners charged with training and managing institutional staff performance in regard to the treatment of behavior disorders will be presented in two formats. First, we will describe a generic model for effectively training and managing different areas of staff performance. Second, we will summarize specific sets of skills that could be targeted with the model that are important for staff to use to successfully treat severe behavior disorders. The skills to be addressed relate to the basic reasons why staff need to be specifically trained to work with residents with serious behavior problems, as discussed earlier. Throughout our discussion, the reader is encouraged to recall the importance noted in the preceding section of not only training staff in certain skills but also managing the appropriate use of those skills in the daily work setting.

A Behavioral Model for Training/Managing Institutional Staff Performance

The behavioral supervision model we are recommending when working with institutional staff is based on results of the investigations conducted with attendant performance as briefly reviewed in the preceding section. The model initially was synthesized from previous research findings by Whitman *et al.* (1983) for use with staff performance, and it subsequently has been elaborated on (Reid & Shoemaker, 1984). In collaboration with our colleagues, we have evaluated various applications of the supervisory model with institutional staff performance in a number of situations and generally have found support for its effectiveness (Faw, Reid, Schepis, Fitzgerald, & Welty, 1981; Ivancic et al., 1981; Korabek et al., 1981; Schepis et al., 1982; Shoemaker & Reid, 1980).

There are five basic steps that comprise the behavioral supervision model, with different implementation components within each step. The first step is to *define performance areas* as observable and countable work outputs or behaviors. For example, Table 3 demonstrates how van den Pol, Reid, and Fuqua (1983) defined desirable staff responses to aggressive resident outbursts in order to prevent harm to both staff and residents. Whitman et al. (1983) also provide a number of examples of behavioral definitions of staff job responsibilities. The second step in the behavioral supervision model, *monitoring*, refers to the systematic collection of objective data on staff performance. One of the most common types of monitoring systems used with staff performance is a time-sampling format that involves a supervisor or appropriate designee periodically performing brief spot checks on staff behavior. Such a system allows a data base regarding what staff are doing at various times

Table 3. *Component Steps for Staff Self-Defense Procedure for Use with Aggressive Resident Activity*

Number	Step
1	Staff member (S) stands within reach of resident (R) within 5 seconds of hit
2	S states R's name and instructs incompatible response within 10 seconds of the hit
3	S physically prompts desired response within 10 seconds of instructions or within 20 seconds of hit
4	S blocks punch with same-side arm, with hand fisted (thumb contacting fingers) and using forearm (between wrist and elbow joint)
5	S blocks kick by raising same-side leg 6 inches with foot partially occluding support leg and torso turning approximately 90 degrees to the side
6	S releases clothing grab by thumb pry within 5 seconds of grab
7	S releases body part grab by thumb or rotating out within 5 seconds of grab
8	S lifts and holds chair between self and R's chair within 5 seconds of attack
9	S states criteria for use of self-defense technique as per policy; to protect people (any) and property

Note. From "Peer Training of Safety-Related Skills to Institutional Staff: Benefits for Trainers and Trainees" by R. A. van den Pol, D. H. Reid, and R. W. Fuqua, 1983, *Journal of Applied Behavior Analysis, 16(2)* 144. Copyright by *Journal of Applied Behavior Analysis.* Reprinted by permission.

across situations in order to better evaluate the effects of particular management interventions. The third step in the model consists of *instructing*
staff as to their expected job responsibilities, using the previously established (Step 1) behavioral definitions to help insure that the responsibilities are clearly delineated. Instructing essentially includes what was
described as staff training in the first part of the preceding section of
this chapter. *Providing consequences* represents the fourth step. This component consists of using events and/or items arranged by a supervisor
to be contingent on identified staff behaviors as described in the second
part of the preceding section. The final step in the behavioral supervision
model is *evaluating*, or reviewing the data collected via the monitoring
system and determining if supervisory procedures (e.g., use of particular
consequences) are producing the desired effect on staff performance.

Obviously, our abbreviated summarization of the behavioral supervision model does not provide enough information for a supervisor to
immediately apply in his or her institution, and the interested reader is
referred to the reports noted earlier that describe the model in considerably more detail. For our purposes here, the model does present a
systematic approach with demonstrated efficacy for improving and
maintaining staff performance. However, we would also like to stress
that this approach is not recommended as a cure-all for institutional staff
training and management problems. Rather, we suggest the model for
practitioners who have a reasonable background in behavior modification for use with clearly identified staff responsibility areas. As an additional precaution for institutional supervisors, a problem area with the
model has been pointed out in that the approach has been effective with
only restricted areas of staff job duties at a particular time as opposed
to the entire set of attendant job responsibilities (Reid & Shoemaker,
1983). Also, the approach can be time consuming for supervisors to use
(Reid & Whitman, 1983).

Specific Skill Areas for Staff Training

This section presents those skills that we believe are among the
most important for staff training/management programs to address in
order for effective attendant involvement in the treatment of resident
behavior disorders. The skills to be discussed are those that should be
useful for working with a wide range of behavior problems of the institutionalized mentally retarded. However, it is probably safe to assume
that *whenever* a formal treatment program is to be implemented for a
severe behavior disorder, the responsible clinician will need to provide

training specifically related to that program for staff who will help implement the treatment regime (e.g., see Katz & Lutzker, 1980).

In situations where a structured, formal treatment program is to be implemented, the behavioral supervision model can be useful for obtaining effective staff involvement. For example, if a required relaxation program (Webster & Azrin, 1973) is being prescribed for aggressive actions of a profoundly mentally retarded woman, the clinician could follow the steps in the model by first behaviorally specifying the exact procedures constituting the required relaxation program, including the target behaviors of the resident that require implementation of the program, the escorting procedures for assisting the resident to an appropriate setting for the program, physical holds to use if the resident continues to dangerously aggress, and so forth. Next, the clinician could instruct the staff in the relevant procedures through a short but comprehensive in-service session consisting of verbal and written descriptions of the procedures, modeling, role playing, and feedback (see Ivancic et al., 1981; Korabek et al., 1981, for descriptions of quick, multicomponent staff instructional procedures). Using the third step of the model, the clinician would intermittently but frequently monitor staffs' use of the procedure, maintain records as to their (in)accuracy in implementation and provide contingent consequences (fourth step) based on how well staff implement the program. Perhaps most easily, the consequences could consist of positive feedback on appropriate implementation by staff and corrective feedback where implementation was not in accordance with the previous instructions. Alternatively, positive feedback could be given to the staff regarding improvement in the *resident's* behavior, such as publicly posted praise statements concerning reductions in the woman's aggressive outbursts (Greene et al., 1978; Korabek et al., 1981). Finally, the clinician could continuously evaluate supervisory effectiveness with the staff, and, as staff performance maintains at a satisfactory level, decrease the supervisory efforts such as reducing the frequency of providing feedback. Although this training and management approach may require a rather considerable amount of time and effort by the clinician, as well as necessitating support for the program from the staff supervisor if the clinician is not in a supervisory role with staff, we have found it is usually worth the investment in terms of eventually remediating serious behavior problems of residents. Similar applications with the behavioral supervision model could be conducted with each of the staff training areas to be described in the remainder of this chapter.

Training in Basic Consequence Application Procedures. Generally it is not possible to predict all varieties of resident behavior problems that direct care staff will face. Hence, training in skills necessary for the effective application of reinforcing and punishing consequences that can be used across situations should be useful, similar to the approaches of the early behavioral staff training programs of the 1960s and early 1970s (Gardner, 1973). However, because of the relative ineffectiveness of classroom-type teaching of behavior modification skills to staff as mentioned previously, we recommend that the classroom-instruction part of the staff program involve less time—a few hours at most—than is the case with many institutional staff development programs on behavior management. The major part of the training should occur in the actual work station with conditions as similar to the day-to-day routine as possible. Using this approach, someone will be required to be in the resident living area or other attendant work station to provide the staff training. For example, staff development and training personnel may need to be assigned to do a significant portion of their job in the attendants' work area. Additional strategies that can be effective in this respect are to (a) first train the supervisor who is usually present in the work station and then have the supervisor train the staff (Page, Iwata, & Reid, 1982); or (b) assign a portion of a competent, experienced attendant's time for the training in a peer-teaching format (van den Pol et al., 1983).

Training in Skills for Evoking Appropriate Resident Compliance. A highly useful skill for direct care personnel in terms of treating severe behavior disorders is evoking resident compliance to staff instructions. That is, if staff have good verbal control over resident behavior, then they are in a better position to prevent and/or stop behavior problems such as disruptive outbursts. For instance, if a resident has been well trained in instruction following and starts to aggress toward another resident, an alert staff member can quickly prevent potential injury by instructing the resident to sit down, go to his or her room, and so forth. Unfortunately, what frequently happens is that consistent, proficient training of residents in instruction following is not conducted by staff, and if staff do attempt to instruct a resident to "stop" when he or she starts to aggress, there is no effect on behavior.

In developing a program for training staff to teach resident instruction following or compliance, we recommend use of a very basic compliance-training paradigm. That is, staff requirements should be as uncomplicated as possible. Whitman et al. (1983) have described a straightforward strategy for teaching self-help skills to the severely and profoundly mentally retarded that can be easily modified for training in instruction following. Very briefly, the strategy includes three rules that staff would need to be aware of and practice during their daily routine. First, a resident should be requested to do something only if the requesting staff person can insure that the resident will comply, even if the resident has to be physically guided. Actually, just the opposite happens frequently in typical institutions in that staff make requests, residents do not comply, and there are no consequences for noncompliance. This latter paradigm is in essence teaching residents not to comply, or at the very least making it difficult to achieve compliance in future interactions. The second rule is that resident compliance to verbal requests should be frequently reinforced with praise, treats, and the like as part of staffs' interactions with residents during the daily work routine. Third, in conjunction with the first rule, if a resident does not respond to a verbal request, then some physical prompting should be used to achieve compliance, thereby prohibiting residents from becoming dependent on staff for physically doing things for them.

In addition to the training approach just described, there are a number of considerably more sophisticated compliance-training procedures that could be taught to staff for use with residents. Nevertheless, we believe that a simple strategy has the advantages of being easy to teach to staff and of making the supervisor's job easier in terms of managing staffs' use of the strategy. The supervision aspect is particularly important because in the short run for staff, it requires less effort not to consistently require compliance of residents, making it likely that the supervisor will have to *actively* involve staff in effective compliance training with residents. In the long run, effective compliance training of residents can make the staffs' job easier as well as reduce the frequency and/or seriousness of resident behavior disorders.

Training in Observation Procedures. Earlier in this chapter, we mentioned the need to involve staff in treatment plans for residents because of staffs' intimate knowledge of resident response patterns. If such knowledge is to be truly useful in treatment regimes, then it is desirable that staff be able to assess and relate resident activities in objective and accurate terms. That is, staff members often need training in the observational skills necessary to record exactly what a resident does in a given situation. Observational skills are important for a variety of reasons, including to help determine the need for a particular treatment program by accurately assessing how serious a behavior problem is as well as to evaluate the effectiveness of a given program for changing the targeted behaviors. For example, a relatively common situation in which skills would be useful in this respect is observing and describing resident tantrums.

Tantrums often refer to a wide variety of undesirable activities including intense self-injury, disruptive outbursts involving property destruction, and aggressive attacks. Each of these types of tantrums may require different treatment interventions for remediation. Hence, it would be of considerable benefit if staff could precisely state the behaviors of concern as well as maintain reliable records as to where, when, and how often the behaviors occur in order to help design, and eventually evaluate, an effective treatment program. Again, staff are in a particularly advantageous position to conduct observations and provide sensitive records on target behaviors because of their frequent contact with residents as part of their usual job routines. Actually, staff have often been involved somewhat in monitoring activities as part of resident treatment programs, but based on our experience, little attention has been given to effectively training staff to be good behavioral observers or given to managing staffs' performance in this area.

Training in the Use of Impromptu Restitutional Overcorrection Procedures. Earlier we emphasized the need to teach consequence application procedures to direct care staff that could be used across a variety of resident problem situations. The rationale for teaching a generalized set of skills was that it is impossible to predict all the problem behaviors staff will face, and they cannot always be prepared for each situation by having a professionally developed and individualized behavioral program to follow. By being skilled in basic behavioral approaches, staff would at least know general rules to follow such as not to reinforce clearly undesirable behavior (e.g., self-injury). If staff members do have these types of skills, an additional concern often arises in that they might know that a particular disruptive behavior such as knocking over a table should be punished but do not know what punishing consequence to use. Hence, a useful area for staff training is the application of a punishment procedure that can be used with novel and unexpected aggressive and disruptive acts by residents. If staff are prepared to deal with a behavior problem via a punishment strategy immediately as it arises, as opposed to waiting for a formal program to be developed when the problem has likely escalated in either intensity or frequency, then the problem will probably represent a less serious situation and should be resolved more easily.

One punishment regime that is well suited for application across a variety of resident problem behaviors, particularly disruptive acts, is restitutional overcorrection (Foxx & Azrin, 1973). The basic procedural component in restitutional overcorrection is that a resident is required to correct the damage that he or she has done to the environment to a level better than that which existed prior to the disruption. Using this explanation as a guideline, the requirements for staff are straightforward. If a resident unexpectedly disrupts the environment and there is not an existing treatment program designed to be implemented, then the resident should be required to correct the damage that has been done. In such cases, the same compliance training sequence described earlier (e.g., verbal instruction vs. physical guidance) can be used with the resident in requiring him or her to reinstate the environment to a level better than its original condition. For example, if a resident knocks over a table, then she or he is instructed to set the table back up as well as setting up any chairs and so forth that were knocked over. A resident who does not comply to the staff request is physically guided through the appropriate activity. Similarly, if a resident throws food during meal-time, then that resident is instructed to clean up the mess and, if need be, is physically guided through the cleaning process.

Our rationale for recommending restitutional overcorrection as a rather generic punishment strategy to use with unexpected behavior problems is threefold. First, it seems to be an easy process for staff to comprehend in terms of determining what should be done following the occurrence of novel behavior problems. Second, it has been shown to be an effective behavior change strategy (see Ollendick & Matson, 1978, for a review). Third, we have found it to be well received by staff relative to other typical punishment strategies. However, it should be noted that such an approach also has its drawbacks. Specifically, at times the procedure requires considerable physical exertion by staff members, and some staff may not be able to physically guide certain residents through tasks unless other staff help is available. Additionally, the impromptu use of restitutional overcorrection needs to be in accordance with a given institution's policies regarding use of behavior management procedures.

Training in Protective and Preventive Techniques. Most of our discussion so far regarding staff training suggestions has focused on teaching skills to staff that will assist in the development, implementation, and/ or evaluation of remedial procedures for resident behavior disorders. A somewhat different but nonetheless important area warranting staff training is methods of preventing harm to staff and residents when seriously aggressive activity occurs. That is, staff should not only be trained in appropriate therapeutic skills to help remediate aggressive disorders, but they should also be trained in skills that will protect themselves and others from harm. Aggressive incidents that result in harm to people are relatively common in institutional settings (Boe, 1977).

Currently, several descriptions of appropriate self-defense skills are available (e.g., Harvey & Schepers, 1977), such as protective maneuvers against resident arm hits and kicks, release procedures from hair pulls and bites, and nonharmful restraining tactics that are designed for use by institutional staff with aggressive residents. In addition, some applied research has been reported that specifically evaluated staff training procedures regarding self-defense skills (van den Pol *et al.*, 1983; see also Table 3 for an example of the types of skills taught). However, again based on our experience, the amount of training and related supervision of direct care staff in these types of skills is quite minimal in many institutions and warrants increased attention.

A related set of skills to those just noted that can be quite helpful to attendants for preventing harm when working with residents with severe behavior disorders is the detection of precursor behaviors that lead up to aggressive or disruptive outbursts. More precisely, if staff are trained to be sensitive to the fact that some clients often exhibit certain behaviors prior to an actual outburst, then such outbursts and potential physical harm can be prevented. For example, one of our former residents who aggressed toward staff frequently made distinctive sounds and began running and flapping his hands prior to aggressing. By intervening to stop the running and hand flapping, the aggression could be prevented. If staff members are trained to observe (see previous section on training staff in observation skills) for such antecedent behaviors that occur prior to an aggressive incident, this information can then be included in the treatment program for a particular resident, and the chain of behaviors that usually leads up to an aggressive act can be interrupted and eventually eliminated.

Training in Behavior Management and Resident Abuse Guidelines. Currently most institutional facilities probably have established guidelines for the application of certain behavior management procedures, particularly the use of aversive techniques with resident behavior problems. If agencies do not have written policies in this respect, it is strongly recommended that the facility's management establish relevant guidelines with input from appropriate professional disciplines. A primary rationale for the importance given to behavior management and related resident abuse guidelines is to protect residents from mistreatment such as being unnecessarily subjected to aversive control procedures. For this reason, it is paramount that the staff who have the most involvement with institutional clients—direct care personnel—be well trained in what procedures are acceptable and unacceptable for use in interactions with residents.

In addition to training staff in acceptable versus unacceptable procedures to protect the rights of mentally retarded residents, such training is necessary for the protection of staff. Frequently, public residential facilities for the mentally retarded prohibit actions by staff with residents that would not be that unusual for a parent to do with his or her daughter or son in a normal home. For example, striking a resident in any way is usually prohibited by regulations in institutions even though it would not be very unusual for a parent, for example, to slap a son's hand for throwing an object that might harm himself or others. If a staff member is unaware of resident abuse guidelines and uses a procedure with a resident such as a hand slap that the staff person is accustomed to using at home, that individual could be terminated. We have seen a number of situations in which staff members lost their jobs, or were "allowed" to resign, for using procedures that they often used at home with their own children.

The example just described pertains to situations in which staff members break a serious facility policy without being aware of the regulation. A similar situation exists in terms of seriousness for staff and residents when a staff person is aware of an abuse policy but in essence loses control while in a demanding or frustrating situation and, for instance, strikes a resident. We recently worked with a new staff member who was performing her job quite well but who, during a training session with an aggressive resident, appeared to momentarily lose control when the resident spit in her face and then responded by slapping the resident. The staff member, in accordance with state law and facility policy, was required to discontinue employment at the institution. Although this is somewhat of an extreme example, we have also seen a number of staff members who had long histories of acceptable performance placed in difficult and tiring job situations (e.g., working shortstaffed with disruptive residents for long periods of time) and, while apparently under duress, respond to an aggressive resident action by striking the resident.

The situations just described are probably best avoided by supervisors being sensitive to conditions that set the occasion for staff to respond impulsively and preventing those conditions from developing. Also, staff should be made aware of what is acceptable to do with residents through an instructional program. Additionally, it may be that some type of staff training in basic self-control procedures such as relaxation exercises or desensitization strategies (Goldfried & Merbaum, 1973) would be helpful for staff who continuously work with very difficult-to-manage residents. The purpose of such training would be to teach staff to be aware of conditions that lead to more impulsive-type reactions as well as to teach them how to remedy such conditions (e.g., changing the activity they are engaging in, calling for relief or assistance from peers and/or supervisors, taking a few minutes to calm down, etc.).

Summary

We have attempted to emphasize the necessity of providing treatment of severe behavior disorders within institutions serving the mentally retarded and the integral role direct care personnel should play in that treatment process. Correspondingly, we stressed the need to actively train attendant staff for assisting in the treatment of resident behavior disorders. Four reasons why staff warrant training in this respect were discussed: the lack of preparation prior to becoming an attendant, prevention of deleterious effects of staff activities on resident behavior disorders, therapeutic utilization of staffs' knowledge about residents, and traditionally low frequencies of therapeutic staff interactions with residents. A brief historical overview of behavioral staff training programs was presented with a resulting emphasis on the importance of both training new skills to staff and *managing* the application of those skills in the daily work environment. Using information obtained from past research, a behavioral supervision model was then summarized for use in improving institutional staff performance. Finally, specific skill areas in which direct care staff warrant training and suggestions regarding how to conduct that training were discussed in relation to effective staff involvement in the treatment of severe behavior disorders. The skill areas addressed included basic consequence application procedures, methods for evoking consistent resident compliance, behavioral observation strategies, impromptu uses of restitutional overcorrection regimes, protective and preventive techniques, and knowledge of agency behavior management and resident abuse guidelines. An underlying contention throughout the chapter has been that by requiring effective training and management of attendant staff performance to be a necessary part of treatment programs for behavior disorders, then the probability of successful resolution of those problems will be enhanced considerably.

ACKNOWLEDGMENTS

Appreciation is expressed to Carole McNew for her very competent assistance in preparing the manuscript.

References

ACMRDD Standards for services for developmentally disabled individuals. (1978). Chicago: Joint Commission on Accreditation of Hospitals.

Andrasik, F., McNamara, J. R., & Abbott, D. M. (1978). Policy control: A low resource intervention for improving staff behavior. *Journal of Organizational Behavior Management, 1*, 125–133.

Baer, D. M., Wolf, M. M., & Risley, T. R. (1968). Some current dimensions of applied behavior analysis. *Journal of Applied Behavior Analysis, 1*, 91–97.

Bassinger, J. F., Ferguson, R. L., Watson, L. S., & Wyant, S. I. (1971). *Behavior modification: A programmed text for institutional staff.* Tuscaloosa, AL: Behavior Modification Technology.

Bensberg, G. J., & Barnett, C. D. (1966). *Attendant training in southern residential facilities for the mentally retarded.* Atlanta: Southern Regional Education Board.

Blindert, H. D. (1975). Interactions between residents and staff: A qualitative investigation of an institutional setting for retarded children. *Mental Retardation, 13,* 38–40.

Boe, R. B. (1977). Economical procedures for the reduction of aggression in a residential setting. *Mental Retardation, 15,* 25–28.

Bricker, W. A., Morgan, D. G., & Grabowski, J. G. (1972). Development and maintenance of a behavior modification repertoire of cottage attendants through TV feedback. *American Journal of Mental Deficiency, 77,* 128–136.

Brown, K. M., Willis, B. S., & Reid, D. H. (1981). Differential effects of supervisor verbal feedback and feedback plus approval on institutional staff performance. *Journal of Organizational Behavior Management, 3,* 57–68.

Burg, M. M., Reid, D. H., & Lattimore, J. (1979). Use of a self-recording and supervision program to change institutional staff behavior. *Journal of Applied Behavior Analysis, 12,* 363–375.

Burgio, L. D., Whitman, T. L., & Reid, D. H. (1983). A participative management approach for improving direct-care staff performance in an institutional setting. *Journal of Applied Behavior Analysis, 16,* 37–53.

Casey, L. O. (1978). Development of communicative behavior in autistic children: A parent program using manual signs. *Journal of Autism and Childhood Schizophrenia, 8,* 45–59.

Dailey, W. F., Allen, G. J., Chinsky, J. M., & Veit, S. W. (1977). Attendant behavior and attitudes toward institutionalized retarded children. *American Journal of Mental Deficiency, 78,* 586–591.

Eyman, R. K., & Borthwick, S. A. (1980). Patterns of care for mentally retarded persons. *Mental Retardation, 18,* 63–66.

Eyman, R. K., & Call, T. (1977). Maladaptive behavior and community placement of mentally retarded persons. *American Journal of Mental Deficiency, 82,* 137–144.

Fabry, P. L., & Reid, D. H. (1978). Teaching foster grandparents to train severely handicapped persons. *Journal of Applied Behavior Analysis, 11,* 111–123.

Faw, G. D., Reid, D. H., Schepis, M. M., Fitzgerald, J. R., & Welty, P. A. (1981). Involving institutional staff in the development and maintenance of sign language skills with profoundly retarded persons. *Journal of Applied Behavior Analysis, 14,* 411–423.

Fielding, L. T., Errickson, E., & Bettin, B. (1971). Modification of staff behavior: A brief note. *Behavior Therapy, 2,* 550–553.

Foxx, R. M., & Azrin, N. H. (1973). The elimination of autistic self-stimulatory behavior by overcorrection. *Journal of Applied Behavior Analysis, 6,* 1–14.

Gardner, J. M. (1970). Effects of reinforcement conditions on lateness and absence among institutional personnel. *Ohio Research Quarterly, 3,* 315–316.

Gardner, J. M. (1972). Teaching behavior modification to nonprofessionals. *Journal of Applied Behavior Analysis, 5,* 517–521.

Gardner, J. M. (1973). Training the trainers. A review of research on teaching behavior modification. In R. D. Rubin, J. P. Brady, & J. D. Henderson (Eds.), *Advances in behavior therapy* (Vol. 4, pp. 145–158). New York: Academic Press.

Gladstone, B. W., & Spencer, C. J. (1977). The effects of modeling on the contingent praise of mental retardation counselors. *Journal of Applied Behavior Analysis, 10,* 75–84.

Goldfried, M. R., & Merbaum, M. (Eds.). (1973). *Behavior change through self-control.* New York: Holt, Rinehart & Winston.

Greene, B. F., Willis, B. S., Levy, R., & Bailey, J. S. (1978). Measuring client gains from staff implemented programs. *Journal of Applied Behavior Analysis, 11,* 395–412.

Halle, J. W., Marshall, A. M., & Spradlin, J. E. (1979). Time delay: A technique to increase language use and facilitate generalization in retarded children. *Journal of Applied Behavior Analysis, 12,* 431–439.

Hart, B., & Risley, T. R. (1980). *In vivo* language intervention: Unanticipated general effects. *Journal of Applied Behavior Analysis, 13,* 407–432.

Harvey, E. R., & Schepers, J. (1977). Physical control techniques and defensive holds for use with aggressive retarded adults. *Mental Retardation, 15,* 29–31.

Ivancic, M. T., Reid, D. H., Iwata, B. A., Faw, G. D., & Page, T. J. (1981). Evaluating a supervision program for developing and maintaining therapeutic staff–resident interactions during institutional care routines. *Journal of Applied Behavior Analysis, 14,* 95–107.

Iwata, B. A., Bailey, J. S., Brown, K. M., Foshee, T. J., & Alpern, M. (1976). A performance-based lottery to improve residential care and training by institutional staff. *Journal of Applied Behavior Analysis, 9,* 417–431.

Jacobson, J. W. (1982). Problem behavior and psychiatric impairment within a developmentally disabled population I: Behavior frequency. *Applied Research in Mental Retardation, 3,* 121–139.

Katz, R. C., & Lutzker, J. R. (1980). A comparison of three methods for training timeout. *Behavior Research of Severe Developmental Disabilities, 1,* 123–130.

Kissel, R. C., Whitman, T. L., & Reid, D. H. (1983). Development of self-care skills in retarded children through an institutional staff training and self-management program. *Journal of Applied Behavior Analysis, 16,* 395–416.

Korabek, C. A., Reid, D. H., Page, T. J., Albrecht, S., & Fitzgerald, J. (1979). *Promoting gross motor development of handicapped children through behavioral supervision of institutional staff.* Paper presented at the Fifth Annual Convention of the Association for Behavior Analysis, Dearborn, Michigan.

Korabek, C. A., Reid, D. H., & Ivancic, M. T. (1981). Improving needed food intake of profoundly handicapped children through effective supervision of institutional staff performance. *Applied Research in Mental Retardation, 2,* 69–88.

Maloney, M. P., & Ward, M. P. (1979). *Mental retardation and modern society.* New York: Oxford University Press.

Marshall, A. M., & Marks, H. E. (1981). Implementation of "zero reject" training in an institutional setting. *Analysis and Intervention in Developmental Disabilities, 1,* 23–35.

McCormick, E. J., & Ilgen, D. R. (1980). *Industrial psychology* (7th ed.). Englewood Cliffs, NJ: Prentice-Hall.

Miller, R., & Lewin, L. M. (1980). Training and management of the psychiatric aide: A critical review. *Journal of Organizational Behavior Management, 2,* 295–315.

Montegar, C. A., Reid, D. H., Madsen, C. H., & Ewell, M. D. (1977). Increasing institutional staff-to-resident interactions through inservice training and supervisor approval. *Behavior Therapy, 8,* 533–540.

Ollendick, T. H., & Matson, J. L. (1978). Overcorrection: An overview. *Behavior Therapy, 9,* 830–842.

Page, T. J., Iwata, B. A., & Reid, D. H. (1982). Pyramidal training: A large-scale application with institutional staff. *Journal of Applied Behavior Analysis, 15,* 335–351.

Pomerleau, O. F., Bobrove, P. H., & Smith, R. H. (1973). Rewarding psychiatric aides for the behavioral improvement of assigned patients. *Journal of Applied Behavior Analysis, 6,* 383–390.

Pommer, D. A., & Streedbeck, D. (1974). Motivating staff performance in an operant learning program for children. *Journal of Applied Behavior Analysis, 7,* 217–221.

Prue, D. M., Frederiksen, L. W., & Bacon, A. (1978). Organizational behavior management:

An annotated bibliography. *Journal of Organizational Behavior Management, 1*, 216–257.

Quilitch, H. R. (1975). A comparison of three staff-management procedures. *Journal of Applied Behavior Analysis, 8*, 59–66.

Reid, D. H., & Shoemaker, J. (1984). Behavioral supervision: Methods of improving institutional staff performance. In W. P. Christian, G. T. Hanna, & T. J. Glahn (Eds.), *Programming effective human services: Strategies for institutional change and client transition* (pp. 39–61). New York: Plenum Press.

Reid, D. H., & Whitman, T. L. (1983). Behavioral staff management in institutions: A critical review of effectiveness and acceptability. *Analysis and Intervention in Developmental Disabilities, 3*, 131–149.

Reid, D. H., Schuh-Wear, C. L., & Brannon, M. E. (1978). Use of a group contingency to decrease staff absenteeism in a state institution. *Behavior Modification, 2*, 251–266.

Repp, A. C., & Deitz, D. E. D. (1979a). Reinforcement-based reductive procedures: Training and monitoring performance of institutional staff. *Mental Retardation, 19*, 221–226.

Repp, A. C., & Deitz, D. E. D.(1979b). Improving administrative-related staff behaviors at a state institution. *Mental Retardation, 17*, 185–192.

Scheerenberger, R. C. (1982). Public residential services, 1981: Status and trends. *Mental Retardation, 20*, 210–215.

Schepis, M. M., Reid, D. H., Fitzgerald, J. R., Faw, G. D., van den Pol, R. A., & Welty, P. A. (1982). A program for increasing manual signing by autistic and profoundly retarded youth within the daily environment. *Journal of Applied Behavior Analysis, 15*, 363–379.

Seys, D. M., & Duker, P. C. (1978). Improving residential care for the retarded by differential reinforcement of high rates of ward–staff behaviour. *Behavioural Analysis and Modification, 2*, 203–210.

Shoemaker, J., & Reid, D. H. (1980). Decreasing chronic absenteeism among institutional staff: Effects of a low-cost attendance program. *Journal of Organizational Behavior Management, 2*, 317–328.

Sneed, T. J., & Bible, G. H. (1979). An administrative procedure for improving staff performance in an institutional setting for retarded persons. *Mental Retardation, 2*, 92–94.

van den Pol, R. A., Reid, D. H., & Fugua, R. W. (1983). Peer training of safety-related skills to institutional staff: Benefits for trainers and trainees. *Journal of Applied Behavior Analysis, 16*, 139–156.

Warren, S. A., & Mondy, L. W. (1971). To what behaviors do attending adults respond? *American Journal of Mental Deficiency, 75*, 449–455.

Watson, L. S., Gardner, J. M., & Sanders, C. (1971). Shaping and maintaining behavior modification skills in staff members in an MR institution: Columbus State Institute Behavior Modification Program. *Mental Retardation, 9*, 39–42.

Webster, D. R., & Azrin, N. H. (1973). Required relaxation: A method of inhibiting agitative-disruptive behavior of retardates. *Behavior Research and Therapy, 11*, 67–78.

Whitman, T. L., Scibak, J. W., & Reid, D. H. (1983). *Behavior modification with the severely and profoundly retarded: Research and application.* New York: Academic Press.

11

Strategies for Evaluating Treatment Effectiveness

Rowland P. Barrett, Patrick K. Ackles, and Michel Hersen

Introduction

Beginning with the preface to this volume and continuing throughout the majority of its chapters, a heavy emphasis has been placed on the concept of *empiricism* and its role in the determination of treatment effectiveness. Simply put, the empirical model involves a quantifiable or data-based approach to clinical decision making that is heavily weighted by *objective* observation and yields information that is *verifiable* through replication. It is unfortunate that within many of the professional disciplines that serve mentally retarded clients, such as psychology, psychiatry, and special education, the empirical model is equated strictly with research and, all too often, is dismissed from its potentially valuable contribution to clinical practice, in general.

A number of journal articles (e.g., Hayes, 1981; Kazdin, 1981, 1983; Schafer, 1982) and books (e.g., Barlow & Hersen, 1984; Chassan, 1979; Kazdin, 1980, 1982; Kendell & Butcher, 1982) have attempted to demonstrate the clinical utility of the empirical model as a facilitator of decision making when addressing issues of treatment effectiveness and the ease with which it may be fully integrated within standard clinical practice. The purpose of the present chapter is similar in nature, with the

ROWLAND P. BARRETT • Department of Psychiatry and Human Behavior, Brown University Program in Medicine, Emma Pendleton Bradley Hospital, East Providence, Rhode Island 02915.   PATRICK K. ACKLES • Illinois Institute for the Study of Developmental Disabilities, University of Illinois at Chicago, Chicago, Illinois 60608.   MICHEL HERSEN • Department of Psychiatry, Western Psychiatric Institute and Clinic, University of Pittsburgh School of Medicine, Pittsburgh, Pennsylvania 15213.

specific objective of extending the applicability of the empirical approach to clinical practice to psychologists, psychiatrists, special educators, and others working in applied areas within the field of mental retardation.

Behavioral Assessment

The most common paradigm of the empirical model, as it pertains to the assessment, diagnosis, and treatment of mentally retarded clients, is represented by the *behavioral assessment* approach (Kazdin & Straw, 1976; Rojahn & Schroeder, 1983; Shapiro & Barrett, 1982). Such an approach consists of gathering information from a wide variety of sources in a number of different ways, but typically from within a standard framework that includes four basic methods: behavioral interviewing, traditional psychological tests, checklists and rating scales, and direct observation.

Behavioral Interviewing

Interviewing is a time-honored initial step in an evaluation process designed to yield a conceptualization of the client and the circumstances that have led to the development of the presenting problem behavior(s). Using the traditional perspective, a client is interviewed, the case formulated, and a treatment plan developed, largely on the basis of information gathered within the interview format. Such is the case even with mentally retarded clients, who are likely not self-referrals and, therefore, rarely interviewed *per se*. The traditional approach with mentally retarded clients is to apply the interview format to "most knowledgeable," third-party informants such as parents, siblings, relatives, and teachers, and base the case formulation and treatment plan on information gathered across multiple interviews with those closely associated and most familiar with the client and his or her problem behavior(s).

In the so-called "behavioral interview," the immediate concern is not with case formulation and treatment prescription but with the conducting of a preliminary functional analysis of the client's presenting problem(s). Although retaining the format of interviewing "most knowledgeable," third-party informants, this approach requires operationally defining, in observable and measurable terms, the behavioral excess and/or deficit that led to referral and obtaining information about the reliably occurring antecedent and consequent conditions that may be serving both to cue the occurrence of the problem behavior and maintain its presence, respectively. In the behavioral assessment literature this is known as the A-B-C format. Antecedents (A) are identified that reliably precede or cue the occurrence of the problem (target) behavior (B) that, in turn, may be strengthened or maintained according to the consequence (C) that is contingently applied (Bijour, Peterson, & Ault, 1968). By example, a child's father may set a limit such as "no more cookies, you've had enough" (antecedent), which prompts a temper tantrum (behavior) on the part of the child, to which the father responds by allowing more cookies (consequence) in an attempt to end the tantrumming. In this example, it is apparent that the child in question is being taught to tantrum in response to limit setting in order to have the limits either suspended or removed altogether. It is also clear from this straightforward example that tantrumming behavior in this particular case may be best addressed by changing the consequences for tantrumming from allowing access to more cookies to, perhaps, ignoring the disruptive acts.

Needless to say, the majority of problem behaviors presented to clinicians will not be so clearly and easily analyzed. As such, the A-B-C format requires obtaining a developmental and medical history in addition to information immediately related to the chief complaint(s), for purposes of examining the client's learning and reinforcement history and ruling out organic factors and/or family-based psychosocial stress as etiologic mechanisms contributing to the disordered behavior.

In sum, the use of the A-B-C interview format is an essential first step in the functional analysis of problem behavior. Even in cases where reliable antecedent or consequent conditions are unable to be identified and organic factors are equally evasive, it is certainly important to recognize what parents and teachers (for example) describe as the problem behavior, their conceptualizations as to the causes or reasons for its occurrence, how they are presently managing the problem, and their speculations as to how it may best be treated in the future.

Psychological Testing

The second step in the behavioral assessment "package" involves the use of traditional psychological tests, such as verbal and nonverbal intelligence tests, psychoeducational and achievement tests, and neuropsychological test batteries. Standardized testing is recommended as the next step beyond interviewing for a number of reasons. First, it allows for a brief period of direct observation of the client. Moreover, it provides an opportunity to directly observe the client under situationally

demanding and possibly stressful conditions relative to task performance, which may serve as antecedent to the occurrence of the problem
behavior being studied. As such, both sets of observations may be helpful in confirming prior data obtained using the A-B-C interview format
or, if such data do not exist, in confirming previous third-party
conceptualizations.

The results of such tests are useful, as well, in terms of identifying
the relative intellectual strengths and weaknesses of the client because
certain aspects of cognitive development will eventually be translated
to adaptive skills (or skill deficits) and bear relevance to the type of
treatment selected. For example, a mentally retarded client with a
Stanford-Binet IQ between 52 and 68 may initially be considered an
appropriate candidate for treatment using a behavior modification
approach such as a token reinforcement program. Indeed, the majority
of clients in the mild range of mental retardation respond quite favorably
to such interventions (e.g., Shapiro & Klein, 1980). However, the best
laid plans for a token reinforcement program may be compromised and
doomed to eventual failure if the client in question does not evince the
conceptual ability necessary to engage numerical reasoning, or what is
otherwise known as 1:1 numerical correspondence.

In addition to the information gathered on the basis of direct observation during the test session, test data are useful if performance is
viewed as a discrete sample of skills that have been acquired (or have
yet to be acquired) through learning. In the previous example, the client
either possesses numerical (1:1) correspondence skills, or has yet to learn
them. Consequently, the client's candidacy for involvement in a token
reinforcement program is deemed either appropriate or inappropriate,
accordingly. However, much caution must be exercised even in the most
straightforward and apparently obvious cases. Samples of ability or skill,
as they are gleaned from standardized psychological tests are, after all,
nothing more than samples. Implications of a fixed ability based on test
findings is inappropriate. It is important to bear in mind that the sample
may or may not be a true representation of the client's potential to benefit
from a particular treatment strategy and is certainly not a valid indicator
of competencies that may be gained through intensive habilation (Kazdin & Straw, 1976; Shapiro & Barrett, 1982).

Although data yielded by a standardized test battery should certainly play a role in the assessment of a problem behavior and the
selection of subsequent treatment forms, it is by no means the final
determinant in either process. In the proper sense, test data should be
used to augment information gained through the initial interviewing
stage and as a steering mechanism to suggest further and more discrete

forms of assessment, such as checklists, rating scales, and direct observation techniques.

Behavioral Checklists and Psychiatric Rating Scales

A third step and frequently used strategy in the behavioral assessment process is the problem-oriented checklist and rating scale. Several reasons underlie the popular use of these instruments as follow-up devices to A-B-C interviewing and standardized tests. First, they are quick to administer. Usually, a checklist or rating scale may be completed in 20 minutes, making it a viable daily assessment form. Abbreviated forms may take even less time. Second, they are efficient and provide a relatively comprehensive survey of problem behaviors. The majority of preferred checklists and rating scales have been carefully subjected to factor analysis and contain normative data, as well as estimates of reliability and validity. Moreover, such instruments yield quantifiable data and can be used effectively for both the assessment of a presenting problem and the objective evaluation of the treatment program designed to address it.

Similar to the A-B-C interview format, the use of checklists and rating scales with mentally retarded clients are not of the self-report variety and require that a knowledgeable informant (e.g., parent, teacher) evaluate, from memory or by direct observation, various client competencies or responses under sets of given conditions. The user of the checklist or rating scale is provided with standardized instructions designed to facilitate objectivity, such that the instrument will yield an accurate quantitative description of the client's behavior. Interobservor agreement may be easily obtained by employing a second independent rater and is considered essential to accurate assessment.

Types of checklists and rating scales are many and varied. They range from assessments of broadly defined psychopathology, such as the parent and teacher forms of the Child Behavior Checklist (CBCL) developed by Achenbach and Edelbrock (1983), which provides indexes on eight separate diagnostic categories according to sex and age cohort, to scales where the focus is on a specific syndrome, such as hyperactivity, where both the *Parent Questionnaire* and *Teacher Questionnaire* originally developed by Conners (1974) have enjoyed widespread use, particularly in their revised forms (Goyette, Connors, & Ulrich, 1979). As examples, such instruments are constructed in Likert fashion (see Anastasi, 1976), with a score of 0 indicating no problem on a particular behavioral dimension and scores of 1, 2, or 3 indicative of progressively greater magnitudes of disorder.

Both the CBCL and the so-called "Conners Scales" have been employed frequently in research protocols designed to assess the incidence of psychopathology in the mentally retarded population and the responsiveness of such clients to empirically based behavior modification and pharmacotherapy treatment programs. It is important to point out, however, that neither scale included mentally retarded individuals in its normative samples and, as such, the clinical utility of these scales as diagnostic tools is severely limited. That is to say, diagnoses of specific types of psychopathologies based on CBCL findings and of hyperactivity based on "Conners Scale" data are not and should not be forthcoming with mentally retarded clients. Although preliminary data suggest that the use of both scales may be applicable with borderline intellectual functioning and mildly retarded individuals (Barrett, Dixon, & Matson, 1984), their use with such clients should be accomplished with much caution.

A recently developed scale entitled the *Aberrant Behavior Checklist* (Aman & Singh, 1983) appears to hold the most promise for use with mentally retarded individuals, particularly those falling within the subtype classifications of moderate, severe, and profound mental retardation. The scale possesses sound psychometric properties (Aman, Singh, Stewart, & Field, 1985a) and was normed specifically on the mentally retarded population. Similar to the CBCL and "Conners Scales," the *Aberrant Behavior Checklist* is a Likert-type scale that has been carefully factor analyzed and includes measures of reliability and validity. Although little research beyond that conducted by its authors is presently available, the scale appears to possess good clinical utility, particularly in the area of ongoing evaluation of both behavior modification and drug treatment protocols. The inclusion of a "hyperactivity" subscale that targets those clients functioning at or below the moderate range of mental retardation represents a marked improvement over the current use of the "Conners Scales" with this population.

In conclusion, it is important to note that, as with the use of A-B-C interview data and information gathered through standardized psychological tests, checklists and rating scales are not sufficiently precise to be used alone in either diagnostic assessment or the evaluation of treatment progress. The utility of such scales is derived from their ability to objectively quantify third-party information as well as to confirm (or fail to confirm) behavior observed during the brief sampling periods afforded by testing. The role of the checklist and rating scale is to objectively assess the problem area(s) under consideration and to provide clinicians with an empirical foundation upon which further, more narrowly defined, and precise assessments may be built.

Direct Observation

The most widely used and well-accepted strategy of the behavioral assessment paradigm is that of direct observation. Indeed, all forms of information gathering discussed to this point serve merely as precursors to this method, which stands as the cornerstone of empirically based assessment. As mentioned throughout the numerous books on the topic (e.g., Hersen & Bellack, 1981), assessment must eventually rely upon direct observation techniques in order to be sufficiently precise. After all, "seeing is believing."

Similar to the A-B-C interview format, direct observation consists of measuring both the behavior selected for treatment (response assessment) and the antecedent and consequent conditions (stimulus assessment) that may be serving to both cue and maintain its presence. Response assessment is necessary to objectively determine the magnitude of the behavior targeted for treatment and to control for the occurrence of reactive changes in the target behavior that may be attributable to the assessment process (see Nelson & Hayes, 1979). Simply put, a client's behavior may change due to the fact that he or she is aware of being systematically observed and not as the result of treatment *per se*. Similarly, it is important to accurately assess the stimulus conditions, both antecedent and consequent, reliably associated with the target behavior. This is necessary in order to objectively determine the functional relationship between the problem behavior and the stimulus events that surround it and to document the effect of a stimulus manipulation, such as a change in consequence, on the behavior targeted for treatment.

The best known strategies for conducting response and stimulus assessments are *event sampling* and *time sampling* procedures. Both methods require that the behavior under assessment be clearly observable, definable, and measureable. That is, observations must be made without reference to inner states or hypothetical mechanisms, response definitions must be without ambiguity, and a final quantitative product must be obtained.

Event sampling is a procedure wherein the frequency or duration of a specific behavior is measured for a given period of time. As a measurement technique, event sampling is thought to be appropriate only if the behavior in question is discrete or has a clearly observable beginning and end. To obtain a frequency measure, the observor merely counts the number of discrete responses that occur within a specified time period. For example, a teacher may wish to assess the magnitude of a client's self-injurious behavior during school hours. By keeping a running tally of the separate incidents of head banging across the school day, the teacher has utilized a form of event sampling known as the "frequency count."

Certain behaviors, however, consume varying amounts of time to perform despite retaining a clearly definable beginning and end. Although the use of a frequency count remains applicable, such a procedure may be misleading both in terms of evaluating the "true" magnitude of the behavior in question and its response to intervention. For example, disruptive outbursts in the form of temper tantrums and destruction of property are certainly clearly observable in terms of their starting and ending points and may be easily tallied by a teacher across the school day. However, the data may be misleading if the tantrums and destructive acts consume varying amounts of time to perform. A total of 7 tantrums per day that climbs to a total of 16 tantrums per day following treatment would seemingly indicate a less than successful intervention program. However, if the mean duration of the 7 daily tantrums before treatment was 20 minutes, compared with a mean duration of 1 minute for the 16 daily tantrums following treatment, there would be little debate over whether the client's behavior was or was not substantially improved. In cases such as these, recording the duration of a specific behavioral event and totaling (or averaging) the time spent engaging in the act may produce a more accurate and, therefore, valid picture of the behavior being assessed and its response to treatment.

The measurement of interresponse time (IRT) is yet another example of event sampling. Here, again, the targeted behavior may have a clearly definable beginning and end and may consume varying amounts of time to perform. However, what may be of interest to the clinician is not (solely) the number of times the behavior occurs within a given time period nor the amount of time consumed performing the response. In some cases, the latency period prior to a first response and the elapsed time between consecutive acts comprise the data of clinical interest. Self-injurious clients and clients who engage in self-restraint, such as wrapping themselves in bedsheets and who, otherwise, appear to work toward being physically or mechanically restrained by staff, provide a good example of the utility of IRT as the event sampling technique of choice. In order to document progress toward freeing the client from self-imposed restraint, it is necessary to measure the increasing period of time before a first attempt at sheet-wrapping each day and, subsequently, between additional attempts at self-restraint throughout the remainder of the day. In cases where self-injury or self-restraint is either high rate, infrequent, or randomly distributed in "break-run" fashion, it is less important to know the actual rate of response as it is to observe the IRT in determining both the basal index of response strength and the client's reaction to treatment.

In cases where a behavior is not discrete, making it difficult to reliably judge when a separate response ends and another begins, *time sampling* may provide the clinician with more meaningful information on the strength of the response and its reaction to treatment. Time sampling is an assessment technique based on units of time rather than events. Among the more common forms of time sampling is interval recording, of which there are two basic types: continuous and noncontinuous. In continuous interval recording, behavior is observed for a given block of time (e.g., 20 minutes) with the time block further divided into shorter observation units or intervals (e.g., 10 seconds). The behavior being observed is then scored as having occurred (+) or not occurred (−) within each separate 10-second interval of observation. Target behaviors are noted as occurring only once per interval and, therefore, may be readily expressed as a percentage of occurrence across the total number of intervals comprising the larger time block. For example, if a client engages in stereotyped eye pressing during 60 of the 120 10-second intervals contained in a 20-minute observation period, it can be stated that he or she performed the behavior 50% of the time while under observation. Repeated assessments of this type will allow for an accurate assessment of response strength and a base rate to which posttreatment comparisons may be made.

In cases where multiple behaviors are targeted for observation, the clinician may find that continuous interval recording does not allow sufficient time for reliable scoring. As such, a noncontinuous interval recording format may be used. This procedure is identical to continuous interval recording with the noted exception of standardized departures from observation following each interval to allow the observor to record the occurrence or nonoccurrence of each targeted behavior. Using the previous example, behavior would still be sampled for 20 minutes using a 10-second observation interval format; however, each interval would be followed by a 5-second pause to allow recording of observations. Thus, the total number of observation intervals (previously 120 during continuous interval recording) would be reduced by one-third to 80, due to the addition of the 5-second recording pause following each interval. Using the nocontinuous interval recording format, the client in the previous example should be observed to eye press in 40 of the 80 observation intervals (50%). Although the cost of utilizing noncontinuous interval recording is one of underestimating behavioral magnitude due to reductions in the numbers of intervals in which observation occurs, the benefit of making additional data simultaneously available (e.g., on-task performance as well as eye-press responding) appears well worth the risk, particularly where the risk may be compromised by simply extending the basic time block by one-third to 30 minutes.

It should also be noted that measurement of interresponse time (IRT), as previously discussed, also may be computed using either continuous or noncontinuous interval recording formats. A quantifiable measure of latency to first response and elapsed time between consecutive responses may be calculated simply by noting the number of intervals to the initial recording of the target behavior, the number of intervals between subsequent observations of the targeted response, and expressing them as percentages against the total number of intervals contained within the larger time block.

As a final note to the discussion of time sampling as a direct observation technique, some mention should be made of *momentary time sampling*. Though interval recording formats are preferred due to their concise and circumscribed nature, such techniques work best in a "laboratory" setting and may be cumbersome in an applied or natural setting, such as the classroom or residential milieu. In these settings it is likely to be more convenient for staff to have specified times, such as every 15 minutes, where they engage in "momentary" observation of the client and record the target behavior as either occurring or not occurring on a prescribed data sheet. It should be noted that use of the term *momentary* is somewhat arbitrary and may be defined variously as 5-second, 15-second, 1-minute or, perhaps, 2-minute intervals of observation, depending on the client, the type of behavior to be observed, and other circumstances relative to the setting in which the sampling is occurring. Using the example of momentary time sampling on a 15-minute continuous schedule, a total of 4 observation intervals are afforded per hour, or 32 separate observations will occur within an 8-hour day. Although such an approach to time sampling is by far less intense than the previously discussed methods of obtaining 80 to 120 separate observations within a 20-minute time block, it allows for the obtaining of behavioral data across an entire day that, across successive days, will prove to be (theoretically) accurate in terms of measuring response strength and the impact of treatment. At worst, such a procedure will yield a serious underestimate of the true magnitude of target behavior; such is the risk with all time sampled approaches to measurement. At best, a daylong ledger of a particular behavior is accurately recorded, including a depiction of "lag" and "peak" periods of responding, a feature inherently omitted from the more intense sampling format of 20-minute time blocks once or twice per day. Ideally, a combination of both procedures should be in effect each day, in order to allow the most accurate and valid appraisal of the behavior being studied.

Approaches to direct observation are, therefore, many and varied. Only a few have been discussed here and, it should be noted, discussed in their most basic forms. Techniques for event sampling and time sampling are limited only by the clinician's creativity with regard to securing accurate and reliable measurements. The interested reader should consult Hartmann (1984) and Hartmann and Wood (1983) for a thorough discussion of observational methods and the training of observers.

Reliability and Interobservor Agreement

The concept of reliability is fundamental to any discussion of an empirical approach to clinical practice. Recall that the basic tenet of the empirical approach is that of objectivity. If a single clinician (observor) completes a rating scale and/or engages in direct observation techniques designed to yield frequency, duration, or time sampled measures of a behavior, such data are reduced to that of subjective impression if, in fact, they are not reliably obtained by additional observers whose role is one of assessing the targeted behavior independent of the primary observer. Similar to the earlier assertion that direct observation techniques serve as the cornerstone to behavioral assessment methodology, the notion of *quality assurance*, whereby obtained data are established as reliable, serves as the foundation to the empirical approach in its entirety. Indeed, it may be stated unequivocally that behavioral measurements must be fully and objectively documented as acceptably reliable in order to meet the basic criterion underlying the empirical approach to clinical practice.

The most popular and, perhaps, straightforward method of obtaining quality control of observational data is represented by the concept of *interobservor agreement*. Simply put, two (or more) observors measure a targeted behavior in independent fashion and compare their findings in accordance with various percentage agreement formulae with estimated values of "reliability" demonstrated on a continuum between 0.00 (no agreement) and 1.00 (absolute agreement). The rule of thumb in behavioral assessment is to accept values of 0.80 and greater as acceptable agreement.

Calculation of agreement values differs according to the observational format used to collect data. By example, when employing a frequency measure, percentage agreement is computed by dividing the smaller of two independently obtained frequency counts by the larger count and multiplying the dividend by 100, as follows:

$$\frac{(\text{smaller } f \text{ count})}{(\text{larger } f \text{ count})} \times 100 = \% \text{ agreement}$$

Percentage agreement for duration data may be calculated in similar fashion, using the time in minutes or seconds in place of the frequency values, as follows:

$$\frac{(\text{less time duration})}{(\text{greater time duration})} \times 100 = \% \text{ agreement}$$

Applications of the percentage agreement formula to time sampled data vary somewhat from the examples used with frequency and duration measures; however, the essential features remain unchanged. By example, when using either continuous or noncontinuous interval recording formats, it is necessary to calculate agreement separately for both occurrence and nonoccurrence of the targeted behavior on an interval-by-interval basis followed by a third computation that yields an overall percentage of agreement. Both Hartmann (1977) and Rojahn and Schroeder (1983) have used the following table to explain this approach.

Table 1. Two × Two Contingency Table of Possible Agreements and Disagreements of Two Observers and the Occurrence (O) or Nonoccurrence (NO) of an Event

		Observer 2	
		O	NO
Observer 1	O	A	B
	NO	C	D

Based on the preceding nomenclature, percentage of agreement on the occurrence of a target behavior, percentage of agreement on the nonoccurrence of a target behavior, and an overall percentage of agreement on both occurrence and nonoccurrence may be calculated using the following formulae:

$$\frac{A}{A + B + C} \times 100 = \% \text{ agreement of occurrence}$$

$$\frac{D}{D + B + C} \times 100 = \% \text{ agreement of nonoccurrence}$$

$$\frac{A + D}{A + B + C + D} \times 100 = \begin{array}{l}\text{overall \% agreement for both occurrence}\\\text{and nonoccurrence}\end{array}$$

Discussion of interobservor agreement as a quality control method in behavioral measurement should also be tempered by the fact that the products yielded by such agreement formulae do not constitute *actual* reliability estimates. In the purest psychometric sense, reliability must provide for measures of data consistency and data stability, assume an underlying observed score and true score variance component, and address the issue of agreement between observers strictly by chance. That interobservor agreement formulae meet none of these criterion is the most commonly cited shortcoming to their use. Although spuriously high levels of what is mistermed as *reliability* is the risk of using various percentage agreement formulae, it should be stated that such formulae adequately address issues of quality assurance and remain particularly applicable to routine clinical practice due to the ease with which they may be integrated within the observational system. It should be noted, as well, that a number of statistical formulae based on weighted agreement (Harris & Lahey, 1978), probability theory (Hopkins & Hermann, 1977), and correlation approaches (Cohen, 1960; Kent & Foster, 1977) exist, whereupon the yield is truly an estimate of data reliability. Although such statistical treatments may initially appear lengthy, burdensome, and anxiety provoking, a basic familiarity with the formula in question will usually do much in the way of dissuading relative fear. In this regard, it is advisable to refer to Wallace and Elder (1980), who present a particularly clear flowchart of suggested techniques to analyze reliability. Interested readers may also wish to consult Rojahn and Schroeder (1983) and the spring volume (*10*) of the *Journal of Applied Behavior Analysis* (1977) for further review of the issue of reliability as it pertains to observational data.

Single-Subject Experimental Designs

The development of empirical case studies using single-subject experimental designs represents the final touchstone in a behavioral assessment process that began with the use of the A-B-C format during the initial interview and continued throughout the use of traditional psychological tests, behavioral checklists and psychiatric rating scales, and direct observation techniques, all of which were aimed at producing a reliable determination that a problem behavior existed, how the problem behavior might best be measured, the extent or magnitude of the disorder, and whether the behavior was being influenced by reliably occurring stimulus events (i.e., antecedents, consequences).

behavior may be unequivocally related to the intervention being applied. To be reviewed are the most commonly employed single-subject design formats, such as the A-B design (Campbell & Stanley, 1966), the A-B-A-B design (Baer, Wolf, & Risley, 1968; Hersen & Barlow, 1976), various multiple baseline design formats, and the alternating treatments design (Barlow & Hayes, 1979), the latter of which has been variously termed the "simultaneous treatment design" (Kazdin & Hartmann, 1978), "multiple schedule design" (Hersen & Barlow, 1976), and "multielement baseline design" (Ulman & Sulzer-Azaroff, 1975).

A-B Design

The A-B format, an example of which is presented in Figure 1, is the simplest of the single-case experimental strategies. Using this format, the magnitude of the behavior targeted for change is measured through repeated observations across two phases of study: baseline (A) and treatment (B).

The baseline, or A, phase represents the natural magnitude of the target behavior under the identified conditions in which treatment will later be implemented. The treatment, or B, phase represents the magnitude of the target behavior after the specific intervention has been introduced. The singular difference between the A and B phases is the introduction of treatment. As such, it may be theorized that any change in the magnitude of the target behavior during the B phase (relative to baseline rates) may be attributed solely to the introduction of treatment.

Although simple and straightforward in both concept and implementation, the A-B design results in rather weak conclusions from a strictly experimental perspective. It is technically quasi-experimental

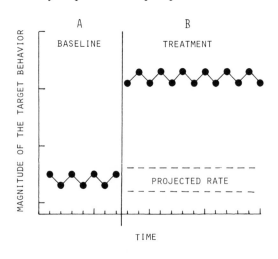

Figure 1. An example of the A-B (baseline treatment) design. The dotted line within the B phase indicate the projected range and magnitude of the target behavior, if treatment had not been introduced.

(Campbell & Stanley, 1966) in nature and, therefore, presents no clear evidence of the functional relationship between treatment and behavior change. Thus, any observed change in client behavior during the B phase of study could be attributable to a host of coincidentally occurring events, such as the simple passing of time. For example, Figure 2 presents hypothetical data for a mentally retarded child who head bangs. The frequency of head banging prior to intervention (A phase) is high. One week following the introduction of a behavior modification program (B phase), decreased rates of head banging were observed. Although it may be speculated that head banging decreased due to the introduction of treatment, the limitations of quasi-experimental findings are such that they offer nothing in defense of the argument that head banging would have subsided even if treatment were not implemented and that changes in the magnitude of behavior were due simply to the passing of an additional week in time or some other coincidental event (e.g., the introduction of a new staff member) extraneous to the prescribed treatment. Although the A-B design most certainly represents a significant improvement over traditional (nondata-based) case study methods and those approaches perhaps best described as B-phase-only studies, the lack of a clearly demonstrated functional relationship between treatment and changing behavior allows attributions of intervention effectiveness to be accepted only with "some major reservations" (Hersen & Barlow, 1976, p. 169).

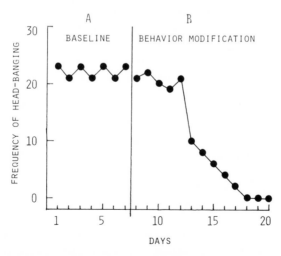

Figure 2. Hypothetical data for a mentally retarded client who head bangs. The baseline (A) phase indicates stable high rates of self-injury. The treatment (B) phase shows a marked decrease in head banging following 5 days of behavior modification. Was the observed change in behavior due to treatment or the introduction of a new staff member on Day 13?

In conclusion, it should be noted that despite its limitations due to a lack of experimental rigor, the A-B design possesses a certain degree of clinical utility. *In field (applied) settings, where control group analyses and/ or systematic manipulations of treatment are either impossible or impractical, the A-B design may yield the strongest empirical conclusion available* (Cook & Campbell, 1979). For similar reasons, Barlow and Hersen (1984) have strongly advocated the use of A-B strategies in private practice settings, and, it may be added here, within facilities such as group homes, classrooms, short-term psychiatric hospital units, and other settings choosing to embark on an empirical approach to clinical practice. Under such circumstances, clinicians are advised to obtain extended periods of baseline observation and pay meticulous attention to the possibility of events occurring coincidental to treatment that may cloud future interpretation of results.

A-B-A-B Design

A logical extension of the baseline-treatment (A-B) design is the A-B-A-B (withdrawal) design, otherwise known as the "equivalent time-samples design" (Campbell & Stanley, 1966). Its use in applied behavior analysis is preferred to the baseline-treatment approach because it allows for a clear demonstration of the functional relationship between the intervention strategy and behavior change through the systematic withdrawal and restoration of treatment upon completion of the initial A-B phases. In this design, baseline and treatment phases are replicated (A-B, A-B) to assess whether change in the magnitude of the target behavior occurred as a function of the manipulation of the treatment procedure or simply by coincidence (chance). If, as in Figure 3, levels of the target behavior prove roughly correspondent across the two independently conducted phases of baseline and treatment, the functional relationship between treatment and behavior change is established, and the conclusion that treatment is the variable affecting the change in behavior is strengthened (Hersen & Barlow, 1976). Of course, no limit exists regarding the number of systematic replications afforded by this design format (e.g., A-B-A-B-A-B-A-B, etc.), with each successive phase of treatment withdrawal and treatment restoration resulting in further strengthening of the conclusion that behavior change is controlled solely by the presence (or absence) of treatment.

Despite the popular use of the A-B-A-B format and its potential to establish clear and convincing evidence of behavior control, the use of this design may be impractical or unethical in certain cases. In the assessment of self-injury, for example, such a systematic manipulation of the

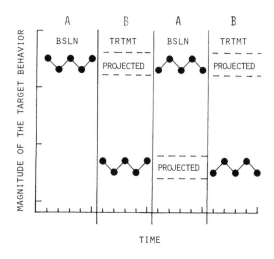

Figure 3. An example of the A-B-A-B (withdrawal) design. The dotted lines indicate the projected range and magnitude of the target behavior, if treatment had not been introduced, withdrawn, and restored in systematic fashion.

treatment procedure would allow the harmful behavior to recover temporarily while treatment was withdrawn, an effect that would be both clinically undesirable and indefensible from an ethical standpoint. In addition, it has been well noted that in many instances behaviors will not revert to original baseline rates upon the withdrawal of treatment, perhaps owing to environmental or learning variables that act to maintain the behavior once some critical level of performance has been achieved (Mann, 1976). In this latter regard, the most commonly cited and descriptive anecdote involves teaching someone how to juggle. Figure 4 presents data indicating that such a person had no basal (A phase) juggling skills but acquired a high degree of juggling ability across a training program (B phase). As could be predicted, the mere cessation of the formal training program, as indicated by the second A phase, resulted in no deterioration of the previously learned juggling behavior. As such, the impact of the training program was not able to be replicated, and the conclusion that participation in training was responsible for the observed increase in juggling ability was reduced in strength to that of a quasi-experimental (A-B) finding. Moreover, it should be noted that this is likely to be the case with the great majority of educational skills such as reading, math, and spelling, where a carryover effect (conversely known as progressive error) from previously learned behavior has a high probability of appearing in an adjacent phase of study.

In sum, if it is not clinically (or ethically) advisable to allow for the temporary recovery of a target behavior, such as in the case of self-injury, or if the behavior in question is a *skill* that is likely to be *mastered* (e.g., juggling, reading) within the course of instructional training, use

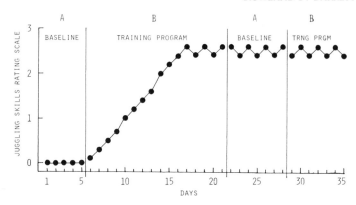

Figure 4. Hypothetical data for a Juggling Skills Training Program using an A-B-A-B (withdrawal) design format. Note the carry-over effect evident in the second baseline (A) phase. Skills previously learned during the initial training (B) phase did not deteriorate upon the withdrawal of active training. Such a result reduces the strength of conclusion to a level commensurate with A-B findings (see Figures 1 and 2).

of the A-B-A-B design is not indicated. Otherwise, the A-B-A-B design provides an easy and straightforward clinical format for empirical behavior analysis.

Variations of the A-B-A-B Design for Use in Drug Evaluation

The basic variation in the A-B-A-B design format to allow for drug evaluation involves the integration of placebo (A_1) and dose titration (B', B", B''') phases. Figure 5 presents hypothetical data for a mentally retarded, hyperactive child being treated with various doses of Ritalin in a placebo-controlled fashion. In this example, the basic A-B-A-B format is varied as follows: $A-A_1-B-A_1-B'-A_1-B''-B_1-B'$, with the A_1 phase serving as the placebo condition and B, B', and B" phases indicating low, medium, and high doses of active drug, respectively. The separate analyses revealed by this particular design strategy are presented in Figure 6, wherein it is shown that each of the three doses of the medication is evaluated within a separate A_1-B-A_1 paradigm and that the design concludes with a final assessment of the dose determined to be most effective in controlling the targeted hyperactive behavior.

Although a convenient format for use with short-acting drugs, the utility of such a design is compromised somewhat in the analysis of phenothiazines and other neuroleptic medications, such as thioridazine (Mellaril) and haloperidol (Haldol), two of the more commonly prescribed behavior modification drugs for mentally retarded clients because the half-lives of these medications are lengthy. That is, they require

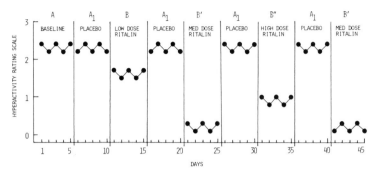

Figure 5. Hypothetical data for a hyperactive mentally retarded client, plotted using a variation of the A-B-A-B (withdrawal design) format. Design variations, such as this one, allow for the evaluation of drug treatment by including both placebo (A_1) and dose titration (B′, B″) phases. In this example, the medium dose of the drug was indicated as most effective in treating the targeted hyperactivity. The design was extended to conclude with a reevaluation of the most effective dose.

repeated administrations across successive days before a behavioral effect will become apparent or, in cases where medication is being discontinued, an extended period of time (e.g., 2 or 3 weeks) before the drug is fully absent from the client's system. In the preparation of an A-B-A-B variant design for drug study, clinicians should take account of the half-life variable when preparing the design protocol. Half-lives of medications are typically accessible by consulting the annual volume of the

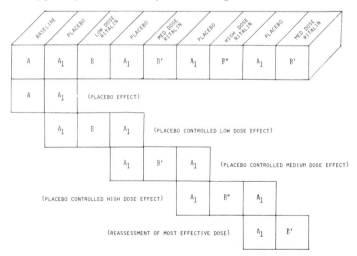

Figure 6. A schematic representation of the (principal) comparative analyses available when employing variations of the A-B-A-B design for drug studies. This schematic breaks down the analyses yielded by the A-A₁-B-A₁-B′-A₁-B″-A₁-B′ format used in Figure 5.

Physician's Desk Reference (PDR). A good rule of thumb is to plan phases of study in a manner that accommodates *at least four times the half-life period* of the drug being used, in order to insure that its behavioral effect (or lack of effect) may be observed. For shorter acting drugs, such as methylphenidate (Ritalin) and dextroamphetamine (Dexadrine), a half-life of 4 to 6 hours poses little analytic difficulty because its behavioral effect will likely be fully exhausted within 16 to 24 hours following administration. However, drugs such as thioridazine (Mellaril), which possesses a half-life of 36 hours, may require 6 days (following administration or upon discontinuation) before behavioral effects are likely to be observed. Individual client reactivity to a particular medication should also be considered as a variable. Different clients may metabolize the same drug faster or slower than the reported half-life values. Polypharmacy or the concurrent use of two or more medications (although not generally a recommended practice) may also affect a clear demonstration of the behavioral effects of a particular drug.

In sum, any analysis involving pharmacotherapy requires a clinician who is as well read in pharmacokinetics as in behavior analysis. The interested reader is referred to Hersen and Barlow (1976) and Barlow and Hersen (1984) for a full discussion of the many single-subject experimental designs available when empirically assessing the effects of drugs on behavior.

Multiple Baseline Designs

The multiple baseline design (Baer, Wolf, & Risley, 1968) is primarily used as an alternative to the A-B-A-B design format when, for the practical or ethical reasons previously discussed, the systematic withdrawal and restoration of treatment is inadvisable. The multiple baseline design, as depicted in Figure 7, employs a series of two or more replications of an initial A-B analysis with the treatment or B phase of the second (and successive) A-B design(s) being systematically delayed until an effect is evident for the target behavior within the B phase of the initial (or preceding) A-B design. A functional relationship between changing behavior and treatment is established if the magnitude of the targeted behavior in the second and successive baseline change only upon the (delayed) introduction of treatment, as it is presented specific to each baseline. Each controlled change of behavior, due to the sequential application of treatment, successively strengthens the conclusion that treatment (and not chance) is the variable influencing changes in the magnitude of the target behavior(s).

The multiple baseline design is flexible to the extent that it may be employed in a variety of clinically convenient formats. Foremost among

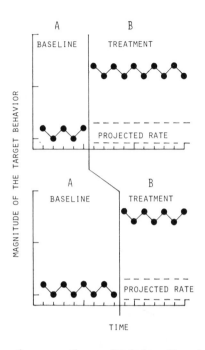

MAGNITUDE OF THE TARGET BEHAVIOR

A
BASELINE

B
TREATMENT

PROJECTED RATE

A
BASELINE

B
TREATMENT

PROJECTED RATE

TIME

Figure 7. An example of the multiple base-line design. The dotted lines indicates the projected range and magnitude of the target behavior, if treatment had not been introduced.

these are the multiple baseline design *across behaviors*, the mutliple base-line design *across subjects*, and the multiple baseline design *across settings*. Combinations of these formats are also possible (e.g., multiple baseline design across subjects and behaviors).

For the multiple baseline design across behaviors, separate A-B analyses are established for two or more behaviors that are targeted for change within a single client. Figure 8 presents data on a hypothetical mentally retarded client who engages in high rates of three distinctly separate forms of self-stimulatory activity (i.e., body rocking, hand motil-ity, stereotyped vocalizing) that, in turn, were treated using a *single* behavior modification procedure (i.e., facial screening). The strategy of delaying treatment to each target behavior until the preceding behavior has shown evidence of responding to treatment, allows the clinician to demonstrate that each of the three forms of self-stimulation is inde-pendently responsive to the facial screening technique. The conclusion that treatment alone was the variable responsible for the observed decreases in body rocking, hand motility, and vocalizing, respectively, was strengthened by the observation that each of the forms of self-stimulation decreased in a sequential manner and only upon the intro-duction of treatment specific to its own unique baseline.

In the multiple baseline design across subjects, separate A-B anal-yses are established for two or more clients who present with a similar

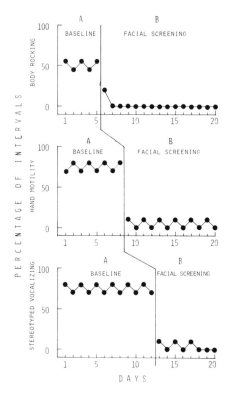

Figure 8. Hypothetical data for a mentally retarded client who presented with three separate forms of self-stimulatory behavior within a single setting. Each of the stereotyped acts was treated using the same intervention. Data are formated using the multiple baseline design across behaviors.

problem behavior within the same setting and who will be treated using the same procedure. Figure 9 presents hypothetical data on three mentally retarded clients, Tom, Dick, and Harry, who exhibited pica habits within the classroom and were treated with overcorrection. Similar to the findings within the design "across behaviors," the observation that each client improved only when treatment was introduced specific to his baseline replicated and strengthened the conclusion that overcorrection was responsible for decreases in pica behavior for all three clients.

In the multiple baseline design across settings, separate A-B analyses are established across two or more settings for a single target behavior within a single client. Figure 10 presents hypothetical data on the aggressive behavior of a mentally retarded child, as it was observed within the separate settings of the classroom, gymnasium, and playground, and its response to treatment using a time-out from positive reinforcement procedure. Similar to the preceding findings in the designs "across behaviors" and "across subjects" formats, the observation that aggression decreased correspondent to the sequential application of

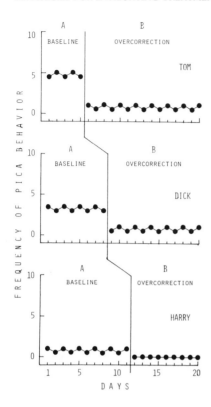

Figure 9. Hypothetical data for three mentally retarded clients, each of whom presented with a pica habit within a common setting. All clients were treated using the same intervention. Data are formated using the multiple baseline design across subjects.

treatment or, only when time-out was applied as a consequence to such behavior specific to the particular setting, strengthened the conclusion that treatment was the variable producing the observed change.

As noted earlier, combinations of the design formats depicted in Figures 8, 9, and 10 may also be conducted. Figure 11 presents an example of a multiple baseline design across subjects *and* behaviors. In this design, separate A-B analyses are established for two subjects who present different problem behaviors within the same setting and who will be treated using an identical procedure. The finding that each subject and behavior responded independently to treatment indicates that the variable affecting the observed changes in behavior was not due to chance.

Although the multiple baseline design has a number of clinical advantages, most notably that it demonstrates the functional control of treatment over behavior change without a temporary withdrawal of treatment (cf. A-B-A-B design), it also has certain disadvantages. In general, two or more baselines of stable response magnitude must be established before treatment can be initiated, and this is time consuming.

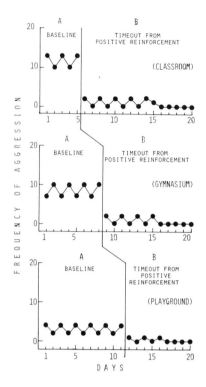

Figure 10. Hypothetical data for a mentally retarded client who presented a single target behavior (aggression) across three separate settings. The target behavior was treated using the same intervention within each setting. Data are formated using the multiple baseline design across settings.

Even then, because of design characteristics (e.g., the same behavior must occur in more than one setting; different behaviors must occur within the same setting and must be treatable using the same procedure; or other clients with similar problem behaviors must be present within the same setting, etc.), certain target behaviors (or clients) remain untreated for relative amounts of time to allow for the sequential application of treatment. It remains, however, that the multiple baseline format serves as the preferred alternative to the evaluation of treatment effectivenss in cases where the systematic withdrawal and restoration of treatment is impractical or unethical (e.g., self-injury) and in cases where a carry-over effect (progressive error) from previous learning (e.g. instructional training) is highly probable. Once again, the interested reader is referred to Barlow and Hersen (1984) for a thorough discussion of the utility of multiple baseline designs in clinical practice.

Alternating Treatments Designs

Single-case experimental strategies for studying behavior change have been greatly enhanced with the advent of the alternating treatments design (Barlow & Hayes, 1979), which allows for a direct comparison of

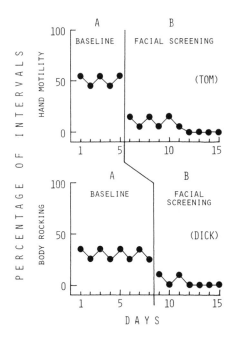

Figure 11. Hypothetical data for two mentally retarded clients who presented different target behaviors within the same setting and who were treated using the same procedure. Data are formated using the multiple baseline design across subjects and behavior.

two or more treatments within the same client. In this approach, which may be conceptualized as an A-B/C-B or C design, a single target behavior is identified and observed for a baseline period comprised of alternating stimulus conditions, such as separate time periods or different therapists, which are conducted in accordance with a future schedule of intervention. After stable response levels across the alternating time periods of baseline (A) are achieved, two or more separate conditions of treatment (B/C) are implemented. During the treatment or B/C phase, each of the separate treatment conditions is presented alternately in counterbalanced fashion across the same stimulus conditions present during baseline. Throughout the course of the B/C phase, an assessment of the differential impact of the separate treatments on the target behavior is made. The design is typically extended to include an additional phase of treatment (B or C), wherein the most effective procedure replaces the less effective intervention.

Figure 12 presents a hypothetical example of a mentally retarded client whose self-injurious behavior is being treated alternately with an omission training (DRO) strategy and a form of contingent punishment. In this example, it can be seen that the baseline (A) rates of the target behavior were stable and did not fluctuate across the alternate time periods in which treatment was later scheduled to appear. However, upon the introduction of the separation conditions of treatment (B/C

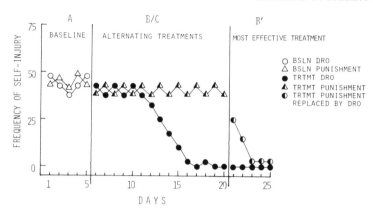

Figure 12. Hypothetical data for a mentally retarded client, whose self-injurious behavior is being alternately treated within the same day using two different interventions. During baseline (A), data are collected in accordance with the future schedule (e.g., time, setting, therapist) of treatment. In the treatment phase (B/C), the separate conditions of active intervention are alternately conducted, yielding a comparative determination of effectiveness. In the concluding phase (B), the least effective treatment was replaced by its more effective counterpart.

phase), a marked differential impact between the two treatments was observed, with omission training proving to be the more efficacious form of intervention. In the concluding phase of the design (B), the least effective treatment (contingent punishment) was simply discontinued and replaced in its scheduled time by the omission training procedure.

Use of the A-B/C-B or C format of the alternating treatments design establishes the functional relationship between treatment and changing behavior in two ways. First, the simple witnessing that the separate conditions of treatment have a differential impact on the targeted behavior is evidence that the behavior is responding independently to the two forms of intervention. As such, the probability that behavior change is occurring due to chance is greatly reduced because chance factors would likely affect both conditions of treatment indiscriminately. The fact that both treatments are applied under identical stimulus conditions and that one is clearly more effective than the other greatly strengthens the conclusion that a functional relationship exists between the changing behavior and the particular treatment observed to be most effective. A second form of control is presented in the B or C phase of study where the least effective treatment is replaced by its more effective counterpart. A correspondent change in the behavior previously not influenced by the least effective treatment replicates the findings of the B/C phase, producing a multiple baseline effect, and further strengthens the conclusion that a functional relationship exists between the target behavior and the treatment initially observed as most effective.

A commonly employed variant of the alternating treatments design is the multiple schedule (Hersen & Barlow, 1976) or multielement baseline design (Ulman & Sulzer-Azaroff, 1975). Using this format, two or more conditions of treatment and a separate condition of no treatment are presented alternately, in either counterbalanced or randomized fashion, with the intent of demonstrating differential impact. Figure 13 presents hypothetical data for a hyperactive mentally retarded child being treated with behavior modification, Ritalin, and a placebo (no treatment). In this example, it is clearly evident that drug treatment was the most efficacious form of intervention. Similar to our previous discussion, the observation of differential impact between treatments (or between treatment and no treatment) under identical stimulus conditions may be taken as evidence that behavior is changing as a function of its relationship to a particular treatment variable. Once again, the probability that chance is the variable affecting the change in behavior is minimized because chance factors must operate in such a manner as to influence all conditions (treatment and no treatment) indiscriminately.

Although designs such as the alternating treatments strategy and multiple schedule format allow for the direct comparison of effectiveness between two or more treatments and stand to be particularly valuable tools in clinical practice, their use may be highly problematic. Beyond the difficulties inherent to the required meeting of numerous counterbalancing and randomization features necessary to insure equivalent stimulus conditions across the design, the mere presence of these required factors serves to predispose the design to threats of internal validity due to *multiple treatment interference* (Barlow & Hayes, 1979). Similar to the

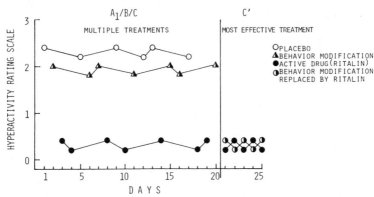

Figure 13. Hypothetical data for a hyperactive mentally retarded client who is being alternately treated across successive days with three separate conditions of intervention. The multiple schedule design format allows for a direct comparison of separate conditions (A_1, B, C) within the same phase. As in Figure 12, the design may conclude with the most effective treatment replacing its lesser effective counterparts in the schedule.

earlier discussion centering on carry-over effects (progressive error), where previously learned behavior contaminates assessment in adjacent phases of study, the effect of more than one treatment occurring within a single phase may also produce assessment contamination. In short, Is the presence of Treatment 1 influencing the client's response to Treatment 2? Is Treatment 2 influencing the observed response to Treatment 1? Would the observed response to either treatment be the same if the other treatment were not present? Can we be sure that we are getting a clear indication of the functional relationship between the targeted behavior and the treatment perceived as being responsible for the observed change? The answer to these and other questions of this nature is a firm "Perhaps." Such questions will likely never be resolved to a point of absolute assurance, and, it may be added, absolute assurance is not being sought. What is being sought, however, is a level of increased confidence (either statistical and/or clinical in nature) that may be applied to the decision-making process surrounding treatment selection. With reference to the example presented in Figure 13, it is both statistically (see Kazdin, 1984) and clinically evident (upon visual inspection of the data) that a confident decision may be made regarding which of the treatments should be continued or discontinued, despite no firm assurances regarding the absence of multiple treatment interference. Whether the decision to select one treatment in deference to another proves to be correct or incorrect is an additional empirical question that may only be answered within the context of ongoing assessment (cf. concluding B or C phase). However, a number of preventative steps may be taken to guard against the occurrence of multiple treatment interference. Foremost among these is the planned use of *discriminative stimuli* that precede treatment and clearly cue the client as to which of the various treatments will be in effect. As regards mentally retarded clients, pictorial cues have served this purpose rather nicely (e.g., Barrett, Matson, Shapiro, & Ollendick, 1981).

In sum, although the alternating treatments design may not be well-suited for use in private practice and settings such as the group home or classroom due to the complex nature of its format, its potential as the most efficacious strategy for studying behavior change is not diminished in settings where counterbalancing, randomization techniques, and the use of discrimative stimuli are easily afforded clinical luxuries. The alternating treatments design yields adequate experimental control without the need to temporarily discontinue treatment (cf. A-B-A-B design) or extend baselines on additional behaviors or clients (cf. multiple baseline design), and the data forthcoming from a direct comparison of two or more treatments within the same client stands to provide the clinician with a unique opportunity around the issue of treatment selection. This latter notion has specific ramifications for mentally retarded clients, who are among the vanguard of patients' rights issues, and with whom least restrictive (intrusive) treatment alternatives may be examined with great scrutiny (see Chapter 12).

Time Series Analysis

To this point, the review of single-subject experimental designs has been confined to those that may be used with practicality in more or less sophisticated clinical settings. Although data from each of the previously reviewed design strategies may be treated statistically (cf. Kazdin, 1984), such analyses are rarely performed. Reasons underlying the lack of use of statistics in determining behavior change are twofold. First, the clinical utility of the design selected stands to be greatly enhanced if statistical treatment of results is altogether avoided. In this case, clinical utility means clinical convenience. A strategy that aids in decision making without the need to apply sophisticated mathematical formulae will be preferred by most clinicians. Second, clinicians will argue that for an effect (change in behavior) to be clinically useful, it must be observable to the extent that statistical treatment of data would be unnecessary and the findings redundant to an obvious conclusion. Suffice it to say, at this point, that such a statement grossly underestimates the complexity inherent to the understanding of data gathered through repeated (serial) behavioral observations.

The requirement to retain clinical utility, including features of convenience in design format and interpretation, although retaining the essential elements of an empirical approach to the study of behavior change, translates to a heavy reliance upon what is known as the "visual analysis of graphic data." That is, one may see the change in behavior by merely viewing the data as it is plotted according to phases on a graph. Visual analysis, in turn, is greatly dependent upon the occurrence of clearly observable differences in *mean* rates of the target behavior, as it is measured across the various phases of study. Although observation of mean differences in rates of a target behavior across successive phases of study (i.e., baseline treatment) may be defended as an adequate method of empirically documenting behavior change, the method is inherently crude and imprecise and will not detect changes in behavior that, by definition, are so discreet that they are impossible to detect simply upon the visual inspection of a graph.

By example, visual analysis of data cannot take into consideration the notion of *serial dependency*, which means that the data are autocorrelated or, simply, that correlations must and do exist among successive data points. As such, any given behavioral observation in time must be recognized as dependent, to a certain extent, upon one or more previous observations of the same behavior under the same conditions. Visual inspection also does not allow for considerations of *changes in level* (behavioral magnitude), *changes in slope* (behavioral gradient), *or the presence or absence of slope* in a particular phase as evidence of the impact of treatment, despite a lack of change in mean rate. Consequently, it may be theorized that significant effects of many treatments may be overlooked upon the mere viewing of data plotted on a graph and go undetected for lack of proper statistical treatment. Conversely, certain effects in terms of behavior change, thought to be significant upon visual analysis, may be explained within the concept of serial dependency as well as level and slope analysis.

Time series designs (e.g., Gottman, 1981) represent a statistical approach to behavior analysis that takes into consideration the notion that data collected across successive observations are serially dependent and that changes in the level and/or slope of such data are indicative of behavior change. The single-subject designs described in this chapter belong to a more specific class of research designs known as "interrupted time series designs" (Glass, Willson, & Gottman, 1974; Gottman & Glass, 1978). The defining attribute of these designs is that they yield two or more sets of time-ordered observations on one or more dependent variables. Univariate time series consist of repeated measures of only one dependent variable (target behavior) for one client across time and may include two or more treatment conditions (e.g., A-B design, A-B-A-B design, alternating treatments design). Multivariate time series result from the simultaneous and repeated measurement of two or more dependent variables (target behaviors) for one client across time (e.g., multiple baseline across behaviors design) or from the simultaneous and repeated measurement of one dependent variable (target behavior) for two or more clients across time (e.g., multiple baseline across subjects design).

The initial task of time series analysis is to remove the element of serial dependency from the data. This is accomplished by examining the autocorrelations existing among data points by employing a correlogram and using these correlations to define the specific structure (and dependency) of the overall data series. The specific structure of the data series is then "best fit" to a selected mathematical model, of which various types exist (Box & Jenkins, 1970; Glass, Willson, & Gottman, 1975). The model then transforms the data such that the serial dependency is removed and the data analyzed in accordance with traditional statistical requirements (i.e., rejection of a null hypothesis). The ultimate yield of a time series analysis is to provide a test of significance regarding changes in the level and/or slope of a measured behavior, while taking into consideration and adjusting to the dependency relationships that exist among serially collected data points.

Needless to say, time series analysis is a far more complicated and meticulous procedure than what has been presented in these few pages. It is a time-consuming approach in which at least 50 (Glass, *et al.*, 1974) and preferably 100 (Box & Jenkins, 1970) observations per phase of study are required in order to allow the analysis to achieve an adequate level of statistical power. For the clinician, such an approach translates to great expense in terms of staff allocation. The expense to the client may be even higher in terms of direct costs (i.e., length of treatment) and the lengths of time in which a problem behavior must go untreated. Generally speaking, it may be argued that the utility of time series analysis is better suited for the laboratory than the applied setting. In most cases, this would be true. Clients have a right to presume they will be treated in the most cost-efficient, efficacious, least restrictive, and least intrusive manner available. Typically, these goals may be accomplished through the use of the earlier reviewed single-subject formats, using the visual analysis of graphic data for decision making. However, there exist those clients who seemingly do not respond to the best laid plans for intervention. As clinicians, we have all encountered (or will encounter in the future) clients who have failed to respond to all traditional forms of treatment and, upon being moved to treatments progressively innovative and radical in nature, continue to show a lack of response. In such cases, time series designs may be helpful in arriving at an understanding of the behavior in question because even the most discreet indication of change will yield optimism and provide guidelines for future treatment. In these cases, the clinician is unequivocally obliged to "step into the laboratory."

Summary

In the preface to this volume it was noted that the behavioral sciences have been severely criticized for their undue and heavy reliance upon subjective, intuitive, and uncontrolled appraisals of human behavior. That psychologists, psychiatrists, and special educators are among the chief offenders to which this criticism applies is evident within the daily course of their respective professional practices. Each day, clients are prescribed medications or entered into other forms of therapy designed to develop or modify some aspect of their behavior, with the clinician's subjective opinion representing the final determination of what was (or was not) accomplished. What is even more frightening and deserving of criticism is the fact that many clients are entered into treatment without any compelling evidence that, indeed, it was warranted.

It will be argued, of course, that certain clients present with such profound clinical symptomatology that treatment is a foregone conclusion. It is obvious that clients who bang their heads against walls or other surfaces at a rate of 2,000 times per day require immediate intervention in the form of behavior modification, pharmacotherapy, or a combination of both and, that the obtaining of baseline data to formally establish the presence of the response would be frivolous and, perhaps, unethical. However, it must be noted that behavior modification approaches are likely to be ineffective if otitis media, a commonly acknowledged organic antecedent to head banging, is the stimulus responsible for cuing the act and that the effect of drugs, other than antibiotics, are likely to be doomed, as well. The role of baseline data may be important in other cases where clients show evidence of a gradual but steady improvement in behavior. It is hardly likely that a client's progress will be recognized if, using the preceding example, head banging is not formally noted as decreasing by 150 incidents per week. Even across a 4- to 5-week period of treatment the decline from 2,000 to 1,000 or 850 daily occurrences of self-injury may be imperceptible to the clinician managing the case, particularly if he or she is dependent upon reports such as "he is still banging his head . . . a lot." Furthermore, it should be stated that the use of empirical methods in case management, including the single-subject designs discussed in this chapter, do not preclude the immediate starting of treatment by using common sense variations of the basic design formats (e.g., B-A-B design vs. A-B-A-B design; multiple schedule design using a single treatment condition while simultaneously time sampling an equivalent condition of no treatment).

The present chapter was intended to provide clinicians with an overview of the basic methods for quantitatively establishing the presence of a problem behavior and fundamental strategies for empirically assessing the effectiveness of an intervention plan used as treatment. Moreover, its intent focused upon the relative ease with which the empirical model may be integrated into the routine clinical practice of professionals who provide services to mentally retarded clients, with the result being credibility for the therapist and increased accountability to the client.

References

Achenbach, T. M., & Edelbrock, C. (1983). *Manual for the Child Behavior Checklist*. Burlington: University of Vermont.

Aman, M., & Singh, N. N. (1983). *Aberrant Behavior Checklist*. Canterbury, New Zealand: University of Canterbury.

Aman, M. G., Singh, N. N., Stewart, A. W., & Field, C. J. (1985a). Psychometric characteristics of the Aberrant Behavior Checklist. *American Journal of Mental Deficiency, 89,* 492–502.

Aman, M. G., Singh, N. N., Stewart, A. W., & Field, C. J. (1985b). A behavior rating scale for the assessment of psychotropic drug effects: The Aberrant Behavior Checklist. *American Journal of Mental Deficiency, 89,* 485–491.

Anastasi, A. (1976). *Psychological testing* (4th ed.). New York: Macmillan.

Baer, D. M., Wolf, M. M., & Risley, T. (1968). Some current dimensions of applied behavior analysis. *Journal of Applied Behavior Analysis, 1,* 91–97.

Barlow, D. H., & Hayes, S. C. (1979). Alternating treatments design: One strategy for comparing the effects of two treatments in a single subject. *Journal of Applied Behavior Analysis, 12,* 199–210.

Barlow, D. H., & Hersen, M. (1984). *Single case experimental designs: Strategies for studying behavior change* (2nd ed.). New York: Pergamon Press.

Barrett, R. P., Matson, J. L., Shapiro, E. S., & Ollendick, T. H. (1981). A comparison of punishment and DRO procedures for treating stereotypic behavior of mentally retarded children. *Applied Research in Mental Retardation, 2,* 247–256.

Barrett, R. P., Dixon, M. J., & Matson, J. L. (1984). *Three year follow-up study of 60 mentally retarded clients hospitalized for severe behavior disorders.* Unpublished manuscript, University of Pittsburgh School of Medicine.

Bijou, S. W., Peterson, R. F., & Ault, M. H. (1968). A method to integrate descriptive and experimental field studies at the level of data and empirical concepts. *Journal of Applied Behavior Analysis, 1,* 175–191.

Box, G. E. P., & Jenkins, G. M. (1970). *Time-series analysis: Forecasting and control.* San Francisco: Holden-Day Publishing.

Campbell, D. T., & Stanley, J. C. (1966). *Experimental and quasi-experimental designs for research.* Chicago: Rand McNally.

Chassan, J. B. (1979). *Research design in clinical psychology and psychiatry* (2nd ed.). New York: Irvington Publishers.

Cohen, J. A. (1960). A coefficient of agreement for nominal scales. *Educational and Psychological Measurement, 20,* 37–46.

Conners, C. K. (1974). Rating scales for use in drug studies with children. *Psychopharmacology Bulletin* (Special issue on children), pp. 24–42.

Cook, T. D., & Campbell, D. T. (1979). *Quasi-experimentation: Design and analysis issues for field settings.* Chicago: Rand McNally College Publishing.

Glass, G. V., Willson, V. L., & Gottman, J. M. (1974). *Design and analysis of time series experiments.* Boulder: Colorado University Associated Press.

Gottman, J. M. (1981). *Time-series analysis: A comprehensive introduction for social scientists.* Cambridge: Cambridge University Press.

Gottman, J. M., & Glass, G. V. (1978). Time series analysis of interrupted time series experiments. In T. Kratochwill (Ed.), *Single subject research: Strategies for evaluating change* (pp. 197–236). New York: Academic Press.

Goyette, C. H., Conners, C. K., & Ulrich, R. F. (1979). Normative data on revised Conners' parent and teacher rating scales. *Journal of Abnormal Child Psychology, 6,* 221–236.

Harris, F., & Lahey, B. B. (1978). A method for combining occurrence and nonoccurrence interobserver agreement scores. *Journal of Applied Behavior Analysis, 11,* 523–527.

Hartmann, D. P. (1977). Considerations in the choice of reliability estimates. *Journal of Applied Behavior Analysis, 10,* 103–116.

Hartmann, D. P. (1984). Assessment strategies. In D. H. Barlow & M. Hersen (Eds.), *Single case experimental designs: Strategies for studying behavior change* (2nd ed., pp. 107–137). New York: Pergamon Press.

Hartmann, D. P., & Wood, D. D. (1983). Observational methods. In A. S. Bellack, M. Hersen, & A. E. Kazdin (Eds.), *International handbook of behavior modification and therapy* (pp. 107–138). New York: Plenum Press.

Hayes, S. C. (1981). Single case experimental design and empirical clinical practice. *Journal of Consulting and Clinical Psychology, 49,* 193–211.

Hersen, M., & Barlow, D. H. (1976). *Single case experimental designs: Strategies for studying behavior change.* New York: Pergamon Press.

Hersen, M., & Bellack, A. S. (1981). *Behavioral assessment: A practical handbook* (2nd ed.). New York: Pergamon Press.

Hopkins, B., & Hermann, J. (1977). Evaluating interobserver reliability of interval data. *Journal of Applied Behavior Analysis, 10,* 121–126.

Journal of Applied Behavior Analysis. (1977). Invited articles: The reliability of measurement. *Journal of Applied Behavior Analysis, 10,* 97–150.

Kazdin, A. E. (1980). *Research design in clinical psychology.* New York: Harper & Row.

Kazdin, A. E. (1981). Drawing valid inferences from case studies. *Journal of Consulting and Clinical Psychology, 49,* 183–192.

Kazdin, A. E. (1982). *Single-case research designs: Methods for clinical and applied settings.* New York: Oxford University Press.

Kazdin, A. E. (1983). Single-case research designs in clinical child psychiatry. *Journal of the American Academy of Child Psychiatry, 22,* 423–432.

Kazdin, A. E. (1984). Statistical analyses for single case experimental designs. In D. H. Barlow & M. Hersen (Eds.), *Single case experimental designs: Strategies for studying behavior change* (2nd ed., pp. 285–324). New York: Pergamon Press.

Kazdin, A. E., & Hartmann, D. P. (1978). The simultaneous-treatment design. *Behavior Therapy, 5,* 912–923.

Kazdin, A. E., & Straw, M. K. (1976). Assessment of behavior of the mentally retarded. In M. Hersen & A. S. Bellack (Eds.), *Behavioral assessment: A practical handbook* (pp. 337–368). New York: Pergamon Press.

Kendell, P. C., & Butcher, J. N. (1982). *Handbook of research methods in clinical psychology.* New York: Wiley.

Kent, R. N., & Foster, S. L. (1977). Direct observational procedures: Methodological issues in naturalistic settings. In A. R. Ciminero, K. S. Calhoun, & H. E. Adams (Eds.), *Handbook of behavioral assessment* (pp. 279–328). New York: Wiley.

Mann, R. A. (1976). Assessment of behavioral excesses in children. In M. Hersen & A. S. Bellack (Eds.), *Behavioral assessment: A practical handbook* (pp. 459–492). New York: Pergamon Press.

Nelson, R. O., & Hayes, S. C. (1979). Some current dimensions of behavioral assessment. *Behavioral Assessment, 1,* 1–16.

Rojahn, J., & Schroeder, S. R. (1983). Behavioral assessment. In J. L. Matson & J. A. Mulick (Eds.), *Handbook of mental retardation* (pp. 227–243). New York: Pergamon Press.

Schafer, A. (1982). The ethics of the randomized clinical trial. *New England Journal of Medicine, 307,* 719–724.

Shapiro, E. S., & Barrett, R. P. (1982). Behavioral assessment of the mentally retarded. In J. L. Matson & F. Andrasik (Eds.), *Treatment issues and innovations in mental retardation* (pp. 159–212). New York: Plenum Press.

Shapiro, E. S., & Klein, R. D. (1980). Self-management of classroom behavior with retarded/disturbed children. *Behavior Modification, 4,* 83–97.

Ulman, J. D., & Sulzer-Azaroff, B. (1975). Multi-element baseline design in educational research. In E. Ramp & G. Semb (Eds.), *Behavior analysis: Areas of research and application* (pp. 377–391). Englewood Cliffs, NJ: Prentice-Hall.

Wallace, C. J., & Elder, J. P. (1980). Statistics to evaluate measurement accuracy and treatment effects in single subject research designs. In M. Hersen, R. Eisler, & P. Miller (Eds.), *Progress in behavior modification* (Vol. 10, pp. 39–79). New York: Academic Press.

12

Administrative Considerations and Responsibilities
Legal and Ethical Issues

ROBERT G. GRIFFITH

Introduction

Organizations exist for many purposes in both the public and private sectors. In a gross economic sense, they may be characterized as for profit or nonprofit, and their ultimate purpose may be manufacturing, sales, finance, or service. One thing they all have in common is that they are composed of people, and people must behave in certain ways in order for organizations to fulfill their purposes (Herbert, 1976). This is true whether they manufacture transistors or attempt to cure people who are mentally or physically sick.

Many of the service organizations are classified under the general rubric of "human services," and these include health care, education, mental health, welfare, and numerous other services to people (Christian & Hannah, 1983). The general function of management in these organizations is to give direction—to define the mission, set objectives, and organize resources in order to produce desired results (Drucker, 1974). The major resource in a human services organization is people; thus the primary administrative task of the human services manager is to optimize the efforts of people in order to serve other people.

There are numerous models of services for mentally retarded people (institution, community residence, etc.), and these are characterized as more or less restrictive depending upon where they fall along a continuum of possible service options (*Halderman v. Pennhurst*, 1982; Turnbull,

ROBERT G. GRIFFITH • Elwyn Institutes' National Rehabilitation Center, Philadelphia, Pennsylvania 19104.

Ellis, Boggs, Brooks, & Biklen, 1981). The nature of program interventions used in these settings constitutes another facet of this concept of restrictiveness; those that are more "normalizing" are construed as being less restrictive, and those that confine, are aversive, or pose risk are considered restrictive. As discussed in numerous chapters herein, the treatment of choice for a significantly maladaptive behavior may be one that poses high risk, thus being greatly restrictive and therefore controversial.

This concept of risk to clients is multifaceted in that it deals with exposure to possible injury, long-term side effects, lack of adequate treatment, or potential violations of rights (Martin, 1975; Turnbull *et al.*, 1981). A necessary corollary in today's litigious society is the nature of risk posed to the employee when working with the volative or dangerous client for whom restrictive or aversive procedures are clinically essential in order to promote adequate habilitation. Typically the major professional emphasis has been on client rights, and these efforts should continue but with more recognition of the safeguards necessary for the employee who is also at risk. The ultimate management goal in a program setting where controversial or "at-risk" strategies are necessary is a proper balancing of the interests and rights of both clients and staff. Such considerations can lead to the development of the legally safe service environment wherein clients are treated with effective, state of the art interventions, and staff may perform without significant or unreasonable fear of liability absent any malicious or irresponsible behavior (Griffith, 1980, 1983).

Organization and Administration

The magnitude of human services is incredibly immense yet the capability of managing these systems if often lacking, in part because of the gulf existing between management theory and practice (Christian & Hannah, 1983). Managers, for example, often look for quick cures when they realize the organization is suffering. *Theory Z* (Ouchi, 1981) was last year's popular contribution to those seeking rapid major change, a direct reference to earlier distinctions between Theory X and Theory Y made by Douglas McGregor (1960) in his classical thinking. Although many think *Theory Z* is a fad brought on by Japanese competition, the manager will find that, as in other responsible management texts, there are presented excellent insights into analysis and long-term strategies for improving organizational health.

Theory is vast and complex and yet often provides the basis for understanding organizations and managers as well as enhancing abilities for planning and service delivery. If used as intended (in most cases), it gives direction to the competent manager to increase the probability of the organization's operating effectively. Unfortunately, there is no faddish theory or blueprint available that will cause a human services organization to run properly (see, e.g., Argyris, 1957) because the complexities of human interaction and vast personality differences preclude this from happening.

It is fairly well accepted that there are no "quick cures" for organizational dysfunction and, in fact, really no substitute for responsible, humane management approaches. Drucker (1974) emphasizes three major responsibilities of management to enable an agency to function and make the proper societal contribution:

1. Perform the specific purpose of the institution (agency)
2. Make work productive and the worker achieving
3. Manage social impacts and responsibilities

The impetus for these derives from the fact that all institutions exist to meet a particular need of at least some segment of society. The specific purpose of a business is economic performance (Drucker, 1974), whereas the specific purpose of a publicly funded human services organization is meeting certain needs of clients. Unlike private enterprise, the human services organizations exist primarily for social reasons; thus there is almost entire overlap between Issues 1 and 3 in the foregoing paragraph. Although it is not always easy to define the purpose of an organization, or to stick to one's primary responsibilities, the major administrative problem in human services remains the matter of making work productive and the worker achieving.

The task of effectively meeting agency goals through properly productive employees is exclusively a responsibility of management. This does not mean that others do not contribute tremendously but, rather, if the organization fails to be effective one cannot blame unions, "lazy" employees, or other forces. Recognize also, however, that often the management of an agency extends beyond the physical boundaries of the agency; for example, the superintendent of a residential institution is often greatly influenced by a central office administrator and is often constrained by the state's fiscal resources.

If an agency provides services to persons who are mentally retarded, there should initially be a statement of purpose, generally a policy, that defines who are the clientele and for what reasons (see Christian & Hannah, 1983). Often, service providers will exclude clients with high frequency or intensity maladaptive behaviors, but because the law recognizes some treatment/habilitation obligations, it generally becomes the responsibility of public agencies to serve this population. And it is often true that if the client demonstrates dangerous or highly offensive behaviors, the service regimen will include something that is restrictive and/ or poses risk, thus being controversial.

The agency that treats dangerous or significantly maladaptive behavior demonstrated by mentally retarded people is meeting a critical social need in terms of protecting clients, their families, and often others. This is not to suggest that these people are criminals but, rather, that their behavior is not always under conscious control, for example, self-injurious behavior (SIB) and aggression. Considering again the high risk inherent in serving this population, it is not unreasonable to impose restrictions, both environmental and clinical, but hopefully on a short-term basis.

Reflecting again upon management theory, and subsequent expectations, the critical administrative concern in providing services to a high-risk population is to develop a productive and effective treatment environment. One primary issue is the development of a proactive staff with the "capacity to respond to problems and prevent their occurrence" (Ziarnik, 1980, p. 291). "Capacity" means that the staff are trained, supervised in a developmental sense, and work in an environment supportive of their rights as professionals. Even though client services is the organization's raison d'être, good management practice dictates strong consideration for the needs of individual employees as they strive to meet organizational demands (Argyris, 1957; Blau & Scott, 1969).

Only a proactive management can develop a proactive staff. Current legal, clinical, and administrative knowledge must permeate the organization in developing systems that support its goals and ethics. One true indicator of organizational success and management effectiveness lies in the impact of management upon those in direct service yet at the lowest level in the administration hierarchy—the operative employees (Simon, 1957):

> In the study of organization, the operative employee must be at the focus of attention; for the success of the structure will be judged by his peformance within it. Insight into the structure and function of an organization can best be gained by analyzing the manner in which the decisions and behavior of such employees are influenced within and by the organization. (p. 3)

This chapter shall examine in detail management mechanisms and considerations in promoting the development of a legally sound, effective service environment.

One final proposition. The appropriate clinical technology exists to adequately deal with most of the severe behavior disorders manifested by mentally retarded persons. The primary reason for the inadequate therapeutic resolution of these is inadequate systems—and this is the critical management problem in human services. Whether the issue is poor supervision, inadequate goals, reluctant employees, or insufficient policies, the general solution lies typically in better management, not in better clinicians. The clinical expertise is available, and the problem is developing effective systems so the treatment is properly delivered to the client.

Treatment Strategies and Management Concerns

General organizational and management responsibilities have been identified in the foregoing sections and are discussed in great detail elsewhere (see, e.g., Drucker, 1974; Herbert, 1976; McGregor, 1960). An understanding of these will provide the impetus for going from the general to the specific, thus taking an identified need or concern and implementing reasonable operational strategies. In an applied sense, it is necessary to specify absolute administrative functions when ensuring the proper development of an environment for treating severe behavior disorders. The following are the most critical:

1. Policies and procedures that are based upon current statutes, case law, regulations, and relevant standards
2. An organizational structure that is designed to meet the goals of the organization and that may be guided by appropriate policies and procedures, under the direction of skilled managers
3. An understanding of the necessity to balance the needs of the clients with those of the organization *and* staff
4. A recognition and understanding of the rights of staff
5. Treatment guidelines designed to ensure the legally safe service environment
6. Proper balance and understanding of the right to treatment, the right to refuse treatment, and the obligation to impose treatment
7. Strategies for the prevention of client abuse
8. A consideration of the ethical issues in using controversial treatment strategies and an acknowledgement of the acceptance of effective technologies

Policies and Procedures

> The purpose of the policy and procedure manual is to ensure that employees
> understand the goals and objectives of an organization and the methods that
> will be employed in their pursuit. Together with the organizational chart,
> the policy and procedure manual serves to integrate the various components
> of the organizational structure to ensure that the organization can be managed
> as a functional unit. There is probably nothing that contributes more to
> organizational malfunction and risk to the consumer than the inadequate
> development of, or ineffective adherence to, prescribed policies and proce-
> dures for program operation. (Christian & Hannah, 1983, p. 47)

Unfortunately, this is an area taken for granted by many people
in managerial positions, and often there is an absence of appropriate
policies. Many view policies as "red tape" obstacles or as formal prohibitions to doing what is essential by clinicians. If thoughtfully planned
and developed, however, policies will guide and influence the organization and its members toward realization of goals (Herbert, 1976).

There is also a legal obligation to have operational policies, particularly when maladaptive behaviors are to be treated with interventions
posing risk to clients and staff. Such an approach may be especially
supportive of the clinician if it, in part, prescribes adherence to current
and acceptable clinical practice without being prescriptive, thus allowing
for creative use of clinical capabilities. Additional considerations for a
behavior management policy are as follows (see also Griffith, 1983):

1. There should be a philosophy statement about treating high risk
behaviors. This should emphasize the necessity for the client to have a
total program, that interactions should be designed to promote positive
reinforcement, and that clinicians should adhere to the concept of least
restrictive, or least intrusive. There should be mention of the recognition
of a balancing of client and staff rights (see section on staff rights).

2. There should be definitions of critical terms, especially those
interventions that pose risk to clients and staff.

3. Abuse should be defined herein, or in a collateral policy. Included
should be reference to procedures that are forbidden.

4. General due process considerations must be enumerated, with
a brief description of each step in the process. Included here is reference
to individual client program plans, peer review, consent, and human
rights committee review (see discussion on treatment guidelines). These
must be developed consistent with current statutes, case law, regulations, standards, and ethics.

5. There must be requirements for monitoring and accountability.

The fact that one adheres to a policy or extant regulations does not
mean one is operating in a truly legal or advisable fashion, inasmuch

as the policy or its "legal" basis may be inadequate for one's program. Consider, for example, the Standards for Intermediate Care Facilities for the Mentally Retarded (ICF/MR) (1978) under Title XIX of the Social Security Act as they deal with behavior modification programs involving aversive stimuli. These interventions may be reviewed and approved by a qualified mental retardation professional (QMRP), yet most professionals who qualify as QMRPs have little or no training in the sophisticated applied behavioral methodology being referenced. Allowing for inadequately trained professionals to design and approve potentially risky procedures is not consistent with the Supreme Court's endorsement of the importance of "deference to professional judgment" (*Youngberg v. Romeo*, 1982). Insufficient or inappropriate policies will not protect the service provider should something go awry during treatment.

In addition to requirements imposed by statutes and regulations, current case law will provide significant issues for consideration for policy development. In *Clites v. State of Iowa* (1980, 1982), for example, a young mentally retarded man suffered severe and permanent disabling side effects from the long-term, improper administration of psychotropic medication. Among other findings the court noted that:

1. The use of the drugs was clinically unwarranted.
2. There was improper monitoring of the drug "therapy."
3. The clinical staff negligently continued to use the drugs after the side effects appeared.
4. The failure to seek consultation with a specialist in drug treatments was substandard medical practice (this is the concept of objective, qualified second opinion).

Without further analyzing this case, it is obvious that the foregoing statements provide numerous issues for consideration in a legally appropriate policy on controversial treatments, or overall behavior management. These matters are all components of due process and are addressed in more detail later. In the instant case, the neglect of proper clinical practice and disregard for due process resulted in an award to the plaintiff of $760,165 for damages; this award was upheld on appeal (*Clites v. Iowa*, 1980, 1982).

Organizational Structure

It is beyond the scope of this chapter to discuss this, for two reasons: (a) the material presented is designed to be most helpful to managers currently operating within relatively well-structured yet flexible organizations, those amenable to change; and (b) this is a thoroughly complex area, the literature is vast, and one could not do justice to the importance of this matter in a few pages. To be fluent in this area requires study and experience and the following are suggested references for pursuing a foundation: Argyris, 1957; Christian & Hannah, 1983; Drucker, 1974; Etzioni, 1969; and Simon, 1957.

Balancing of Needs

The major program goal of an agency providing treatment to clients with severe behavior disorders is to move toward diminishing the undesirable behaviors while increasing the likelihood of acceptable, adaptive behaviors. The direct service staff (clinicians) will concentrate primarily on the clinical concerns, especially diagnosis, ethics, program design, and implementation of therapies. The program administrators are charged with properly supporting these efforts while making sure there is strict adherence to current laws, regulations, standards, and policies. It is not unusual for these two roles to conflict, though by definition they should be complementary.

Everyone in an organization has expectations and perceptions as to how others should behave in their respective roles, and incumbents are greatly influenced by the formal structure, formal role definitions, and certainly their individual backgrounds and personalities (Getzels, 1958). Clinicians generally represent a particular clinical discipline; thus their authority derives from their knowledge base and discipline orientation; the authority of administrators is often ascribed by virtue of their position in the power structure as well as being enhanced by broad legal factors (Blau & Scott, 1969). Their respective performances should be tempered by consideration of the others' responsibilities, but invariably the balance resulting from cooperation will be offset.

As an example of these roles conflicting for legitimate reasons, consider the situation wherein the clinical staff recommends the application of contingent electric shock because a client's self-injurious behavior is life threatening; this may be the least intrusive treatment available. The state, however, has an unwritten but understood policy that proscribes the use of shock, and thus the administration is bound by this. Such a situation is going to cause the compromise of one or more roles; there are a number of possible solutions to this dilemma, and these will become clearer as this discussion develops.

The primary concern for administrators in these situations is to ensure the availability of systems that generally support the use of necessary clinical interventions, giving full consideration to legal constraints. Because some of these are highly controversial, however, they cannot be left entirely to the discretion of clinicians. Yet there must be sufficient support for the clinicians so they do not feel "regulated" or controlled, thus allowing for the existence of conditions that meet their professional practice needs and allow for job satisfaction and professional growth (Argyris, 1957; Herzberg, 1966; Maslow, 1954).

It is obviously desirable to give clinicians as much freedom as possible, yet impractical for them to perform autonomously considering legal constraints and the constant reminder that the administrator is typically the named defendant in the lawsuit for damages (Griffith, 1983). How much regulation there is depends upon numerous variables, including the risk posed by both client behavior and proposed treatments, the competence of the staff, the legal authority for the operation of the agency, and current law and regulation. It is not legitimate for clinicians to argue that *they* will assume responsibility for their actions because they cannot indemnify their employer; ultimate accountability and responsibility lies with the agency management. Current legal considerations demand reasonable administrative surveillance (Martin, 1975; Sheldon-Wildgen & Risley, 1982), but in a fashion that will promote acceptable and current clinical practice.

Although the primary service goal of the agency is to meet client needs, it is critical that this not be done totally at the expense of the needs of the organization and its employees. This is a terribly sensitive issue, however, considering the current pressure to "do everything" for clients who are disabled; this is further confounded by the fact that there often exists the perception that those who work with the handicapped are themselves "special" people and provide service (only) because they are altruistic. Perhaps we should not shatter this myth, even though that is exactly what it is.

Considering the additional constraints created by limited resources, all parties—clients, clinicians, administrators—must recognize the role played by compromise. This may be a distasteful word to the idealist, but then so often is *reality*. The following is one of the most basic and essential concepts in managing complex organizations:

> In an important sense, all decision is a matter of compromise. The alternative that is finally selected never permits a complete or perfect achievement of objectives, but is merely the best solution that is available under the circumstances. The environmental situation inevitably limits the alternatives that are available, and hence sets a maximum to the level of attainment of purpose that is possible.
>
> This relative element in achievement—this element of compromise—makes even more inescapable the necessity of finding a common denominator when behavior is aimed simultaneously at several objectives. (Simon, 1957, p. 6)

The administrator in representing the organization must recognize the concept of *needs compromise* and apply it in developing effective systems. Clinicians should also be aware of the necessity for this, and it is additionally desirable (though not always realistic) that clients and their representatives comprehend why it is essential. This concept means reciprocity of consideration by all parties in understanding roles, responsibilities, and capabilities in order to deliver quality services with limited resources. The basic elements of needs compromise in programs treating severe behavior disorders are as follows:

1. Top management, those developing and implementing policy, must recognize and respect the needs of employees to be creative, productive, and independent in carrying out their responsibilities within the organization. This is accomplished, in part, by minimizing regulation that interferes with professional/clinical practice, by enhancing communication throughout the organization, and by appropriate participation of employees in goal setting and problem solving. The major factor in the issues under consideration is the development of a treatment environment that promotes and (legally) supports current clinical practice without undue restraint.

2. The organization should only accept for services clients whose needs may be reasonably met; implicit here, however, is the mandate for public services to adapt in order to be more flexible and, in some cases, less exclusionary. It is not suggested tht agencies become "all things to all clients" but, rather, that there exists in the public sector a properly defined continuum of services so there is the elimination of unnecessary duplication of services, thus promoting more service options for the difficult-to-manage client. The major consideration for the individual agency is a clear policy on who can be served, so that expectations for staff are relatively clear. Recognize that agencies are often criticized for being exclusionary and only taking the "easiest" clients, but this is generally a systems problem and not one to be resolved by the individual agency.

3. The employee must recognize that the agency management must impose reasonable treatment guidelines, especially if they are serving high-risk clients. Properly developed guidelines protect the rights of clients *and* staff and should maximize the potential for clinical success while minimizing risk of liability should something go wrong during the treatment regimen. This is not meant to imply that guidelines will protect anyone if negligence occurs but, rather, that they will minimize the potential for negligent behavior. The employee who is offended by these "controls" must be made aware that the agency is almost always liable for the improper or capricious behavior of its employees, and top management are the first to be sued in cases of injuries resulting from irresponsible treatment. The clinician who wishes to operate autonomously and free from administrative oversight should be in private practice.

4. Management must decide upon which clients are accepted for services, and this must be understood and accepted by the clinical staff. Generally the pressures of the "system" will dictate who has the greatest need for services, and agencies may periodically alter admission requirements in order to better serve the general public. Employees must not be locked into the mentality of "we only serve this type of client." Employees must constantly be prepared to adapt to working with clients with varied needs.

5. Clients (usually their representatives) must recognize that organizations cannot meet all their needs and that public resources are limited; thus services may only meet certain priority needs. Understandably this is a very sensitive and controversial statement, more or less so depending upon whether one is a client, advocate, service provider, or government agent. The shrinking human services dollar during the recession of the early 1980s is evidence of the reality behind this position, however. One would be wrong to expect clients to *agree* with this, but this perspective is a reality nonetheless.

6. Clients will be expected to participate in programs that are clinically reasonable, including the application of aversive or restrictive interventions if necessary for the treatment of severe behavior disorders. There is no categorical or absolute right to refuse treatment if one expects or desires to participate in publicly funded programs. There must be some deference, therefore, to the role and responsibility of the competent clinician, especially those working in a legally sound, well-managed agency.

It is apparent in considering these six concerns that there exists a commonsense rationale for supporting and understanding reciprocity of responsibilities and feelings, or needs compromise, on major issues. Figure 1 depicts this graphically. The major weakness in this proposition is the suggestion that each party will (or can) understand and respect the positions of the other two. It is naive to think that clients and their representatives will be as enthusiastic about these considerations as those who are employed. But the reality of the shrinking human services dollar will continue to influence all parties toward the importance of compromise.

Staff Rights

It seems almost anathema today not to show an overwhelming concern for client rights, and perhaps rightfully so. Although this topic occupies volumes and is the central issue in innumerable court cases, there is very little recorded about the rights of staff in treatment settings. The risks to staff in providing necessary treatment for severe behavior

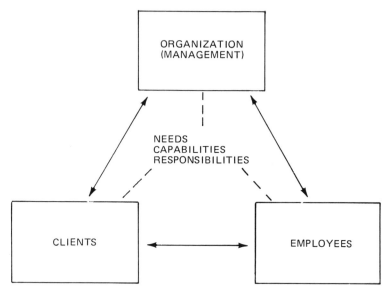

Figure 1. Needs compromise.

disorders, however, causes one to wonder "if staff rights might be the other side of the patients' rights coin" (Rachlin, 1982, p. 60).

In seeking greater recognition and acceptance of staff rights one need not diminish the importance of clients' rights, that is, this is not an area that demands great compromise if the rights of both are to be supported. What is essential is a clear understanding of what it is that constitutes the rights of staff in the treatment settings discussed herein. Gibson (1976), for example, proposed the following for mental health settings while he was president of the American Psychiatric Association:

1. The right of staff to have sufficient resources to provide adequate health care
2. The right of staff to participate in the allocation of resources and the setting of priorities
3. The right of staff to be accountable for clinical matters to the highest governing authority
4. The right of staff to the free and complete exercise of clinical judgment and skill under conditions that will not cause the deterioration of the quality of care
5. The right to have clinical practice reviewed by peers
6. The right of staff to practice without excessive and unnecessary regulation
7. The privilege of staff members to practice their profession

One thing fairly predictable is that if things go badly—if staff are exposed to great risk or if someone is seriously injured—management will be taken to task to generate mechanisms to minimize these difficulties or their future potential. It is administratively more responsible to develop a proactive approach to defining and guaranteeing some reasonable staff rights, rather than having to respond in time of crisis and agitated employee feelings. In this sense "staff rights" become "employer obligations," and if properly in place these contribute to the overall professionalism and legal safety of the clinical working environment (Griffith, 1984). The following are critical:

1. *Philosophy of treatment.* This is a statement of the general purpose of the agency and the nature of the population served, including some indication as to the general approaches to treatment. This should be discussed with all applicants for employment, as well as be an indication as to the potential risk to employees in working with mentally retarded clients with severe behavior disorders. People who accept employment aware of these risks should view this philosophy as a commitment to seriously disabled individuals.

2. *Appropriate policies and procedures.* These establish the parameters of the scope of one's employment, and outline general courses of action for meeting the goals of the organization (see preceding discussion on policies and procedures). This is especially significant in the area of guidelines for treatment, discussed later.

3. *Current technology.* This is a training/consultation obligation of the employer, and its goal is to ensure the best possible availability of clinical expertise for staff.

4. *Staff development.* This is a continuous training process designed to enable staff to meet the myriad demands of meeting client needs and overall agency goals.

5. *Staff* should be free to practice their areas of qualified clinical expertise without excessive regulation.

6. *Identification of client rights.* This should be done through a general policy statement so staff have a clear understanding of these matters prior to implementing or imposing treatments. It is imperative that such a statement distinguish between rights and privileges.

7. *Adequate and visible supervision.* This is a continuous process of assigning and clarifying responsibilities, implementation of tasks, observation, feedback, retraining or consultation, and ultimate evaluation. This should be viewed as a helping function designed to facilitate professional growth.

8. *Objective investigation of incidents by qualified personnel.* Few administrators are sophisticated enough by training and experience to conduct

a legally defensible investigation of a serious incident, for example one involving client abuse. There are numerous legal considerations for clients and staff in such investigations, and the subtleties of these should not be left to those lacking sufficient skills and background.

Staff will recognize a serious effort toward incorporating these obligations into the personnel practices of an agency as a demonstrated interest in their welfare. One reason, perhaps, is that to ensure adequate attention to these, management will have to interact extensively with line supervisors and direct service staff. In addition, as long as there is a logical legal rationale, staff will understand when something is in their best interest and is not just another bureaucratic annoyance.

Treatment Guidelines

With the ever-present risk of injury and the escalating probability of lawsuits it is little wonder there is often administrative reluctance to endorse the use of controversial interventions, primarily those from behavior modification technology, for treating severe behavior disorders. These concerns impact significantly upon the behavior of clinicians as well.

> Therapists are continually confronted with legal and ethical issues, sometimes to the extent that they become preoccupied with those issues rather than the issue of providing the best possible therapy. This concern about liability and lawsuits is understandable in today's legal climate where consumers are seeking monetary judgments against professionals at an increasing rate. Yet, therapists have a right to put their skills to the best possible use without a constant fear of legal recourse. To have this right, however, therapists must accept certain responsibilities, including the responsibility of relinquishing total control over the client–therapist relationship. (Sheldon-Wildgen, 1982, p. 169)

What therapists must relinquish in regard to the use of controversial treatments in public settings is clinical autonomy; they will be able to practice their trade if they follow reasonable guidelines. These due process considerations must be legally sound and administratively supported, with serious attempts at minimizing red tape.

Although there has been strong concern from a few professionals (Goldiamond, 1975; Stolz, 1977; Stolz & Associates, 1978) that guidelines for behavior modification will stifle responsible research and treatment activity, this has rapidly become a moot issue in many respects. Most states now have some form of regulation or guidelines in their residential and community programs serving mentally retarded people; the public schools are following suit in some areas but they do not typically "treat" the difficult-to-manage client being discussed herein. Continuing court cases and statutory enactments indicate more scrutiny and protection of clients' rights (Martin, 1981), and guidelines support this concept as well as ensuring protection for professionals, barring any malicious or negligent behavior (Griffith, 1980, 1983). The following components should be considered.

Statement of Policy. As previously discussed, this will provide employees with the philosophy, goals, and objectives of the organization (Christian & Hannah, 1983), and a formal policy on behavior management is essential in any publicly funded or supported program using controversial techniques (Griffith, 1983). The policy must make clear the degree to which the agency supports the use of necessary, clinically appropriate controversial techniques, and in addition should include:

1. Adherence to the principle of the least drastic, least intrusive, or least restrictive means (see, for example, Turnbull *et al.*, 1981)
2. Definitions of critical terms; as well as an indication of interventions which are absolutely forbidden (e.g., corporal punishment)
3. Acknowledgment of the interdisciplinary team approach to planning for clients
4. Required review mechanisms, i.e., peer review, human rights review committee
5. Mandate for legal consent
6. Define abuse and what constitutes abusive action; or do this in a separate policy on abuse
7. Requirements for data collection and monitoring

Interdisciplinary Team Process. The proposal to use a necessary controversial intervention should originate with the client's program planning team, or in conjunction with a consulting expert in such procedures. Whereas not all staff members with programming responsibility will have the requisite skills to develop clinically defensible interventions, they will have much to contribute regarding the client's behavior. Unless extremely controversial or esoteric techniques are used, all those in direct service should be trained to apply them on a client-specific basis, with proper monitoring and follow-up by the clinical experts (Risley, 1975).

The use of such teams is currently standard practice in habilitative and educational programs. In a legal sense, the total involvement of the interdisciplinary program planning team in recommending and applying such interventions adds to the credibility of the overall treatment process. Administratively, this type of participation encourages employees to actively participate in the development of service delivery mechanisms, especially if planning sessions are designed to foster input and communication.

Peer Review. Following recommendation by the interdisciplinary team, the next logical step is some sort of peer review. Christian (1983) and Christian and Hannah (1983) have identified two types: (a) case consultation, which applicable in this instance because it is client specific; and (b) program review, which is more comprehensive and looks at service components. Case consultation, the only type to be discussed and hereafter referred to as "peer review," involves the examination by one or more experts (in this case in behavior management and related areas) of the client's treatment plan for appropriateness, and subsequent recommendations for change if necessary.

Peer review may be conducted by one or more persons, either employed by, or external to, the agency. In general, peer reviewers will not have been involved in the original recommendation to use a controversial intervention, and their role is to render a "second opinion," similar to what has become standard in medical practice. The types of reviewers necessary will vary but usually will include professionals with backgrounds in psychopharmacology, various psychological approaches, physical and mechanical restraints, medicine, and treatments involving aversive stimuli (Griffith, 1983). Because of the complexity of procedures and the subsequent risks, a small committee is preferable to a single reviewer, although one expert could feasibly review proposals involving low-risk interventions.

Peer review is an excellent example of proactive management (Christian & Hannah, 1983). One significant benefit is that it assures those outside the program environment that treatment procedures are justified and clients' rights are of concern (Sheldon-Wildgen & Risley, 1982). Peer review also develops a logical link between the administrators and those performing the treatment:

> Since committees should not be responsible for the administration of programs, the role of the peer review committee is to advise the agency management personnel as to the feasibility of implementing all proposals reviewed. They must be aware of the potential risks to clients and staff as well as any anticipated public reaction to the recommended technology. It is not, however, the committee's decision to implement a particular procedure but rather their sanction that properly influences program managers to do so. (Griffith, 1983, p. 332)

The general standard for determining appropriateness in sanctioning procedures has two major components. First, the intervention must meet the test of "least restrictive" or "least intrusive." Second, the techniques must be professionally justified, that is, have support in the *current* professional literature (Sheldon-Wildgen & Risley, 1982). Those involved in peer review may also play a significant role in monitoring and follow-up of clinical interventions, thus expanding their consultative role.

Legal Consent. The term informed consent is probably somewhat a misnomer, inasmuch as "informing" is but one of three elements necessary to make consent truly legal. Therefore, *legal consent* seems more appropriate here and the requisite criteria are the following (American Association on Mental Deficiency, 1977; *Kaimowitz v. Department of Mental Health for the State of Michigan*, 1973; Martin, 1975):

1. *Capacity.* People generally have capacity if they have reached the age of majority (usually 18) and have the ability to acquire information, process it, and use it to make rational decisions about what will happen to them. Mentally retarded people often lack capacity, especially at a level required to deal with complex matters. Retarded persons for whom controversial treatments have been legitimately recommended typically do not have the capacity to consent to these procedures, especially considering the current behavioral state of the person that necessitates the application of this technology.

2. *Information.* In order to decide whether or not to participate in a particular program, clients and/or their representatives must be presented with a description of the interventions, their purposes, risks, side effects, and anticipated outcome, or benefits. To be legally sound, this informing process must occur in a fashion designed to be understood by the client/representative, without a profusion of professional jargon; this means presenting the information in the primary language of the service recipient, as well.

2. *Voluntariness.* It is not legal to coerce consent from clients/representatives because truly proper consent depends upon the free will of the person affixing his or her signature. Coercion could occur directly or subtly by suggesting, for example, that a lack of willingness to comply would result in certain repercussions affecting other areas of programming, such as discharge from services. This issue is particularly sensitive in institutions for additional reasons, especially if someone feels compelled to consent to something in order to facilitate release or movement to a "better" program.

One issue of great concern occurs when consent is needed from an adult mentally retarded client who has not been adjudicated incompetent to handle his or her personal affairs, but neither has there been the appointment of a legal guardian (the parent is almost always the guardian of a minor child and decides consent). A literal interpretation of existing statutes indicates that consent must be sought directly from this person, yet we know from experience that the client often lacks the capacity to deal with the complex matters at hand, especially when the issue is controversial treatments. In this instance, capacity is the critical element, and if the person cannot comprehend and decide rationally then he or she cannot give legal consent, irrespective of his or her status under the statutes.

Ideally, when such a situation arises there should be a petition to the court of proper jurisdiction in order to determine the competency of the individual and in cases of incompetence the subsequent appointment of a guardian to act in behalf of the person. This is logical in long-term planning for clients but generally impractical when severe behavior disorders need immediate attention. The *tradition* in the law will usually allow the treating agent to turn to the parent or next of kin for consent for interventions that are controversial yet considered to be acceptable, current clinical practice. Because concerns in this area vary from state to state it is essential that service providers acquire competent legal counsel when establishing consent processes.

A second major concern arises when a client refuses to consent to what we deem a necessary (though controversial or aversive) procedure. Perhaps the first thing to ask is who in their right mind would give their permission for someone else to inflict pain or discomfort upon them? The refusal must be examined to determine if it is truly informed and comes from someone with the capacity to make such a decision. It takes as much cognitive ability to responsibly refuse as it does to consent, and generally mentally retarded persons displaying behavior warranting controversial interventions lack the capacity to decide complex program issues for themselves (see the discussion on the "right to refuse" in the next section).

Generally consent is the sine qua non in any reasonable treatment program wherein risk is posed. Although it might not be available in all instances of necessary controversial treatment, it is the most critical element to be sought prior to commencing the intervention. Legal consent will offer the most protection for staff should there be any question as to the propriety of the intervention or its consequences in a setting where it has been responsibly delivered (Griffith, 1983). It also ensures the thorough participation of clients and their representatives in exercising some control over the treatment regimen (Christian & Hannah, 1983).

Human Rights Committees (HRC). In addition to helping ensure protection of client rights to humane and necessary treatment, human rights committees also help add credibility to what an agency does clinically. Their role is especially significant in programs using controversial treatments with severely debilitated clients, where clinically necessary procedures may be highly objectionable to the general public, if taken out of context (Sheldon-Wildgen & Risley, 1982). In the area of controversial interventions, a HRC should review, and sanction or reject, proposals for programs posing significant risk from a perspective of the community at large and should be prepared to publicly support the agency when it is using necessary but controversial treatment strategies that have withstood the scrutiny of legitimate due process review.

The HRC should advise the administration on numerous rights and program issues but should not assume the posture of "rubber stamping" administrative proposals or practices; thus the majority of members should come from outside the agency in order to minimize the potential for administrative control (Griffith & Henning, 1981). The HRC should operate under the auspices of an administrative policy with clearly defined roles and functions, including review of the application of controversial treatment strategies (Risley & Sheldon-Wildgen, 1980). Because most properly established HRCs are comprised primarily of volunteers, their overall responsibilities must be limited to those that may be reasonably managed within the time available.

In addition to reviewing controversial treatment strategies, other logical areas of responsibility include review and assistance in the development of policies that affect client rights, and investigating legitimate grievances of clients and representatives about the conditions or availability of treatment/habilitation. Some areas are too technical and/or administrative by nature, such as investigations of alleged abuse, and should not be relegated to a committee; this is especially true because of the necessary concern for the rights of staff (Griffith & Henning, 1981).

Legal Rights

The courts have used the term *right to habilitation* with the mentally retarded as being generally synonymous with the concept of *right to treatment* with the mentally ill; *habilitation* is more appropriate for services to the retarded and includes education, training, and care (*Halderman v. Pennhurst*, 1977; *Romeo v. Youngberg*, 1980). Extensive litigation has developed parallel and overlapping findings in establishing statutory and constitutional rights of both classes of mentally disabled persons, either to treatment, or to refuse treatment. It is therefore reasonable to use the terms *treatment* and *habilitation* interchangeably for the purpose of discussing legal rights and principles in this vastly complex area of mental disability law.

Right to Habilitation. The idea of a right to treatment is no longer novel, having been established to some degree in most states and federal court jurisdictions (see, e.g., *Rouse v. Cameron*, 1966; *Welsch v. Likins*,

1974; *Wuori v. Zitnay*, 1978; *Wyatt v. Aderholt*, 1974). Although historically, the level and intensity of treatment expectations seemed to accrue
in gradual increments, more recent litigation has resulted in vastly
enlightened opinions and subsequently the establishment of broad-based
service requirements (*New Jersey ARC, Inc. v. New Jersey Dept. of Human
Services*, 1982):

> This case concerns the rights and liberties of mentally retarded citizens in
> public institutions in New Jersey. The parties disagree on the extent of the
> protection and freedom granted those individuals by state statutes. Today
> we interpret those statutes to grant mentally retarded children in State facil-
> ities the legal right to a thorough and efficient education suited to their
> individual needs and abilities. We further conclude that all mentally retarded
> adults in those facilities have the legal right to adequate training, habilitation,
> education, care and protection in accord with their individual needs. Finally,
> we hold that all mentally retarded citizens have the right to these services
> in the setting which is least restrictive of their personal liberty. (pp. 705–706)

Traditionally, matters of rights to services were decided within the
state or federal court systems, thus precluding the development of any
binding national standards or requirements. Recently the U.S. Supreme
Court examined on a limited basis the right to habilitation for involuntarily committed mentally retarded persons (*Youngberg v. Romeo*, 1982).
Although the full impact of the Court's opinion is still evolving, it is
clear the constitutional rights cited will have far-reaching effects upon
mental retardation services (American Bar Association, 1983) and particularly in programs treating severe behavior disorders.

The Court acknowledged certain basic rights, including adequate
food, shelter, clothing, and medical care (*Youngberg v. Romeo*, 1982). The
critical determination, however, was a constitutional right to "such training as may be reasonable in light of respondent's liberty interests in
safety and freedom from unreasonable restraints" (pp. 14–15). A partial
analysis of what this means is:

> Thus, at a minimum it would appear that residents of institutions are entitled
> to habilitation designed to provide them with the skills necessary to avoid
> injury caused by themselves or others and the skills which would allow them
> freedom of movement. (Ellis, 1982, p. 198)

This has particular relevance for clients with severe behavior disorders, especially considering the danger for physical or intellectual damage. There now exists an affirmative obligation on the part of
administrators of public residential institutions to establish programs to
properly treat this behavior in order to minimize its pernicious effects;
whether this requirement will accrue to other types of programs remains
to be seen. The Court was careful not to specify the course such treatment

should take, reinforcing its current stance on the role of professionals in clinical treatment matters (see also *Parham v. J. R.*, 1979; *Secretary of Public Welfare of Pennsylvania v. Institutionalized Juveniles*, 1979):

> In determining what is "reasonable"—in this and in any case presenting a claim for training by a state—we emphasize that courts must show deference to the judgment exercised by a qualified professional. . . .[T]he decision, if made by a professional, is presumptively valid; liability may be imposed only when the decision by the professional is such a substantial departure from accepted professional judgment, practice or standards as to demonstrate that the person responsible actually did not base the decision on such a judgment. (*Youngberg v. Romeo*, 1982, pp. 15–16)

The message from this opinion is very positive from a staff rights perspective. Although there is imposed an obligation to treat, the course of treatment is to be decided by those delivering the service. The standard for determining liability, should something go wrong during treatment, greatly favors the responsible clinician who is operating consistent with current professional practice; what is "current" in settings treating severe behavior disorders is adherence to standard practice *and* reasonable guidelines fashioned after the due process considerations previously discussed. The course of judicial scrutiny has been altered significantly:

> Thus, it appears that mental health professionals will be allowed to set their own standard of care, and this standard will very likely be determined by examining the published literature as well as expert opinion. (Sheldon-Wildgen, 1982, p. 167)

The substantive treatment rights established in *Youngberg v. Romeo* will surely be available to voluntarily admitted retarded persons as well as those who are committed, as was the case with Nicholas Romeo. Unlike mental health, in retardation facilities there is generally no major differences between clients who are committed and those who enter "voluntarily." The clients usually lack the capacity to participate in the decision to institutionalize, and the same circumstances may lead to either voluntary admission or commitment, depending upon the jurisdiction (see *ARC of North Dakota v. Olson*, 1982; *Halderman et al. v. Pennhurst State School & Hospital*, 1977). The liberty interests behind the concept of "least restrictive" should bring more of the *Romeo* treatment requirements into community programs as well (*ARC of North Dakota v. Olson*, 1982; *Halderman v. Pennhurst*, 1982).

Right to Refuse. Coincidental to the right to treatment/habilitation exists the possibility that clients will not wish to participate in certain activities or treatment regimens. Such a refusal, at least around the use of controversial treatments, will most logically occur during the consent process. Remember that one option when consent is sought is for the client or representative to say "no" (Griffith & Coval, 1984). Administratively, there are numerous options following a refusal, and a careful analysis of the issues should yield a reasonable course of action.

Client rights have been secured at an astounding pace during the past decade. This has resulted in vast increases in the availability of habilitation services generally geared around the concept of services to the individual based upon needs, and encouraging extensive involvement in planning by clients and/or their representatives. The sensitive complexities of serving clients with severe behavior disorders demand thorough understanding of options and obligations, yet it is virtually impossible to maximize client rights and needs simultaneously and still optimally deal with treatment refusals (Mills, Yesavage, & Gutheil, 1981). The most reasonable way to face up to this is through the implementation of a system of procedural safeguards (described previously) and subsequent strategies for managing refusals.

There are numerous reasons why clients might refuse to participate in certain interventions (Griffith & Coval, 1984; Martin, 1975):

1. *Too intrusive.* To decide whether or not something is too intrusive involves consideration of current clinical practice in conjunction with the legal principle of "least drastic means":

> In a series of decisions this Court has held that, even though the government purpose be legitimate and substantial, that purpose cannot be pursued by means that broadly stifle fundamental personal liberties when the end can be more narrowly achieved. The breadth of a legislative abridgement must be viewed in the light of less drastic means for achieving the same basic purpose. (*Shelton v. Tucker*, 1960, p. 488)

This is generally synonymous with the more popular designation, "least restrictive alternative" (Turnbull *et al.*, 1981).

By definition, the more intrusive or restrictive the treatment the more it poses risk of side effects, restriction of rights, or usually both. Yet if one's behavior is seriously maladaptive or dangerous, it is likely the treatment regimen will involve some risk, and therefore be deemed restrictive. Especially valuable in using controversial treatments is the concept of a hierarchy of potentially effective interventions (Roos, 1972), and the proper choice is that that has a reasonable probability of effectiveness while minimizing the risk of undesirable side effects (Griffith & Coval, 1984).

Clients have the right to refuse interventions that are unnecessarily restrictive, and these often are recommended by overly zealous clinicians in programs lacking the procedural safeguards discussed previously. Levick and Wapner (1975) have suggested some general guidelines for assessing the restrictiveness of an intervention:

a. The extent to which the intervention has been demonstrated effective in dealing with a client's behavior
b. The degree of change in the client's personality that may result from the intervention
c. Possible side effects
d. The extent to which it requires physical intrusion into the client's body
e. The degree of pain and discomfort involved
f. The extent to which an uncooperative client can avoid the effects of the intervention.

2. *Improperly placed.* Refusals on these grounds have occurred most dramatically with clients who felt their placement in residential institutions was too restrictive (*ARC of North Dakota v. Olson,* 1982; *Barbara C. v. Magnone,* 1981; *Halderman v. Pennhurst,* 1982; *Wuori v. Zitnay,* 1978). The regulations (42 *Federal Register,* 1977) promulgated subsequent to passage of P.L. 94-142 (1975) spell out rigid due process mechanisms in order that parents may seek the least restrictive environment for their children. Generally, if there exists significant incompatibility between a client's needs and the restrictiveness of the environment, the matter is legally challengeable.

3. *Not legitimate treatment.* Nicholas Romeo, through his mother, challenged the excessive use of mechanical restraints imposed upon him in a residential institution (*Romeo v. Youngberg,* 1980). These were used allegedly for misbehavior and aggression, yet without benefit of a specific, overall treatment program. The U.S. Supreme Court decided he was entitled to something more—basically professional treatment that would obviate the frequent use of restraints (*Youngberg v. Romeo,* 1982).

Other cases have upheld the rights of clients to refuse, or be protected from, interventions that do not meet the standards of current, acceptable clinical practice: excessive and punitive restraint (*Wheeler v. Glass,* 1973); forced administration of drugs as punishment for undesirable behavior (*Knecht v. Gillman,* 1973; *Mackey v. Procunier,* 1973); seclusion without due process *Morgan v. Sproat,* 1977); and, electroconvulsive therapy (*Wyatt v. Stickney,* 1972). Risley (1975) found the following examples of "punishment" in his investigation of one public residential facility for the mentally retarded: forced public masturbation, excessive seclusion, withholding of food, and forced lack of sleep. All of these are certainly punitive, but in no way do they resemble clinically justifiable punishment interventions (Axelrod & Apsche, 1983).

4. *Case law prohibitions.* Litigation often results in significant changes in the conditions of services to large classes of mentally disabled clients

or in further enumeration of rights. In some jurisdictions, for example, the courts have decided that psychotropic medication may be refused unless it is deemed to be clinically essential and consistent with current medical and psychiatric practice (*Mills et al., Pelitioners, v. Rogers et al.,* 1982; *Rennie v. Klein,* 1981). In a seemingly more drastic move a court directed, by agreement of the parties, that all services may be refused (*Barbara C. v. Magnone,* 1981):

> Nothing in this Proposed Plan For Relief shall be construed to prohibit or interfere with the right of any class member to refuse or reject any or all of the required services or requirements of this Proposed Plan For Relief. In the event that any class member rejects services or requirements pursuant to the terms of the Proposed Plan For Relief, he/she or his/her guardian shall be required to sign a written waiver which specifies the service or requirement rejected. (p. 47)

5. *Relevant regulations and standards.* Most publicly funded mental retardation services operate under regulations that impact on a client's right to refuse services, especially because the use of consent processes has become relatively standard practice. Residential programs supported by the Medicaid program (Standards for Immediate Care Facilities for the Mentally Retarded, 1978), for example, are closely scrutinized, and legal consent is required for the use of aversive stimuli or time-out devices. It is beyond the scope of this chapter to expand on this topic, but thorough knowledge of relevant regulations will often clarify many client rights issues concerning refusals to participate.

There are other reasons clients and/or their representatives might refuse, but space does not permit additional discussion here. Clients may withhold consent to participate if the intervention interferes with religious beliefs, is experimental or unusually hazardous, is designed to prolong life of someone terminally ill, constitutes cruel and unusual punishment, or invades privacy. The administrator must recognize that a refusal is often an indication that something is wrong with the proposed program, not the thinking of the client, thus warranting thorough administrative and clinical analysis.

Managing Refusals. The refusal by a client/representative to participate should not be viewed in an adversarial sense: in other words, do not initially assume the client is "being difficult." It is a basic right to refuse unwarranted or unwanted interventions, and when a legal consent mechanism is in place (as it should be) there will be instances when clients decline. Inasmuch as there are many possible scenarios underlying a refusal, it is better viewed as an administrative and clinical challenge that needs further scrutiny and action.

Agency management must weigh the impact of the refusal, if it is allowed, upon all parties. Will the client pose additional risk to self or others? What is the risk to staff of the refusal to participate in a program involving a controversial intervention? Will the agency be able to continue to provide the client with a meaningful overall program based upon needs? What other options must be pursued?

One response might be to allow the refusal and leave the client's program plan as it was. To determine this as an appropriate course of action demands thorough scrutiny of all relevant concerns, but would not usually be an acceptable response to a refusal of treatment for a severe behavior disorder. Initially, therefore, the agency must determine the adequacy and necessity of the proposed intervention based upon the concept of least intrusive, and then proceed appropriately (Griffith & Coval, 1984).

Perhaps at this point the agency might consider discharging the client using the rationale "If we can't meet the needs of this client he can't remain, especially when there are others waiting for this service." This option is much more viable in the mental health system where the legal concept of "voluntary" and "involuntary" are more applicable, and "uncooperative patients" can often leave, perhaps to seek alternative treatments elsewhere. Because of diminished capacity, this is not a reasonable course of action for a retarded client, nor is it likely there will be alternatives if the client has severe behavior disorders.

Depending upon the concerns of the client/representative, it might be most reasonable to redesign the program. Typically you will not find clients/representatives opposed to *all* interventions that might be effective, and it is worth the time to negotiate, as well as further educate those who will be giving consent ultimately. Recognize that it is not unusual for a planning team to recommend something excessively restrictive the first time, out of legitimate concern for helping the client to rapidly bring his or her behavior under better control.

It may be necessary to impose the recommended procedure over the objections of the client/representative, even though this is an extremely sensitive proposition. This decision may come about, for example, because of the affirmative obligation of the agency to provide reasonable, appropriate treatment for a particularly difficult or dangerous behavior. Inasmuch as significant support for responsible professional judgment has come from the courts (*Rennie v. Klein*, 1981; *Youngberg v. Romeo*, 1982), this should be a legally safe strategy if the proper foundations are in place:

> The two interventions most likely to be refused by mentally retarded persons or their parents/guardians are aversive behavior modification interventions and psychotropic medications. These may be highly intrusive, at best uncomfortable, but often have great (short-term) therapeutic value in management of disruptive, aggressive or bizarre behavior. Unless there is great risk to a

client a reasonable set of due process safeguards will allow the agency to
manage most refusals in a legally sound fashion. (Griffith & Coval, 1984,
p. 260)

The option of imposing treatment against the wishes of the client,
although very sensitive, is quite realistic in cases of severe behavior
disorders, especially when one considers the potential consequences to
the agency of *not treating* the problem behaviors. Are you more negligent
if you withhold appropriate treatment, or proceed against the client's
wishes with what is clinically recommended? Assuming the client remains
in your program, he or she will minimally require emergency intervention such as mechanical or chemical restraints, but this is the Band-Aid
approach to dealing with seriously maladaptive behavior. The imposition of clinically appropriate and necessary treatment is often preferable,
assuming there are no legal barriers to proceeding in such a fashion.

Abuse

One common manifestation of severe behavior disorders is overt
actions that are hazardous, or potentially so (see Chapter 2). Typically
there is a positive correlation between the magnitude of dangerousness
of a behavior and the amount of risk (to client and staff) involved in
treating it. Because the potential for unwanted or undesirable side effects
is relatively high, there also exists a high probability for charges of abuse,
even in the most sophisticated programs. The repercussions from abuse
allegations present nightmares for administrators, whether or not the
agency is at fault.

The degree to which an action is deemed to be abusive depends,
in part, upon the characteristics of the client. Consider, for example, the
difference in the public outcry toward a situation wherein someone
punches a juvenile delinquent versus one in which the person punched
is a mentally retarded child. I am not suggesting there should be a
different standard but rather pointing to the perception that one type
of client is certainly "more helpless" and therefore more vulnerable.

The restrictiveness of the program environment will influence the
degree to which physical discipline is legitimate. Although corporal punishment is categorically prohibited in public residential facilities for the
mentally retarded, the Supreme Court has ruled that it is allowable in
public schools and would not be construed as being abusive if judiciously
applied (*Ingraham v. Wright*, 1977):

The openness of the public school and its supervision by the community
afford significant safeguards against the kinds of abuse from which the Eighth

Amendment protects the prisoner. In virtually every community where corporal punishment is permitted in the schools, these safeguards are reinforced by the legal constraints of the common law. Public school teachers and administrators are privileged at common law to inflict only such corporal punishment as is reasonably necessary for the proper education and discipline of the child; any punishment going beyond the privilege may result in both civil and criminal liability. (p. 670)

Proactive strategies for preventing abuse often arise out of an analysis of the elements necessary to define abuse. One general paradigm comes from the literature on child abuse (Gil, 1982):

1. *Physical abuse.* Physical, sexual and emotional abuse perpetrated by a professional caretaker or foster parent.
2. *Program abuse.* When programs are substandard, have extreme or unfair policies, or rely on inhumane or clinically unacceptable techniques.
3. *System abuse.* Occurs when a service system is too large, too complicated, or too political to meet needs; often fraught with waste, inefficiency, and clients who fall "between the cracks."

A broader, yet more specific perspective comes from a synthesis of current treatment issues with stated definitions from the National Center on Child Abuse and Neglect (Dept. of Health, Education & Welfare, 1977):

1. *Physical abuse.* This falls into the following subcategories: (a) client/client; (b) staff/client; (c) outsiders/client; and (d) self-inflicted. The term *abuse* seems to denote *physical abuse*, at least in popular usage.
2. *Physical neglect.* Examples include failure to notice a physical problem, lack of programming, enforced idleness, and improper diet. This may actually be more harmful than physical abuse inasmuch as the effects are more likely to be permanent.
3. *Medical abuse.* The major concern in programs for the mentally retarded is the improper use of psychotropic medication. (For an indication as to the extent of possible liability see *Clites v. State of Iowa*, 1980, 1982, wherein damages in excess of $750,000 were awarded to the plaintiff because of misuse of psychotropic medication.)
4. *Environmental abuse.* Blatant deficiencies in the living and program environments are the most common types: for example, uncovered radiators, scalding tap water and broken equipment.
5. *Sexual abuse.* This may be the most sensitive type of abuse, as well as the most abhorrent.

6. *Seclusion.* Placement of a client in a locked room, without legal authorization nor defined treatment goals, is prohibited in most mental retardation programs.
7. *Emotional/psychological harm.* Most obvious are acts of harrass-ment, threats, and denigration; it could also include lack of stimulation or opportunities for growth.
8. *Punishment disguised as treatment.* The application of punitive consequences that are not clinically justifiable and therefore would not withstand the scrutiny of a series of procedural safeguards (see section on guidelines).
9. *Unauthorized restraint.* Excessive use of unjustifiable restraint is prohibited (*Youngberg v. Romeo*, 1982).
10. *Deprivation of rights.* There are certain recognized basic rights afforded to clients because they are people and citizens. These may not be denied without rigid due process procedures.

Working with behaviorally disordered clients certainly generates the potential for bringing out undesirable behaviors in employees. Abuse often occurs when adults are unable to cope with stress (Durkin, 1982), and the logical ways to deal with this are to change the person's coping mechanisms or alter the environment to relieve stressful situations and stimuli. Because the former involves changing personalities (which is terribly complex), the latter seems a more appropriate avenue for the administrator confronted with extant abuse. Significant attention to the matter of staff rights is a most viable approach to improving the "mental health" of the work environment, thus representing a preventive approach to this nefarious phenomenon.

It is apparent that the potential for several types of abuse thus far described may be minimized by sensitizing staff through training. It may not be unusual for staff members, for example, to assume they may approach client discipline in the same manner used with their own children, including spankings. The point is that abuse is not as obvious as it appears at first glance, especially when some normative child-rearing practices are inappropriate in program or treatment settings. The same logic may be applied in addressing the more subtle types of abuse, such as withholding rights or the existence of environmental flaws.

Staff development represents the positive approach to the problem, but that is not generally enough inasmuch as there are people who are not sufficiently affected by it. These are employees who, for whatever reason, devalue mentally retarded (and often other) persons to the extent they will inflict harm in response to annoying or other undesirable behaviors. There must be harsh consequences for proven abusive acts, including termination of employment and prosecution in the legal system, if a crime can be established. Although these words sound noble, administrators must be cautioned about proceeding in a cavalier fashion when abuse is suspected.

Abuse is hard to prove, especially if there is an investigatory procedure considerate of the due process rights of staff members. Many client injuries, even those occurring while in physical contact with an employee, are accidental or result because the employee was inadequately trained. If we expect staff to work with behaviorally disordered clients in a truly therapeutic fashion, then we must recognize the risks. There will be injuries to both staff and clients. One cannot organize a witch-hunt following injury to a client.

The investigation process in such instances must be developed so that it is perceived as being thorough and fair, by employees as well as clients/representatives and advocates. There should be only a few management personnel allowed to conduct such investigations, and these people must be trained to do so. This is critical because the complexities of such investigations often parallel those in situations where a crime has occurred. In fact, if an abusive act has resulted in injury, then a crime may have been committed, and external authorities, usually police, must be notified. Because of the complexities in such situations and differences in state laws and regulations, legal advice should be sought if there is any question on how to proceed.

The primary responsibility of management personnel is to be proactive on this issue, by attention to training and broader staff rights issues. Abuse must be discussed at new employee orientation, including its definitions, techniques for managing undesirable behaviors, as well as the administrative and legal consequences for committing such an act. Employees must be shown how systems are developed to protect their rights, that there is an understanding that injuries will occur, but that they must recognize the difference between intervening that is consistent with their training and malicious behavior.

Ethics of Controversial Strategies

Entwined with the obligation to treat severe behavior disorders is the realization that generally the interventions of choice will pose not only risk but will be painful or uncomfortable as well. Progressive strategies often come from the behavior modification technology, typically involving combinations of accelerative techniques, usually positive reinforcement, with decelerative approaches, primarily aversive interventions, or punishment (see Axelrod & Apsche, 1983). Because many, as

alluded to earlier, see clinical punishment as being "punitive" or even
abhorrent, ethics often as much as legal matters will influence decisions
on using these approaches (Braun, 1975; Carrera & Adams, 1970). (See
Chapter 7 for discussion on the ethics of pharmacotherapy.)

Some professionals, it has been noted, charge that behavior modification techniques treat only symptoms rather than the underlying
causes of aberrant behavior (Bucher, 1969; Cooke & Cooke, 1974). The
argument that aversive interventions lead to undesirable side effects is
not warranted, providing clients have a properly developed, total program of habilitation (Azrin & Holz, 1966; Harris & Ersner-Hershfield,
1978). Others have rejected these strategies as mechanistic and gim-
micky, without proper recognition of the laudable success rate of many
behavior modifiers (Barrish, 1974; Tanner, 1973). Finally, there are those
who oppose it as a matter of principle *only*, which leaves little basis for
discussion or negotiation (Bucher, 1969).

Granted that the client should be at the center of the planning
process and influence as much as possible the course of therapy (see,
e.g., American Psychological Association, 1977; Stolz & Associates, 1978),
but the clients addressed herein typically lack the cognitive ability or
behavioral control to make rational decisions, or participate in any meaningful manner. Part of the ethical question is: how much shall we impose
upon this client in order to promote the alteration of his or her behavior?
And: what does it mean as far as basic human rights are concerned if
highly restrictive and sometimes painful interventions are imposed upon
someone who cannot understand or participate? Does not the application
of these interventions fly in the face of normalization?

Human rights are not absolute, and there is always a quid pro quo
when one is granted rights. One has the right to freedom of speech as
long as one uses it responsibly; the right may be abridged if one uses
it to cause unjustifiable harm. The clients addressed in this book are so
mentally disabled and distressed that it is unlikely they are making
conscious, rational decisions to act the way they do; this is really a
paradox because rational thinking would not likely induce such behavior. Ethics demand the imposition of the necessary appropriate clinical
interventions within a legally responsible and sound system. As for
normalization:

> It can be argued, therefore, that selective application of aversive conditioning
> can be a highly humanitarian procedure. It can free individuals from crippling
> behavior, enabling them to interact more meaningfully with their environ-
> ment and thereby enhancing their opportunities to develop their human
> qualities. In short, while deviating from the principle of normalization in its

procedures, aversive conditioning has been successful in yielding more normative behavior. (Roos, 1972, p. 146)

Conclusion: Some Final Thoughts

From the literature comparing institutional and community-based mentally retarded clients (e.g., Lakin, Hill, Hauber, Bruininks, & Heal, 1983; Scanlon, Arick, & Krug, 1982; Sutter, Mayeda, Call, Yanagi, & Yee, 1980), one surmises that the major difference is that institutionalized clients demonstrate significantly greater amounts of maladaptive behaviors, especially those that are dangerous or potentially harmful. According to Eyman and Call (1977) "it would seem that physical violence, property damage, and self-violence are the discriminating problems much more common for institutionalized individuals than for those living in the community" (p. 142). And it is difficult to prove that institutions cause this type of behavior (Eyman, Borthwick, & Miller, 1981), inasmuch as these seem to be some of the predominant factors contributing to institutionalization.

One might read this literature and conclude that there is a technology gap—that we cannot treat or correct certain pernicious behaviors in the community and therefore the safest, or at least societally most desirable, placement is a residential facility. Furthermore, one might conclude that the residential institutional setting must have the highest probability of successfully treating these disorders because so many admissions and readmissions occur due to these problems. Obviously, such conclusions would not be based upon logic, but rather they evolve as excuses for systems failures.

From the literature and research presented and cited in this text, it is quite apparent that the technology is available for addressing most of the behavior disorders manifested by mentally retarded persons. It is not used in a clinically responsible fashion in many cases, and this is a systems management problem, more so than one of insufficient clinical input. With no intent to malign those working in institutions, behaviorally disordered clients get sent to these facilities because such a move is expedient, not because there is a high probability of receiving treatment more appropriate than could be developed elsewhere.

Behaviorally disordered clients are not properly treated in most settings because of numerous factors, some legitimate and some attitudinal. It is legitimate if some programs do not deal with these clients because most programs cannot and should not be "all things to all people." Unfortunately, we often find lack of consideration of this issue as a systems problem, and nobody bears proper responsibility. This is a major management problem.

Lack of resources is a frequent and recurring program reality and one that seems to penalize the behaviorally disordered clients inordinately. They become low priority in times of tight money. They may be the most recalcitrant because of the way they are viewed within many programs—as being too hard to manage. It is quite remarkable what a good dose of clinically appropriate and responsibly delivered intervention can do for these clients, especially if this occurs as the behavior is evolving.

Simplistic thinking? Maybe. But I come back to what is probably the critical point in the habilitation of mentally retarded clients with severe behavior disorders. The technology for treating "unmanageable" behavior is quite good and effective, but the systems, the processes for environmental applications, are inadequate. Clinical research and education should continue to be emphasized, but the ultimate challenge in services to these clients is acceptance and improvement of the administrative role.

References

American Association on Mental Deficiency. (1977). *Consent handbook*. Washington, DC: Author.

American Bar Association. (1983). Commission on the Mentally Disabled, summary and analysis. *Mental Disability Law Reporter, 7*, 67–69.

American Psychological Association. (1977). *Standards for providers of psychological services* (rev. ed.). Washington, DC: Author.

ARC of North Dakota v. Olson, No. A1-80-141 (D.N.D. Aug. 31, 1982) as reported in *Mental Disability Law Reporter*, (1982), *6*, 374–376.

Argyris, C. (1957). *Personality and organization*. New York: Harper & Row.

Axelrod, S., & Apsche, J. (Eds.). (1983). *The effects of punishment on human behavior*. New York: Academic Press.

Azrin, N. H., & Holz, W. C. (1966). Punishment. In W. K. Honig & W. Staddon (Eds.), *Handbook of operant behavior: Areas of research and application* (pp. 380–447). New York: Appleton.

Barbara C. v. Magnone, No. C-2-77-887 (5D. Ohio, Oct. 19, 1981).

Barrish, I. J. (1974). Ethical issues and answers to behavior modification. *Corrective and Social Psychiatry & Journal of Behavior Technology Methods and Therapy, 20*, 30–37.

Blau, P. M., & Scott, W. R. (1969). Dilemmas of formal organization. In A. Etzioni (Ed.), *Readings on modern organizations* (pp. 138–147). Englewood Cliffs, NJ: Prentice-Hall.

Braun, S. H. (1975). Ethical issues in behavior modification. *Behavior Therapy, 6*, 51–62.

Bucher, B. (1969). Some ethical issues in the therapeutic use of punishment. In R. D. Rubin & C. M. Franks (Eds.), *Advances in behavior therapy* (pp. 59–72). New York: Academic Press.

Carrera, R., & Adams, P. I. (1970). An ethical perspective on operant conditions. *Journal of the American Academy of Child Psychiatry, 9,* 607–623.

Christian, W. P. (1983). Professional peer review: Recommended strategies for reviewer and reviewee. *The Behavior Therapist, 6,* 86–89.

Christian, W. P., & Hannah, G. T. (1983). *Effective management in human services.* Englewood Cliffs, NJ: Prentice-Hall.

Clites v. State of Iowa, Iowa District Court for Pottawattamie County (Law No. 46274, Aug. 7, 1980). Affirmed, Court of Appeals of Iowa (No. 2-65599, June 29, 1982).

Cooke, T. P., & Cooke, S. (1974). Behavior modification: Answers to some ethical issues. *Psychology in the Schools, 11,* 5–10.

Department of Health, Education and Welfare. (1977). *Child abuse and neglect in residential institutions: Selected readings on prevention, investigation, and correction.* Washington, DC: National Center on Child Abuse and Neglect.

Drucker, P. F. (1974). *Mangement: Tasks, responsibilities, practices.* New York: Harper & Row.

Durkin, R. (1982). Institutional child abuse from a family systems perspective: A working paper. *Child & Youth Services, 4(1,2),* 15–22.

Education for All Handicapped Children Act. (1975). 20 U.S.C. § 1401 *et seq.,* PL 94-142.

Education for Handicapped Children, Implementation of Part B of the Education of the Handicapped Act. 42 C.F.R. (1977). *Federal Register,* 42474–42518.

Ellis, J. W. (1982). The supreme court and institutions: A comment on *Youngberg v. Romeo. Mental Retardation, 20,* 197–200.

Etzioni, A. (Ed.). (1969). *Readings on modern organizations.* Englewood Cliffs, NJ: Prentice-Hall.

Eyman, R. K., & Call, T. (1977). Maladaptive behavior and community placement of mentally retarded persons. *American Journal of Mental Deficiency, 82,* 137–144.

Eyman, R. K., Borthwick, S. A., & Miller, C. (1981). Trends in maladaptive behavior of mentally retarded persons placed in community and institutional settings. *American Journal of Mental Deficiency, 85,* 473–477.

Getzels, J. W. (1958). Administration as a social process. In A. W. Halpin (Ed.), *Administrative theory in education* (pp. 150–165). Chicago: University of Chicago.

Gibson, R. W. (1976). The rights of staff in the treatment of the mentally ill. *Hospital and Community Psychiatry, 27(12),* 855–859.

Gil, E. (1982). Institutional abuse of children in out-of-home care. *Child & Youth Services, 4,(1,2),* 7–13.

Goldiamond, I. (1975). Singling out behavior modification for legal regulation: Some effects on patient care, psychotherapy, and research in general. *Arizona Law Review, 17,* 105–126.

Griffith, R. G. (1980). An administrative perspective on guidelines for behavior modification: The creation of a legally safe environment. *The Behavior Therapist, 3(1),* 5–7.

Griffith, R. G. (1983). The administrative issues: An ethical and legal perspective. In S. Axelrod & J. Apsche (Eds.), *The effects of punishment on human behavior* (pp. 317–338). New York: Academic Press.

Griffith, R. G. (1984). Client abuse: Broadening the perspective. *Superintendents' Digest, 2,* 46–52.

Griffith, R. G., & Coval, T. E. (1984). The mentally retarded and the right to refuse habilitation. In S. E. Breuning, J. L. Matson, & R. P. Barrett (Eds.), *Advances in mental retardation and developmental disabilities* (Vol. 2, pp. 237–268). Greenwich, CT: Jai Press.

Griffith, R. G., & Henning, D. B. (1981). What is a human rights committee? *Mental Retardation, 19*(3), 61–63.

Halderman v. Pennhurst, 673 F.2d 647 (3d Cir. 1982).

Halderman, *et al*. v. Pennhurst State School & Hospital, 446 F. Supp. 1295 (E.D. Pa. 1977).

Harris, S. L., & Ersner-Hershfield, R. (1978). Behavioral suppression of seriously disruptive behavior in psychotic and retarded patients: A review of punishment and its alternatives. *Psychological Bulletin, 85*(6), 1352–1375.

Herbert, T. T. (1976). *Dimensions of organizational behavior.* New York: Macmillan.

Herzberg, F. (1966). *Work and the nature of man.* Cleveland: The World Publishing Co.

Ingraham v. Wright, 430 U.S. 651 (1977).

Kaimowitz v. Department of Mental Health for the State of Michigan. No. 73-19434-AW (Mich. Cir. Ct., Wayne County, July 10, 1973) as reported in *Mental Disability Law Reporter,* (1976), *1*, 147–154.

Knecht v. Gillman, 488 F.2d 1136 (8th Cir. 1973).

Lakin, K. C., Hill, B. K., Hauber, F. A., Bruininks, R. H., & Heal, L. W. (1983). New admissions and readmissions to a national sample of public residential facilities. *American Journal of Mental Deficiency, 88*, 13–20.

Levick, M., & Wapner, A. (1975). Advances in mental health: A case for the right to refuse treatment. *Temple Law Quarterly, 48*, 354–383.

Mackey v. Procunier, 477 F.2d 877 (9th Cir. 1973).

Martin, R. (1975). *Legal challenges to behavior modification.* Champaign, IL: Research Press.

Martin, R. (1981). Legal issues in preserving client rights. In G. T. Hannah, W. P. Christian, & H. B. Clark (Eds.), *Preservation of client rights* (pp. 3–13). New York: The Free Press.

Maslow, A. H. (1965). *Motivation and personality.* New York: Harper & Row.

McGregor, D. (1960). *The human side of enterprise.* New York: McGraw-Hill.

Mills *et al.*, Petitioners, v. Rogers *et al.*, U.S. Supreme Court, No. 80-1417 (1982).

Mills, M. J., Yesavage, J. A., & Gutheil, T. G. (1981). *Continuing case-law development in the right to refuse treatment.* Boston: Commonwealth of Massachusetts, Department of Mental Health.

Morgan v. Sproat, 432 F. Supp. 1130 (5 D. Miss. 1977).

New Jersey ARC, Inc. v. New Jersey Department of Human Services, 445 A.2d 704 (N.J. Sup. Ct. 1982).

Ouchi, W. G. (1981). *Theory Z.* Reading, MA: Addison-Wesley.

Parham v. J. R., 443 U.S. 584 (1979).

Rachlin, S. (1982). Toward a definition of staff rights. *Hospital and Community Psychiatry, 33*(1), 60–61.

Rennie v. Klein, 653 F.2d 836 (3rd. Cir. 1981).

Risley, T. R. (1975). Certify procedures not people. In W. S. Wood (Ed.), *Issues in evaluating behavior modification* (pp. 159–181). Champaign, IL: Research Press.

Romeo v. Youngberg, 644 F.2d 147 (1980).

Roos, P. (1972). Reconciling behavior modification procedures with the normalization principle. In W. Wolfensberger (Ed.), *Normalization* (pp. 136–148). Toronto: National Institute on Mental Retardation.

Rouse v. Cameron, 373 F.2d 451 (1966).

Scanlon, C. A., Arick, J. R., & Krug, D. A. (1982). A matched sample investigation of nonadaptive behavior of severely handicapped adults across four living situations. *American Journal of Mental Deficiency, 86*, 526–532.

Secretary of Public Welfare of Pennsylvania v. Institutionalized Juveniles, 442 U.S. 640 (1979).

Sheldon-Wildgen, J. (1982). Avoiding legal liability: The rights and responsibilities of therapists. *The Behavior Therapist, 5,* 165–169.

Sheldon-Wildgen, J., & Risley, T. (1982). Balancing clients' rights: The establishment of human rights and peer review committees. In A. Bellack, M. Hersen, & A. Kazdin (Eds.), *International handbook of behavior modification* (pp. 263–289). New York: Plenum Press.

Shelton v. Tucker, 364 U.S. 479 (1960).

Simon, H. A. (1957). *Administrative behavior.* New York: Free Press.

Standards for Intermediate Care Facilities for the Mentally Retarded, 43 C.F.R., subpart 442-400 (1978).

Stolz, S. B., & Associates. (1978). *Ethical issues in behavior modification.* San Francisco: Jossey-Bass.

Sutter, P., Mayeda, T., Call, T., Yanagi, G., & Yee, S. (1980). Comparison of successful and unsuccessful community-placed mentally retarded persons. *American Journal of Mental Deficiency, 85,* 262–267.

Tanner, B. A. (1973). Aversive shock issues: Physical danger, emotional harm, effectiveness and "dehumanization." *Journal of Behavior Therapy and Experimental Psychiatry, 4,* 113–115.

Turnbull, H. R., Ellis, J. W., Boogs, E. M., Brooks, P. O., & Biklen, D. P. (1981). *The least restrictive alternative: Principles and practices.* Washington, DC: American Association on Mental Deficiency.

Welsch v. Likins, 373 F. Supp. 487 (D. Minn. 1974).

Wheeler v. Glass, 473 F.2d (7th Cir. 1973).

Wuori v. Zitnay, Civil Action N. 75-80 S.D. (D. Me. July 21, 1978).

Wyatt v. Aderhold, 503 F.2d 1305 (5th Cir. 1974).

Wyatt v. Stickney, 344 F. Supp. 373, 344 F. Supp. 387 (M.D. Ala. 1972).

Youngberg v. Romeo, 102 5 Ct. (1982).

Ziarnik, J. P. (1980). Developing proactive direct care staff. *Mental Retardation, 18,* 289–292.

Index

Vomiting
  medical factors, 171–173
  parent and family training, 260

Workshops. *See* Vocational habilitation

XXY syndrome. *See* Klinefelter's
  syndrome

Zero reject principle, 276
Zones. *See* Activity zones